Praise for *Stokoe, Sunderl...*

'Remember when football wasn't just abou...
BBC's *Final Score*, Hardy relives the greate...
Sunderland defeated Leeds by a single goal' *GQ*

'The angel is in the detail of such a loving work; you really get to know the players who beat Leeds United at Wembley'

Patrick Barclay, *The Times*

'Hardy evokes this period exceptionally well . . . It's an excellent read'

Salut Sunderland

'Setting the match in its sporting and social context, it's an enjoyable slice of nostalgia for footie fans of a certain age' *Choice*

'Hardy's meticulously researched tale, supported by a host of specially commissioned interviews, brings the period into vivid relief'

Northern Echo

'An essential piece of British football history for fans of any club. Brilliantly researched and written with an undisguised passion'

Guy Mowbray of BBC's *Match of the Day*

'From trilbys to tracksuits to daft red-and-white plastic hats, this well-researched book provides a fascinating insight into the intricacies of the event no one even knew existed' *A Love Supreme*

'Anyone who loves football will love it. The insights it offers into how the game was run during the '60s and '70s are compelling' *Sentinel*

'A brilliant book' Henry Winter

'It is a remarkable book, dense with detail, rich in anecdote and full of little-known or untold tales alongside the standard facts of the story'

Sunderland Echo

'I very much warmed to a familiar story, given added depth by amusing material, genuine feeling and honest appraisal' *When Saturday Comes*

Lance Hardy is a writer and television producer. He has worked at numerous sporting events around the world, including four World Cups, two European Championships and two Olympic Games. The 1973 FA Cup final between Sunderland and Leeds United was the first football match he ever saw. He lives in London.

STOKOE, SUNDERLAND AND '73

The Story of the Greatest
FA Cup Final Shock of All Time

LANCE HARDY

An Orion paperback

First published in Great Britain in 2009
by Orion
This paperback edition published in 2011
by Orion Books Ltd,
Orion House, 5 Upper St Martin's Lane,
London WC2H 9EA

An Hachette UK company

1 3 5 7 9 10 8 6 4 2

Copyright © Lance Hardy 2010

A CIP catalogue record for this book
is available from the British Library.

ISBN 978-0-7528-8340-3

Typeset by Input Data Services Ltd,
Bridgwater, Somerset

Printed in Great Britain by
CPI Group (UK) Ltd, Croydon, CR0 4YY

The Orion Publishing Group's policy is to use papers that
are natural, renewable and recyclable products and
made from wood grown in sustainable forests. The logging
and manufacturing processes are expected to conform to
the environmental regulations of the country of origin.

'Saturday Gig' words and music by Ian Hunter © 1976,
reproduced by permission of EMI Songs Ltd, London.

Every effort has been made to fulfil requirements with
regard to reproducing copyright material. The author and
publisher will be glad to rectify any omissions at the
earliest opportunity.

www.orionbooks.co.uk

For those who dare to dream.

'Saturday Gig'

'Oh, Seventy-three was a jamboree
We were the dudes
And the dudes were we.'

Ian Hunter, Mott the Hoople

CONTENTS

CONTENTS

ACKNOWLEDGEMENTS

This book could not have been written without the co-operation of many people. First and foremost my gratitude to those connected with Sunderland AFC in that extraordinary 1972–73 season who generously gave me their time, trust, respect and recollections: Jim Montgomery, Dick Malone, Ron Guthrie, Dave Watson, Ritchie Pitt, Bobby Kerr, Billy Hughes, Vic Halom, Dennis Tueart, Dave Young, coach Arthur Cox and the late chairman Keith Collings, who sadly recently passed away. Of course there were others involved in this story who I could not request interviews with at the time of writing, for they are regrettably no longer with us: Bob Stokoe, Billy Elliott and Ian Porterfield. All three men feature on the front cover and this book is dedicated to their memory. Thanks also to Ian's widow, Glenda, for her contributions.

I interviewed players from each of the sides Sunderland beat in the 1973 FA Cup run as well as players from each of the clubs Bob Stokoe managed before he arrived at Roker Park. Thanks to: Peter Lorimer (Leeds United), Bob Wilson (Arsenal), Viv Busby (Luton Town), Willie Donachie (Manchester City), Tommy Youlden (Reading), Les Bradd (Notts County), George Jones (Bury), Keith Peacock (Charlton Athletic), Reg Jenkins (Rochdale), Stan Ternent (Carlisle United) and Jimmy Armfield (Blackpool). Thanks also to Charlie Hurley, a Sunderland player between 1957 and 1969 and Reading manager in 1973.

Three friends and colleagues from the world of television shared their reminiscences and football libraries with me, helping my research into this era and the many characters featured within these pages. Thanks to: Barry Davies, John Motson and Gerald Sinstadt.

Then there are the Sunderland supporters, from famous names to friends of mine for over twenty years. Thanks to: Sir Tim Rice, Steve Cram, Paul Dobson, Steve Hodgson, Paul Mulley (and his programme collection), Bill Peverley and Pete Sixsmith.

Many other people gave interviews, helped to arrange interviews, arranged permissions, checked information and provided books and newspaper articles for my research. Sadly there are too many names to mention but my gratitude to all, and particular thanks to the following: David Barber, Gordon Banks, Leslie Barrett, Steve Clark, Stuart Clarke, John Cole, Robin Daniels, Alfred Dipper and members of 189 Roker Mess, Dave Dixon, David Downes, Bob Gardam, Allan Graham, Rob Mason, Dianne Moxon, Suzanne Pakarian, Arthur Pearson, Richard Platford, Ken Pollard, Margaret Sinstadt, Steve Smith and Susan Swinney. Thanks also to Ian Hunter, who generously allowed me to use his lyrics at the start of this book.

Libraries have played an essential part in my research. Thanks to the helpful and professional staff at five in particular: the British Newspaper Library at Colindale, London; East Sheen Library, London; Central Library, Leeds; Sunderland City Library; and Worksop Library.

Many thanks to Ian Preece, my editor at Orion, for advising me and guiding this work to completion and thanks to Vicki Harris for her constructive comments and improvements and Jane Sturrock for her assistance. Thanks also to David Luxton, my agent, for getting this project off the ground for me.

Love and thanks – as always – to Mum, Dad and Adelle, not least for sitting me down in front of a television set on 5 May 1973 and telling me to support the team in the red and white stripes. My father will be relieved to know that this is the final version of the manuscript! Love and thanks also to my girlfriend Lijana Sutich for her love and support.

Lance Hardy
Barnes, London
December 2009

AUTHOR'S NOTE

A brief word on the text: the story is written from the time it took place; therefore certain team names – Atlético Bilbao, Hartlepools, Orient, Swansea Town for example – have since changed. They appear as they were at the time. Sunderland's nickname during this period was the Rokerites. 'Saturday Gig' is the registered title of the song more commonly known as 'Saturday Gigs' by Mott the Hoople.

Sunderland's achievement in winning the FA Cup in 1973 has been called the 'greatest FA Cup final shock of all time'. This, then, is how it happened . . .

Prologue
A DATE WITH DESTINY

The rain has been pouring down almost all day, all along Wembley Way. The football pitch is soaked through. This is not what you would call normal FA Cup final weather – but then this is not what you would call a normal FA Cup final. For the old arena is celebrating the fiftieth anniversary of its first Cup final in 1923 with the biggest 'David and Goliath' encounter it has ever witnessed: current holders and massive favourites Leeds United versus Second Division outsiders Sunderland.

Deep inside Wembley Stadium's famous tunnel stands the country's most successful football club manager, Don Revie, clean and dry in his lucky blue suit. Behind him stands the star-studded international line-up that currently makes up the nation's most successful football club, sock tags and all: captain Billy Bremner, David Harvey, Paul Reaney, Johnny Giles, Norman Hunter, Trevor Cherry, Peter Lorimer, Eddie Gray, Mick Jones, Paul Madeley, Terry Yorath and Allan Clarke. This Leeds side features eleven full internationals. It's some team.

Ten of these players won the FA Cup for Revie twelve months ago against Arsenal; only the recently retired Jack Charlton is missing from that side and he is not too far away, sat high up in a television studio looking down on what he and most others in the media feel will amount to little more than a workout for Leeds ahead of their European Cup Winners' Cup final against A C Milan in Greece next week. The sunshine of Salonika may seem a long way from the cascading rain in London, but these two matches mark the eighth and ninth major Cup finals for Revie's all-white machine in less than a decade – simple statistics that sum up this team's achievements, both at home and abroad.

This is already Leeds' third FA Cup final of the seventies. In 1970 they lost – after a replay and extra-time – in an ugly encounter to Chelsea. Two years later they won – courtesy of Clarke's diving header – against the Gunners. In between those two finals Leeds crashed out of the 1971 competition in the fifth round at Fourth Division Colchester United 3–2, having somehow trailed 3–0 after less than an hour. That remains the biggest embarrassment of Revie's managerial career to date, and provides a constant reminder to him of a most unpredictable and unforgiving foe – the FA Cup underdog. But Leeds are the hottest Cup final favourites of all time today. Surely lightning cannot strike again? No matter how bad the weather.

Alongside the suited and booted Revie stands his opposite number Bob Stokoe, a man dressed from head to toe in a brand-new bright red club tracksuit. A bigger managerial contrast on Cup final day would be hard to find: while Revie has guided Leeds to the First Division title, the FA Cup, the League Cup and the Inter-Cities Fairs Cup; Stokoe has flitted around the lower divisions of the Football League with the likes of Bury, Charlton Athletic, Rochdale, Carlisle United and Blackpool before landing the job of saving relegation-threatened Sunderland from a first-ever drop into the Third Division less than six short months ago. He has claimed one trophy in his managerial career so far: the rather inferior Anglo-Italian Cup, which he won with Blackpool in 1971, just a few weeks after the club had been relegated to the Second Division.

But Stokoe is full of optimism and pride as he looks confidently down the tunnel at his team, long hair, sideburns and all: captain Bobby Kerr, Jim Montgomery, Ritchie Pitt, Micky Horswill, Dick Malone, Dave Watson, Ron Guthrie, Ian Porterfield, Billy Hughes, Dennis Tueart, Dave Young and Vic Halom. There is not one full international cap between these young men, but they are giant-killers. Sunderland have already beaten two of the best sides in the country – Manchester City and Arsenal – and they now believe the unbelievable: they can go one better and topple the mighty Leeds at Wembley. It's some dream.

In appearance and achievement Leeds United and Sunderland are worlds apart. In appearance and achievement Don Revie and Bob Stokoe are worlds apart. But the two managers have met before, most notably as players in this very same tunnel and on this very same occasion eighteen years ago, when Stokoe, then a centre-half with Newcastle United, won an FA Cup winners' medal against Revie's Manchester City.

That was the highlight of Stokoe's playing career; yet it hardly ever crosses his mind when he thinks of the famous and successful manager stood just a few yards to his right. Instead he remembers a meeting with him that took place in the early 1960s when both men were at the start of their managerial careers. The sheer thought of that day has apparently made him feel ill ever since. In his own mind, some form of retribution can be found here today. There would never be a better time or place to do so.

Leeds fans occupy the tunnel end of the stadium, much to the annoyance of Stokoe, who feels this will give Revie's side an unfair advantage. But you would never know it from hearing the crowd as the teams emerge from the tunnel: 'Stokoe – Stokoe; Sunderland – Sunderland' is all that can be heard as the players glance up to see a sea of red and white in front of them from the far end of the arena. Most of the 100,000 capacity crowd are shouting for the team in red and white stripes and the man in the tracksuit at the helm; most of the country, sat at home and watching on television, is doing exactly the same.

Revie's Leeds may be the strongest FA Cup final favourites of all time but Stokoe's Sunderland are, by far, the most popular FA Cup final underdog of all time. As the two men lead their teams out on to the famous Wembley turf, Stokoe – trying his best to avoid small-talk with Revie – proudly lifts up his head, pushes back his shoulders and begins to dream of causing the greatest ever shock in FA Cup final history.

1.

ONE GOOD FRIDAY AFTERNOON

There was no bright red tracksuit or lucky blue suit around when Bob Stokoe and Don Revie first came face to face as managers in April 1962. The Lancashire mill town of Bury appeared almost monochrome that day: the sky was dull and overcast and the atmosphere was wet and cold. It was a perfect setting for the first of two crucial Second Division relegation clashes to be played that Easter between Bury and Leeds United.

The sixties were just about to start swinging. The previous week a gritty film version of Stan Barstow's book *A Kind of Loving* had been released; featuring similar cobbled streets to those near to Bury's football ground on Gigg Lane, it was part of the New Wave movement in British cinema and would soon speak for a generation. There was a new music scene evolving too, with the Beatles in Liverpool, the Rolling Stones in London and the Animals in Newcastle. D. H. Lawrence's *Lady Chatterley's Lover*, first printed in 1928, could now be purchased in bookshops and, possibly most significant of all, the contraceptive pill was available on the National Health Service.

Football was to become a major part of this cultural revolution. That spring hopes were high that England – with players such as Bobby Charlton, Jimmy Greaves and Bobby Moore – would perform well in the forthcoming World Cup in Chile. They could even win it, some of the newspapers said. Domestically the game was in good health too: the maximum wage for players had just been abolished; Greaves and Denis Law were on their way back to the First Division after spells in Italy; attendances were on the up; and television was being tentatively discussed as the way forward.

Anglia Television was the pioneer in football highlights on the small screen, and regularly featured Ipswich Town on *Match of the Week* that season as future England manager Alf Ramsey successfully steered the club from the Third Division South to the First Division title in just five seasons. Any manager at any level on the league ladder now harboured similar ambitions after this remarkable achievement in Suffolk.

But there was also a sobering moment for football to ponder that Easter, for the Football League suddenly comprised just ninety-one clubs after Accrington Stanley – based only a few miles north of Bury – resigned. Already prevented from making transfers due to their debts to other league clubs, an emergency fund was set up to raise £20,000 to keep them in business; but this failed miserably when only £450 was collected. With little in the way of funds and a diminishing support, the club folded. Never before had the divide between winners and losers in the game seemed so vast, and nowhere was that felt more sharply than in Lancashire, a county that had supplied half of the twelve original Football League members back in 1888, including a team from Accrington.

As the 1961–62 season drew to a close those two new inductees into the managerial game – Revie and Stokoe – were both fighting to keep their clubs in the Second Division. Leeds, with just seven wins all season and no fewer than eight defeats since Christmas, looked particularly vulnerable.

Gigg Lane had been Bury's home since the late nineteenth century. The Shakers had played there when they won the FA Cup in 1900 and 1903, and the old ground still had a Victorian aura with its dark corridors and austere woodwork. The six decades that had passed since those two triumphs had brought little success to the club's supporters, but there had been something of a renaissance over the last few years with an all-time record crowd of 35,000 for a Cup match against Bolton Wanderers in 1960 and promotion to the Second Division the following season. Stokoe had been the skipper of that side.

Born south of the River Tyne in the Northumberland hamlet of Mickley in 1930, Stokoe was the son of a Sunderland-supporting coal miner. But he learned his trade in the nearby football-rich mining village of High Spen and joined Newcastle United from Spen Juniors as an apprentice in 1947. He scored on his first-team debut as a centre-forward against Middlesbrough on Christmas Day 1950 before gradually establishing himself at centre-half and going on to make a total of 261 league appearances for them. It was only the supremacy of England captain Billy Wright that denied him an international cap.

Stokoe had been reluctant to move to Bury in exchange for John McGrath and £24,000 in February 1961. He felt let down by the club he had served for almost fourteen years. But he soon put that disappointment behind him to lead his new team on an unbeaten run of eighteen league matches, which secured the Third Division title. When Newcastle were relegated from the First Division the following week, Stokoe openly admitted to grinning like a Cheshire cat. The love and loyalty he felt for the Magpies was completely overshadowed by personal pride.

Stokoe became player-manager at Gigg Lane in December 1961 after the man who signed him, Dave Russell, suddenly and surprisingly left to take over at Fourth Division Tranmere Rovers. The Bury directors were unanimous in their managerial choice and this was backed 100 per cent by the players. At thirty-one years old Stokoe became the second-youngest manager in the Football League and was given just one task by his chairman Major George Horridge: avoid relegation. He was given no money to spend, but he quickly set about improving a highly physical side with his commanding presence at the back. He made Bury difficult to beat by shoring up a leaky defence and giving his players a new belief in their abilities with regular and rousing team talks. Due to this an improved run of results had almost secured the club survival by the time the Easter fixture list came around.

By contrast Leeds were involved in a real dogfight to stay up, much to the dismay and disappointment of their fiercely ambitious young manager, who had bravely changed the team's colours from blue and gold to all-white in recognition of the great Real Madrid side that had won five successive European Cups in the late 1950s and early 1960s. (The Spanish greats wore all-white in reverence of Corinthians, a London club founded in 1882 that became legendary for fair play.) Despite Leeds' lowly league position, Revie, aged only thirty-three himself, already had a conviction that, one day in the future, his team could reach similar heights as the most successful club side the world had ever seen.

It was some target, for the club was based in a predominantly rugby league area – a fact celebrated in David Storey's book and forthcoming film *This Sporting Life*. Leeds was home to one of the best-supported rugby league teams in the country – plus two others in Bramley and Hunslet – which often challenged nearby Wakefield Trinity for the top honours in the game. The city also housed the best county cricket side, at Headingley: Yorkshire dominated the sport, winning the County Championship four times in five years. The city's football club – with no major honours and struggling at the bottom of the Second Division – was seen as inconsequential in comparison and often played in front of as little as 8,000 spectators. But Revie's motto was 'If you think small then you will stay small.' He saw potential at Leeds, particularly within a group of youngsters he had inherited from previous manager Jack Taylor.

Born in Middlesbrough, Revie began his playing career at Leicester City in the wartime league in 1944, and a number of things happened during his time there that helped to shape his young managerial mind: he met and married manager John Duncan's niece, Elsie; he was introduced to intelligence reports on opposing teams, compiled by Septimus Smith, a former England international; and he helped the Second Division club reach the 1949 FA Cup Final by scoring two goals in a semi-final win over First Division Portsmouth at Highbury – then sat at home in despair as a burst blood vessel in his nose cruelly denied him his place at Wembley. Revie was forced to listen to radio commentary of the Cup final as Leicester were swept aside by Wolverhampton Wanderers. He later reflected that 'fate was so unkind', and spoke of the 'fickle wheel of fortune'. Unwittingly he would become, by his own admission, one of the most superstitious people ever seen in football. His rituals spread from wearing lucky suits to walking to and from a certain set of traffic lights on home match days.

An intelligent forward, Revie was capped six times by England and won the prestigious Football Writers' Footballer of the Year award in 1955, largely due to his role in an exciting free-flowing formation at Manchester City that became famous as the 'Revie Plan' where he played as a deep-lying centre-forward – essentially an attacking, free-running midfielder – connecting defence with attack in a style reminiscent of Hungary's Nándor Hidegkuti, the man who starred alongside Ferenc Puskás when his country had annihilated England 6–3 at Wembley Stadium and turned international football on its head in November 1953.

The Revie Plan won the FA Cup for Manchester City in a 3–1 victory over Birmingham City in 1956. After his personal disappointment in missing out on the 1949 final, and defeat against Stokoe and Newcastle in the 1955 final, Revie was not going to leave anything to chance this time around and took along two pieces of wood – apparently given to him by a gypsy – to the Wembley dressing room for good luck. His team-mates looked on astounded but Revie's performance – and the success of the Revie Plan – marked him out as a manager for the future. Although he was always quick to point out that the Plan involved the whole team rather than just one man, here was a deep thinker and a strategist with a tactical mind. He wrote about his ideas and methods in some detail in his book *Soccer's Happy Wanderer*, which was published while he was still playing the game.

After accumulating a combined record total of transfer fees by moving from Leicester to Hull City to Manchester City to Sunderland to Leeds, Revie was offered his first managerial opportunity by the debt-ridden Elland Road outfit in March 1961, mainly due to director and future chairman Harry Reynolds being so impressed by his football brain and his style of play.

Revie had a vision for the club. He wanted his team to play the way he had in his playing days. But this did not work so well in the lower reaches of the Second Division. By March 1962 Leeds were at the bottom of the table and staring at the prospect of relegation. Revie had used over thirty players in a variety of positions – Jack Charlton had featured as an emergency centre-forward for most of the season – but to no avail, and with time running out the manager had even played himself at Huddersfield Town. It was his first appearance in months and it would be the last of his career as Leeds lost again. The club's record of never having played outside the top two divisions was now in jeopardy.

Then – in the very same week that he hung up his boots – Revie produced a rabbit from a hat. He somehow convinced Everton manager Harry Catterick to sell him the combative Scottish international mid-fielder Bobby Collins; somehow convinced Collins to leave a side riding high in the First Division for one that was propping up the Second Division; and then somehow convinced the cash-strapped Leeds directors to part with £25,000 to buy him. It proved to be a masterstroke. Collins was made club captain and immediately toughened up the side, Charlton went back to centre-half and Leeds went to Bury on an unbeaten run of five matches. But they were still very much in relegation trouble and desperately needed to take points from their remaining four matches to survive. And two of those were against Stokoe's Shakers.

When Stokoe arrived at Gigg Lane over an hour before kick-off that wet Good Friday, he locked up his car and made his way towards the home dressing room, stepping over the mud and the puddles that covered the car park along the way. His mind was completely focused on extending his team's winning run in the league to five matches. He entered the ground via a wicket gate and promptly came face to face with Revie, who was waiting on the other side. They had a conversation; it was brief, to the point and over in a matter of moments. But what was said so outraged and shocked Stokoe that he immediately went upstairs to the Bury boardroom to tell his chairman and vice-chairman about it. His description of events was damning.

According to Stokoe, Revie said to him, 'I've got £500 in my pocket for you if you take it easy today.' The Bury player-manager replied, 'Not bloody likely.' Revie then asked him: 'Well, can I have a word with some of your players?' He was told: under no circumstances. A some-what scorned Stokoe was advised by his chairman to say nothing about the matter and to go out on to the pitch and win the match.

The allegation formed part of the *Daily Mirror*'s 'Revie File' in September 1977 – over fifteen years after the match took place – and according to journalist Richard Stott Stokoe wept uncontrollably when he recounted his version of events from that day. He was to repeat his claims regularly over the next twenty-five years.

'This was against all the things I stood for: the honesty, the fairness, the competitiveness I have always loved,' he said. 'The fact I had only been a player-manager for about four months and he was asking me to jeopardise my career. I was very bitter towards him.'

These events created a distance between the two men that would last for ever, living with one of them for the rest of his life and haunting the other long into his retirement, continually questioning his managerial achievements and morality within the game.

Stokoe played himself in a fiercely fought 1–1 draw that day, watched by a crowd of 13,313 despite the heavy rain. Bury were on top for most of the match and missed several chances before sixteen-year-old striker George Jones scored his first-ever goal for the club to put them ahead just before half-time. Charlton equalised for Leeds with a header on the hour. Bury fought for every ball and every opportunity in the latter stages of the match, but Leeds held on to claim a vital point.

'I think in many ways the players supported me and it made them more determined that it was going to be harder for Leeds to get a result than it might have been because we didn't have too much at stake other than our pride,' Stokoe said. 'After that match I lost all respect for Revie. On the Tuesday night we went to Leeds, Revie never spoke but I had one of the finest games of my life and we drew 0–0.'

That draw at Elland Road left Leeds one point above the relegation zone with one game left to play. Revie's men still needed a win in their last game to be sure of Second Division safety. As it was, both Bury and Leeds avoided relegation. Bury ended the campaign eighteenth, on the same points total as the seven teams above them, while Leeds stretched their unbeaten run to nine matches and finished fourth from bottom after a 3–0 win at Newcastle on the last day of the season. Bristol Rovers and Brighton & Hove Albion went down.

Revie had won more time to plot his revolution at Elland Road; the signing of Collins may even have saved him his job. Within a few years Leeds would be challenging for the Football League title, the FA Cup and European honours. Stokoe meanwhile would continue to make do in his own way but – given what he was to say many years later – the following comment from the main character, Vic Brown, on the final page of *A Kind of Loving* would no doubt have resonated with him: 'There's right things and there's wrong things and if you do wrong things, wrong things happen to you – and that's the punishment.' Stokoe made sure that Revie was never able to forget that one Good Friday afternoon.

2.

FROM BURY TO BLACKPOOL

Bob Stokoe was appointed Blackpool manager in late 1970. The team in tangerine were by far the biggest of the five clubs he had managed so far and one that, he hoped, could realise his ultimate ambition of winning honours. He also hoped that he was joining a club not reliant on selling the best talent, something that had been a feature of his early managerial career up and down the country and up and down the divisions.

Blackpool had won the FA Cup in 1953 with a thrilling 4–3 win over Bolton Wanderers and the club was steeped in the history of Stanley Matthews, Stan Mortensen and Bill Perry. The 'Matthews Final' was the club's biggest triumph, as golden as the mile on its famous seafront. A commendable First Division runners-up spot behind Manchester United – the best-ever finish in the club's history – followed three seasons later as the Seasiders enjoyed thirty unbroken years as a First Division side under the management of just two men, Joe Smith and Ronnie Stuart.

But the sixties were a difficult decade, and after six successive bottom-half finishes in the top flight, Blackpool finished bottom of the table at the end of the 1966–67 season and were duly relegated to the Second Division. The club quickly lost managerial stability. Stan Mortensen came in as manager in 1967 but lasted little more than two years. Les Shannon took over and won promotion back to the top flight in 1970 but a few months into the following campaign – with the club again rooted to the bottom of the table – he resigned after his team had thrown away a 3–0 lead against Chelsea and lost 4–3. Stand-in manager Jimmy Meadows had to take charge of team affairs. After two managers in thirty-two years, Blackpool were now looking to make a third full-time appointment in as many seasons.

The club's directors decided to go for someone who they thought could bring back the good old days to Bloomfield Road and a smile back to the faces of the players and the fans. They also needed to find a troubleshooter. The target was found at Carlisle United; his name was Bob Stokoe. Blackpool chased Stokoe and eventually they got him. It was a new challenge for him: the first time he had ever managed in the top division, albeit at the bottom of it. But it was common for him to join a club in trouble; he had previously saved Bury, Rochdale and Carlisle from the drop. On this occasion survival was to be unachievable and after just one league win in five long months Blackpool were relegated.

'Only a miracle could have saved Blackpool,' Stokoe said. 'Possibly in lower divisions it is a little bit easier to get out of trouble? I managed to do a rescue operation at Carlisle when they were right at the bottom but that wasn't in the premier division. You can't go and pinch points at Arsenal and Chelsea and other clubs of their standard.'

It had been some rescue operation by Stokoe at Carlisle. The Cumbrians had won just three points from their opening ten games when he arrived there in October 1968. When he left them two years later, they were in the Second Division promotion pack. In two short years he had brought back the good times to Brunton Park, and that had not gone unnoticed in Blackpool.

Alan Ashman had taken Carlisle from the Fourth to the Second Division in the mid-1960s, but when he left to take charge of West Bromwich Albion in 1967 the club fell apart. Ashman's successor was Tim Ward, who was quickly dismissed, and this led to the arrival of Stokoe, who secured two mid-table finishes and two impressive Cup runs before mounting a serious challenge for promotion early into the 1970–71 season. Stokoe was a loyal manager but, when it came, he eventually found the offer of managing in the First Division too much to turn down.

Stokoe was essentially a man manager, as strong on discipline as he had been in a tackle in his playing days. But he was also a man with feelings, a family man who adored his dog. He loved the music of Frank Sinatra, whom he copied by often wearing a trademark trilby to cover the developing bald patch on his head. He enjoyed bridge, golf and snooker and quiet evenings at home, watching Westerns on television, particularly the American series *Bonanza*. He was passionate about events on the pitch but he also had personal skills off it. It was said he often made his mind up quickly and players could find themselves 'in' as easily as they could find themselves 'out'. He was brash, honest and a born winner. He had a talent for motivation and he despised losing. His defensive prowess as a player was his starting point at every club he managed: shore up the defence and work forward from there. Time and time again it proved to be a successful formula for him.

Stokoe found the mood at Blackpool not too dissimilar from what he had found at all his previous clubs, starting at Bury and his first managerial appointment back in 1961. The Shakers had been near to the bottom of the Second Division table when he took over. Stokoe might have been inexperienced in the managerial game at that time, but he soon became an inspiration to his players. He toughened them up – mentally and physically – and turned them into a difficult side to beat, quickly moving them away from the danger of relegation.

The following Christmas Bury were involved in the promotion race in the Second Division alongside much bigger clubs such as Chelsea and Sunderland. But the coldest winter of the twentieth century plus a long-term knee injury to their player-manager ended any chances of First Division football. After beating Sunderland twice in four days over Christmas, Bury played just two more league games before March, and when the football programme fully resumed they still had to face an enormous twenty-one-game run-in to the end of the season. The build-up of postponed fixtures eventually proved too much for Stokoe's small squad and his team faded to finish the campaign in eighth place, five points behind promoted Stoke City and Chelsea.

'We had a cracking season in 1962–63 and we should have won promotion,' former Bury forward George Jones says. 'We did the double over both Sunderland and Leeds that season. We had a really good spirit going and were difficult to beat, particularly at home. Bob Stokoe was a lovely bloke. He was a real gentleman and a quiet man off the pitch but he put over what he wanted from us. Some managers just have the ability of making you want to play for them. He did that. He could change on the field – he was very competitive and he didn't like losing – but you knew where you stood with him.'

Eighth place in the Second Division was a commendable achievement. To this day it remains Bury's highest league finish since the Second World War. That season also provided the Shakers with their best-ever run in the League Cup, when they got all the way to the semi-finals before bowing out 4–3 on aggregate to Birmingham City.

Stokoe consolidated Bury's position as a Second Division side – the job he was brought in to do – for two more seasons. He finally hung up his playing boots in 1964 and began to concentrate full-time on team management. During this period he nurtured a lot of young talent into his first team, including future Manchester City and England midfielder Colin Bell, who was given his first professional contract at Gigg Lane by Stokoe. But the manager was continually frustrated by an enforced need to sell a lot of the club's young jewels for economic reasons, and this was to lead ultimately to his departure.

'Colin Bell came into the first team in the 1963–64 season,' Jones says. 'Funnily enough he made his debut for us against Manchester City at Maine Road and scored in a 1–1 draw. I played about ten games with Colin but then I was sold on to Blackburn Rovers at the age of eighteen. I was one of the first of that team to leave. Bob didn't want to sell me; he used to tell me, "You will leave Bury over my dead body," but I think money just spoke in the end. He got £30,000 for me. He wished me good luck and said it was a good opportunity for me to join Blackburn. But he was clearly disappointed that I had to go.'

In August 1965 – after more than three and a half years of wheeling and dealing and keeping Bury up – Stokoe received an approach from another Second Division outfit, Charlton Athletic. He promptly accepted the offer and moved south.

Football was about to hit boom time as London prepared to host England matches in the World Cup finals the following summer, but the Valiants – one of the capital's eleven Football League clubs – were an outfit heading in the wrong direction. A First Division team from 1936 to 1957 and FA Cup winners under Jimmy Seed in 1947, Charlton had spent eight fruitless seasons searching for a return to the top flight. Furthermore, two of the previous three seasons had seen near-flirtations with relegation to the Third Division. Stokoe had, in fact, guided Bury to a higher league position than Charlton in his last season in Lancashire. But Charlton were recognised as a bigger club than Bury and, with the likes of Mike Bailey, Billy Bonds and Keith Peacock on their books, one with a lot more potential.

As had been the case at Bury, it soon became apparent to Stokoe that he would have to sell his young talent. So Bailey moved to Wolverhampton Wanderers for £40,000, where he went on to make

360 league appearances, and Bonds moved up the road to West Ham United for £49,500, where he went on to play 655 league games and famously lift the FA Cup twice for the Hammers.

Losing both players was a big blow to Stokoe: 'I had no option [but] to sell,' he later said. 'The team badly needed strengthening in other positions. I had to raise money to cover these. Yet most of what Bailey and Bonds brought in was not made available to me for team building. Neither would have been allowed to leave if I'd had my way and the club's finances had been stronger.'

One player who remained at The Valley was Keith Peacock. Stokoe created history when he made him the first-ever substitute in English football on the opening day of the 1965–66 season against Bolton at Burnden Park: 'I remember that my name was in the programme – which in those days meant that you were going to play – and yet I was left out of the team,' Peacock says. 'Bob Stokoe must have had a change of heart. It was very disappointing for me but then our goalkeeper Mick Rose suffered a severe injury and I came on. John Hewie went in goal. In doing so I became the first substitute to be used in the Football League.

'My childhood team was Newcastle United so I knew all about Bob,' Peacock adds. 'My parents came from South Shields and we were all Newcastle fans. I saw Bob play in the flesh for Newcastle and the very first Cup final I watched as a youngster on television was the 1955 final, when he played and Newcastle won. Bob was hands-on in training at Charlton and quite different to the suited managers of that time. He loved to join in the five-a-sides on a Friday before a match and he took no prisoners. I always found Bob to be a very honest man. I was fairly young and learning my trade but he always had such a nice way about him. He was a strong character but underneath all that passion and determination there was sensitivity. The only game he ever missed when he was manager of Charlton was when his dog died. He stayed at home that day. That kind of thing was unheard of at the time but it said a lot about the kind of man Bob was.'

Two disappointing finishes at sixteenth and nineteenth in the Second Division were deemed not good enough by the Charlton board, and when the 1967–68 season began without a win in the first five matches Stokoe was dismissed by chairman Michael Gliksten and quickly replaced by Eddie Firmani, a man who had begun his league career at the club and then spent several seasons in Italy before Stokoe brought him back to The Valley as a player just a few months before getting the sack.

This was to be the lowest point in Stokoe's managerial career. 'I thought the bottom had dropped out of my world the day Michael Gliksten told me I was finished,' he later said. 'For the first time I had tasted real failure. I might have got my will-to-win spirit across to the players but I certainly failed to inspire the club directors.'

'It was a surprise to me when Bob was sacked,' Peacock says. 'It was a surprise that it happened so early on in the season. I thought he was very unfortunate to lose his job. But the chairman loved Eddie Firmani's history. Eddie had played in Italy either side of two separate spells with us. So he sacked Bob and brought Eddie in. Bob felt – probably quite justifiably – that he was never given a fair crack of the whip at Charlton. He always felt that. It clearly hurt him and I know that hurt stayed with him.'

Stokoe, a man who had spent the first thirty-five years of his life in the north of England before accepting the job at The Valley, vowed never to manage a club in London or the south of England ever again. He never did.

This was the first time in his life that Stokoe had been without a job. But his work with Charlton had not been wasted: a young teenager, playing at left-half after having been unearthed from a South Derbyshire mining town, was handed his first professional contract and his league debut during this time. His name was Vic Halom. In years to come he would play a significant part in Stokoe's managerial career.

As Stokoe pondered his immediate future, he was grateful to accept an offer from Orient manager Dick Graham to do some coaching and scouting for the sum of £10 per week. Stokoe had employed Graham as his assistant at Charlton before the managerial post at Brisbane Road had become vacant. The pair's friendship and Graham's subsequent loyalty to his former boss in what was an hour of need cannot be overstated: Graham played an important role at this time, keeping Stokoe busy and involved in the game. But Stokoe's motivational methods also rubbed off on Graham – as was seen a few years later when his Colchester United side shocked Leeds United in the FA Cup.

During this low point in his life Stokoe must have considered how things were turning out so differently for his old rival Don Revie, who was making the headlines by spending £100,000 on Sheffield United striker Mick Jones to boost Leeds' bid for the league title. It was simply a world away from having to sell the best players on your books at Bury and Charlton and then earning your keep from coaching and scouting for a friend at a lowly Third Division club.

In the end Stokoe was out of football management for just a matter of weeks. Then, while his nemesis was again riding high at the top of the First Division with Leeds, he went all the way down to the bottom of the Fourth Division to take over as manager at struggling Rochdale. Five years on from that Good Friday encounter at Gigg Lane, the gap in league status between these two managers could not have been wider: Spotland was a far cry from the glamour and glitz that Revie was enjoying in the top flight and European competition.

Rochdale was about as unfashionable as you could get in the Football League at that time. Founder members of the new Division Three North in 1921, the club remained in that division until the reorganisation of the league in 1958 and the introduction of a national Third and Fourth Division to replace the north–south divide. This reorganisation had given the club perhaps the biggest success so far in its sixty-year history as clubs were selected for the inaugural season in the Third and Fourth Divisions by their final position in the Division Three North and South tables at the end of the 1957–58 season: teams finishing in the top half of each were placed in the Third Division and teams finishing in the bottom half of each were placed in the Fourth Division. Rochdale finished tenth in Division Three North – avoiding the bottom half of the table on goal average – and were therefore elected as members of the new Third Division. Alas the club lasted just one season before a bottom-placed finish resulted in relegation to the bottom tier in 1959. And there they stayed. And there they slumped.

Stokoe arrived at a club that had twice had to apply for re-election to the Football League in the last two seasons – 1965–66 and 1966–67 – on account of finishing in the bottom four of the Fourth Division. On both occasions Rochdale received the fewest number of votes out of the four re-elected league teams, but they had managed to survive as a league club. Things did not start well in the 1967–68 season, with just one win before the end of October, and nobody at Spotland could face or risk the prospect of a third re-election. This was now rock bottom: the ground only had one stand and that had a hole in its roof after collapsing under the weight of heavy snowfall earlier in the season! But for the new manager this was a chance to get back into the managerial game. The only way was up.

'I remember Bob Stokoe coming to Rochdale halfway through the 1967–68 season,' Rochdale's all-time record goal scorer Reg Jenkins recalls. 'We were struggling in the Fourth Division and he wanted to move me from up front to centre-half. He called me in and he told me that he wanted to try me at the back. I remember we lost 4–0 against Luton and Malcolm MacDonald scored three against me.' Luton went on to comfortably win the Fourth Division title that season as Stokoe started to slowly sort out the Rochdale defence. The centre-forward-cum-centre-half improved and the team began to pick up points. But with three games remaining they were still placed in the bottom four.

Rochdale went on to beat Halifax Town and Workington but then lost at Southend United the night before the season ended. With their league programme completed the club would once more face re-election if three of the teams below them won on the final Saturday. It was a nerve-racking afternoon for all involved. Stokoe sat at home watching the teleprinter on *Grandstand* and contemplating fate and his future. Luck was to be on his side and the results went Rochdale's way. The club finished the campaign sixth-bottom and therefore avoided a third successive and possibly unsuccessful re-election, which would in turn have brought an end to their forty-eight-year Football League membership.

Having managed to keep the club in the league, Stokoe now set about changing his first-team squad from top to bottom ahead of the new campaign. By the end of that summer only a handful of players remained at the club. There were no fewer than seven debuts on the first day of the following season and only one of them had cost any money. This huge gamble paid off: by the autumn Rochdale were riding high in the Fourth Division. The transformation under Stokoe had been remarkable.

'Bob had a big clear-out that summer and only four of us remained,' Jenkins explains. 'He just kicked everyone else out. I think Bob was the type of man who either liked you or he didn't. I was lucky – he liked me and I could always talk to him, although you couldn't argue with him: he was very headstrong and he was very competitive. He was a hard, strict man and he had a saying about the opposition: "They can't run without their legs." If he didn't like you or if you didn't do the business for him, that was it. He liked players who gave a hundred per cent and I would like to think that I was one of those.'

Yet again Stokoe had started off by making his defence solid. Rochdale lost just one of their first ten league matches at the start of the 1968–69 season. Jenkins returned to centre-forward and scoring goals, and soon a first-ever promotion for the club began to look like a possibility, particularly when Bradford City were trounced 6–0 at home. But the revolution at Spotland did not go unnoticed elsewhere, and just two months into the season Carlisle made an approach for Stokoe and the manager was gone.

His leaving remark was directed at Gliksten, the man who had sacked him at Charlton the previous year: 'I think when something like that happens you tend to take stock, you tend to get a little bit more determined, you tell yourself: "You'll show them, you'll win."' He had once more shown the football world that he was a survivor and that he had potential. His reward was a return to the Second Division, albeit to a club that was cut adrift at the bottom.

Under two other Geordies, Len Richley and Dick Connor, Rochdale went on to finish third in the Fourth Division that season and in doing so achieved their first-ever promotion. The following season the club finished ninth in the Third Division – so far their highest-ever finish in the Football League. Richley and Connor celebrated these achievements, but Stokoe was the man who put this team together and is therefore credited for revitalising the club.

'Most of the players in the promotion team were players that Bob brought in, and nearly all of them were free transfers too,' Jenkins says. 'But Carlisle came in for him and I suppose it was a better offer for him. I remember we played one match and got back to Rochdale on the coach at something like six o'clock the following morning. Bob had a chance to go somewhere else and he took it. Everybody at Rochdale respected Bob. He was a hard, strict man but he was a very, very passionate man as well. He was a winner.'

Like Rochdale, Carlisle had spent their formative years in the Football League in Division Three North before Alan Ashman had come along and turned the club around. But when he left, the club went into decline. A famous FA Cup win over Newcastle in 1968 glossed over a disappointing campaign and two months into the following season –

without a single win and some heavy defeats – Carlisle were heading for the Third Division. It was familiar autumn territory for Stokoe. Once again he remodelled the team's defence, demanded 100 per cent commitment and effort and soon hauled the club free from the threat of relegation into a comfortable mid-table position.

'I think I'm right in saying that when Bob Stokoe got the Carlisle job the other names in the frame were Lawrie McMenemy, who was then a coach at Sheffield Wednesday, and Ian MacFarlane. They were on the shortlist but Bob got it,' former Carlisle player Stan Ternent says. 'Bob was a good guy to play for. He had a great knowledge of the game, was infectious, tough and a winner. He was definitely the boss and what he wanted, he got. If he didn't get it, he would do something about it.'

Carlisle prospered in Cup competitions under Stokoe, who quickly made a name for himself by guiding his new side past Second Division leaders Huddersfield Town and First Division Chelsea – later to be crowned FA Cup winners that season – to reach the semi-finals of the League Cup. Carlisle were denied a place at Wembley by West Brom (still managed by Ashman) 4–2 on aggregate after a gutsy 1–0 win at Brunton Park had given them a first-leg lead. This was the second time Stokoe had achieved the feat of taking a lower-league club to the last four of this competition, following his achievement with Bury in the 1962–63 season. But behind the glory of this Cup run there was frustration: star striker Hugh McIlmoyle had been sold to Middlesbrough and the manager had to once more grudgingly accept that he was working for a selling club.

'Carlisle was always a side that needed money,' Stokoe later reflected. 'Hugh McIlmoyle was clearly our best player and here he was being removed without any real consultation with either myself or him. Football club directors back then were just like accountants, making a profit on the books was all they cared about.'

The FA Cup had been something of a stumbling block for Stokoe as a manager. A dismal run of six successive defeats in the competition ended in 1970 when Carlisle caused a third-round shock by dumping First Division Nottingham Forest out after a replay. The Cumbrians then beat Aldershot in the fourth round to set up a fifth-round clash against Middlesbrough at home. In front of 27,603 – the highest attendance ever recorded at Brunton Park – Carlisle went down 2–1 to a Boro side that included McIlmoyle. But this was the first time Stokoe had ever got to the last sixteen in the Cup as a manager, and it equalled Carlisle's best run in the competition.

There is no doubt that Cup runs suited Stokoe, though. The pride and passion they brought to the towns where he managed was the stuff he had been brought up on at Newcastle. But it was his reputation for getting teams out of trouble and then reviving their fortunes that led to his fifth managerial appointment in December 1970 when Blackpool lured him away from Carlisle to take over at Bloomfield Road.

Ternent pays his former manager this testimony: 'Bob was an out-and-out winner. He took Carlisle to the semi-finals of the League Cup, we maintained our status in the division comfortably and a few years later we won promotion to the First Division. He was never frightened to be first and he was a hard taskmaster. He was tough but his bark was worse than his bite really. Football management was a way of life for him. He had a desire to improve players and he treated them as men. He didn't suffer fools gladly but he was a fantastic guy and I got as close to him as anyone. Bob was immaculate in his dress. He loved his Chester suits and his Church's shoes. He loved his family, he loved his dog and he loved the golf course. We became good friends. He was a big influence on me.'

Blackpool had been interested in Stokoe for a while. They had approached him at the end of the 1968–69 season after Stan Mortensen left, but he had turned them down: he had been at Carlisle for just a matter of months at that time and he was not interested in leaving. But in October 1970 Blackpool went for Stokoe again – and again and again. At the fourth time of asking, they finally got him.

'Blackpool persisted and persisted,' Stokoe said. 'I think they had made up their minds that I could be the salvation of the club. They felt that I was the one to lead them. This influenced me more than anything: the fact that I was wanted so much. I started to waver. Eventually I said: "If Carlisle are prepared to release me from my contract, I will join you." Everything was sorted out by the two chairmen.'

Stokoe's first match at Blackpool was the FA Cup third-round tie against West Ham. A match that was made famous by the skills and goals of Tony Green and the subsequent suspension of Bobby Moore and Jimmy Greaves by the Hammers after the England internationals had broken a pre-match curfew the night before. Blackpool won 4–0. It was the highlight of a dismal season for them, but while Stokoe was present at the game, he did not pick the team; that had been the last task of Jimmy Meadows, who then blotted his copybook by being quoted as referring to Moore as 'the world's worst defensive player'.

The first public task for Stokoe at Bloomfield Road was to make an apology on behalf of Meadows: 'I know I would have been very upset if Ron Greenwood, the West Ham manager, had said something like that about a Blackpool player,' he said. 'I don't think a club has any right to criticise someone else's players.'

Stokoe's first match as Blackpool manager came in the First Division the following week, against Liverpool at Anfield. It finished in a 2–2 draw. In total he was in charge of eighteen top-flight games that season – including a 1–1 draw against Revie's Leeds – but had to wait until the penultimate fixture of the season, at home to Crystal Palace, to celebrate his first-ever managerial win in the top flight. Blackpool finished eleven points away from safety and were promptly relegated back to the Second Division. It was the first relegation in Stokoe's twenty-three-year career as both a player and a manager.

'We weren't good enough,' Stokoe said. 'Those four or five months in the First Division were frightening. I never want to go back unless I am ready – it is cruel.'

'I think Bob Stokoe made his mind up pretty soon that the team was not going to survive in the First Division,' Blackpool's record appearance holder and former England international full-back Jimmy Armfield says. 'In my opinion he made his mind up too quickly about that. But he was very experienced, realistic and always looking to the future. The team was struggling. I had a bad knee injury and watched a lot of games that season from the sidelines. I came back into the side and played in the very last game of the season against Manchester United at Bloomfield Road. That was the last match of my career.

'As a footballer, Bob was an old-fashioned stopper,' Armfield adds. 'But off the pitch his temperament was nice and gentle, with a soft side. He was good to me. I started coaching the Blackpool youth team that season and we got to the final of the Lancashire Youth Cup, where we lost to Bolton. At the end of the season I was approached by both Blackburn and Bolton and asked if I would be their manager. I was thirty-five at the time. I told Bob about it and he said to me, "I would have jumped at Bolton at your age, I'd take it." I went to see Sir Matt

Busby and he told me the same.' Armfield accepted the Bolton job offer and within two years he had led them back up to the Second Division.

While Armfield took over at Bolton in the summer of 1971, Stokoe guided Blackpool to their first piece of silverware since the FA Cup in 1953, in the shape of the Anglo-Italian Cup. This summer competition was usually contested by a dozen sides from the lower reaches of the First Division and Serie A, plus a handful of invited Second Division teams. Blackpool's place was only assured after Brian Clough's Derby County had pulled out of the tournament at the end of the season. Victories over Hellas Verona and Roma were followed by a 2–1 extra-time win over Bologna in the final, played in front of a partisan 40,000 crowd at the city's Stadio Communale on a warm June evening. This was Stokoe's first trophy as a manager and the morose mood of relegation that had overcome Blackpool the previous month was instantly lifted. The promenade was packed with cheering fans the following day when Stokoe and his team arrived back at the town hall.

'It was all well and good winning the Anglo-Italian Cup but, while he enjoyed winning it, I think Bob had a long-term view for Blackpool,' Armfield says. 'I thought he would go on and win promotion back to the First Division. They won the Anglo-Italian Cup and the only thing they had lost was me. Bob had some good young players – Tony Green, Tommy Hutchison, Bill Bentley, John Craven, Glyn James, Alan Suddick and so on.'

But Blackpool did not win promotion back to the First Division and Stokoe soon had to sell Green to Newcastle, rebuffing a bid from Revie and Leeds in the process. 'I want Newcastle to have Tony Green,' Stokoe said defiantly at the time. Later on he admitted he had also tried to attract other sides into signing the midfielder in an effort to spurn Revie's advances: 'I tried to get Liverpool interested,' he said. 'When Bill Shankly asked me why I was set against the offer from Leeds, I told him about the thing with Revie at Bury. Bill went silent. I don't think he ever again saw Revie in the same light.'

Blackpool finished sixth in the Second Division that season, and Stokoe enjoyed another good Cup run when his team reached the quarter-finals of the League Cup. They also relegated Charlton – the only club ever to sack him – on the last day of the season. It was the first time the Valiants had sunk below the top two divisions since 1935. Stokoe was ecstatic.

'We went up to Blackpool and we needed a result to stay up,' Peacock recalls. 'I remember Bob standing in the corridor as we were coming out on to the pitch and telling the Charlton players, "You're going to get nothing from me today." I perhaps didn't care for his remarks but I can understand it. He was fired up and he had his team fired up too. It was clear to me that this was his chance for revenge and he wanted to prove a point. He was clearly still hurting from his dismissal. Blackpool beat us 5–0 and we went down. It was a terrible moment for us. Bob popped his head around the dressing-room door afterwards and told us that he was glad we had gone down. He said he had wanted to see us get relegated. He had been hurt and this was his moment of satisfaction. There were only a few of us that remained from his time at Charlton but his feelings were not directed at any of the players. It was not personal as such. He wanted the club to suffer. I remember he told us: "This is a moment I have to enjoy." That was Bob.' It was almost five years since Charlton had sacked Stokoe, but the character of the man could not forgive and could not forget even after he had found some form of retribution.

The 1972–73 season started well for Blackpool and by the end of November Stokoe's side were positioned third in the table and were again through to the quarter-finals of the League Cup, knocking out First Division Newcastle and Birmingham in the process. The future looked bright for Stokoe and the Seasiders.

Blackpool-born journalist Robin Daniels had just completed his book *Blackpool Football*. It came out in October 1972 and a whole chapter was dedicated to Stokoe, in the manager's own words, and makes interesting reading. Stokoe told Daniels: 'We want to re-establish ourselves as a First Division club. But we want to re-enter the First Division from a position of strength. We want to have a good chance of staying up.' It seemed apparent he had no intention of leaving the club. Meanwhile chairman Frank Dickinson told Daniels: 'The longer Bob Stokoe is with us, the more my faith in him is justified.'

'My impression of Bob Stokoe at that time was that he was a man who got respect not from fear but from a natural dignity,' Daniels recalls. 'He had a natural charm but I think he may have underestimated himself a little bit. He wasn't particularly proactive in looking for new opportunities and therefore he was usually headhunted by other clubs. He had a strategic sense of building a team on a budget and he had a deep sense of responsibility and commitment. But he was also a very competitive man. I remember going to one match with him on the team coach and he was at the front, kneeling down, watching a horse race on the small television set. He had placed a small bet – maybe £1 – on this horse at four to one or something and he was on his knees shouting, "Come on, baby!" He was like that about everything, even if he was playing a game of chess.'

By now Stokoe had learned the credentials of his own managerial style, putting an emphasis on loyalty and respect: 'A manager who doesn't have the respect of his players might as well give up,' he said. 'My relationship with players is the most important aspect of my job. If you don't get them to play for you, you have no chance.'

At this time a return to the First Division looked possible for Blackpool, but it was not to happen. In fact until 2010 Blackpool had not played in the top flight since the very day Armfield retired from playing in that match against Manchester United back in May 1971. During the following six seasons they were always near the top of the Second Division or thereabouts, but promotion was never achieved. Nor did it ever look quite as likely as it had in the autumn of 1972 when the club was placed third in the table and in the last eight of the League Cup – just days before Stokoe received a telephone call that was to offer him the chance of a lifetime and a return to his native north-east.

3.

A DISCIPLE OF DISCIPLINE

Raich Carter and Len Shackleton were living legends in football; their faces adorned old cigarette-card collections and their names tripped off the tongues of generations of football supporters. In County Durham they remain icons to this day and merchandise featuring both of them continues to sell at the Stadium of Light.

These two England internationals sum up a large part of the history of Sunderland: the cool and talented Carter captained the club to their sixth (and last) league championship in 1936 and to a first-ever FA Cup triumph the following year; while from the late 1940s onwards Shackleton did more than anyone to create the famous 'Roker Roar' – an overwhelming wall of sound that reverberated around the home ground on match days. Shack was the greatest entertainer ever seen in a red-and-white-striped shirt. A genius on the ball with tricks to burn, he made Sunderland supporters laugh as much as cheer and happily lived up to his title of the 'Clown Prince of Soccer' from week to week for ten seasons.

During this period Sunderland became known as the 'Bank of England club' on account of the large sums of money paid to attract a plethora of international stars to the north-east in a seemingly never-ending search to win silverware. The 1937 FA Cup win remained the last in the club's long list of honours for some time. The true glory days had come a long time before, with the 'Team of all the Talents' claiming three Football League crowns before the end of the nineteenth century. Two more titles were won before the outbreak of the First World War. Furthermore the league and Cup double was almost achieved in 1913 when a league-winning side led by another legend, Charlie Buchan, was narrowly beaten 1–0 by Aston Villa in the FA Cup final at Crystal Palace in front of 120,081 spectators.

The Cup eluded Sunderland for a very long time. The supporters always loved the competition and flocked to Roker Park for matches – the biggest attendance ever recorded there was 75,118, for a quarter-final replay against Derby County on a Wednesday afternoon in 1933 – but success in it remained comparatively thin. The 1937 triumph, achieved with a televised 3–1 win over Preston North End at Wembley in front of King George VI, was celebrated more than any of the club's six league titles. The team's homecoming was spectacular: a special Pullman train brought them through packed platforms full of men, women and children waving red-and-white scarves at Doncaster, York and Darlington; and when the players stepped off the train at Monkwearmouth Station, tugs and ships on the River Wear hooted and blew their sirens to welcome them home. As the trophy was paraded around Roker Park fans clad in red-and-white suits and dresses danced up and down the terraces. The party went on until the early hours of the following morning. The recently married Carter had by then departed on his delayed honeymoon. The Cup had always mattered to Sunderland fans, but a deep and true love affair with it began at this very moment.

As the stylish Shackleton strutted his stuff to rapturous applause throughout the 1950s, Sunderland twice more reached FA Cup semi-finals but lost on both occasions. After the Second World War the club became more famous for entertainment than silverware, and it was soon two decades since they had won anything, no matter how hard manager Bill Murray tried, and no matter how much local furniture manufacturer Bill Ditchburn, the club chairman, and his board of directors spent to lure the top stars to the club.

Murray had played at right-back for the Rokerites in the 1935–36 championship-winning season. He returned to take over as manager at the beginning of the 1939–40 season, which was subsequently abandoned due to war, and was in charge for eleven full seasons from 1946 to 1957. However, despite taking Sunderland to those two semi-finals in 1955 and 1956 and finishing third in the First Division in the 1949–50 season, his name will always be synonymous with events that were to spearhead the sudden demise of the club and lead in turn to the arrival of one Alan Brown, a disciple of discipline and a manager who would gradually bring together most of the team that would one day bask in the glory of Sunderland's greatest-ever achievement.

Shackleton was Murray's first big signing for Sunderland. He joined the club from Newcastle United for a British record fee of £20,050 in early 1948. Shack was a maverick: highly skilful yet controversial. His comments often made him as famous as his footwork and his popular remark, 'I am not biased when it comes to Newcastle, I don't care who beats them' is still happily quoted by Sunderland fans.

Supporters surged to Roker Park to see him play. A new league attendance record of 61,084 was set at the ground against Blackpool in April 1948, and was broken twice within the next eighteen months. But the fervour that followed him often hid some poor results: Sunderland came close to losing their First Division status in the 1947–48 season and were on the receiving end of one of the greatest FA Cup shocks of all time when they went down 2–1 after extra-time on the sloping Huish pitch at Southern League Yeovil Town to an amateur side full of workers from the local glove factories who were managed by Alec Stock, in January 1949. 'The world's best 11 players wouldn't make a team, you must have blend,' Shackleton, helped by hindsight, later wrote in *Clown Prince of Soccer?*.

Murray and the Sunderland directors responded to the Yeovil defeat by bringing out the chequebook: inside-forward Ivor Broadis was signed from Carlisle United for £18,000, and two days later winger Tommy Wright joined from Partick Thistle. The new signings paid off as Sunderland became the top-scoring side in the First Division in the 1949–50 season with eighty-three goals, and finished third in the table – the club's highest position since the last championship win. Had it not been for an inexplicable home defeat by bottom-of-the-table Manchester City in April, the Rokerites would have won the title. As it was they finished one point behind both Portsmouth and Wolves. Meanwhile the crowds just got bigger and bigger, resulting in a record league attendance of 68,004 against Newcastle in March 1950. The average home attendance was 47,785. The aggregate home attendance exceeded one million. Football had become the nation's number-one entertainment industry, and in Shackleton Sunderland had the greatest entertainer of them all. The gate money was burning a hole in the club's pockets.

During that season Ditchburn took over as chairman. His instinct was to keep on spending. It was a quick-fix formula to win honours: big-money transfers for top-quality superstars. More new signings arrived, in the shape of Wales international centre-forward Trevor Ford for a new British transfer record fee of £30,000; Northern Ireland winger Billy Bingham; and Scotland half-back George Aitken. Suddenly everyone wanted to play for the Rokerites: 'I wanted to go to Sunderland,' Leeds United, Juventus and Wales legend John Charles later admitted. 'Everybody wanted to go to Sunderland because they were getting good wages. They were getting overpaid, I think, and everybody wanted to play for Sunderland at that time.' This, of course, was still the era of the maximum wage.

In January 1953 Sunderland were top of the First Division and seemingly closing in on the title, but a terrible run of six draws and six defeats left them in ninth place at the end of the campaign. Ditchburn and his directors again splashed the cash in a bid to buy success and forked out a further £62,000 on three more international players within a fortnight – Scotland goalkeeper Jimmy Cowan, Wales centre-half Ray Daniel and England winger Billy Elliott. The 'Bank of England club' tag was now well and truly established and famous throughout the football world. So much so that when South African Ted Purdon, who cost £15,000, arrived at Sunderland early the following year and went over to Daniel, Elliott and Shackleton – all £20,000-plus signings – to say hello, Shackleton joked to him, 'You mustn't mix with us. Go and talk to the other serfs and peasants.'

Sunderland now started to attract support from outside County Durham. One of the club's most famous supporters is Buckinghamshire-born lyricist Sir Tim Rice, who began following the fortunes of the Rokerites from afar when he was at school. He says: 'I have no connection with Sunderland at all. I didn't even know where it was. But I thought the name conjured up images of calypso beaches and palm trees and it sounded fantastic. After about three matches I realised that I had picked a team that could hardly have been further away from where I was, but I stuck with it and I carried on caring about how they did each Saturday.'

Despite a truly breathtaking forward line Sunderland could still struggle on the pitch. The club inexplicably finished the 1953–54 season in eighteenth place and were knocked out of the FA Cup in the third round by Second Division Doncaster Rovers at Roker Park. Never has there been a better example of talented individuals being unable to make a successful team, prompting Shackleton's famous quote. So yet more new players arrived, including Scotland centre-forward Charlie Fleming.

Sunderland improved, to finish fourth in the table in the 1954–55 season, and were only denied a place in the FA Cup final in a 1–0 semi-final defeat by Don Revie's Manchester City at Villa Park – this was the nearest the competition has ever been to a Tyne-Wear Cup final to this day. The Rokerites reached the last four again the following season, when two goals from Bill Holden secured a satisfying quarter-final victory over Newcastle, the holders, at St James' Park – Jackie Milburn, Bob Stokoe and all.

'That had to be the worst feeling any Newcastle supporter or player could have,' Stokoe admitted. (Incidentally, Holden went on to play with the future Sunderland manager at Bury and featured in *that* match against Leeds in April 1962.) The Rokerites were comfortably beaten by Birmingham City in the FA Cup semi-finals.

'It's a bitter experience to lose a semi-final,' Elliott, who played for Sunderland in both those semi-finals, at outside-left in 1955 and inside-left in 1956, later said. 'There was a lot of fuss about Revie then – he was playing with a number 9 on his back but lying very deep – and the papers were full of the "Revie Plan". Sunderland didn't have a tactician, a leader or a driver and that is why we failed to win anything, even though we had a great side.' Revie and Manchester City went on to win the 1956 FA Cup final, and the man himself was duly signed by Sunderland a few months later in a £20,000 deal.

Then the walls caved in at Roker Park. Towards the end of 1956 the Football League received a letter signed by a 'Mr Smith' citing financial irregularities and undeclared payments to players at Sunderland. The Football League's management committee asked to see the club's books and, in the following March, a joint Football League and Football Association commission saw Murray, Ditchburn, director W. S. Martin and secretary George Crow at the Royal Victoria Station Hotel in Sheffield. Three weeks later the entire Sunderland board, plus Murray and Crow, were summoned to a second hearing. When the commission published its findings, Sunderland were damned. The inquiry found that illicit payments had been made to players totalling £5,427 14s 2d. The club was said to have paid contractors – dealing in straw and tarmac – excessive amounts of money, which were then returned as treasury notes and subsequently handed out to players as payments.

This was in breach of the permitted maximum-wage regulations and therefore illegal.

The commission threw the book at Sunderland: Ditchburn and Martin were suspended permanently from any involvement in professional football, vice-chairman Stanley Ritson and director L. W. Evans were suspended *sine die* and other directors were severely censured. The club was fined £5,000 and ordered to pay full costs. It was the biggest fine ever imposed in the history of the game. The 'Bank of England club' was no more.

Six players – four of whom were still at Sunderland – were then summoned to the FA to answer allegations regarding illegal payments. Five of them appeared but under advice did not answer any questions and were suspended *sine die*. Three weeks afterwards, at another meeting, they admitted the charge and the suspensions were lifted, but each of them was made to forfeit qualification for benefits.

Murray was fined £200 after the commission took into account that he had acted under instruction. After an association with Sunderland as a player and a manager for close on thirty years, he handed in his resignation to the new club chairman Colonel John Turnball on 26 June 1957. He continued to live in the town and remained a regular supporter of the club until his death just four years later in 1961.

'Mr Smith' was never named, but the *Daily Express* saw a copy of the letter that was sent to the Football League and reported: 'Smith gives enough facts to show he is well acquainted with the Sunderland club and that his object is the punishment of individuals.' More than fifty years on, the identity of the mysterious Mr Smith remains unknown.

Long after the dust had settled, the Association of Football Players and Trainers' Union – dubbed the 'Players' Union' by the press – collected thousands of names of other footballers who admitted to having received similar payments elsewhere. The case essentially highlighted the fact that football's maximum-wage system was out of date, and within a few years it would in fact be abolished. Elliott, one of the Sunderland players caught up in the scandal, later said: 'I felt that if they were going to accuse us of illegal payments they had to accuse everybody, because it was happening throughout football.'

Sunderland paid the highest price, morally as much as anything else. On the field the team managed to scrape enough points together at the end of that tumultuous 1956–57 season to avoid relegation and keep up the club's long-standing unbroken record in the top flight, but the damage was deep and the scars would take a long time to heal.

No club had been in the First Division longer than Sunderland, and this was a lasting achievement that the fans proudly held on to; the matchday programme featured the words 'Only club which has never played in any other than the First Division' on the cover. But those days were numbered; Sunderland were now a club in crisis.

The new chairman needed to appoint a new manager quickly. The directors were looking for someone who could turn the club's fortunes around and take them forward into the new decade and beyond. More pressingly, they needed to find someone who could move the club on from this mess. Raich Carter – who was by then the manager of Leeds – was the popular choice among the supporters and also reported to be the favourite for the job but, instead, the position was offered to Alan Brown, who readily accepted it.

Brown was a man who both craved and demanded respect; and he was feared as much as he was respected. Those attributes are clearly what attracted the new regime at Roker Park.

He was also a manager who believed whole-heartedly in the power of youth. Born in Consett in County Durham – close to the northern border with Northumberland – in 1914, Brown attended Hexham Grammar School and played football for the successful Spen Black and Whites, based in High Spen, in his youth. He supported Sunderland from boyhood and grew up with happy tales of the 'Team of all the Talents'. Sunderland had one of the proudest histories in the game and nobody would have been prouder to manage them at that time than this man, who had once played at centre-half for Huddersfield Town, Burnley and Notts County.

As a player, Brown's biggest honour was an FA Cup runners-up medal with Burnley, whom he captained in the 1947 final defeat by Charlton. He retired from football the following year and trained as a policeman, but was persuaded to come back into the game in a coaching capacity after receiving a flattering letter from FA secretary Stanley Rous.

Brown subsequently spent four seasons as trainer-coach at Sheffield Wednesday before securing the managerial post at Burnley under the chairmanship of Bob Lord in 1954. With small crowds and limited funds, Brown set up a youth system at Turf Moor and impressively nurtured young talent. He also made famous names such as Jimmy Adamson and Jimmy McIlroy dig out ditches with him as he developed futuristic outdoor training amenities. An imposing character, Brown would often sweep the dressing-room floor himself in front of his young players. He had always believed the best way to learn was by tough example.

Within six years Burnley were crowned Football League champions, but by then Brown had moved on and Harry Potts – who managed them to that success – subsequently took the credit. Brown was renowned as an energetic, hard-working manager with innovative ideas – particularly around free-kicks, set pieces and training techniques – plus a football brain that was said to be years ahead of its time. But his main prowess as a manager undoubtedly lay in discovering and grooming young talent. Therefore, inheriting the superstar remains of the 'Bank of England club' era at Sunderland was not to his liking.

Shackleton played just one game under Brown – the opening fixture of the 1957–58 season – before abruptly announcing his retirement on medical advice. Shackleton had caused a reaction in the Sunderland dressing room during the close season by refusing to sign the Players' Union 'confession'. Possibly more significantly, he was also a Murray man.

Brown seemed undeterred by this. He had already set about the task of finding new, improved training facilities for the club on the old gun site between Cleadon and Whitburn, and led the way in creating the North Regional League for reserve teams. He also recruited Scottish scout Charlie Ferguson, who had worked with him at Burnley, and challenged him to find the best young talent around. Slowly Brown started to reshape the look of the Sunderland side by putting the emphasis on youth, something he had done so successfully at Turf Moor, but something that was not popular at all among the senior players at Roker Park.

Right-back Allan Graham was one of the youngsters drafted into the first team by Brown and made his debut in the third match of the 1957–58 season in a 5–0 defeat at Wolves: 'The best players in the British Isles had been attracted to the club in the Bill Ditchburn era,' he says. 'These were international players who knew how to play entertaining and skilful football. It was a nice, settled life for them and they were looked after pretty well. But then it all got very different. Alan Brown wasn't very well liked. He was the sergeant-major type and he would stroll on to the pitch on training days in just a pair of shorts, bare-chested and with no shoes. It was a big shock when they got this chap. He took the squad on a pre-season walk down to the sea at Roker, then a run along the seashore, and then a run back to the ground. Once back at the ground, he ran us around the track. The senior players didn't take too much to that and there was a lot of whispering going on.

'I think Len Shackleton would have lasted longer if Bill Murray hadn't gone – but of course only Shack knew how bad his knee was,' Graham adds. 'The crowd used to go wild for Shack. It was one and threepence very well spent, I can tell you. I watched him myself as a ten-year-old boy from the Roker End. He was one of a long-established team of international players at Sunderland. This was the team that I joined. Then this new guy comes in and tries to teach them all a lesson. He picked a lot of young fellows and he threw us in, to be honest. The team wasn't doing very well and I think he was trying to tell the older players that their places weren't guaranteed. He did that by bringing in youngsters like me. There was a reaction to it and it wasn't very nice. It wasn't a pleasant time at the club.'

Sunderland stuttered and spluttered on the pitch more than ever under Brown. Supporters, used for many years to the entertaining fare served up by Shackleton and co., became disenchanted and began to openly criticise the manager. The Rokerites were thrashed 7–0 at Blackpool and 6–0 at Burnley, but Brown remained unmoved.

Those two defeats heralded the beginning of the career of Charlie Hurley at Sunderland. The stylish centre-half would become one of the most important signings ever made by Brown, and helped shaped the future of the Rokerites for the next decade. The circumstances surrounding his move from Millwall to Sunderland say a lot about the manager who was now known within the game as 'the Bomber': 'Alan Brown spent three whole days talking me into going up to Sunderland,' Hurley says. 'I was happy in London and a few clubs were interested in me. I spoke to my mum and dad about it and I told them how I felt but he talked them around. I had my own car and it took me ten hours to get up there. I swear I went through every town and village and

I thought I was going to come to the end of the earth. But it was the greatest move I could ever have made. The man was a father figure to me. He was a real hard bastard and he didn't stand any nonsense but you knew where you stood with him. The players were frightened to death of him.'

Hurley replaced Aitken in a changing Sunderland line-up: Bingham, Daniel and Fleming all played just one season under Brown, while Elliott and Revie lasted little more than that. But what a season it turned out to be: it was a complete and utter disaster. More heavy defeats followed – 7–1 at Luton and 6–1 at Birmingham – and the campaign ended with a first-ever relegation to the Second Division. The long, proud unbroken run of the Rokerites was finally over. Among those in the team relegated at Portsmouth on 26 April 1958 were Billy Elliott and Don Revie.

Revie was the club captain at Sunderland. He would always remember one particular home match against Everton that season, when his manager was subjected to chants from the terraces for him to be sacked. Brown faced the crowd and the criticism, man to man, at the end of the match. Revie, who saw it all happen, later said: 'I am certain I learned a great deal from him in that unhappy moment.'

Revie was seen to be the man who would lead Sunderland back into the top flight. But within weeks of the start of the new season he had fallen out with Brown, after being banished to the reserves to make way for younger players, and was duly placed on the transfer list, where he was quickly purchased by Leeds. Revie learned a lot about man management and the power of youth from his days spent under Brown, and when he eventually became manager at Elland Road he built a young team from scratch that lasted for a generation.

Brown convinced the Sunderland board that he was building for the future and that youth was the way forward. Sadly things got worse before they got better. The club's first-ever fixture in the Second Division ended in a 3–1 defeat at Lincoln City and the side never recovered after that. More heavy defeats followed: 5–0 at Swansea Town, 6–0 at Sheffield Wednesday and 6–0 at Leyton Orient.

Sunderland finished their first campaign outside the top flight in fifteenth place. The following term they finished sixteenth. The glory days were long gone and as a result attendances were down to the lowest level since the Second World War. The knives were now out for the manager, but he continued to count on the support of his board of directors, led by new club chairman Stanley Ritson – and so he stuck to his principles, handing right-back Cecil Irwin a first-team debut at sixteen while establishing another youngster, Len Ashurst, at left-back. Brown would, in time, be proved right here: both players became Sunderland's first-choice full-backs until the early 1970s.

Slowly but surely a new side was being built around a new captain, Stan Anderson. The local wing-half was the one first-team player who remained from the 'Bank of England club' days, which was ironic given that he had cost the club nothing more than a signing-on fee. He would soon be capped twice under Walter Winterbottom for England.

Sunderland finished the 1960–61 season in sixth place in the Second Division and knocked out Arsenal, Liverpool and Norwich City in the FA Cup before taking on Tottenham Hotspur – placed nine points clear at the top of the First Division – at home in the quarter-finals. In front of 61,326 spectators, Sunderland trailed 1–0 at half-time but put on a second-half display that rocked Spurs. Willie McPheat equalised, prompting a raucous pitch invasion, and in the end Tottenham had to hold out for a draw. Sunderland lost the replay but the point had been made, particularly when Spurs went on to win the league and Cup double that season.

'We absolutely pulverised them at home and the crowd were going berserk,' Hurley recalls. 'Danny Blanchflower later told me that the last fifteen minutes of that match were the hardest fifteen minutes he ever played. We had a chance to win the FA Cup in 1961.'

Brown was now developing a young team of real potential, with youngsters like Jimmy Davison, Jimmy McNab and Nick Sharkey breaking through. McNab and Sharkey were both found in Scotland by Ferguson. Two other Scots, George Herd and George Mulhall, arrived from Clyde and Aberdeen respectively, while Martin Harvey, a future Northern Ireland wing-half, was also picked up. It was an impressive first-team squad and featured no fewer than seven players who had come through the youth system, including possibly the greatest capture of them all: Jim Montgomery.

Montgomery had been taken down to Burnley at the age of fourteen for trials by the club's north-east scout Jack Hixon – the man who later discovered Alan Shearer for Southampton in the 1980s – and could easily have been lost to the Lancashire club. Coincidentally, Hixon began working for the Clarets due to Billy Elliott – whom he knew from serving alongside in the Royal Navy on HMS *Tobago* during the Second World War – who asked him to keep an eye out for good local youngsters. Hixon worked under Brown during his managerial reign at Turf Moor but when 'the Bomber' moved up to Sunderland the scout rejected an opportunity to join him at Roker Park and decided to stay put.

In the end Montgomery was dissuaded from joining Burnley by the high number of quality goalkeepers already on the club's books. He returned home and – after some quick intervention by Sunderland physiotherapist Johnny Watters – was signed up by his home-town club as an apprentice.

'I came home after five weeks at Burnley and Johnny Watters was stood on my doorstep the next day with Mr Alfie Lavender, one of my schoolteachers at St Hilda's School in Sunderland,' Montgomery says. 'I signed for Sunderland straight away.'

Watters was a real character behind the scenes at Roker Park. A short and stocky Scotsman, he would often play the bagpipes to accompany the players as they trained and was rarely seen without his greased black hair and white coat and a pipe in his mouth. But it was his sense of humour that made him so popular with the players. For example, he would think nothing of bringing a greyhound into the dressing room before a match and suggesting that the dog was worth a bet later that night at the races.

The fair-haired Montgomery measured five feet ten inches and was a goalkeeper with a fabulous natural agility and stunning reflexes. He made his first-team debut for Sunderland at Roker Park against Walsall in the second round of the League Cup in October 1961, just five days before his eighteenth birthday. He made his league debut for the club the following February against Derby.

Then came another example of Brown bravado: the signing of Brian Clough. By the end of the 1960–61 season Clough, aged twenty-six, had two England caps to his name and 204 career goals in 222 appearances for Middlesbrough; but he had still not played in the First Division. That summer he arrived at Southampton Docks with his wife at 5 a.m. following a Mediterranean cruise and there to meet him on the quayside was the Sunderland manager, who had in turn broken his own family holiday in Cornwall in an attempt to seal the signing of the talented centre-forward.

As Clough recalled in the book *Cloughie: Walking on Water*:

I'm known as the one who speaks his mind, who gets to the point without fuss, but Browny was the master at it. He tipped the porter a couple of bob, heaved our luggage on to a trolley, looked me straight between the eyes in a way that made lesser men freeze to the spot, and asked: 'Would you sign for Sunderland?' I didn't know Alan Brown personally, but I knew of him. I was aware of his reputation as a strict and honest man. I took him at his word.

Clough returned home and signed for Sunderland.

There had been a petition set up by some Middlesbrough players to remove Clough as their team captain, such was his reputation at Ayresome Park, but Brown referred to the signing as 'the shortest, sweetest deal you ever saw – and this was supposedly the most awkward bloke in the game'. 'I didn't worry about his reputation,' the Sunderland manager said. 'I had the same reputation myself. We both called a spade a spade.'

Clough's signature cost Sunderland £40,000, but he never played for the club in the famous strip of red-and-white shirt and black shorts. Brown controversially decided to change the colour of the team's shorts to white just before the start of the 1961–62 season and in doing so he announced a new future for the club and visibly declared that the days of Carter, Shackleton and those before them were well and truly in the past. His decision was not a popular one among supporters but, once again, he remained unaffected by that. No supporter could argue with the improvements on the pitch: Sunderland narrowly missed out on returning to the First Division in the next two seasons and on both occasions were denied in heartbreaking fashion. In 1961–62 the Rokerites missed out by a point to Leyton Orient after a final-day draw against relegation-threatened Swansea; a win would have put them up on goal average. The following season they missed out on goal average to promotion rivals Chelsea, after losing 1–0 at home to them in their final match of the season; a draw would have put them up. But that season was completely overshadowed by what happened to Clough in front of a crowd of 42,407 at Roker Park on Boxing Day.

Clough had made an instant impact at Sunderland. He hit twenty-nine league goals in thirty-four appearances in his first season, and added twenty-four league goals in twenty-four appearances in the early part of the following season. In all he recorded no fewer than seven hat-tricks in that time and there is little doubt Sunderland would have won promotion had he not been so cruelly taken from them midway through his second season at the club.

The winter of 1962–63 was the coldest on record since 1739–40. Heavy snowfall, ice and freezing fog brought havoc to the country for months. The Football Pools Panel was created to deal with the never-ending weekly list of postponements, and the Christmas football programme was decimated. Few matches survived that Boxing Day but Sunderland versus Bury – led by player-manager Bob Stokoe – went ahead. The fact that it did inadvertently led to the premature end of one of the brightest careers in English football.

'The weather was that bad on the way to the ground that Bob Stokoe telephoned Sunderland from Scotch Corner to check that the match was still on,' Bury player George Jones remembers. 'When we got to Roker Park we saw workmen on the field using braziers to melt the ice. The pitch was soft on top for about one-quarter of an inch but it was rock-hard underneath. It was treacherous actually.'

Thirty minutes before kick-off there was a deluge of hailstones and the pitch was turned into a mudbath. During the match Clough collided with Bury goalkeeper Chris Harker as he chased a loose ball in the penalty box and his cruciate ligament was ripped apart by the impact of the oncoming goalkeeper's shoulder. Watters raced through the driving sleet towards the stricken striker. The physiotherapist later said that what he saw when he got over to Clough made his heart sink and he knew immediately that the player's career was over.

As a bloodied Clough attempted to crawl on his hands and knees – unable to push himself up from the ground – he heard the words 'Get up, get up' from a Bury player nearby. This was followed by another comment from the same player to referee Kevin Howley. The words that followed would remain with Clough for the rest of his life: 'Come on, ref, he's only codding,' the player said. A desperate and distraught Clough looked up and realised those words had come from the mouth of Bury's player-manager. Clough would never forgive Stokoe for that.

'They beat us 1–0 and Charlie Hurley missed a penalty for us ten minutes or so before Brian Clough was injured,' Montgomery remembers. 'You always wonder, If we had been 1–0 up, would Brian have gone for it? It was a bad injury in those days and I think we all knew he was never ever going to make it.'

Both Brown and Watters knew deep down that there was no way back for Clough, but they decided to keep that truth from him. 'It would have shattered him,' Watters later said. 'He needed to have some hope as the next few months went by.' Brown personally supervised Clough's rehabilitation, often running beside him up and down the steps of the Fulwell End at Roker Park.

By the 1963–64 season Brown's young Sunderland side were maturing into a team that was too strong and too good not to go up, and the Rokerites were promoted back to the First Division after six long seasons alongside Revie's Leeds, after a battle at the top of the table that kicked off an intense rivalry between these two clubs that was to last for years – largely due to two feisty matches that were played over the Christmas period.

'The rivalry with Leeds all started back in the promotion season when they just kicked us and kicked us at Roker Park,' Sunderland supporter Pete Sixsmith says. 'It was the only time I ever saw Charlie Hurley lose his temper at Sunderland. I was stood at the front of the Fulwell End and clearly saw Leeds' centre-forward Ian Lawson follow through on Jim Montgomery and kick him in the head. Hurley had hold of Lawson by the throat. It took Len Ashurst, Martin Harvey and Jimmy McNab to drag him off. He was furious. We all thought they were just a dirty, nasty, horrible side from then on.'

Sunderland enjoyed another good run in the FA Cup in 1964 and provided Roker Park with one of its most famous nights in the process. It is possible that had the Rokerites not lost a two-goal lead in the closing minutes against Manchester United in the quarter-final at Old Trafford the long wait for silverware could have ended that year. As it was, the tie went on to last for 300 minutes before finishing in a second replay – and a Sunderland defeat – at Huddersfield.

Three home wins in the competition had already attracted three large crowds, including the highest attendance recorded at Roker Park since 1954 when 62,817 spectators turned up to watch a memorable 3–1 win over Football League champions Everton in the fifth round.

Arthur Pearson was a pianist with a dance band that played regularly at the Roker Hotel, on the seafront, at this time: 'I remember those nights when the Roker Roar was in full force,' he says. 'We couldn't hear ourselves play and the dancers couldn't hear any music to dance to. It was that loud.'

Two Johnny Crossan goals helped to put Sunderland 3–1 up in front of a crowd of 61,700 at Old Trafford. But Montgomery was concussed late on and the game suddenly changed. Bobby Charlton and George Best scored, to agonisingly force a 3–3 draw and earn the Cup holders a replay – and another chance – at Roker Park.

'Denis Law smacked one from six yards straight into my face,' Montgomery recalls. 'I was knocked out a bit. But that is how I stopped it. From a goalkeeper's point of view, it doesn't matter how you save them or with what. Sadly they came back after that and grabbed a draw. We had been in a good position to reach the FA Cup semi-finals.'

Thirty miles away, at Anfield, Swansea caused the shock of the season by defeating Liverpool 2–1; and with Preston North End, another Second Division club, also through to the semi-finals, the competition was wide open. If Sunderland could win their replay against Manchester United the trophy was well within their reach. Cup fever spread throughout the town.

Stories persist to this day that close to 100,000 people turned up at Roker Park for the replay. The official attendance was recorded at 46,727, but due to a large gate collapsing under the weight of the crowd the actual figure remains unknown. One man, who lived in a street nearby, left home to buy a packet of cigarettes, was carried into the ground by the momentum of the surge when the gate collapsed and ended up in the Roker End. He eventually returned home, minus cigarettes and his slippers. Some reports suggested that as many as 90,000 people could have been in the ground to see the match, with many others outside on the streets following the action via the roars from the terraces.

In the first volume of his autobiography, *My Manchester United Years*, Sir Bobby Charlton vividly remembers this match: 'The noise generated by all those fans crammed into the dark, and what must have been extremely dangerous, terraces was amazing. It was as though we were playing beyond ourselves, carried on by the fervour of the crowd and an unwillingness, after so much effort, to abandon the fight.'

Sunderland took the lead again in the replay, this time through Sharkey. Law equalised to force extra-time. Sunderland again took the lead – after a Maurice Setters own-goal – and once more looked set for the semi-finals until another late goal from Charlton just two minutes from the end of time sent the tie into a second replay.

The following day dozens of shoes – and at least one pair of slippers – were found scattered around the ground and in the adjoining streets. The roofs of parked cars were found dented as people had escaped from the crush. There were sixty-one casualties and fourteen people were detained in hospital overnight.

In the second replay Sharkey gave Sunderland the lead once again, but United replied with five goals – including a hat-trick from Law – to progress comfortably into the semi-finals, 5–1. Sunderland's brave attempt at knocking out the Cup holders was finally at an end.

'My big ambition was always to lift the FA Cup,' Hurley says. 'We had a great chance in 1964 and the vast majority of our side were Alan Brown's boys from the youth system. Manchester United hammered us in the last game but we led 3–1 at Old Trafford and were unlucky at Roker Park too. We were fantastic in the first two games and, had we won, the draw would have opened up for us. I was absolutely desperate to get to a Cup final but fate didn't grant me that wish. That year was my last chance really.'

A total of 322,080 spectators had seen Sunderland play six matches in the Cup that season – an average of 53,680 per match. The true figure, of course, will never be known given the events surrounding the sixth-round replay at Roker Park. But what is known is that Sunderland would never again host such a match without making it all-ticket.

West Ham United beat Manchester United in the semi-finals and went on to win the FA Cup, defeating Preston in the final. Charlton suggested in his autobiography that the three matches in nine days it took to get past Sunderland possibly had an effect on his side's attempt to reach Wembley. West Ham captain Bobby Moore later said that he was pleased when the Rokerites had been knocked out.

Moore won the Football Writers' Footballer of the Year award in 1964, while Hurley finished runner-up. 'Who knows? I may have won the award had we been FA Cup winners,' the former Sunderland captain jokes. Hurley's fine achievement in finishing second to Moore while playing in the Second Division says a lot about his performances for Sunderland that season, and a lot about that Sunderland team as well.

*

The 1964 FA Cup run – and the huge support it generated – summed up the strength and potential of Brown's side. Promotion was secured shortly afterwards and the long-awaited return of First Division football to Roker Park was eagerly anticipated. But before a ball had even been kicked the following season, the club was suddenly searching for a new manager.

While the Sunderland players were awarded a cash bonus on winning promotion to the First Division, Brown reportedly was not. Furthermore he claimed that he had a verbal agreement to receive one. The board was unforthcoming and so, after seven hard seasons moulding his dream and finally getting the club back into the top flight, Brown simply walked away. He returned to Sheffield Wednesday as manager shortly afterwards.

The Sunderland fans were aghast: 'It was ludicrous,' Sixsmith says. 'The board made no attempt to keep him. In all the years I have watched Sunderland, the biggest opportunity the club ever wasted was in 1964. We went up with a really good side but the club fell out with Alan Brown and we ended up not having a manager until November, by which time the impetus we had taken into the First Division was lost.'

'I was not on the board at that time and I was not party to any knowledge about bonus payments or anything,' future Sunderland chairman Keith Collings, son of Syd Collings, who was chairman at the time of Brown's departure in 1964, says. 'But I do remember, because I was travelling with the team at that particular time, that when we played the FA Cup replay at Huddersfield I saw him in the corner of a room with Eric Taylor, who was then the secretary with Sheffield Wednesday. I thought it was odd that these two were closeted in one corner of the room, particularly in front of Sunderland officials. I thought it was a bit blatant, so it came as no surprise when shortly after that he departed.'

Some weeks after his departure from Roker Park, Brown gave an interview to Tyne Tees Television about his decision to resign: 'I never regret anything. I think it is a waste of time,' he said. 'I have no reason to change my mind at all. I am a little sad about it, losing friends and connections perhaps temporarily, but football is rather a small world so we don't entirely lose each other.'

But Brown was to have one regret, as he later admitted to Tony Francis in *Clough: A Biography*:

'When a footballer's getting over a bad injury he is mentally ill as well. It showed in Clough's behaviour. He was under dreadful strain – frightened to death about what would become of him after football. I wasn't as understanding as I might have been. My intention was to get him on to the coaching staff but I didn't tell anyone, least of all Cloughie. I realise now I should have done. It would have eased his anxiety,' he said.

So Sunderland started the 1964–65 season without a manager. George Crow, the club secretary and the one man who came out of the investigation into the illegal payments scandal in 1957 unscathed, took over team affairs and was forced into overseeing a major decision in the opening match of the season when a hand injury sustained by Montgomery left fifteen-year-old Derek Forster as the only option in goal. Forster made his debut in a 3–3 draw at home to Leicester City. But by mid-September – eight games into the new campaign – the Rokerites were still without a league win and, more pertinently still, without a manager.

The Sunderland board decided that the solution might be found 100 miles south of the town in the shape of the club's former captain. Syd Collings travelled to Yorkshire in an attempt to lure Revie from a team placed at the top of the First Division to one placed at the bottom. He came close to securing his signature too.

The Leeds manager was reportedly attracted by the prestige and potential of Sunderland. Billy Bremner, for one, believed Revie was on his way to Roker Park. In *Bremner!* he recalls hearing reports – after Leeds had played Leicester at home in September 1964 – that Revie was set to leave: 'It was very difficult to come to terms with that. It meant a return to his roots for Revie but, to the rest of us, it meant that he was leaving us and joining our rivals,' he said. 'Perhaps most people might have thought that we looked upon him as a traitor – but we didn't at all. He had made us and, even if he did leave, we could never thank him enough for what he had done for us as individuals and as a team,' Bremner added. 'We were determined that we should win his farewell game, and win it well as a gift to him to show him what he had created.'

Leeds beat Blackpool 3–0 in what appeared to be Revie's last match in charge at Elland Road. But then the story turned around and Revie decided to stay put. 'Then came the news that the boss was not leaving at all,' Bremner said. 'The newspapers had turned a vague possibility into an actual event and we had all swallowed it. He called all the players together and told us to forget about any idea that he might be going somewhere. He had started a job at Leeds and he was going to see it through.'

It would not be the last time Revie was linked with the Sunderland manager's job. But he was to stay at Leeds for another ten years until England came calling for his services. It is interesting to speculate what the future might have held for both Sunderland and Leeds had Revie moved back to Roker Park in 1964. One thing is indisputable: the history of English football would never have been quite the same.

The new manager of Sunderland was eventually unveiled three months into the season. George Hardwick had won thirteen caps for England as a player but had not managed a club since leaving Oldham Athletic in the summer of 1956. He had spent the intervening years as a coach at PSV Eindhoven in Holland and later at Middlesbrough. Hardwick had been working as a newspaper journalist for some time and one day, while sitting in the Roker Park press room, was asked if he would go to the chairman's office.

Hardwick thought he was going to be told the name of the new Sunderland manager. He was flabbergasted when he was offered the position himself. He promptly accepted and agreed to work without a contract, although he claimed he shook hands with Collings on a gentleman's agreement which, he believed, meant a long-term deal if relegation was avoided. Sunderland suddenly found form under Hardwick and hauled themselves up the table with a stunning home record of ten wins from fourteen matches to avoid the drop.

The future managerial talent of Clough also began to emerge at Roker Park that season. After almost two years out of the game he had returned briefly to play three matches for the first team early in the 1964–65 season, but he broke down again and it was clear to all that his playing days were finally over. (Incidentally the one and only goal Clough ever scored in the top flight was against Leeds.) When Hardwick arrived at Sunderland Clough was still receiving treatment and still contracted to the club until the end of the season. Hardwick was asked by the directors to find a role that could go towards justifying the striker's wages, so the manager gave him the job of coaching the youth team.

'Cloughie was hanging around the place like a miserable and persistent North Sea fret,' Hardwick wrote in his autobiography *Gentleman George*.

His much heralded comeback had failed and, although he was trying to keep himself physically fit, he had no focus in his life. But I was determined to give him one. I called Brian into my office and told him that I had a job for him. I informed him that he was going to work for me, training the youth players. It was heart-warming to see Brian's positive and immediate reaction. He jumped at the chance, just as I knew he would. The appreciation was written all over his face as he warmly put his arm around my shoulder and said: 'You'll do for me, boss.'

Clough had been a lost soul since sustaining his sickening injury, and by his own admission he was looking for a new direction. He flirted with politics and may even have stood as a parliamentary candidate for the Labour Party in the North Yorkshire seat of Richmond in the 1964 general election had Brown not put a stop to it.

More emerging youth talent continued to arrive at Roker Park. One of the last youngsters to have joined Sunderland under the Brown regime was the diminutive Bobby Kerr, who hailed from Alexandria, a small town near to the southern shore of Loch Lomond in Dunbartonshire. The tiny Scot appeared almost fragile at first glance, but within this small frame there was a fearless competitor.

'Charlie Ferguson came from Dumbarton and the joke was that he liked to come home to visit his mum and so that is why he picked so many Scottish lads up,' Kerr says. 'I came down to Sunderland in May 1963 with my dad and we stopped at the Roker Hotel. Sorry, I should say I stopped at the Roker Hotel – my dad and Charlie went out and got absolutely kaylied!

'The story about me is that when he saw me Johnny Watters said, "Has Alan Brown seen him yet, Charlie? Has he seen the size of him? Look at him – he's about seven stone wet through." I never changed. I was always like I was – busy, chasing, running around.

'The manager spent a lot of time on the youth team at Sunderland. We used to play at Hendon police ground and sometimes got crowds of 3,000 to 4,000 there, so that told you what was going on. I remember his statement to us was: "You are not here to clean boots." So basically I started my football career at Sunderland playing football. I would have tidied up and all that, but I don't remember cleaning boots. The manager saw you as men, even though you were only fifteen years old or so.

'Coming to Sunderland was a major culture change for me,' Kerr adds. 'I was brought up in Aggie and Pop Fenwick's digs at 5 Hampden Road, right next to the famous Roker Pie Shop with George Herd, John O'Hare and Norman Clark. George was the king. He was fed on steak while I only got bananas. I once told Aggie that I liked banana sand-wiches and so that is what I got for six months. She would give me my tea and say, "There you go, Bobby, it's your favourite." What could I say?'

O'Hare was in the Sunderland youth team set-up at this time as well. Another Scot, Billy Hughes, came down from Coatbridge Schools, on the outskirts of Glasgow, a little later while two local youngsters – Colin Suggett and Colin Todd – were also on the club's books. All of them were put under the tutelage of Clough.

'We were once told to go and clean George Hardwick's car by Brian Clough,' Kerr recalls. 'My partner in crime was Billy Hughes and we didn't want to do it and we stuck by our guns. We went to see Brian and we said, "We are not here to clean cars." He said, "Well, do it this time for me and I will never ask you again." And he never did.

'I played in some reserve games with Cloughie when he was coming back from his injury,' Kerr recalls. 'In those days we all played a similar system, so if a first-team player got injured then the reserve-team player came into the team and so on. I moved up from the youth team into the reserves and at that time Cloughie was in the reserves making his comeback. We played in one game together against Halifax Town and we beat them 7–1 at Roker Park and Cloughie scored a hat-trick. It was just after this match that he got back into the first team, scored against Leeds, and then sadly that was it. But he scored this hat-trick against Halifax and I am sure I heard the centre-half saying to him afterwards, "It has been a pleasure playing against you, Mr Clough." I thought to myself, Cloughie's just banged in a hat-trick against him! But that was his stature in the game.

'Brian was a carbon copy of Alan Brown,' Kerr continues. 'The one thing he had that Browny didn't have was man management. Cloughie treated every player as an individual but Browny tried to teach every-body the same. He would sometimes try and belittle Charlie Hurley in front of the young lads and we all looked up to Charlie. Cloughie had some crazy ideas but then Browny had some crazy ideas too.'

'Cloughie was the spitting image of Alan Brown,' Montgomery agrees. 'Both had big characters and both would never be wrong: whatever they said went and that was it. There was an incident once with Cloughie and a few of the lads. We used to like a cigarette in them days and we would go to where the counting house was, beside the laundry women, and have a sly one. I will always remember Cloughie walking in one day and giving us the biggest bollocking of our lives for smoking. I thought he was a lovely, smashing fellow and a likeable person but it just depends how you take people, you know. Some got on with him and some didn't get on with him. I think if he had ever been offered the job at Sunderland he would have walked up here to take it.'

The youth-team players responded to Clough. The results were immediate and within a few months the side had reached the last four of the FA Youth Cup, a competition that had been dominated by the Busby Babes of Manchester United in the early years. United won the first five competitions with many of the players who would go on to become household names and some who would sadly lose their lives in the Munich air disaster of 1958. Their success set a hallmark. Clough aimed high in his first season with the youngsters at Roker Park and took them as far as the semi-finals, where they lost to Arsenal. His reward for this achievement was to be released from his duties.

'I went up to Scotland for the summer holidays and I read in the newspaper that they had sacked Brian Clough, for what reason I couldn't tell you to this day,' Hughes says. 'I just couldn't understand why they got rid of him, but Brian being Brian, he was always forthcoming in his opinions and maybe in that day it wasn't welcome. He was always arrogant and confident in his own ability. I suppose, in hindsight, if they had stuck with him who knows what would have happened? We all know the history now, so it was our loss. But I was glad to see him go on and achieve what he did. He was a brilliant manager and even then – as a young player – the confidence he bred in you was brilliant. I had a lot of time for him even though it was a short period in my life. I can understand why he went on to better things.'

'I had known from the start that Brian's appointment was not going to be a popular one in the boardroom,' Hardwick wrote.

In fact I didn't immediately tell the directors about my plans for Brian. When I was finally forced to mention his name at the next board meeting, their reaction was one of controlled anger. It was obvious they didn't want Cloughie on the coaching staff. In fact, they would have preferred to have him out of the club altogether. So when I suggested my long-term objective, which was to appoint him as my right-hand man with the first team, I thought some of the directors were going to have seizures.

At the end of the 1964–65 season both Hardwick and Clough were independently told there was no future for them at Roker Park. Former Scotland manager Ian McColl became the ninth manager of Sunderland, and his first task was to tell Clough he was to be released from the club. Several years later, on the BBC chat show *Parkinson*, Clough spoke openly about the pain this had caused him: 'I was with a club called Sunderland at the time, who were life to me,' he told Michael Parkinson. 'They were life to me. I was under contract. I started training some young boys, coaching the third team actually. Then a new manager took over and he said there was no room for me, and it kind of shattered me for a period of time. It broke me up in actual fact.'

Sunderland received £40,000 in compensation for Clough, who apparently got just £1,500. A crowd of over 31,000 later turned up for a testimonial match at Roker Park for him, raising £5,000 towards his welfare. That summer Hardwick was offered the job of manager at Fourth Division Hartlepools. He declined, but suggested Clough to Pools chairman Ernie Ord. Shackleton – who was by now a journalist with the *Sunday People* – also made the same recommendation to Ord. In October 1965 the most famous managerial career of the late twentieth century began in earnest. On taking up his new position Clough was advised by Shackleton to go and appoint his former Middlesbrough team-mate – and his one true friend during his time at Ayresome Park – Peter Taylor, then manager of non-league Burton Albion, as his assistant. The two of them were to famously create a formidable partnership.

Within a few months of his arrival at the Victoria Ground, Clough had a public-service vehicle licence and was driving the Hartlepools team bus. Within a few years he would return to Roker Park and take O'Hare and Todd – two of his former youth-team players – from the Sunderland first team and turn them into Football League champions at Derby.

Through his contacts, Shackleton played a big part in arranging Clough's move to the Baseball Ground in 1967. Clough soon persuaded O'Hare to drop down a division to join him, and by the time Todd signed, four years later, the Rams were a very good side indeed. The Sunderland board would soon regret letting Clough go. Clough, and the Sunderland fans, would never forget it.

Meanwhile Alan Brown was beginning to rebuild another club in crisis. Sheffield Wednesday were facing the ignominy of having had three first-team players – including two full England internationals – involved in a match-fixing scandal that was to rock English football to its foundations the year before the country hosted the 1966 World Cup finals.

The players – Peter Swan, a member of the 1962 England World Cup squad; Tony Kay, who was expected to feature in the 1966 England World Cup squad and had by now moved to Everton; and David 'Bronco' Layne – were found guilty of match-fixing in the infamous bribes trial of 1965. Each was sent to prison and banned for life. The match in question was between Ipswich Town and Sheffield Wednesday in March 1962. Ipswich won the match and the three players were found guilty of placing bets on their team to lose. Despite a number of other players at lower-league clubs also being charged and sentenced over other results, it was this match that caught the headlines, these players that were to be reviled, and Sheffield Wednesday that emerged from the scandal with the biggest stain of all.

Brown was now a member of the Moral Rearmament movement, a mid-twentieth-century international spiritual organisation that was based on honesty, purity, unselfishness and love. In his autobiography *Setting the Record Straight*, Swan tells of how one day Brown called him into his office at Hillsborough and told him to go home and pray to God for forgiveness for what he had done. 'God will then look after you. Trust in the Lord and you won't have a problem,' he claims Brown told him.

It was no easy task to lift Wednesday from this sorry state of affairs. But lift them Brown did, by doing what he knew best. He focused on youth and within two years took a side featuring no fewer than three teenagers to the 1966 FA Cup final. The Owls led Everton 2–0 at Wembley with just over half an hour to play, but lost the match 3–2. Brown then broke with protocol by instructing his players to do a lap of honour around the pitch. It was the first time in the history of the competition that a losing side had ever done this.

In keeping with what Brown had previously done at Sunderland, the Owls had a new strip that season as well. The manager wanted to rid the club of the famous blue-and-white-striped shirt associated with the match-fixing scandal, and so he replaced it with a blue shirt with white sleeves. This strip remained with Wednesday as long as Brown did; when he left, the club reverted to playing in blue and white stripes.

In the summer of 1966 Roker Park hosted four World Cup matches, including a quarter-final. As a result the Fulwell End got a roof and the Clock Stand gained some seats. Meanwhile McColl signed the mercurial Jim Baxter for £72,500 from his old club Rangers. Although possibly past his best, Baxter was still the most gifted player seen at Sunderland since Shackleton, and he became an instant hero on the terraces. He won ten caps for Scotland in two and a half seasons at Sunderland, including his most famous appearance in the dark blue shirt when he mischievously juggled the ball at Wembley in the 3–2 win over England in 1967. But Baxter was also a serious drinker, and McColl failed to control that. This soon led to a split in the dressing room as Hurley and some of the other players felt ostracised by this new regime. In his autobiography, *Left Back in Time*, Ashurst refers to this period as 'the Bacardi Years'. 'It doesn't take much to upset the very fine balance and pecking order of a dressing room,' he wrote. 'Baxter's arrival wrecked Sunderland's. Worse, Baxter brought a new culture of drinking into the club.'

'Jim Baxter was an absolute genius, way ahead of his time and brilliant to play with,' Hughes says. 'Yes, Jim liked to enjoy himself and it was a shame he liked alcohol more than people should, because if he had stayed on the straight and narrow he would have been the best player they had ever seen in Scotland and in England.'

It was Baxter – not McColl – who told Hughes that he was to make his first-team debut for Sunderland against Liverpool in February 1967: 'That's how it was at that time,' Hughes adds. 'It wasn't very disciplined, but Jim was very good to me and very fair to me and he encouraged me. These are things that you don't forget.'

Hughes had been offered the chance to leave Sunderland for Celtic – the team he supported as a boy – the previous year. A subtle and versatile attacking player, he was offered terms by both clubs but chose Sunderland, much to his father's disappointment. 'Sunderland offered me professional forms to sign when I turned seventeen,' Hughes explains. 'My father came down and he wasn't too happy with the money I was offered so he took me back up to Scotland. At that time I had no say in the matter. I spent six weeks with Celtic and played a couple of reserve games. Jock Stein was the Celtic manager and I was offered more money to play for them but my brother John played for Celtic and Scotland at that time and I felt that I didn't want to be compared. He was a very famous player there. I felt if I was going to make it, I would like to do it on my own without any comparison so that was the reason why I went back to Sunderland. My father never spoke to me for a year and a half! What can I say? I was a Celtic man and Ian McColl was a Rangers man.' When Hughes informed Stein of his decision to sign for McColl and Sunderland, the Celtic boss wished him well and then told him: 'I have got more knowledge in my little finger than he has got.'

Two other notable signings came down from Scotland in the shape of Neil Martin, who joined from Hibernian for £80,000, and George Kinnell, who signed from Oldham Athletic for £20,000. Within a short space of time McColl had a first-team squad with a true Scottish backbone – Baxter, Herd, Hughes, Kerr, Kinnell, Martin, Mulhall and the Derby-bound O'Hare. Not since the all-conquering days of the 'Team of all the Talents' – which featured eight Scots in the first team – had there been so many players from north of the border at Sunderland.

So it was perhaps unsurprising that when Baxter left the club to join Nottingham Forest McColl went back up to Scotland to find a replacement. Ian Porterfield joined Sunderland from Raith Rovers for a fee of £45,000 just after Christmas 1967. There were numerous similarities between Baxter and Porterfield: both started off their careers at Raith, both wore the number 6 shirt and both became cult heroes at Roker Park. But the temperaments were different: Porterfield was more placid. He was also much more of a midfield conductor than a midfield maverick.

Leeds, another club with a strong Scottish presence, had shown an early interest in Porterfield after a chance meeting between the player's mother and Revie's wife in a corner shop in his home town of Lochgelly, in Fife, led to a trial.

'Duncan's was the shop where my mother used to go for the groceries, it was owned by relatives of Don's wife, Elsie, and as a result Elsie and Don often used to pop up to Lochgelly during the close season,' Porterfield explained in his own story of the 1973 FA Cup win, *The Impossible Dream*. 'My mother was always talking about my infatuation with football and the word got back to Don, who was then a player with Leeds.' This amazingly led to a kick-about between the thirteen-year-old boy and the former Sunderland captain at Gardiner's Park – the home of local junior side Lochgelly Albert – and, later on, a month's trial for the youngster at Elland Road.

'Revie was first class,' Porterfield said. 'He made sure I was looked after and he invited me up to his own house for the night. I vividly recall him going upstairs and getting his Player of the Year trophy to show me.'

Porterfield trained every morning and afternoon and played in a couple of trial games but returned after a month homesick. 'When I got back home Revie approached me again to return to Elland Road but I never went,' he said. The youngster signed for Raith and first came to Sunderland's attention a few years later when he played in a Fife Select side against the Rokerites in support of the Michael Colliery Disaster Fund, which was set up following the loss of nine men in a fire at the pit in East Wemyss, Kirkcaldy, in September 1967. Porterfield scored one goal and made two more in a 4–2 win.

He could have signed for Manchester City had the Raith board accepted a £35,000 bid, but this was rejected as they held out for a higher fee. At the press conference to announce his move to Sunderland, McColl was asked why the player had cost so much money. Before the manager could answer, his new recruit cheekily interjected, 'He's got a bargain.' Indeed he had. Porterfield made his debut for Sunderland the following day in a 3–3 draw against Newcastle at Roker Park. His ability to find space immediately stood out, along with his calm and composed interplay in midfield. He was a natural footballer.

McColl took Sunderland to two bottom-six finishes in the First Division – nineteenth and seventeenth – and one decent FA Cup run in 1967 which ended after an infamous three-match fifth-round encounter against their bitter rivals Leeds. This epic tussle turned out to be another chapter in the ongoing history of bad blood between the two clubs.

Sunderland had home advantage in the first match, which was the first time the BBC's *Match of the Day* cameras had been at Roker Park. A crowd of 55,763 turned up to see it. The game finished in a 1–1 draw but the headline was a broken leg sustained by Kerr in a collision with Norman Hunter. The replay four days later drew a record attendance of 57,892 to Elland Road. The match again finished in a 1–1 draw but football was almost an irrelevance after a crush barrier gave way and more than thirty people were taken to hospital with injuries.

A second replay was held at Hull City's Boothferry Park ground. This was also level at 1–1 after ninety minutes. Peter Lorimer recalls that in the team discussions leading up to extra-time Revie told his players: 'If anybody gets anywhere near the box, get down.' Jimmy Greenhoff – appearing to be outside the box – was later brought down and referee Ken Stokes gave a penalty. Sunderland had both Herd and Mulhall sent off for protesting at the decision. Johnny Giles scored from the spot to put Leeds through.

'I thought we were a little bit hard done by on the night,' Montgomery says. 'But those were three big Cup games. Sunderland and Leeds games were always like that at that particular time. They were always frenetic. It was like a local derby really and it was probably the nearest derby we had when Newcastle and Middlesbrough weren't in the top division. We have always had spicy games against Leeds.'

Kerr would be out of first-team action for eighteen months, for after recovering from the initial injury he then rebroke the same leg in a reserve game at Ashington and had to remain on the sidelines until September 1968. It was a cruel halt to a career that had started magnificently. 'When my first break happened I was on a high,' Kerr says. 'I made my debut in place of George Herd against Manchester City and scored. I stayed in the team and scored seven goals before my injury. My shots were classed as "banana shots" as they seemed to bend, I don't know how. My second break happened well into my comeback trail. I think it was going to be my last game in the reserves before I went back into the first-team pool. I went to block a ball and my leg broke again. I felt the full force. It opened up at the back, so obviously it hadn't healed a hundred per cent the first time. I remember I came back to the club in an estate car and Johnny Watters put me on the bench and just walked past me and knocked it. I think he did it to see if there was any reaction. It was X-rayed and confirmed as a break. I was out for a long time. But in a sense I was lucky. The best thing was that it happened to me when I was young.'

By the time Kerr returned to the Sunderland first team McColl was long gone, sacked following a shock FA Cup defeat at home to Second Division Norwich in a third-round replay in January 1968. The name of the new manager was announced immediately afterwards and it came as a complete surprise.

'I liked Ian McColl very much but he lost control of the players,' Keith Collings says. 'We had a number of considerably older directors at that time – two of us were fairly young but the rest were old – and they wanted a disciplinarian. Of course they knew Alan Brown from the previous time he had been there and they felt – particularly in Jim Baxter's days – that Ian McColl lost the players. It was true he did lose them. The older directors wanted the discipline of Alan Brown back and so we asked him to come back.'

Despite Brown's achievements at Hillsborough, Sunderland fans were not overwhelmed by the news of his return: 'The feeling was that it wasn't the right move at the time. It was seen as going backwards: if the board didn't think he was good enough in 1964 then what makes them think he is good enough now? It certainly wasn't met with a huge amount of cheering and shouting,' Sixsmith says.

Brown's status at this time is summed up by the respected football writer Arthur Hopcraft in his celebrated book *The Football Man*, which was published the same year the manager left Sheffield Wednesday for Sunderland. Brown is one of five men featured in Hopcraft's chapter entitled Managers. Stan Cullis of Wolves, Stan Mortensen of Blackpool, Sir Matt Busby of Manchester United and England manager Sir Alf Ramsey are the others. Each is given a particular strength. In Busby's case it is virtuosity, in Ramsey's case it is strategy. Brown's prowess is considered to be absolute trust.

'There are many honest men in football, but Brown is fiercely attached to protecting integrity in the game as its central factor,' Hopcraft wrote.

It is more important to him than brilliance; success without it is to him deceit. His first value to football, which may not be of total satisfaction to his directors or his team's supporters, is that he is one of the counter-balances to the utter ruthlessness elsewhere in the game. If every team was conducted as Brown conducts his there would be less drama, less thrill, less interest in football; if every team was run as some other managers run theirs there would eventually be no sport in the business at all.

'I believe I have to inculcate absolute trust, and that applies even to triviality,' Brown told Hopcraft. 'I allow myself to be involved when someone comes along with some problem, however small it sounds. It is important to me that I am considered absolutely trustworthy.' Even more pertinently, as each of his Sunderland players would find out, Brown also said, 'I ask – no, I demand – the highest code of conduct.'

'Alan Brown was like a sergeant-major and he frightened you,' Kerr says. 'You could tell he was once a policeman; he looked like a policeman. To this day I have never worn a pair of jeans in my life and that comes from him. You always had to be smart and you did as he said. He would not allow you anything on your chin or anything on your lip. I grew my moustache after he left Sunderland.

'Once Browny walked into a room he had control,' Kerr adds. 'We all started talking from one side of our mouths because he was that good, he could lip-read. He knew some people were having a drink but he didn't want to see it and if he saw it he would crucify the lads. He even threatened to take testimonials off a few of the senior players.'

'When Alan Brown came back to Sunderland he had changed religiously and was now a member of the Moral Rearmament group,' Montgomery adds. 'The first time around we used to have miniatures on the train after a meal and play cards, but not any more. He wouldn't even let us have two Cokes, never mind a drink or anything else.'

Something else that had changed from the first time around was the Sunderland youth system. In 1968 Brown inherited a set-up that was now flourishing. It had, of course, been created by his own fair hand and nurtured by others including, of course, Clough, his protégé. An attacking side featuring the likes of Hughes, Kerr and Suggett and aided by the much-talented Todd at right-half reached the Youth Cup Final in 1966, where they lost 5–3 on aggregate to Arsenal. The following season the Rokerites won the trophy, beating Birmingham 1–0 both at home and away in the final. Hughes scored in the first leg and Albert Brown scored in the second leg. It was the club's first form of silverware at any level for thirty years.

A Newcastle schoolboy by the name of Dennis Tueart played for Sunderland in the competition against Manchester United that season. He scored one goal and made another in front of a home crowd of over 11,000.

'Sunderland took a gamble on me,' Tueart says. 'I was a centre-forward at that time and I was quite small. Charlie Ferguson signed me on schoolboy forms for a year. I became a right-footed left-winger at Sunderland. Newcastle United watched me but wouldn't take a risk on me. You can imagine the reaction in Newcastle when it appeared in the local newspaper that I had scored for the Sunderland youth team.'

Tueart was given his first-team debut by Brown a few weeks after his nineteenth birthday in a Boxing Day draw with Sheffield Wednesday at the end of 1968. 'Alan Brown was very much a disciplinarian and very well organised but he was well ahead of his time tactically,' Tueart adds. 'He was something of a guru to up-and-coming coaches; people like Malcolm Allison really respected him. He was astute and innovative and his training programmes and ideas were well ahead of his time.'

Brown introduced shadow play to the Sunderland training sessions: a routine where he would sit and watch from the stand as his players moved the ball around from back to front within their allocated positions and roles on the pitch. The catch was, there were no opponents. It was purely a functional theory to get his team thinking as one. Nearly thirty years later Arsène Wenger brought something similar to the Arsenal training ground with the use of mannequins and soon took his team to the league and Cup double. But at Sunderland in the late 1960s the reaction to such a method of training was mixed, to say the least.

'I couldn't get the gist of it,' Hughes says. 'Let me give you an example from a few years later: there was Dennis Tueart on the right, me on the left and Dave Watson at centre-forward. We played this shadow thing and Alan Brown was sitting on his own up in the directors' box. The ball gets played up to Dave and he comes deep and knocks it back down to Ian Porterfield – remember there are no opponents – and Ian then switches it out to the right wing for Dennis, but Dave is now out of position, so I came in from the left-hand side and make a near-post run. Dennis crosses the ball and I put it in the back of the net. Brown stands up and shouts, "Stop!" and comes down and gives me a bollocking for scoring a goal. "What the hell are you doing in there? That's Dave's domain, you stay on the left," he says. "A lot of people say the man was a genius but I found him very difficult: he either did it his way or no way at all. I also found it hard with the system that he wanted to play. I disagreed with it but I had to go along with it because if you didn't do what your manager said then you weren't in the team.'

'From a goalkeeper's point of view it was boring,' Montgomery says. 'You got the ball, threw it out and stood there until it came back to you. But it was good in as much as it showed the lads where to run, how to overlap and where to be in a given situation. The only thing that was missing was obviously physical contact and man-marking.'

'I thought it was like formation dancing and we got it to a tee in the end,' Kerr adds. 'A lot of the lads thought that it was wrong to do it but through time it is getting used quite often today and I think that says a lot about Alan Brown.'

While the senior players got to grips with the futuristic training methods, the youth system continued to blossom. Sunderland won the Youth Cup again in 1969 with a side coached by Billy Elliott, who had now been brought back to the club by the same man who had given him his cards as a player. Elliott had spent time coaching in Libya, West Germany and Belgium as well as at Sheffield Wednesday before being appointed trainer-coach at Roker Park shortly after Brown's return. This successful youth side featured no fewer than ten players who would go on and play for the Sunderland first team, including Keith Coleman, John Lathan, Mick McGiven, Bobby Park, Ritchie Pitt and John Tones. Pitt was an England Schoolboy international and had represented his country six times at that level, including one match against Scotland at Wembley. A 3–0 away defeat at West Bromwich Albion in the Youth Cup final was overturned by a fabulous 6–0 victory at Roker Park. Paddy Lowrey scored a hat-trick for Sunderland while West Brom had Len Cantillo and Asa Harford sent off.

Brown's youth policy would again be key to Sunderland's future. With limited funds to spend, 'the Bomber' had little choice. But he was as enthused as ever about once again building from the bottom: 'In the course of a long experience in the game of football, the signing of a promising young player has always been the most exciting event to me,' he said.

'Alan Brown took a great interest in the youth team,' Pitt says. 'He knew all our names and he would come in in a morning and say, "Hello, Ritchie, how are you doing? I watched you last week, you need to do some work on this," and so on. He had me running up a ninety-degree wall just to strengthen my legs. He would have me doing that twenty times a day just so I would be able to jump higher. I would manage two or three steps – "One, two, three, touch" – with a piece of chalk in my hand to draw a line, so we could see how high I could reach up the wall. If I didn't beat the previous day's mark then I had to keep going until I did. I would do that twenty times a day in the gym after training. He had these slightly unusual methods, but they worked. A lot of it was psychological. If I thought I was getting higher then it increased my confidence and so on. He was very good with young kids.

'Charlie Ferguson was the main person who got me to sign for Sunderland,' Pitt adds. 'I think it was the fact that I was playing for England Schoolboys and I was probably the same size as I am now! The club had a good reputation at that time, not only due to having a good network of scouts but also because we were the team that everybody wanted to play for in the north-east, due to the youth system. We had a good crop of lads coming through, including some lads who didn't really make it.'

All the energy Brown had spent in establishing a successful youth system at Sunderland in the late 1950s was now paying dividends. Those two Youth Cup wins at the end of the 1960s suggested a bright future. Now, just as he had done previously at Burnley, once before at Sunderland and also Sheffield Wednesday, he started to blood youngsters into his first team. Pitt was given his senior debut at Coventry City at the age of just seventeen.

'Alan Brown would stick with you even if you had a bad game, and I had a few of those when I first went in,' Pitt says. 'But I learned quickly and the manager could see that. He made me into the player that I was. He was quite strict, in the sense that he gave you a role in the team and you had to play that role but, all in all, I thought he was an excellent manager.'

Pitt continued playing in the Sunderland youth team until the end of the 1968–69 season when the Youth Cup was won. Other members of that youth side were also given games in the first team: Lowrey, aged eighteen, made his debut against Arsenal in early April and came off the bench to score against Burnley a few weeks later, while Colin Beesley, aged seventeen, was named as substitute on three occasions. Malcolm Moore, aged twenty, a Youth Cup winner in 1967, was also given a run in the side and scored two goals.

Brown had set about his second stint as Sunderland manager in much the same way as he began his first: he oversaw the building of a new training complex, comprising four pitches and a gymnasium, at Washington, and soon replaced older, established stars with up-and-coming youngsters. He was the ultimate totalitarian and had the same traditional tactical formation in place throughout all three levels at the club – youths, reserves and first team – keeping faith with the 2–3–5 system long after England had won the World Cup without it. He stringently instructed his players to play to their number and position and rarely allowed exceptions. He remained the ultimate hard task-masker, both on and off the pitch.

'Alan Brown made us build the bloody gymnasium at Washington by the way,' Hughes says. 'He used to go in there and rip nettles out with his bare hands. Once the gym was up he had us laying flagstones and cementing them in and all that. At one time on a Friday before a game there were five players on the treatment table with lime burns and that was because you couldn't turn around and say, "I'm not doing that." If you didn't do it, he wouldn't pick you, so we all had to do it; that was the type of man he was.'

Brown's immediate task when he returned to Sunderland had been to save the club from relegation. This he managed to achieve, and on the last day of the 1967–68 season his side went to championship-chasing Manchester United and won 2–1. Manchester City, 4–3 winners over Newcastle, claimed the title as a result. Sunderland's performance that day was their best of the season, with Porterfield inspirational in midfield. Two weeks later United beat Benfica 4–1 at Wembley to become the first English side to win the European Cup.

But Sunderland's form was sporadic. Relegation was avoided again the following season but there were many heavy defeats, including an 8–0 thrashing at West Ham where Geoff Hurst scored six. Another embarrassing result came in the FA Cup when the Rokerites crashed out 4–1 at home to Fulham in the third round, a side that would finish the season bottom of the Second Division. This was the second of what would soon become a run of four successive third-round defeats in the competition for Sunderland, all of them by Second Division opponents and three of them coming at Roker Park.

Hurley and Mulhall were given free transfers, while Herd never appeared for Sunderland again and Ashurst played just one more season before leaving to become player-manager at Hartlepool United. Brown had signed them all, and they had been prominent members of his promotion team in the 1963–64 season, but he moved them all on without hesitation.

It was clear that the free-spending days of the 'Bank of England club' and, to an extent, the McColl era were over. West Brom offered a club-record fee of £100,000 for Suggett in the summer of 1969, and the bid for the twenty-year-old inside-forward was quickly accepted. This had a negative effect on Sunderland and a dreadful start to the 1969–70 season left the club stranded at the bottom of the table. A solitary strike from Todd in a 2–1 home defeat by Sheffield Wednesday was the only goal the team scored in the first six matches of the campaign.

Brown was trying to blend emerging but relatively raw young talent with experience: Montgomery was in his ninth season in the goalkeeper's jersey, Ashurst and Harvey were still featuring at the back, while former England internationals Joe Baker and Gordon Harris were playing up front. But after ten matches Sunderland were still without a win and a battle against relegation was already on the cards.

During this time Porterfield remained on the outside after an argument with Brown at a pre-season training camp in Denmark. The Scot was left out of the first team for an entire season. As Sunderland struggled for points, Brown stubbornly made a point.

Porterfield asked to be put on the transfer list but Brown refused. The midfielder later wrote a letter to the new Sunderland chairman Jack Parker, who had taken over that season, asking to be put on the list. The request was accepted but all bids appeared to be blocked. Porterfield had been frozen out. On one occasion he was even sent home from the training complex due a lack of space. He watched in disbelief as the first team and a few reserves trained without him.

'The coming of Brown heralded a big change for me,' Porterfield later said. 'I hadn't only to adapt to English soccer but to a new manager as well and I got a feeling straight away that I wasn't going to be one of his blue-eyed boys.' Porterfield had to seek solace from his wife and children at this time and by reading a scrapbook, which detailed happier moments in his playing days with Raith. 'Looking back on those days,' he added, 'I feel that I was made an example by Brown to show others what would happen if they stood up for themselves.'

Without Porterfield Sunderland recorded just six wins and thirty goals in the First Division – the lowest number of points and goals so far in the club's history – and were relegated back to the Second Division. They could have survived had they beaten Liverpool at home in the final game of the season, but they lost 1–0 and went down. Yet again Brown was the man at the helm. But while the relegation of 1957–58 had seemed unthinkable to the club's loyal supporters, the relegation of 1969–70 met with a rather sober acceptance.

Added to the poor league form, the Rokerites had again gone out to lower-division opposition in both Cup competitions. Leicester City beat them 1–0 in the third round of the FA Cup, and Third Division Bradford City won 2–1 at Roker Park in the League Cup. It is doubtful whether the mood of the fans had ever been so bleak. It was now over thirty years since Sunderland had won any major silverware, and while the Youth Cup successes pointed to a brighter future, the competition was not the FA Cup or the Football League championship. 'The Bank of England club' had become a sleeping giant.

Questions were asked about the manager, both in the press and by the supporters. Why had he left Porterfield out of the side while his team struggled at the foot of the First Division table? Could it really have been just to prove a point? But Parker stoically stood by Brown, believing he was the right man to return the club to the First Division.

The only thing Sunderland fans had to look forward to during the summer of 1970 was the World Cup in Mexico and the possible inclusion of Montgomery as one of the three goalkeepers in the England squad. There had once been hopes that Baker and Todd would also make the trip, but the goalkeeper was the last realistic one left.

Montgomery had been listed in the original squad of forty and was expected to feature in the final twenty-two. But in the event Gordon Banks, Peter Bonetti and Alex Stepney all made the trip and Montgomery was left at home. The extremely agile Sunderland goalkeeper –

who won six England Under-23 caps and made one other senior England squad against France at Wembley in March 1969 – never won full international honours. In many circles he is still regarded as the finest goalkeeper never to have been capped at full international level by England.

'I was in the forty in 1970 and I had all the injections because you had to have them so long beforehand,' Montgomery says. 'I was disappointed not to make the trip because Alex Stepney wasn't having the best of times in the league. I felt Gordon Banks and Peter Bonetti spoke for themselves really but when the four of us were named in the original squad I thought I would get in there ahead of Stepney – but that was the manager's choice.'

Emotions still run strongly among some Sunderland supporters over this: 'I have never followed England since 1970, when Monty was left out of the squad for Mexico,' Sixsmith says. 'He should have gone to Mexico. He was certainly better than Stepney at that time and probably better than Bonetti as well. I have never cared for England since.'

That summer Sunderland took part in the Anglo-Italian Cup for the first time, losing to both Lazio and Fiorentina on foreign soil after a respective win and a draw at Roker Park. Collings recalls an incident during that tour of Italy concerning Brown and his trainer-coach, Elliott, a man renowned as one of the hardest players of his era. What follows says a lot about Brown's management style and the fear factor that ran throughout the club at this time.

'Billy Elliott and I were relaxing one day in Italy, sitting at this table by a lakeside, and we both had a brandy with us,' Collings says. 'Alan Brown came around the corner and sat at the same table with us. I quickly had to pick up Billy's brandy and move it away from him. There was no way that Billy wanted to be seen drinking in front of Alan Brown.'

As Second Division football returned the following season Brown remained resolute concerning his team and indeed his own managerial approach: 'We have already laid the foundations for a successful team,' he said. 'Relegation is merely a temporary setback.'

After just four wins from the first eleven matches, it looked to be a little more than that. The manager, who continued to be backed by the Sunderland board, now reached for the chequebook and made what would prove to be two inspired signings: Dick Malone arrived from Ayr

United for £40,000 in October, and Dave Watson signed from Rotherham United for a club-record fee of £100,000 two weeks before Christmas.

Malone, a lean and tall right-back, had been watched by a number of English clubs during his six years at Ayr and once came close to signing for Fulham: 'I went down there and Vic Buckingham, the manager, said he wanted me to be an attacking sweeper. I had never heard of that phrase and I didn't think he could be right in the head. Those two words – "attack" and "sweep" – were a bit of a contradiction to me. He took me out into the middle of the park and said, "This will be all yours – you will be the king of Craven Cottage." I thought to myself, Get me out of here! It just wasn't right for me and so I decided to stay at Ayr.

'My manager at Ayr was Ally MacLeod, who later managed Scotland in the 1978 World Cup finals. I rate him as one of the best managers ever. He was a pure football manager and very positive in his outlook. His method of defence was attack, and I regularly scored over ten goals a season as a full-back. He had been a left-winger and he told me that wingers hate to chase back, so that is how I played: I made runs and I got forward a lot.

'But one day the manager accused me of not trying and I said to him, "That is the last time you will ever say that to me." I put my letter in on the Monday and I was transferred to Sunderland on the Tuesday. I believe they had been watching me for about two years. I later found out that Leeds had chased me for two years as well. It is ironic, given what followed, that they were interested in me. But the Bomber came in for me and I signed for him straight away. I made a commitment to myself that I would sign for the first manager that I liked. Alan Brown was the first manager to come in for me and he was the first manager that I liked, so I signed for him.'

Watson spoke of a similar experience: 'Alan Brown was about fifty-five or so when I signed for Sunderland, but he was probably the strongest person in the squad in terms of strength and physique. Apparently he had once specialised in armed combat and nobody ever stood up to him. But he was a good man: I stayed at his house on the seafront at Roker when I first moved up there and was there for a couple of months on my own until my wife and I found a house. That says a lot about him. He was a disciplinarian but footballers and young adults need discipline, I firmly believe that. He guided us like children, like we were his boys.

'I was the youngest of eight children and I had four brothers who all played football,' Watson says. 'Peter played for Nottingham Forest and was the twelfth man in the 1959 Cup final against Luton Town in the days before there were any substitutes; he was ten years older than me and played at centre-half. Tony was a centre-forward and a decent header of the ball too. My two other brothers, Fred and Jack, played as well. We all played, although Peter and I were the only two who went on to do so professionally. We used to kneel on the grass a couple of yards apart and head the ball to each other, keeping it up in the air. I did that from a young age with all my brothers in a field close to a dairy farm nearby. That gave me a good grounding in how to head the ball and connect with it to make it go in a certain place and so forth. You would always find us on that bit of grass, heading the ball to each other. I also used to hit a ball against the wooden panels of a disused railway carriage with my left foot and right foot. I always used both feet.

'I never had any real ambitions to play professionally. I was working as an electrician but was made redundant at the age of nineteen and redundancy forced me into professional football. Tony was instrumental in getting me a trial at Notts County. I got signed up as a centre-half and after playing three games in the reserves I was put in the first team. Once I had decided to play professionally I was determined and hungry to succeed. Notts County were near the bottom of the Fourth Division when I signed for them and the big thing back then was re-election. We could have gone out of the Football League one season but it didn't happen – it rarely did in those days, as self-interest from the clubs at the bottom meant that everyone looked after each other when it came to re-election.

'I was only a professional for about six or seven months when Tommy Docherty came in for me at Rotherham. I remember I went in to pick my wages up, which in those days was some cash in a little envelope with a slip of paper telling you what you had paid in tax and National Insurance and everything – there wasn't much money in that envelope, I can tell you – and Billy Gray, the Notts County manager, shouted out to me, "Tommy Doc has been on; he wants to sign you for Rotherham." He then looked me straight in the eyes and said, "Go and see him." I think he knew that if I signed I would do well and it would be good for me. I didn't really understand how football worked at that stage and I was happy to just keep playing for Notts County and get paid for it. I never once considered a transfer or moving away. I signed for Rotherham, who were then in the Second Division. We talked about money but I would have been happy with anything because I was on a pittance at Notts County. As it was, it was a huge leap for me in wages at that time.'

Docherty soon left Rotherham to take over at Queen's Park Rangers and Jimmy McAnearney took over at Millmoor. Soon afterwards the new manager asked Watson if he would help him out by playing up front for a while during an injury crisis. He had previously played in both positions during his time at Notts County.

'Rotherham had a plethora of centre-backs at that time and so I said I was quite happy with that and agreed. I was playing centre-forward at the start of the 1970–71 season and I had scored twelve goals when Sunderland came in for me, out of the blue,' Watson says.

One of those goals came at Grantham Town, of the Midland League, in the second round of the FA Cup on 12 December 1970. Rotherham won the match 4–1 and within forty-eight hours the Millers were rewarded with a home tie and a Yorkshire derby against Leeds United in the third-round draw. But by then Watson was a Sunderland player, after quickly agreeing terms with Brown.

'When I played for Rotherham, I lived in Carlton-in-Lindrick, near Worksop, in Nottinghamshire,' Watson says. 'Whenever we played in the south the team bus would pick me up and drop me off *en route* at a hotel car park nearby. After the Grantham game, I got off the coach, said goodbye to the lads as usual and then I realised that Jimmy McAnearney had followed me off the bus. He took me to one side, put his arm around me and said, "Alan Brown has come in for you at Sunderland with £100,000. I want you to go and talk to him." I didn't know where Sunderland was. I remember asking him, "Where's Sunderland?" He said it was in the north-east and that it was a massive club.'

While Rotherham had been beating Grantham, Sunderland had been losing at Cardiff City. McAnearney arranged for Brown to meet Watson at a service station on the A1 at eleven the next morning. 'I was flattered but it was a bit of a shock to me,' Watson recalls. 'Alan Brown had booked a room in the hotel by the services and when my wife Penny and I got there he asked to meet me privately to discuss money. She had to wait outside, which seemed a little odd. He told me: "I've got a dual player here – you are a centre-forward and a centre-half." So he must have seen me play in both positions. He then offered to double my wages – I didn't know just how big a club Sunderland was. He told the press he was signing a "dual player" too. I accepted it. I could play in two positions, mainly because I was good in the air – but I always saw myself as a defender.

'The fee was £100,000 and that was a lot of money, especially for a Second Division club. The press asked me how I was going to pay the fee back and I told them, "It's not my valuation; the clubs have come to that arrangement and I don't get any of that money." It seemed to me that they were trying to put pressure on me. Maybe they wanted me to say that I was going to score twenty goals in my first season or something. I guess the expectancy at Sunderland was something I hadn't encountered before,' Watson adds.

When Watson arrived at Sunderland, Joe Baker made a point of introducing himself straight away. The expectation – in the team and on the terraces – was that the two would play up front together. But within a month Baker had been sold to Hibernian for £12,000.

Sunderland's record signing made his home debut against Middlesbrough on Boxing Day 1970 in a 2–2 draw watched by a crowd of 42,617. 'The place was packed,' Watson says. 'I had come a long way from crowds of three thousand or so at Rotherham and even less at Notts County.'

The Sunderland team that day was Jim Montgomery, Dick Malone, Martin Harvey, Colin Todd, Ritchie Pitt, Ian Porterfield, Brian Chambers, Bobby Kerr, Dave Watson, Gordon Harris and Billy Hughes. Bobby Park was substitute. But Dennis Tueart was missing. It was now the young winger's turn to fall out with the manager.

'I had a set-to with Browny,' Tueart recalls. 'We had a fall-out over contracts and I was after a new one. To be fair to him, he always had to work within budgets at Sunderland and he didn't have much money to spend.' Brown was to leave Tueart out of his side for three months. Tueart scored on his return against Blackburn Rovers in January 1971.

'We were all on our guard with Alan Brown, but that is not

necessarily a bad thing,' Watson says. 'Billy Hughes told me that when Browny got angry the vein in his neck used to stick out and that was the time to back off. There was also a story that one of the older players had gone in to see him to ask for a rise and he was given his cards instead!

'I played as a centre-forward for him for two years solid,' Watson adds. 'I was happy to get a game and so I would play wherever he wanted me to play, but in my heart I was always a centre-half. I remember him telling me that I was the only player he wanted to see shooting from outside the penalty box. In theory it never happened but that underlines his strictness that midfield players are midfield players et cetera and so they shouldn't do anything else.'

It was not only the players that needed to be on their guard. Brown had by now brought in a ballroom dancer, Lenny Happell, to help with the players' balance. Porterfield later spoke very highly of the work Happell did and Brown certainly valued him very much, so much so that once, when he was driving with Happell to a match, Jack Parker – the chairman who had stood by him more than anyone – was given short shrift when he invited himself along for a ride. Parker had sat himself, uninvited, in the front seat of Brown's Audi 500 coupé until he was instructed by his manager to get in the back.

Unbeknown to the manager, behind the scenes there were moves being made to suggest a replacement: 'I was not at all happy about the situation with Alan Brown so I went to see Jack Parker and I expressed my views that I wasn't happy, I didn't think the supporters were happy and that I thought we should make a change,' Collings says. 'Jack Parker asked me for my loyalty; he said he wanted to keep Alan Brown and asked if I would be loyal to him and the club, which I of course was. But I certainly talked with him personally about changing the manager at this time.'

The money spent on Watson and Malone had an effect on the club's bank balance, particularly as attendances were not generally getting any better. It was therefore somewhat expected on the terraces that a first-team player would soon have to be sold. It turned out to be Todd. The man who signed him was Clough. The fee was £175,000. It was a severe blow in more ways than one.

Todd was a real Sunderland hero. He hailed from County Durham and had joined the club straight from school. He was calm and confident in his approach; quick and strong in the tackle; fast and accurate with his passing from defence. He had been a consistent and fundamental feature of the first team for four years, but now he was leaving, at the age of just twenty-two.

Graffiti, simply saying TODDO, written on a wall near to Roker Park summed up the legend and is epitomised in an image of two elderly gentlemen walking by in a famous photograph taken by Peter Robinson at this time. This photograph symbolised to Sunderland fans that a once powerful buying club had, in effect, become a selling club. Promotion was also, by now, no longer on the agenda.

'I remember the discussions,' Collings says. 'We didn't want Colin Todd to go and we said to him, "Be loyal to us for another year while we try and get ourselves back to where we should be and if we haven't done this within a year, then we will listen to your request." So, in the end, we had to let him go.'

Clough lured Todd away from Roker Park by telling him, 'You will never ever win a Cup final or championship medal with Sunderland or any other team. But you'll do it with me and that is a guarantee.' By the end of his first full season at the Baseball Ground, he had.

Todd's transfer to Derby was disappointing and frustrating for Sunderland supporters in equal measure. The fact that it was Clough who signed him hurt them: Clough had had Todd in his youth team at Sunderland and now he was taking him away from Sunderland. 'Our fans have always loved local lads getting into the team,' Sunderland supporter Steve Hodgson says. 'Colin Todd is a good example. He was a class apart and it was a big blow to everybody when he was sold for all sorts of reasons. He was going from Roker Park – where a World Cup quarter-final had been played just a few years earlier – to Derby. It really rubbed it in as well that the man who signed him was Brian Clough.'

The last game Todd played for Sunderland was a 4–0 home defeat by Cardiff, watched by a crowd of just 11,566. 'He was the next big thing in football but that season the crowds just weren't there to see him play and it wasn't enough to justify him staying really so the club took the money. We became resigned to the fact he was going to go in the end,' fellow fan Paul Dobson adds.

Sunderland finished their first season back in the Second Division in thirteenth place. Progress in both Cup competitions was again short-lived, with Orient winning 3–0 at Roker Park in the third round of the FA Cup and Lincoln City – who had to apply for re-election to the Football League at the end of the season – knocking the club out of the League Cup in the second round. The Rokerites had now gone three years without a win in either competition.

Apathy began to show on the terraces: the home match against Swindon in April 1971 was watched by 8,596, the lowest crowd recorded at Roker Park in almost two decades. How could Sunderland attract a crowd of over 42,000 for one match over Christmas and then be seen by just eight and a half thousand souls a few months later? The support for the team was clearly there, but Brown had to find a way of tapping into that potential.

The 1971–72 season kicked off with another disappointing home crowd of just 9,749 turning up to watch Sunderland play Birmingham. This was the lowest opening-day attendance ever recorded at Roker Park. Those that were there witnessed Bobby Park – playing at left-back – break his leg. Brown was clearly unsure of whom he should play in the number 3 shirt, for six different players were to wear it that season, including seventeen-year-old Joe Bolton.

A respectable fifth-place finish was a big improvement and suggested a proper promotion charge could begin the following August. Tueart and Watson each scored thirteen goals in the league campaign while Hughes added another six, despite only starting half the games. Brown was reluctant to play Hughes and Tueart – two equally exciting players – in the same side.

Sunderland now had a new captain, in the shape of Kerr, who took over from Harvey after he had sustained an injury at Norwich in March 1972. 'That was the type of thing Alan Brown would do,' Kerr says. 'He had no hesitation in putting a young lad in as captain, but I was well tuned in by then. Having said that, I once made a decision – I moved Ritchie Pitt from centre-half to centre-forward during a game – and Browny later came over to me and said, "It is not in our ways to make decisions like that – we'll not say anything about it this time but it will not happen again." So, in other words, any changes came from the touchline. But I made sure I never did it again. I think, as captain, I led by example by running and chasing. I always thought, If you keep on going, even if you know are getting beaten, you have a chance, so keep on battling. That was always my belief, both as a player and as a captain.'

At five feet four and a half inches, Kerr was the smallest skipper in the club's history. But he had plenty of heart and had already shown great courage in how he had recovered from those two broken legs as a teenager. He seemed a natural captain, one who led by example.

The average age of the Sunderland team was getting younger and younger. Micky Horswill, a rather striking-looking nineteen-year-old redhead, was given a run in the side towards the end of the campaign. Brown had watched the tough-tackling and hard-running ball winner playing for Stanley Boys against Newcastle Boys in 1968 and personally went around to his house afterwards to sign him up. As he did so, he told the player's father, 'You have just lost a son because I am his father from now on.' Horswill played the final seven games of the season in place of the missing Harvey. The number 4 shirt would soon become his own.

First Division football remained the aim for Brown. Sunderland supporters had once expected it; now they just lived in hope of a return any time soon. As for the Cup competitions, the dismal run continued: Third Division Bristol Rovers knocked the Rokerites out of the League Cup, and although the club did manage to force a first win in the FA Cup in five seasons by beating Sheffield Wednesday, they then succumbed to Cardiff in a fourth-round second replay at Maine Road after a first replay that had been watched by a crowd of 39,348 at Roker Park, comfortably the highest attendance in another season affected by poor gates. The competition remained a massive attraction to Sunderland fans, even though the manager did not appear to list it as a priority.

Sunderland had a rich history. In addition to the trophies, when the 1971–72 season came to a close only Everton and Aston Villa had played more seasons in the top flight than the Rokerites. But while a seventh Football League championship looked a long-distant dream, the greatest knockout competition in the world still gave supporters hope.

What those supporters would have given for a repeat of the glory of 1937! These fans were long overdue a second trip to Wembley, but the bookmakers gave them little chance of doing so and priced an FA Cup win for the club at odds of 250–1 or even higher pre-season. Some optimistic supporters began to talk about symmetry in football – how the number 37 when reversed became the number 73 – but this was dismissed by the majority as nothing more than a pipe dream.

4.

BACK TO BLACK

The national football headlines at the end of the 1971–72 season were all about the new Football League champions Derby County and their thirty-seven-year-old manager Brian Clough. Seven years after he had been relieved of his youth-team duties at Sunderland, this man was now the most famous manager in the country.

The race for the First Division title had been the most exciting and open for years. Manchester City led the table by four points in the middle of March but lost three times in the run-in to drop out of the race. Derby took over at the top of the table on the final Saturday of the league season, but the initiative was with Leeds United and, to a lesser extent, Liverpool, both of whom still had a game left to play. Leeds required just a draw at Wolverhampton Wanderers to clinch the championship, while the Reds needed to win at Arsenal and hope that Leeds lost. Clough – believing only a miracle could win the Rams the title – sent his players to Majorca on a team holiday and went off to the Scilly Isles with his family.

Leeds and Arsenal were due to meet in the FA Cup final, Wolves were in the UEFA Cup final and the Home International Championship began the following weekend, so Football League secretary Alan Hardaker controversially ordered the two remaining league fixtures to take place on the evening of Monday 8 May, just over forty-eight hours after the Cup final. Leeds manager Don Revie was said to be speechless at the decision.

With Billy Bremner playing up front in place of Mick Jones, who had dislocated his shoulder in the 1–0 Cup final win over Arsenal, Leeds had three penalty appeals turned down as they went down 2–1 at Molineux. Liverpool had a last-minute John Toshack goal ruled out for offside and drew 0–0 at Highbury. Remarkably, Derby won the title on fifty-eight points, one point ahead of Leeds, Liverpool and Manchester City. Revie was, again, said to be speechless.

'Leeds were as nervous as kittens that night,' BBC commentator Barry Davies recalls. 'They only needed a draw to win the double and on one occasion the Wolves player Bernard Shaw had two hands on the ball in his penalty area. There was a split second when he was actually carrying the ball. I was there, I saw it, but the referee didn't give a penalty.'

The *Sunday People* later claimed that three unnamed Wolves players were offered £1,000 apiece to throw the game in Leeds' favour. FA and police investigations found no evidence of any wrongdoing, yet speculation surrounding this match will not go away and in the recent publication *Running with Wolves* by Peter Lansley, former Wolves player Frank Munro claims that manager Bill McGarry was informed about an alleged approach before the match and called his players together to tell them: 'If I hear about any of you even thinking about taking a bribe, you'll never kick a ball again as long as I'm manager.' It has since been suggested that, fired up by such talk, Wolves went out to prove a point that night; either way Leeds lost the match and with it went the chance of the double. It was the fifth time in eight seasons that Revie's side had finished runners-up in the First Division.

The championship success became the making of Clough. He made two remarks after this achievement that had resonance in Sunderland. The first suggested he would one day like to manage the Rokerites – this comment would remain with supporters for generations – while the second paid tribute to his mentor, Alan Brown, the biggest influence on him as a manager.

As Clough made plans for the European Cup with Derby, his former boss walked the Pennine Way, planning and plotting the next step in Sunderland's patiently awaited revival. Brown was now in his thirteenth season in charge of Sunderland and this was to be his ninth spent in the Second Division with them. But he had displayed certain leadership qualities during this time that had been copied far away from Roker Park, certainly by one young man. He had also built a youth policy that would very soon play a significant part in a glorious and unexpected triumph.

Brown had hardly changed at all since his early managerial days at Burnley. What he said still went, no matter how bizarre and unreasonable it may have seemed to his players: 'There was one training session when Alan Brown introduced a golfball for the defenders to head,' Dave Watson recalls. 'He threw it up in the air and headed it and then he threw it for young Freddie McIver to do the same. Freddie went up like a swallow and *whack*: you could feel his pain. Dick Malone was next but he dodged it. Browny had a go at Dick over that. He wanted the older players to set an example for the younger ones and he wanted us to accept that nothing could hurt us.'

'I remember that incident,' Dick Malone adds. 'I thought he was joking so I didn't head it. But he wasn't best impressed with me. After that I headed those golfballs for him. He used to tell me, "Those muscles up there in the forehead, son, they need to toughen up." I thought it was a bit severe, but there you go. He ruled the club with an iron fist.'

Sunderland began the 1972–73 season with a 2–1 defeat at Middlesbrough but then went on an unbeaten run of seven games that saw them climb to seventh in the table by the middle of September. This was again largely achieved without the flamboyant skills of Billy Hughes, who was left out of the first eleven for the first eight games of the season by Brown.

'Alan Brown and I were having fall-outs all the time,' Hughes says. 'I just disagreed with his sergeant-major attitude towards players. He got players playing with fear and I disagreed with it, so we were at loggerheads and I fought with him all the time. I thought he was wrong and I voiced my opinion and at that time you didn't do that. So he used to make me train on my own, all these sorts of things.'

On the last day of September Sunderland crushed Nottingham Forest 4–1 at Roker Park. Hughes, recalled to the starting line-up the previous week, scored his first goal of the campaign, while John Lathan struck twice to take his tally to six for the season. He was now at the top of the Second Division goal-scoring charts, alongside the likes of Leighton James (Burnley), Brian Joicey (Sheffield Wednesday), Don Givens (Queen's Park Rangers) and Vic Halom (Luton Town). Sunderland were placed just behind the promotion pack and Brown's pre-season optimism seemed to be justified. Then October arrived and the wheels came off.

The big turning point came at the half-time interval between Oxford United and Sunderland on 7 October 1972. Sunderland led 1–0 with a goal from Bobby Kerr but the team was nursing four serious injuries after a highly physical first half. With just one substitute allowed, Brown replaced Hughes and the three other casualties had to limp on. The team was patched up and under strength, and Oxford ran out 5–1 winners. It was Sunderland's biggest defeat for three seasons; the days of "the Bomber" were numbered.

In terms of results Sunderland never recovered after that heavy loss at the Manor Ground. Luton inflicted a first home defeat of the season – Halom scored in a 2–0 win for the Hatters the following week – and then QPR won 3–2 at Loftus Road with two goals from Stan Bowles.

Sunderland slumped into the bottom half of the table but those three successive defeats belied the fact that the team was actually playing quite well: Lathan hit the post early on against Luton, and QPR, placed second in the table, had scored twice late on to take the points. The Londoners also gave new £165,000 signing and England Under-23 international Dave Thomas his debut on the wing in that match. The stark contrast between their spending power and their league position was not lost on Sunderland fans or the local press. The Rokerites had not paid out a fee for a player for almost two years since Watson had arrived at the end of 1970.

Keith Collings had now taken over as club chairman, following the death of Jack Parker. He reported a loss of £103,000 on the year with liabilities of nearly £250,000 at the annual meeting in October 1972. As the club desperately searched for ways to find an injection of new funds, *Sunderland Echo* football correspondent Bill Butterfield, who wrote for the newspaper under the pseudonym of 'Argus', was becoming impatient, writing that the Rokerites were now 'the only North East club which has made no attempt to invest in success'.

'Alan Brown has been required to build with home-developed talent and if the time element could be set aside then the verdict must be that he is making excellent progress,' Argus wrote.

The production lines have already filled key positions in the team and there is a wave of talent coming along which promises more exciting progress still but time is not on their side and with attendances at their present level losses mount weekly at a substantial rate. There is no indication of progress towards the development [to] which club chairman Keith Collings referred at the annual meeting of finance becoming available to allow for team building. In the absence of such progress, the long, slow haul towards improvement will continue and the hardcore of supporters who still make Roker Park their Saturday afternoon will go on hoping for miracles.

That hard core of support was dwindling. The home match against Fulham attracted the lowest attendance of the season, 11,618. The game finished in a goalless draw and while it ended a run of three successive defeats, one point out of a possible eight left Sunderland just three points clear of the relegation zone. Furthermore, the average attendances from the previous two seasons – 15,764 and 15,905 – had plummeted below the 20,000 mark for the first time since the Second World War and, worryingly, the average home gate in 1972–73 so far was much lower than both of those figures at 13,409.

With attendances forever falling, Sunderland took the desperate step of advertising forthcoming matches in the local newspaper. Malcolm MacDonald's £180,000 transfer from Luton to Newcastle United the previous season had poured salt in the wound, and while Sunderland fans rallied to Geordie chants of 'SuperMac' by chanting 'SuperDick' as the popular, towering Malone made his regular charging runs – often accompanied with some unorthodox dribbling – down the flank from full-back, it was clear they were desperate for some new signings to inject some strength up front and at the back.

'We weren't really that bad, but we were getting really bad press,' Malone says. 'The crowd responded to that by not turning up. I can understand that. I know supporters say they want good, attacking football, but they want their team to win as well, and if you don't get the results then that affects the crowd. The manager also treated the press with a bit of contempt: he never really told them anything and if ever someone said something unjust about a player, he would call him in and ask him to apologise. So they resented him and any time they could get a dig into him they did. They picked up on the bad points even if the good points outweighed the bad. The press is a powerful tool and I think that brainwashed the supporters to an extent.'

On top of those poor attendances, the league position and the lack of funds, Brown became upset by the Sunderland board's refusal to acknowledge his request to open renegotiations on his contract, which was due to expire at the end of the season. This proved to be the final straw, and he abruptly resigned from the club for a second time on 1 November 1972 after fourteen matches into the new season, approximately one-third of the league programme. He was fifty-eight at the time. He never managed again.

Syd Collings had been chairman of Sunderland when Brown resigned in 1964 and now it was the turn of his son, Keith, to experience a similar fate: 'I read it in the press, or, should I say, I was told by the press,' Collings says. 'He had pushed for a new contract and I said that we were not prepared at that stage to give him a new contract and that we would leave it until the end of the season. The next thing I knew the local newspaper rang me up and told me he had resigned.

'Many people have mixed views about Alan Brown,' Collings goes on. 'It is no secret that I was instrumental to some extent in getting him to resign because I didn't think he was all that good a manager. I think he would have been excellent for a youth team but I didn't see him in the same universe as the more senior players. I think he was too strict in some ways. I never felt he was very popular with the public and probably him going did lift some of the supporters.'

Hughes had met Brown in his office just a week before his resignation and his recollection is telling: 'We had a heart-to-heart,' he says. 'I just told him about his attitude and that he put the fear of God into the young players and they were all frightened of him. He said to me, "I treat them as my sons; they're not footballers, they're my family." Tears came into his eyes. I was amazed – it was the first time he had ever let himself go. I didn't say anything to anybody but maybe he knew something was going on. I didn't get to know the man until then and I had been at Sunderland for years. A week later, he was gone.'

'Everybody was in a state of shock when Browny left,' Watson recalls. 'I just thought he was going to be there for ever because he was so commanding and demanding. He had principles and he would never change those principles. It was a big blow to me personally when he left.'

'I felt sad for the man; he wanted to sign a few more players, but the club would not or could not give him the money,' Malone adds. 'But it took the pressure off a little bit when he left because the fans and the press were pillorying the club something rotten. I felt the criticism was unfair but I have always said that it is better to be lucky than good. I have known managers do everything right and get the wrong results and I have known managers do everything wrong and get the right results. Now, who is the good manager? It's a difficult call.'

Brown's two spells at Sunderland make him the second-longest-serving manager in the club's history, yet to this day he is associated with those two relegations more than anything else. His greatest triumph was undoubtedly winning promotion in 1963–64, and while it is unlikely – to say the least – that Sunderland would have recovered in the 1972–73 season with him in charge and gone on to the success they later achieved, it should be recorded that without him a large part of that team may not have even been at Sunderland to achieve the glory that awaited them: Jim Montgomery, Micky Horswill, Ritchie Pitt, Bobby Kerr, Billy Hughes and Dennis Tueart all came through the youth ranks at Sunderland, while Dick Malone and Dave Watson signed for him. Without doubt Brown's youth policy was his biggest contribution to the club.

At around this time it was confirmed that three new directors had joined the Sunderland board, in the shape of Maurice Berwick, Alan Martin and Fred Stewart. Former chairman Stanley Ritson and fellow director Jack Cooke gave up their seats and accepted positions as life vice-presidents. 'We wanted to have a younger balance on the board and we needed spaces to do this,' Collings explains.

The new board's first task was to find a new manager. The fans' favourite was overwhelmingly Clough. Undeterred by the fact that he had signed a new improved contract at Derby the week before, supporters remained hopeful that the man who held Sunderland's post-war record for goals scored in one season would now return to manage them.

The *Sunderland Echo* ran a poll and Clough topped it handsomely. The comments from supporters on the streets of the town ranged from hope to hysteria: 'Sunderland should sell Dave Watson or even the whole of the team to buy Brian Clough for manager,' said one fan. 'I have read that Clough would like to come to Sunderland and I would like to see him as manager, he would certainly get us promotion,' said another. Perhaps the most considered comment came from seventeen-year-old Nigel Bruce of Chester Road, Sunderland, who said, 'The new manager, whoever he might be, would have the nucleus of a good team for the future, thanks to the building work of Alan Brown.'

But Clough appeared to be out of reach. Newspaper speculation quickly turned towards another former Sunderland player, Len Ashurst, who was player-manager at Hartlepool United. In fact, speculation became so rife that Hartlepool chairman John Curry issued a 'hands off' warning:

Let anybody touch Len Ashurst and they will have to answer to me. If anybody approaches a player before he approaches the club that holds that player's contract, he is in trouble. That applies to all levels in the game. I am quite convinced that if Brian Clough and Peter Taylor had not already signed their new contracts, they would have been favourites. I brought Brian to the Victoria Ground and I feel certain that he would have been glad to join Sunderland given the opportunity.

Another rumour going around was that Jack and Bobby Charlton could be offered a joint role at Roker Park. Both brothers were still playing at the time, but each had indicated his wish to go into management. By the end of the season both of them would have retired from playing and taken over managerial positions at Second Division clubs – but not here. The Sunderland board advertised the vacancy and in the meantime handed trainer-coach Billy Elliott the role of managing team affairs on a caretaker basis.

Some forty-eight hours later local bookmaker Gus Carter, on Norfolk Street, offered the following odds on the new manager: Jack Charlton 6–1; Len Ashurst (Hartlepool United) 7–1; Brian Clough (Derby County) 8–1; Stan Anderson (Middlesbrough) 9–1; Billy Bingham (Greece) 10–1; Alan Ashman (Carlisle United) and Lawrie McMenemy (Grimsby Town) 12–1; Don Revie (Leeds United) and Tommy Docherty (Scotland) 14–1, Jimmy Hagan (Benfica) 16–1; Bobby Charlton, Billy Elliott, Charlie Hurley (Reading) and Brian Doyle (Stockport County) 20–1; George Aitken (Workington) and former Sunderland players George Herd and Arthur Wright 25–1; two more former Sunderland players, Raich Carter and Ken Chisholm, 33–1; journalist and another former hero Len Shackleton 50–1. In all, thirteen of the twenty names listed were former Sunderland players.

'We want the best man available,' Collings told the press. 'I think it is a plum job and we are prepared to pay a good salary. This is a club with fine traditions and the manager has always had free scope. It is important to the continuity of the team that a new manager be appointed with all haste.' In answer to growing speculation concerning the Charlton brothers, he replied, 'I can state categorically that we have made no approach to anyone whatsoever. We have decided to advertise the vacancy and that is how it stands.'

Elliott made four changes to the side for the visit of third-placed Aston Villa to Roker Park, including recalling Hughes up front and moving Kerr to right midfield. The biggest home crowd of the season so far, 18,717, saw Hughes fire Sunderland ahead after just fifty-five seconds. The game finished 2–2 with Kerr – now wearing the number 7 shirt – scoring Sunderland's other goal.

In his second game in charge – away at Carlisle – Elliott decided to move Watson from number 9 to number 5 and from centre-forward to centre-half. After playing for two years in attack, Watson was to finally make his first appearance for Sunderland in his favoured position at Brunton Park. Pitt made way at the back and youngster Jimmy Hamilton – who had been given his debut by Brown at just sixteen the previous year – came into the side at centre-forward. Elliott believed that Watson would tighten up the defence and his aerial presence would break up opposing attacks. But the caretaker manager was keen for the player's power in the air not to be lost up front, and encouraged him to continue to go forward for set plays.

'Billy Elliott always thought I was wasted at centre-forward and that I had much more to give the team as a centre-half,' Watson says. 'I had done all right as a centre-half playing centre-forward, but I felt much happier playing at number 5. I think Billy saw that and he thought that I should be playing at the back so he moved me there at the earliest opportunity.'

It was a somewhat auspicious start to the new line-up: Sunderland started the match sluggishly and trailed 3–1 at half-time, but as Watson began to apply his strength and industry to the defence Porterfield started to control the midfield and, after Lathan replaced Hamilton up front, the Rokerites fought back to draw level at 3–3 before Stan Ternent won it seven minutes from time for the home side.

As the season entered the second half of November there was still no new manager at Sunderland. The only news to emanate officially from the club regarding the vacancy was that despite over

100 postal applications the standard was 'disappointing' and the search continued. But behind the scenes tentative moves were being made. The club aimed high – right to the very top in fact – and approached the men in charge of the two top sides in the country: the current Football League champions and the current FA Cup holders. Both managers had previously played in the red and white stripes of Sunderland under Brown.

Collings reveals that he met and interviewed both Clough and Revie at this time in the hope of offering the vacant manager's position at Roker Park to one of them.

'I went to Don Revie's house in Leeds with my vice-chairman Jack Ditchburn and we spent an evening in his house and discussed the matter,' Collings says. 'Unfortunately there were things he asked of me which I was not prepared – and was not able – to do. Similarly with Brian Clough. We met him at a friend's house in Holmfirth in West Yorkshire and a similar situation arose, that he made demands which I was certainly not at all happy with. But one always looks for the best and Sunderland supporters always expect you to look for the best. The names that automatically came to the front were Revie and Clough. They were the ones that the supporters wanted and the club wanted really, I suppose.'

With both those avenues closed, the search for a new manager continued. The press remained way off the mark: 'None of those names mentioned were in the frame really,' Collings says. 'Not Len Ashurst, not Billy Bingham and not the Charltons.'

Clough maintained that he 'always had a passion for Sunderland', but in *Provided You Don't Kiss Me*, Duncan Hamilton's award-winning book about his close working relationship with him, it is suggested that the man's interest in the vacancy at that time was all to do with Bob Stokoe. 'Putting himself in contention for the vacancy at Sunderland was done solely to get back at Stokoe,' Hamilton writes. 'Sunderland, after all, were near the bottom of the Second Division and there was no way that Clough was going to abandon a league-championship-winning side for them. He hadn't climbed the ladder, rung by desperate rung, only to voluntarily descend it again.'

Revie meanwhile had now had the opportunity of managing Sunderland twice – having turned down Syd Collings eight years before when it looked likely he would accept.

Sunderland – without a win since September – had now slipped into the bottom six of the Second Division. Elliott kept making changes in the hope of a turnaround. Impressed with Lathan scoring as a substitute at Carlisle and the display of John Tones for the reserves in midweek, he brought the small striker back into the side to replace Hamilton and put Tones on the bench for the visit of Hull City. Elliott's thinking was sound: Tones, at six foot two and thirteen stone, could play at centre-half, and Lathan had worked well before with Watson up front. Should Sunderland need to chase a game, Watson could be pushed into attack and Tones could take over at the back. The match against Hull was drawn 1–1 but it began a substitution policy that would continue for months.

On that same day the first round of the 1972–73 FA Cup took place, and the main shock was provided by Sunderland old boy Cecil Irwin, manager of non-league Yeovil Town, as his side knocked out Third Division Brentford 2–1 on the same sloping pitch where that famous Sunderland side of Len Shackleton and the rest had succumbed almost a quarter of a century before. More upsets were provided by Hayes, who beat Bristol Rovers 1–0; Margate, who beat Swansea City 1–0; Bangor City, who won 2–1 at Rochdale; and Walton and Hersham, who defeated Exeter City 2–1. The competition was well and truly under way.

And then the big news broke: 'Stokoe is the man if . . .' ran a single-column news story on the front page of the *Sunderland Echo* on Monday 20 November 1972. The narrow strip was overshadowed by the main headline of the day, CONGRATULATIONS, which celebrated Queen Elizabeth and Prince Philip's silver wedding anniversary, but it did reveal that Bob Stokoe would be the next Sunderland manager if the Blackpool board agreed to release him from his existing contract.

The story had broken in Blackpool, not Sunderland. The Seasiders' chairman Frank Dickinson told of a chairman-to-chairman approach from Roker Park the day before, requesting permission to speak to Stokoe: 'I turned this request down,' Dickinson said. 'I would not give permission because we are a nine-man board and this permission must come from the board. Mr Stokoe did not apply for the job and he still has twelve months to run on his contract with us. Obviously it has come as a shock to me, I am disappointed because he has done well for us and we should be loath to see him go.'

Blackpool were riding high in the Second Division – two points below the promotion positions – and still involved in the League Cup with a quarter-final tie against Wolves to be played the following night. After a three-hour board meeting the Blackpool directors agreed to allow talks between the chairmen and vice-chairmen of both clubs to take place later that week.

With speculation about Stokoe mounting, Blackpool almost pulled off a win at Molineux when Keith Dyson gave them a first-half lead, but Jim McCalliog equalised to force a replay. This result delayed any hopes Sunderland had of a quick appointment. It did appear that Stokoe could be on his way back to the north-east, but he made little comment himself: 'My hands and tongue are tied until after this meeting,' he said. 'I cannot prejudge the issue.'

'We invited Bob Stokoe over while he was still at Blackpool, as these things happen,' Collings says. 'He came over and had a chat with us and we were impressed with his honesty and straightforwardness. He had no particular airs and graces about him. He was a thoroughly nice man. We felt that he had the right attributes. He had got enough character, we thought, to control players and his reputation in the lower divisions was quite good too so my vice-chairman and I went over to Blackpool to talk to his chairman and vice-chairman, and they were prepared to release him.'

It was the fourth time in Stokoe's managerial career that he had been poached by a bigger club, and Blackpool – who had had to pay Carlisle compensation when they lured him to Bloomfield Road – requested compensation from Sunderland. This was agreed at a sum of £12,000 and a deal was finally done. But there was one last sting in the tail; at his own request, he was to stay with Blackpool until after the League Cup quarter-final replay with Wolves the following Tuesday: 'All I can say is that obviously I wanted to leave the club in the right way and this has been done,' Stokoe said. 'The decision had been reached between the two chairmen and I am quite happy with it.'

'I think the thing about Bob Stokoe was that he was always hoping to get a job at a big club, even when he was at Blackpool,' Jimmy Armfield says. 'Blackpool were the biggest team he had managed in his career but then he got that chance at Sunderland and they were really a First Division team playing in the Second Division, so he took it.'

Yet this Sunderland team were heading in the wrong direction: Bristol City beat them 1–0 at Ashton Gate the following weekend and that result left the Rokerites fourth from bottom of the Second Division at the time of Stokoe's appointment. In fact, they were only placed out of the bottom two relegation places on goal average.

On Tuesday 26 November, Blackpool lost their quarter-final replay against Wolves and Stokoe said goodbye to his players, his board of directors and the Blackpool fans. BBC commentator John Motson saw it all, having been assigned to cover the story of Stokoe leaving Blackpool for Sunderland for that weekend's *Football Preview* – a forerunner of *Football Focus* – which ran at the top of *Grandstand* on BBC1 on Saturday afternoons.

'I went into the Blackpool dressing room after the game and the players seemed quite down,' Motson says. 'I interviewed Glyn James, the centre-half, who had been there a long time and I asked him how the players felt about losing their manager and I remember he told me what an honest guy Bob Stokoe was.'

The next morning the BBC crew followed the new Sunderland manager across the Pennines by road for a 9.30 a.m. appointment at Roker Park. Stokoe gave his first-ever national television interview to Motson that day.

'As soon as we got up to Roker Park, Bob told us that he had to go upstairs to deal with a situation that we couldn't film,' Motson recalls. 'I think it was to do with Billy Elliott. My understanding was that Bob was going to sack him.' But Stokoe did not sack Elliott; not, at least, on this occasion.

'Bob then came downstairs to meet the players and they all came out on to the pitch for a photo shoot. They were all there gathered around him and I remember they were all smiling and this was literally just after he had met them,' Motson adds.

This photo shoot would later become famous: the mood of the Sunderland squad – all black polo-necks, tank tops, flared trousers and smiling faces – was in stark contrast to their lowly position in the Second Division and the atmosphere that had clouded the club in recent months. The players surround their newly appointed manager and jostle around him in front of the waiting cameras, laughing out loud in the process. Stokoe had already brought something to the club. It could be seen instantly in these brief but brilliant pictures.

'Bob Stokoe had done well at Blackpool and he was a very solid and very well-organised manager plus a good motivator,' Motson says. 'But coming from Blackpool to Sunderland at that time, he had given up a team that were in line for promotion and taken on a team that were threatened by relegation. He had a lot of enthusiasm and a drive to succeed which would have definitely translated itself to the players that day and – as we later found out – it wasn't that Sunderland had a bad team, it was just in need of some redirection. I think when Bob arrived it lightened the mood and that was probably the reason why that famous shot of him and the players out on the pitch at Roker Park shows everyone relaxing.'

'My view of Bob Stokoe was that he was more of a heart manager than a head manager,' Barry Davies says. 'He was a very emotional man and he could see things in the future as colourful, successful and so forth. In fact, he would have loved the perfect day. I found him to be very different in his outlook as a manager than he had once been as a player, that is for sure. He was a very determined, no-nonsense centre-half in his day. As an appointment at Sunderland I think it was surprising. But he got the job and he seemed to have a look at what was there and decided not to tinker with things. I think he soon realised the players were maybe capable of sorting themselves out. He was also a totally different character to Alan Brown and that was a major factor in my view.'

'Bob Stokoe was always thought of as a guy who knew his way around the lower divisions,' adds writer and broadcaster Gerald Sinstadt. 'But he had a talent for making players better than people thought they were. He was a motivator and a passionate man – I think that was part of why he got results. I considered him to be an example of the inspirational manager rather than the great tactician. There was a big difference between him and his predecessor at Sunderland: I think it is fair to say that you tended to respect Alan Brown and that you tended to like Bob Stokoe.'

'I personally had never heard of Bob Stokoe and everybody was surprised when they picked him,' Hughes admits. 'But you just knew there was going to be a difference as soon as he arrived. I certainly felt that.'

The new Sunderland manager told the press that the chance of managing a big club in his native north-east had been too big to turn down: 'I am delighted to be here and could not be more excited about the prospects of the job I am taking on,' he said. Stokoe announced that he would soon be bringing his own trainer-coach to the club, probably within the next week. But for now Elliott remained.

'I have always wanted to get back to the north-east. I played for Newcastle and since I became a manager I have spent the years working hard to gain the kind of experience that would justify me getting a chance back home,' Stokoe said.

Now I have it and I am delighted. Two points from the bottom of the table is not a very happy position but there is still a long way to go. We will be fighting very hard to improve. I have been too long in the game to set targets and we will be taking each game as it comes but I am confident things will go well. Words can come very easily and we can talk about ambitions and all kinds of things but everything depends on the players and they are the people upon whom we will be depending for success. There was no lack of effort under Alan Brown nor since he left and I am sure we will get the same effort on Saturday.

Brown's ears must have been burning when Collings then added, 'Money will be made available for Mr Stokoe if he requires it.'

'I consider myself to be a players' man, to try to know what makes each one of them tick, to distinguish their different sense of humour, to understand who needs to be driven, who to be coaxed and I demand dedication,' Stokoe said. 'It is a team game. I try to make all players equal, not to show favours to players who might be a little more valuable.' The north-east press pack – denied decent copy for so long by Brown – scribbled frantically away in their notebooks.

But the announcement of the new manager did not immediately placate the fans. There was one man and one man only that they wanted to take over at their club, and it wasn't Bob Stokoe.

'When Bob Stokoe got the job I was very disappointed,' Sunderland supporter Steve Hodgson says. 'I really wanted Brian Clough. He seemed young, brash, exciting and full of ideas, while Stokoe looked like a bald old man and a tired has-been. He had mainly managed teams like Bury and Rochdale and the fact he was a Magpie came into it as well. Cloughie was far and away the fans' number one choice. I think he wanted to manage Sunderland and I think he should have managed Sunderland.'

'I always wanted Brian Clough to manage Sunderland. I was stood in the Roker End when he suffered his injury against Bury in 1962 and

I can still remember the agony on his face,' Sunderland fan Bill Peverley adds. 'I followed his managerial career step by step and I always liked him. I can remember when he suggested he would like to come back to Sunderland. That struck a strong chord with Sunderland fans of all ages. All I knew about Bob Stokoe was that he had played for them-up-the-road. I didn't associate him with the Clough injury until it made the newspapers later on. I had always associated Chris Harker, the goalkeeper, with that.'

So Stokoe had two obstacles to overcome before he could start work in his new position, and he couldn't do too much about either: he had played for Newcastle and he was not Clough. In the circumstances he played a blinder: he immediately changed the colour of Sunderland's shorts from white back to black. His first game in charge – at home to Second Division leaders Burnley that forthcoming Saturday – was the first time the Rokerites had played in their famous black shorts since the 1960–61 season. Stokoe's brainwave went down a storm among supporters: he understood history; he understood passion; he understood what was required.

'The older fans were very pleased with his decision concerning the shorts,' supporter Pete Sixsmith says. 'It took them back to the glory days of Raich Carter and so on.'

'Bob Stokoe also fixed the clock on the Clock Stand roof,' fellow fan Paul Dobson adds. 'It had sat there for years and it wasn't working but he got it fixed. It is dead simple really: you walk into a ground and there is a clock there so let's make it bloody work. That clock sort of summed up what was wrong with the club at that time. It had slowed down and eventually it had given up. Stokoe got it going again and that was a symbol of what he was doing. It was exactly the same with the shorts going back to black.'

Stokoe may have got the clock on the Clock Stand roof to work but the tall grandfather clock that stood in the corner of his office at Roker Park – among the ornate trimmings of oak panels, parquet edges and wall-to-wall Axminster carpet – remained unworkable for some time to come. It did not seem to bother him unduly in his day-to-day duties at the club, however.

The new manager changed one other thing on his arrival at Sunderland: he moved the midweek home matches from a Wednesday to a Tuesday evening. 'I remember in the 1960s at night games there would be a lot of men in overalls who had just finished their shift and would come to see the match straight from the shipyards after a few pints,' Sixsmith recalls. 'Stokoe changed the midweek matches to Tuesday so that the ship workers could work overtime shifts and still come to the match. Wednesday was an overnight shift at the shipyards so he switched the days around. He could see straight away that it would be better for the community to do that and he could see straight away that there would then be bigger crowds.'

But he made no change in the club captaincy. 'When Bob Stokoe came in I went to see him and I told him I was quite happy to relinquish the job of captain so that he could do what he wanted,' Kerr says. 'But he said to me, "No, we'll just leave it as it is and take it as it comes." Hence it just went on. There were a lot of rumours at the time that he wanted Dave Watson to be captain. One or two others were mentioned too. But nothing was ever said or done and so I continued in the role.'

In his programme notes for his first match in charge Stokoe wrote:

I was brought up in these parts so I know how knowledgeable the people of Durham and Northumberland are about their football. I know also how desperately the supporters of Sunderland want success. To these faithfuls of Sunderland, I say: 'I am no miracle worker.' I make you only one promise that I shall do absolutely everything in my power to put Sunderland where they belong – right at the top of the tree.

He concluded the article by saying, 'I dream of Roker Park being packed to capacity in the future to see the kind of successful team this area deserves after so many lean years. We start this afternoon on the job of turning this dream into a reality.'

Stokoe retained the same starting line-up that Elliott had used for the previous two matches and then watched – before a much-improved crowd of 16,812 – as Sunderland were narrowly beaten 1–0. It was their eighth league defeat of the season. The Rokerites held the upper hand for most of the match as Burnley played a holding game, but the winning goal came from Paul Fletcher on seventy-two minutes. Defeats for both Brighton & Hove Albion and Portsmouth plus a postponement for Cardiff City were all that kept Sunderland out of the relegation zone at the beginning of December.

'They gave everything they had and I thought they did well enough to get a point,' Stokoe said afterwards. 'I was disappointed for them and for the fans, because this was a tremendous effort against a very good team. I am quite confident we can work one or two things out and get the job going well. We will go like a bomb in the second half of the season.'

Stokoe made a point of seeing every single player on Sunderland's books within his first week in the manager's chair. Following the first team's defeat by Burnley, he watched Sunderland Youths beat Hull Youths 4–1 in the Northern Intermediate Cup and then saw Sunderland Reserves win 2–1 against Barnsley Reserves. Both teams were doing well in their respective leagues.

Bobby Park had made a welcome return to the reserve team after the serious injury he had sustained on the opening day of the 1971–72 season, and due to his form and fitness Stokoe included him in his thirteen-man squad to travel to Portsmouth, a team placed just one position below Sunderland in the table.

An injury to Lathan meant a reshuffle for the long trip south for Stokoe's second game in charge: Hughes was handed the number 9 shirt, Horswill was switched to number 8 and Mick McGiven was drafted into defence. Tones was again on the bench and so Park just missed out.

The changes paid off and Sunderland achieved a first win in ten games, coming from 2–1 down with two late goals to win 3–2. The turnaround was again influenced by Tones coming on as substitute, which allowed Watson – who had scored his first goal of the season in this match – to push up front and make his presence felt. Hughes equalised with a header on eighty-seven minutes, and Kerr produced a diving header from Tueart's cross in injury time to clinch the win in front of a crowd of just 5,783 at Fratton Park – the second-lowest attendance at a Sunderland match since the Second World War.

The second round of the FA Cup took place that afternoon. Two Southern League outfits progressed into the third round courtesy of a draw that had created two all-non-league affairs. Chelmsford City thrashed Telford United 5–0 and Margate defeated Walton and Hersham 1–0.

The Sunderland players were keen to enjoy their first two points since September. It promised to be a long but joyous coach journey back to the north-east. The new manager was about to make it even more enjoyable.

'Back in the Alan Brown days you would never be allowed to touch alcohol at all,' Hughes says. 'It got to the stage at one time that if you wanted an extra glass of Coke, Charlie Hurley had to go up to where he was sat – at the top of table like the master – and ask if it was all right. Now sometimes he would say yes and sometimes he would say no. So after our first away match with Bob Stokoe, we stop off at a café for a bite to eat. We're sitting there and three or four of the lads went up to the bar. We were only there for a couple of minutes before Bob got off his chair and came straight over to us. We feared the worst but he just said, "Excuse me, I'll see to all these." Well, from being like that for four years under Brown and then having this was incredible. He just said to us, "Look, you're all men together – you know when the right time is and you know when the wrong time is." He gave us a responsibility but he immediately gave us a certain freedom as well.'

One player who would sadly never fully experience that freedom was Park. A freak accident during a training session at Washington just days after the Portsmouth game broke the same leg that had caused the player to previously miss a season and a half of first-team football. He had fought back so bravely to the verge of the first team that when he broke down again it was devastating to all connected with the club. Park would not recover this time and he retired from football at the age of twenty-three in 1975.

The third-round draw of the FA Cup was made on Monday 11 December 1972 and pitched Sunderland away to Notts County. The Third Division side had already reached the quarter-finals of the League Cup that season, eventually losing to First Division Chelsea after knocking out both Southampton and Stoke City from the top division in the early rounds.

Stokoe, desperate for a good Cup run to boost attendances, was upbeat about his team's prospects: 'Obviously I am disappointed that we have been drawn away, but it could have been a lot worse. I am confident we can get a result out of this one, even if it means a second game.'

The manager's immediate task when he had been appointed was 'Keep us up and bring the crowds back.' Frustratingly, despite the win at Portsmouth there was a drop of over 5,000 from the previous attendance at Roker Park and the lowest home crowd of the season

(11,529) saw a 0–0 draw against Preston North End. This was not a good sign for Stokoe or the club.

Jackie Milburn, who was working as a journalist with the *News of the World*, later recalled throwing his pen at one Sunderland fan who heckled his former Newcastle team-mate on the way to the tunnel after this match with the words 'Get back to the black-and-whites, Stokoe.'

The Sunderland team that lined up against Preston had a new look about it: Jim Montgomery in goal; Dick Malone at right-back, Keith Coleman at left-back; Dave Watson at centre-half, John Tones at left-half, Mick McGiven at right-half; Ian Porterfield and Micky Horswill supplying and supporting Billy Hughes, Bobby Kerr and Dennis Tueart up front. Stokoe also made an interesting numerical switch, with Porterfield – the talented playmaker – given the number 10 shirt. He would now famously wear it for the rest of the season.

'I am still experimenting,' Stokoe said. 'We will get a lot of goals from Hughes, Tueart, Kerr and Porterfield. That is a very useful quartet and we will get greater value from their work if we can tighten things up a little at the back.' Stokoe's first three games in charge had heralded three points – one win, one draw and one defeat – and so Sunderland remained in relegation trouble.

But Stokoe was steadily moulding his team. Wherever he had managed, defence had always been his first priority, and he achieved the club's first clean sheet in seven matches against Preston. As someone who had played at centre-forward as well as centre-half in his early career at Newcastle, he may well have made the positional change with Watson himself sooner or later, but it was Elliott – the man he considered getting rid of as soon as he stepped into Roker Park – who did it, and it is Elliott who should get the credit for making that switch.

Everything was then stopped in its tracks when a flu virus spread through Sunderland and brought the town to a virtual standstill. Stokoe was one of the first at the club to be struck down and remained bedridden for over a week. At one stage only four squad members were fit enough to report for training. The club's medical adviser, Dr Jim Scott, recommended closing down Roker Park and the training ground immediately to prevent further spread of the infection. As the number of cases in Sunderland soared to epidemic proportions, club secretary Ron Linney managed to get the Football League to authorise the post-ponement of all three of Sunderland's fixtures over the forthcoming

Christmas programme. Apart from the war years this was the first time since 1886 that Sunderland had not played a match over the festive period. The next time the Rokerites would be in action would be in 1973.

5.

THE BLEAK MIDWINTER

'It's a matter of principle, principle of what we're fighting for – equality,' Terry Collier, alias Sunderland-born actor James Bolam, said in *Whatever Happened to the Likely Lads?*, shown on BBC1 at the beginning of 1973. 'You take away a man's work and you take away his pride.'

Rising inflation, rising unemployment and regular strikes dominated British society. This whole cycle would eventually lead to an energy crisis, the three-day week, a national pay freeze and the end of Edward Heath's Conservative government. Heath had survived the miners' strike of 1972 – felt keenly in the north-east – but he would soon succumb to another one. Recession hit the street, there was little money in the pocket and the mood was dark, not helped at all by the lights having to go out at 10 p.m.

The majority of Sunderland's male support worked locally in the mines and shipyards that had once made the town a flourishing port. At one time Sunderland was the biggest shipbuilder in the country, and the north-east was the prime provider of coal. But in the 1960s the collieries and the shipyards began to close. Over seventy mines in the area were shut down within a decade, with the loss of more than 60,000 jobs.

During the first week of 1973 there were concerns that the situation in County Durham and Northumberland was going to get even worse when Sam Potts, the area director of the National Union of Mineworkers, told a meeting of local miners that 'King Coal' no longer ruled. As he said this, 2,500 workers at Coles Cranes in Sunderland were out on strike in protest over 300 job losses, barricading the entrance to the plant with three twenty-ton cranes. It was a bleak time.

Glam rock lifted the mood a little. After the fantasy – the glitter of Marc Bolan and the glory of David Bowie – came the reality: an army of imitators, all long hair and make-up, and 1973 was to be their year:

'Blockbuster!' by Sweet and 'Cum on Feel the Noize' by Slade were the big anthems of the winter, and with colour television sets fast becoming the must-have consumer item – either to purchase or to rent – and *Top of the Pops* the must-watch television programme, pop music provided something of an antidote to the gloom.

In Sunderland there would soon be a different type of bedroom-wall pin-up. Footballers such as Jim Montgomery, Billy Hughes, Bobby Kerr, Dennis Tueart and Dave Watson resonated with the local people far more than the likes of Bolan, Bowie, Slade or Sweet. What's more, they played in the town every other week. During this time of political unrest nothing could give the locals more pride than their football team. The New Year marked a new start for the Rokerites and their new manager. The flu virus that had ravaged the club was finally at an end and, after the enforced lay-off, Bob Stokoe could get back to work.

'The pressure came off a little bit at that time and we were able to relax a bit more,' Dick Malone says. 'We had three weeks without a game over the Christmas period and I think it did us all the world of good. It was like starting a new season again after having that break.'

During his fortnight away from work Stokoe pondered the areas where he needed to recruit experience to his side. He focused on three positions: centre-forward, central defence and left-back. On returning to his office at Roker Park the first call he made was, ironically, to Brian Clough at Derby County. The target was John O'Hare, the former Sunderland striker who had been sold by Ian McColl in the summer of 1967. Unable to reach Clough personally by telephone, Stokoe had no option but to put his offer in the post: 'It would be on Brian's desk this morning and I am awaiting the outcome,' he said. Clough turned down the offer.

Stokoe had no such problem in contacting his best friend Joe Harvey, the manager of Newcastle United, the best man at his wedding and the man whose boots he used to clean at St James' Park back in the 1940s. He asked for permission to speak to two of his underused squad players, one a left-back and the other a central defender.

Ron Guthrie was built like a tank. A couple of inches under six feet, he weighed close to thirteen stone. He was also twenty-eight years old. Stokoe had recognised the emerging talent of Joe Bolton at left-back but also the inexperience of the seventeen-year-old. Alan Brown had chopped and changed at number 3 and Sunderland needed stability in the position. It came in an accomplished player who had both First Division and European experience.

Guthrie had joined Newcastle as a left-winger but after suffering a cartilage injury he was switched to left-back. He made his debut on the opening day of the 1966–67 season at Aston Villa and was understudy to Frank Clark for the next seven seasons. His biggest honour at the club came as a member of the 1969 Inter-Cities Fairs Cup-winning squad: Guthrie played in the third-round match against Real Zaragoza and thereby qualified for a winners' medal. He also played in the competition against the likes of Anderlecht and Porto in later years. He had made a handful of league appearances in the 1972–73 season and scored against Norwich City in October. His last appearance for the Magpies had come at Derby on 16 December 1972.

Dave Young, aged twenty-seven, was an experienced and versatile defender. He made his debut for Newcastle in the 1969–70 season at West Bromwich Albion in place of the injured right-back David Craig, and went on to play in a variety of roles for the club in both midfield and defence. But his preferred position was at number 6. He had also played in Europe, against the likes of Anderlect and Inter Milan. His last game for the Magpies was at Coventry City on 16 September 1972.

Both Guthrie and Young were Northumberland-born and Newcastle fans. This was, of course, familiar territory for Stokoe, and the manager did not foresee a problem with crossing the divide. The supporters may not have been so relaxed about it, but both players settled quickly.

'Keith Burkinshaw, Newcastle's first-team coach, asked me to go and see Joe Harvey in his office,' Guthrie recalls. 'I went in and there was Joe, Jackie Milburn and Bob Stokoe. Joe said to me, "Bob would like you to go to Sunderland." Bob then told me I would be his first choice left-back if I signed. I think he had seen me play in a couple of reserve games and obviously he liked what he saw. I said, "OK." Wages weren't even discussed.'

'Joe Harvey told me Bob Stokoe had come in for us,' Young adds. 'I said I would like to talk to him. Of course going from black and white to red and white was difficult for both Ron and me, but it all happened very quickly. Bob said, "I'm going to build a team here; it is red-and-whites – I know all that – but I want to get some good players in and Joe tells me you will do a good job for me." Bob convinced us. He was quite persuasive and at our ages we didn't want to be in the reserves so we just moved across to Sunderland. We didn't even move house, we just went through the Tyne Tunnel.'

Young went straight into the Sunderland team to face Brighton & Hove Albion – partnering Watson in defence – but Guthrie's signature was delayed when he went down with the same flu virus that had affected Sunderland just before Christmas, so Bolton played at left-back. John Lathan – still the club's top goal scorer with the seven goals he got before Stokoe arrived – returned at centre-forward, while Hughes and Tueart were given wide attacking roles and a 'licence to roam' and 'freedom to express themselves' by their manager, who had now decided to adopt a more exciting 4–3–3 formation.

After shoring up the defences at his previous clubs, Stokoe's tried and tested method was to focus next on his attacking options. He had been lucky to have the likes of an emerging Colin Bell at Bury, Hugh McIlmoyle at Carlisle United and Tony Green at Blackpool. He soon found that he had inherited much more at Sunderland. He was also quick to realise that the tough tactics of his predecessor had inhibited certain players. Against Brighton, he gave this talent a chance to shine.

'Bob Stokoe just said to us, "Go out and show me what you've got,"' Hughes says.

There were no tactics as such and so this natural way of playing just occurred. We weren't told to do things and I suppose you got a feeling in the way he spoke to you and the way he spoke to other people that he may not be brilliant tactically, but you just felt so comfortable in his company. I think with the tightness of Alan Brown and the realisation of the freedom Bob gave us, we were suddenly no longer playing out of fear. We were now playing for a man who respected us. That comment he made in the café told me I could play for him. I could play for a manager that treated me like an adult rather than a kid. That is the way I got on with him. It wasn't his team talk as such but the atmosphere he brought into the dressing room.

The result was immediate: Sunderland hammered Brighton 4–0. Hughes, showing glimpses of the swashbuckling style that would soon entrance the nation, scored two goals and Tueart scored one. The crowd was low – 12,573 – and the club remained nineteenth in the table, but the signs on the pitch were more than encouraging, regardless of the fact that Brighton were bottom.

Malcolm Musgrove, who had been relieved of his coaching duties at Manchester United following the sacking of Frank O'Farrell, was at the match, and the press reported that he would soon be joining the Sunderland staff as coach. But no announcement was made after the match and so, for the time being, Billy Elliott continued to work in that role.

'Bob Stokoe and Billy Elliott didn't get on particularly well,' Watson says. 'I think this went all the way back to the Newcastle-versus-Sunderland matches in the 1950s when they had played against each other. Billy was a tough player and – for his size – a very hard man. Malcolm Musgrove was a big mate of Bob's and I think Bob really wanted to bring him in.'

Prior to FA Cup third-round weekend Sunderland held their first board meeting of 1973. Stokoe later reflected with relish on the suggestion by one of the club's new directors, Maurice Berwick, to back the Rokerites at 250–1 to win the competition. 'I had £2 in my pocket and I gave it to him without thinking,' he said.

The third-round draw had thrown up some interesting ties. There were five all First Division matches, including Cup holders Leeds United at Norwich; league leaders Liverpool were at Second Division leaders Burnley; and the two surviving non-league sides – Chelmsford City and Margate – were at home against Ipswich Town and Tottenham Hotspur respectively. Sunderland's visit to Notts County was nowhere near the spotlight but it was an opportunity for both clubs to progress in the competition. 'There is nothing like a Cup run to excite the supporters of teams in the north-east,' Stokoe proclaimed on the eve of his side's trip down to Meadow Lane.

The rather eccentric Jimmy Sirrel had guided Notts County from the lower reaches of the Fourth Division to the verge of the Second Division in three seasons. However, the 1972–73 campaign had been hard to fathom: they had beaten two top-flight teams on the way to the quarter-finals of the League Cup but were placed just above the relegation zone and had struggled past two Northern Premier League outfits to reach the third round of the FA Cup. 'We played at Altrincham in the first round and that was a tough match,' Notts County's all-time record goal scorer Les Bradd says. 'Kevin Randall won it for us with a second-half penalty but we weren't playing particularly well at that time. We beat Lancaster City 2–1 at home in the second round, which was a little easier, but we still weren't playing well. Then we drew away at Bolton Wanderers, who were top of the Third Division, on Boxing Day and our season just took off. That result really turned us around and we won eight out of our next nine league games. By the time we were due to play Sunderland in the Cup the mood was a lot better and our confidence was high.

'Jimmy Sirrel was a real character. He talked in riddles a lot and relaxed us with names like "Aston Vanilla" and things like that. But it was amazing how he got your concentration. He worked with every player and we believed in ourselves. Jimmy only talked about us, never about the opposition. We never talked about Sunderland before we played them, even though Jimmy was a great friend of Bob Stokoe. It was all about us and how we played. His mindset was that we were going to win the match. There was no fear attached at all. We had some good players and so we thoroughly expected to go through, particularly as we were at home.

'The only player in the Sunderland side I knew was Dave Watson,' Bradd adds. 'Dave took me under his wing when I joined Notts County. He was playing at centre-forward by then and I made my debut along-side him against Crewe Alexandra in 1967. We were near the bottom of the Fourth Division and Crewe were near the top but we won 1–0 and Dave scored the goal. He was always a very strong player and could hold his own against any defender. I knew how good a centre-half he was too, for he would sometimes mark me in practice matches!'

Both Guthrie and Young were unable to play at Meadow Lane due to the timing of their registration with Sunderland and so they had to watch from the stands. Stokoe selected John Tones to partner Watson in central defence and kept Bolton at left-back. Jackie Ashurst came into midfield and Mick McGiven was named substitute. This gave Stokoe the standby option of playing either Ashurst or McGiven in defence alongside Tones and pushing Watson into attack if needed.

'We had the extra forward against Brighton last week,' Stokoe said on the eve of the match. 'Tomorrow we tighten up again but we are not going to be defensive-minded. Kerr can stay up at the front with Hughes and Tueart and I am sure we will get goals. Notts County have one or two really big fellows who need to be taken care of.'

One of those big fellows, Bradd, gave Notts County the lead on twenty-seven minutes when he scored from close range after Mont-gomery pushed out a fiercely struck angled drive from Randall. The home side – with Don Masson and Arthur Mann dominating the midfield – were in control of the match early on and Randall went close again before half-time. Sunderland's best opportunity in the first forty-five minutes fell to Tueart, whose well-hit shot was comfortably saved by goalkeeper Roy Brown.

Sunderland improved in the second half but still trailed with less than twenty minutes to go. Stokoe then replaced Ashurst with McGiven and sent Watson up front into the attack. This was now a tried and tested Plan B, but it was also a gamble, and it almost cost the Rokerites at the other end when Bradd found himself in space in the penalty box and connected powerfully with his head. It looked a goal all the way but Montgomery, diving backwards, managed to produce a brilliant one-handed save to tip the ball away for a corner. It kept Sunderland in the Cup.

Years spent honing his reactions and reflexes on the training ground had paid dividends for the nimble Sunderland goalkeeper: 'I trained for those moments,' Montgomery says. 'We didn't have a goalkeeping coach at that time so I would do things with the lads on my own. I did a lot of "on the turn" stuff with them where I would stand and face them and get them to knock the ball either side of me, so I had to get down and get up; it was repetitive, it was physical and it was hard. I trained for saves like the one I made from Les Bradd as well: one of the lads would get a ball in his hand on the penalty spot, I would run off my line, touch the ball and they would then throw it over me towards one corner or the other. So I had to get back, dive up and get to the ball. It is all about good feet: good feet backwards, push off and keep it out. We used to work on that so when that happened at Notts County it wasn't something that came out of the blue, it was something that I had worked on in training. It might have been that I never needed to make that particular save all season but then one game comes along and that saves you a goal, or it saves you a point, or it keeps you in the FA Cup.'

Sunderland's support at Meadow Lane was boosted by several hundred exiles now working in the Nottinghamshire coalfields after the spate of pit closures in County Durham during the previous decade. The attendance of 15,142 included the strongest Sunderland away following of the season so far. Paul Dobson and Pete Sixsmith were among them and both remember Montgomery's save well: 'It was a cracking header and I thought that was it: game over,' Sixsmith says. 'I was stood right behind the goal where it happened,' Dobson adds. 'The ball went over Monty and I thought it was in but somehow he got his hand behind his head and hooked the ball back up over the bar. It was a tremendous save and it kept us alive.'

But Sunderland still needed to find a goal to stay in the competition. One minute after Montgomery made that vital save, Watson forced home an equaliser. There were eleven minutes left on the clock.

'It was a free-kick close to the touchline, near to the halfway line, and it was angled towards the far post,' Watson recalls. 'Bill Brindley, the Notts County right-back, was marking me and I rose well above him to head it into the goal by the near post. We rescued a draw in that match. We were minutes from going out.'

'We could easily have gone out against Notts County and we would have done had it not been for Monty,' Kerr adds. 'I always said that Monty could save balls that were going into the net, if you know what I mean. He wasn't just a good goalkeeper. He was a top-notch goalkeeper. We were used to Monty doing those types of save. He saved us lots of times.'

It was a sombre mood in the home dressing room afterwards: 'I can still remember the disappointment,' Bradd says. 'We felt we should have won the game. We had our chance and we didn't take it. The result took the wind out of us completely but our manager had taught us how to win up and down the country and we believed in ourselves away from home.'

'They played the better type of Cup football in the first half than we did and we were fortunate to be only one goal down at half-time,' Stokoe told the press after the match. 'It certainly made a big difference when Watson moved forward. We left ourselves stretched at the back but we had to go for it. They have had their chance at home and now we have ours.'

Lady Luck smiled down on Sunderland in the FA Cup fourth-round draw by offering them a potential home encounter against Fourth Division opposition. Reading's third-round match with Doncaster Rovers had been postponed due to an injury crisis at Doncaster. Both clubs were currently positioned in the lower half of the bottom division and one of them would now play the winners of the Notts County–Sunderland replay for a place in the fifth round. For the Rokerites – still placed fourth-bottom of the Second Division – there could not have been a better opportunity to progress into the last sixteen: 'This is wonderful,' Stokoe said on hearing the news. 'I am delighted with this one and it will be a tremendous incentive for us. It may not be the most attractive of ties but results are important and this is one we can win, providing we get the right result tomorrow night.'

Stokoe brought McGiven into his defence for the replay against Notts County and played Watson – with a number 5 on his back – at centre-forward. It was essentially the side that had finished the match at Meadow Lane. Lathan was brought back as an attacking option on the bench and Ashurst was dropped.

Neither Bradd nor his team-mates had any experience or expectation of what the crowd could be like at Roker Park on big Cup nights and the atmosphere it could generate. Furthermore the attendance for the replay – 30,033 – almost doubled the gate at the first match. The Roker Roar was back.

This was only the third time the ground had attracted an attendance greater than 30,000 since the club's relegation from the First Division in 1970. The tall, imposing floodlight pylons that gleamed over the rows of terrace houses around Roker Park picked out a growing number of supporters making their way to the stadium for the evening kick-off. The excitement among these fans could be felt in the cold North Sea breeze that enveloped them that night.

'There was a fair deal of excitement about the replay as the fans knew we would play either Reading or Doncaster if we won,' Sixsmith recalls. 'It was a big crowd and I think it was then that you began to feel that something could be happening at the club, you know: Hang on, this is interesting – thirty-thousand-plus for a replay against a team from a division below. Stokoe had tapped into something, and moving the midweek matches to Tuesday was a great decision by him.'

'I have never felt a noise like it to this day,' Bradd says. 'I had played at Villa Park and later on I played at Old Trafford and it doesn't compare. Why is that? Maybe the acoustics of the stand threw the noise levels down on you at Roker Park? I don't know what made the atmosphere like that but it was an amazing experience to play there.'

Notts County had chances again in the early stages of the replay: Masson went close with a first-half free-kick and Montgomery saved well from Jon Nixon at the start of the second half. But other than that

Sunderland were in control and from early in the second half the visitors had to defend in growing numbers as the Rokerites moved up the gears.

A Kerr cross was headed over the crossbar by Dave Needham and Bradd had to do the same to keep out a dangerous corner from Ian Porterfield minutes later. The deadlock was finally broken on fifty-four minutes: Porterfield won the ball in midfield and pushed it through on the left, and Kerr allowed it to run on to the advancing Watson, who ran towards the edge of the box before hitting a right-foot shot across Brown and inside the far post.

Once Sunderland had the lead, they dominated the match. With three minutes remaining Lathan came on for Micky Horswill and with seconds remaining Tueart whisked the ball away from a hesitant Needham: it sailed over Brown and into the net off the foot of the post. Some fans invaded the pitch to celebrate the 2–0 win. Stokoe was a relieved man.

'When it comes to Cup games, league positions and form do not matter a jot,' Malone says. 'You've got to match any team that you are playing – regardless of which league they are in – for effort first of all. If you are better than them the class will show. We didn't play particularly well in the first game against Notts County but we got the draw and we managed to come through in the replay.'

'We played well that night,' Watson adds. 'I remember Don Masson mentioned to me during the game, "We can't get anything here." We fully deserved to win.' With Watson playing at centre-forward, Sunderland's back four that night was Bolton, Tones, McGiven and Malone. This would be the last time they would ever play together and only the tall Scottish right-back would remain in Stokoe's Cup side that season.

'The match at Roker Park was totally different to the one at Meadow Lane,' Bradd concedes. 'We were under the cosh, the atmosphere was charged and Sunderland responded to it. They were sharper to the ball and much stronger. Sunderland controlled the game that night and deserved to win. But make no mistake, the support of the crowd was a factor too.'

Reading defeated Doncaster 2–0 the following night to set up an emotional fourth-round return to Roker Park for their manager and former Sunderland skipper Charlie Hurley, who had famously been chaired around the ground when he captained the Rokerites to their first-ever promotion in the 1963–64 season. Notts County went on to win fifteen games in the second half of the season to finish second in the table and secure a return to the Second Division after an absence of fifteen years.

There were few surprises from a third-round draw that had promised so much excitement: Second Division Swindon Town knocked out First Division Birmingham City 2–0 and Fourth Division Bradford City beat Second Division Blackpool 2–1. And that was it. In the all-First Division encounters, Arsenal, Leeds and Manchester City all progressed: Manchester City defeated Stoke 3–2 at Maine Road while Arsenal, 2–1 down at home to Leicester with just three minutes remaining, required a replay at Filbert Street to go through. Leeds needed two replays to get past Norwich but after 1–1 draws at Carrow Road and Elland Road, Don Revie's side thrashed the Canaries 5–0 at a neutral Villa Park. Allan Clarke scored a hat-trick. Norwich boss Ron Saunders accused Leeds of 'extreme professionalism' afterwards but Revie publicly refuted the claim.

The stocky Guthrie finally made his Sunderland debut at left-back in a rain-soaked league match at Swindon the following weekend. Watson played at centre-forward again, with Ashurst partnering Young in central defence. McGiven was ruled out with a cartilage injury and required an operation the following week.

The match ended in a 1–1 draw – Porterfield scored Sunderland's goal – to stretch the Rokerites' unbeaten run to six games in all competitions. But the position of eighteenth in the table remained a concern. As did the long-term solution at centre-forward. Stokoe's interest in O'Hare was now at an end and Charlie Ferguson's frequent trips to Scotland – reportedly to check out Drew Busby at Airdrieonians – had yet to produce anything tangible.

The Sunderland manager said he was after a big, strong, attacking player with plenty of experience who could hold the ball up as well as score goals. He believed he had finally found his man at Crystal Palace, and promptly paid out £30,000 for the bustling former Scottish international and Celtic star John Hughes.

Hughes had made his name under Jock Stein at Parkhead, where he won five Scottish League championships. He was a member of the 1967 European Cup-winning squad, although he did not play in the final in Lisbon. He did play in the 1970 European Cup final defeat in

Milan against Feyenoord and scored one of the goals that defeated Leeds in the so-called 'Battle of Britain' semi-final that year at Hampden Park. Interestingly Hughes was given his Scotland debut in Ian McColl's last match in charge of the national team in 1965. He was capped eight times over the next six seasons. He signed for Crystal Palace in 1971 and enhanced his reputation in England by scoring a terrific goal against Sheffield United that was screened on *Match of the Day*. But Sunderland fans knew all about him anyway, for he was Billy's older brother.

'I thought it was a great move when we signed John Hughes,' Sixsmith says. 'I had seen him play a few years before for the Scottish League against the Football League at St James' Park on an icy pitch that was just lethal, and he had a game that you would just die for. Billy was at Sunderland by then so there was always a lot of interest in his brother and that night on that pitch he was like a ballet dancer. He was brilliant. He was a legend at Celtic and he had also done quite well at Crystal Palace so I was pleased when we signed him.'

'He is a big, strong player and he can do a job for us by filling a gap at the front,' Stokoe said. But the new recruit could not provide an option for him against Reading as he was Cup-tied, having already played for Palace in the third round against Southampton.

After turning down the chance to play alongside his older brother at Celtic at the beginning of his career, Billy Hughes was now set to be joined by him at Roker Park, but he claims he had nothing to do with the transfer: 'John was a really good player and he was available, but Bob Stokoe signed him, it had nothing to do with me,' he says. 'I did have a little bit of a reputation for enjoying myself, you know, and Bob knew that, so maybe he brought John in to try and be a steadying influence on me. I might be wrong but I think that had a little bit to do with it. I think the manager felt, If I can't manage him, then I'll get somebody in who can.'

Both of the Hughes brothers could play up front or on the wing, but in appearance they looked very different: Billy was five feet nine inches tall and weighed under eleven stones, while John was six feet two inches tall and weighed over thirteen stones. This was a big man who was nicknamed 'Yogi' by the Celtic fans, who likened him to the cartoon character Yogi Bear. A favourite chant at Parkhead in the 1960s was 'Feed the Bear!' The brothers became the first siblings to play in the same Sunderland side since Frank and Warney Creswell at Blackburn Rovers in September 1926. At the first opportunity he got – a home league match against Millwall – Stokoe played his big new signing at centre-forward. This, importantly, allowed Watson to move back to centre-half (Ashurst was the man to make way). This was the type of line-up Stokoe had been looking to create. The other new boys – Guthrie and Young – also played.

But Stokoe's new signing was to suffer a knee injury in the opening minutes of the game and although he fought on, the pain was so bad that he eventually had to come off. Only the two brothers were aware of the injury during the match.

'John came running past me and said, "My knee's gone." The crowd started getting at him but he just wouldn't go off,' Hughes says. 'He didn't say anything at half-time and tried to play the second half but his ligaments were knackered and it cost him, because he didn't play again. I didn't react very well to the crowd booing him and I have often wondered if he hadn't had the injury, had stayed with us and was having a bad game, how it would have affected me. I was playing well at that time and I can remember that was my worst game because the crowd affected me. At the end of the day it is your brother, you know?'

Kerr and Tueart scored Sunderland's goals in a 2–0 win over Millwall – the third victory in all competitions since the start of the year. The Rokerites ended the month in seventeenth place in the table, with three games in hand on most of the teams around them due to the postponements caused by the flu virus.

Attendances were also on the up, with 22,781 fans watching the win over the Lions: the highest home league gate of the season and over 10,000 more than the previous league match against Brighton. But the highest attendance of the month – and the season so far – had come against Notts County. A late equaliser, a replay win and a for-tuitous fourth-round draw had began to stir Cup fever, and Sunderland's first appearance in the fifth round of the competition in six years was within touching distance. Only Hurley and his Reading side stood in the way.

Ritchie Pitt was substitute against Millwall – due to an injury concern over Watson – and came on for the last ten minutes. This was his first appearance under Stokoe and it could quite easily have been his last, for a £15,000 bid from Graham Taylor – who had just been appointed manager at Fourth Division Lincoln City – had been accepted.

Pitt had made over 100 league appearances under Brown but was told early on by Stokoe that he had no future at Roker Park. This may have been due to personalties, or maybe the manager found the England Schoolboys pedigree was at odds with the no-nonsense approach he had displayed in his playing days and looked for in his players now. He had little time for training courses at Lilleshall and coaching certificates either. Pitt, who remains at a loss concerning Stokoe's grievance to this day, was also a staunch supporter of Brown. Whatever it was that led to him being frozen out by Stokoe, the defender met Taylor at Washington Services to discuss a possible move to Sincil Bank.

'There were a lot of problems between Bob Stokoe and me,' Pitt says. 'He didn't want me. He wanted to sell me and he tried to sell me. I would actually have been Graham Taylor's first signing as a professional manager had I signed for him. We met and we had a chat about Lincoln but I didn't want to go all the way down to the Fourth Division. I genuinely thought I was a better player than that. I rang Graham up the following day and explained my decision. Therefore I remained a Sunderland player, albeit one that was not in the first team.'

6.

A ROYAL RETURN

The visit of Reading to Sunderland was big news in Berkshire and County Durham, but elsewhere it seemed to matter little on FA Cup fourth-round weekend. The national media hardly mentioned the contest at Roker Park between sides placed in the bottom half of the Second Division and the bottom half of the Fourth Division.

The main focus was on two all-First Division clashes – Derby County versus Tottenham Hotspur and Liverpool versus Manchester City. Brian Clough's Derby were the reigning Football League champions and Bill Nicholson's Spurs side – UEFA Cup winners the previous year – were still challenging on three fronts, having won through to the final of the League Cup and the quarter-finals of the UEFA Cup. Bill Shankly's Liverpool were also in the last eight of the UEFA Cup and sat at the top of the First Division, while Malcolm Allison's Manchester City could – on their day – be the most exciting team to watch in the country.

Elsewhere in the competition, Cup holders Leeds United were at home to Plymouth Argyle; Arsenal were at home to Fourth Division Bradford City; Ipswich Town – fourth in the First Division – were at Chelsea; while Newcastle United – sixth in the First Division – were at home to Second Division Luton Town. No fewer than thirteen sides from the top flight were expected to make it into the last sixteen. Ladbrokes bookmakers listed Leeds (6–1), Liverpool (9–1) and Arsenal (10–1) as the top three favourites for the competition. It had been a disappointing draw for the romantic and it promised to be a difficult day for the underdogs.

Reading manager Charlie Hurley – nicknamed 'King Charlie' on the Roker Park terraces in his playing days – decided to play a five-man defence at Sunderland by moving experienced midfielder Barry Wagstaff into a sweeper position behind the back four. The Royals had the best defensive record in the entire Football League despite having the smallest goalkeeper in the four divisions in Steve Death, who measured just five feet seven inches. Reading could also have had the best mid-fielder in the Fourth Division had they been able to find £20,000 to buy him just a few months before.

'I tried very hard to sign Ian Porterfield from Sunderland earlier that season,' Hurley recalls. 'Alan Brown was prepared to sell him but I couldn't get the money together. To be honest I'm not sure Ian really wanted to come down to Reading at that time. I may be wrong but I think his wife had a lot of clout and she didn't want it. Isn't it funny how things work out?'

Reading's main goal threat came from Les Chappell, who had found the net eleven times that season. Chappell, like Les Bradd at Notts County, was another striker who had once played alongside Dave Watson at the start of his career, this time at Rotherham United.

'Our defensive record was very good at that time and we were doing quite well in the Fourth Division,' Reading defender Tommy Youlden says. 'We had a fairly strong defence with a great shot stopper behind us. Steve Death was an outstanding goalkeeper and very agile. The only reason I can think why he did not move on in his career was his height – goalkeepers are expected to be six feet tall and he was a lot smaller than that – but he made some super saves for us.'

Bob Stokoe had former Newcastle duo Ron Guthrie and Dave Young available for selection for the fourth round, so youngsters Joe Bolton and John Tones – who had both featured against Notts County – made way at left-back and number 6. This brought experience and added strength to the Sunderland rearguard as Young partnered Watson in central defence. The pair had gelled immediately and had conceded just one goal in three Second Division matches so far. This was to be their first outing together in the FA Cup.

'It was fantastic playing alongside Dave Watson,' Young says. 'He used to tower and power and I used to sweep around, read things, get the ball, gee people up, whatever. It was really good. He was totally commanding, a fantastic centre-half and great to play with.'

Up front Stokoe opted to play John Lathan – a late substitute in the Notts County replay – at centre-forward. This would prove to be a mistake, for his lack of height – he was also only five foot seven – would be no match for the Reading rearguard. But with Watson back in defence the manager's options were limited. Jackie Ashurst was named

substitute, meaning there was yet again no place for the unwanted
Ritchie Pitt.

'We can throw the league table out of the window and concentrate
on a flying effort to crack this one,' Stokoe said. 'If we can go into the
hat for Monday's fifth-round draw it will keep interest alive and bring
a lot of excitement. We want to win this one and the enthusiasm
and atmosphere within the team tells me that it is well within our
capabilities.'

It was to be an emotional return for Hurley, who had played alongside five of Sunderland's starting line-up that day during his time at
Roker Park: 'I used to say to my players at Reading, "Roker Park: you
have no idea!" and when we got Sunderland in the FA Cup, I said to
them, "Now you will find out what I mean." What a reception I got; it
was "Charlie – Charlie – Charlie – Charlie" all around the ground,' he
says. 'All the people stood up when I walked out. It was quite a strange
day for me, of course. But I think it was fate to draw Sunderland in the
Cup, especially in that year. The reception I got was magnificent – you
would have thought I was playing for Sunderland, not managing a team
against them.'

'Charlie Hurley helped us by taking the attention away from us,'
Youlden says. 'He soaked it all up himself and he loved all that. But,
importantly, what that meant for the team was there was no pressure
on us.'

'I wasn't at Roker Park for the Reading match,' Pitt says. 'I'd had
words with the manager the day before and he told me that he didn't
want me to be at the game. It was a shame because Charlie Hurley is a
really nice bloke and he got a tremendous reception.'

The match presented a fabulous opportunity for both sides: Sunderland had not reached the fifth round of the FA Cup since the three-
match epic against Leeds in 1967, while Reading hadn't been there
since 1935. The highest attendance of the season so far at Roker Park –
33,913 – turned up to watch it. Special arrangements were made to
broadcast live radio commentary to hospitals in Sunderland, Durham
and South Shields as well. There was a growing expectation among
most red-and-white supporters that a place in the last sixteen was
almost assured.

Within fifteen minutes of kick-off those supporters were in shock.
A corner from the left by Gordon Cumming was met by the head of

Chappell, who flicked the ball past an outstretched Jim Montgomery to score at the Roker End. There was silence. Sunderland, unbeaten in seven matches and with no goals against them at Roker Park in the three matches since the turn of the year, trailed 1–0 at home to Fourth Division opposition.

'It was a great start for us,' Youlden says. 'We didn't concede many goals and so when we took the lead we knew we had half a chance of winning. We felt relaxed and all the pressure was suddenly on Sunderland.'

Billy Hughes started to fear the worst: 'You did think to yourself, There goes another Cup run out of the window,' he says. 'Our recent history in the competition had not been good. We had lost to teams placed in lower divisions for two or three years running by that time and a few of those were at home as well. So you begin to fear the worst.'

Sunderland fought back but found Death in inspired form. He made fine saves from Hughes, Porterfield and Bobby Kerr in the first half. This performance was later rated as the best in his twelve-year career for the Royals. Ironically it was his one and only mistake in the match that led to Sunderland's equaliser. Eight minutes before half-time Hughes made space on the left and put the ball across the six-yard box. Death got both hands to the ball but failed to hold on to it and Dennis Tueart was on hand to force it over the line.

In the second half the Rokerites pushed hard for a winner but still they found the Reading goalkeeper unbeatable. And when he was beaten the woodwork saved him, as Dick Malone found out when he saw his shot crash down from the underside of the bar.

Death also clawed a shot from Tueart back from under the bar and saved another effort from the winger before a goalmouth scramble denied both Hughes and Lathan. Death saved again from Hughes and Tueart in the closing stages of the match. Kerr picked up an injury and was replaced by Ashurst, and Watson was pushed up front to add extra height to the attack. Lathan had the ball in the net in injury time but his effort was ruled out for offside: Reading somehow survived to earn a draw and a replay.

'I think with the aura of Charlie Hurley coming back to Roker Park we were a little bit apprehensive and not particularly confident going into the match,' Young says. 'He was bigger than life at Sunderland really and I think we felt much happier knowing we were going down to play them in the replay at Reading than we had been playing them at home.'

As the Sunderland players returned to their dressing room, results began to filter through of some astonishing results elsewhere in the FA Cup, with four Second Division sides knocking out First Division outfits: Millwall had won 2–0 at Everton; Hull City had beaten West Ham United 1–0; Carlisle United had shocked Sheffield United 2–1; and, perhaps greatest of all, Luton Town had won 2–0 at St James' Park against Newcastle United, much to the embarrassment of former Hatter Malcolm MacDonald, who had said in the newspapers before the match that he would score a hat-trick against his old side and had been made captain for the day.

'We attacked and they didn't,' Luton manager Harry Haslam said afterwards. 'There is a heck of a lot of attacking football in the Second Division but clubs aren't getting the credit for it that they deserve.'

'A lot of teams lost today but we have got another chance and we have everything to look forward to,' Stokoe said after hearing those results. 'We are still in there fighting.'

When Sheffield Wednesday later put out First Division strugglers Crystal Palace with a Brian Joicey hat-trick, it meant that half of the sixteen clubs left in the competition would come from the lower divisions. The fifth-round draw that took place at lunchtime on Monday 5 February 1973 was eagerly anticipated up and down the country. There was hope for the underdogs after all. The big names left in the hat were Arsenal, 2–0 winners over Bradford with goals from Alan Ball and Charlie George; Leeds, 2–1 winners over Plymouth with goals from Allan Clarke and Mick Bates; and two teams from Derby or Tottenham and Liverpool or Manchester City, who had to replay.

As usual, the draw was transmitted live from the Football Association headquarters at 16 Lancaster Gate, London, on BBC Radio 2 at 12.30 p.m. Fans up and down the country – players, managers and chairmen alike – would be glued to transistors and car radios.

'The draw always took place during the full FA Challenge Cup committee meeting held in the Centenary Room on the first floor of the building,' Steve Clark, a member of the FA competitions department at that time, explains. 'In the room there was a glass-topped table and chairs presented to the FA by the respective football associations of Scotland, Northern Ireland and Wales in recognition of our centenary in 1963, hence the name. Each chair was embossed with the crest of the respective football association and the room was full of artefacts from each of them too. At the top of the table sat the chairman of the FA, Sir Andrew Stephen, the chairman of the Challenge Cup committee Sam Bolton and FA secretary Denis Follows.

'Next door to the Centenary Room was the library, where the BBC set up with all their equipment. Radio vans were parked outside and cables ran up through the window. The broadcaster Bryon Butler and engineers would be situated in the library. Microphones had already been set up and cabled into the library.

'At around twelve-twenty p.m. I would go into the library and signal to Bryon that the committee was ready for the draw to take place. Bryon would then stand and wait in the corridor outside. At a given signal Bryon would then start his commentary with the words, "I am leaving the library and entering the Centenary Room." He would then say, "The next voice you will hear is that of Denis Follows, the secretary of the FA." The chairman of the FA would call out the home teams, the chairman of the Challenge Cup Committee would call out the away teams and Denis Follows would call out the draws. The matches were all played on a Saturday. There were no Sunday matches back then.

'The chairman of the Challenge Cup Committee would have the velvet bag resting on the table in front of him,' Clark adds. 'There would be empty boxes for the balls placed on the table too. They were polished maroon balls with white numbers. We had used them for the FA Cup draw since the Second World War. It was very exciting and FA staff would listen to the draw eagerly from the corridors. At the end of the draw Bryon would resume his commentary and move back to the library to conclude the broadcast. I would close the Centenary Room door behind him as he did that. It was quite dramatic.'

Stokoe listened to the draw from his office on the first floor at Roker Park. He did not have to wait long to find out whom his team would play should they survive the replay at Elm Park. Sunderland or Reading was the second ball out of the velvet bag and Liverpool or Manchester City had been the first. The Sunderland–Reading replay was now to be played for higher stakes than either Stokoe or Hurley could ever have imagined – the winners would be going to either Anfield or Maine Road in the next round.

'It is not the sort of game I would have picked but we won't let it worry us,' Stokoe said. 'We will be playing our fourth FA Cup tie of the season on Wednesday night and after we have won that one we will start thinking about what comes next. We must not fail at this hurdle because we want to give our supporters the next game against Liverpool or Manchester City. They have been wonderful to us. We don't want to let them down and I am sure we won't.'

Leeds were installed as 4–1 favourites to retain the FA Cup. Arsenal were second favourites at 9–2, Liverpool and Tottenham were 9–1, while Manchester City and Wolverhampton Wanderers were 10–1. Neither Sunderland nor Reading were initially priced after the draw.

After listening to the draw the Sunderland manager then finalised some outstanding business. Nine weeks into the job, he was finally able to appoint a head coach. But it was not – as had been widely expected – Malcolm Musgrove. Stokoe found his man at Preston North End and it was to be an inspired move. His name was Arthur Cox. As a result of this appointment Billy Elliott was sidelined, but still remained at the club.

Cox had been with Coventry City in the late 1950s before a broken leg curtailed his playing career at the age of nineteen. He became a coach at Highfield Road and later moved on to Walsall, Aston Villa and Halifax Town. He once had a spell as caretaker manager at Villa Park. He then joined up with Alan Ball Sr at Deepdale and Preston won the Third Division title in 1970–71. They were currently placed four positions higher than Sunderland in the Second Division table.

'I used to play golf at the Open championship course at Lytham & St Annes during my time at Preston, and that is how I got to know Bob Stokoe, when he was manager at Blackpool,' Cox explains. 'There was a centre-forward at Preston called Hugh McIlmoyle, who Bob had at Carlisle United. When Bob got the Sunderland job, Hughie told him to take me with him but Bob fancied Malcolm Musgrove instead. Malcolm iffed and butted and eventually decided he didn't want to go and then the call came. Bob told me, "We need a little lift and the time is right for you to join us, Arthur." Sunderland had to pay Preston compensation for me. It was the first time anything like that had happened with a coach. Alan Ball Senior had an uncomfortable time at Preston due to me leaving. The directors were not happy but Alan saw it as an opportunity for me to go forward in my career.

'When I got to Sunderland I noticed there was an extremely good morale among the players,' Cox adds. 'Most of them had grown up together and it was very noticeable at that time that the players were very, very together. Every one of them wanted to do better and improve. They were all hungry and had receiving ears.'

Cox's first match in the Sunderland dugout was the replay at Reading. The trip down south was expected to be the last one that Pitt – and Keith Coleman – ever made with the club, for Stokoe had agreed with Arsenal manager Bertie Mee to allow the two defenders to spend a month on loan at Highbury with a view to permanent moves.

'Bob Stokoe called me into his office on the Monday morning after the home game with Reading and told me that Arsenal wanted Keith Coleman and me to go on loan but that Arsenal would only take Keith if I went too, so the whole thing hung on my decision,' Pitt says. 'I said I would like to go and so Keith and I travelled down to Reading with our own bags because the Arsenal assistant manager, Dave Smith, was going to meet us after the match and take us to London.

'When the players went out on to the pitch pre-match at Reading, Keith and I just stood on our own in the centre circle, not really knowing what to do,' Pitt adds. 'Then, while the players went off into the goalmouth, Stokoe came over to me and said, "You're playing tonight." I said, "I'm sorry, I don't understand: I'm going on loan to Arsenal because you don't want me." He said, "I'm playing you tonight because I want to Cup-tie you!" The only reason he picked me that night was so he could Cup-tie me. That way I couldn't play for any other club in the Cup that season, including Arsenal – who were still in the Cup, of course.'

Pitt made his first-ever start under Stokoe alongside Young in defence as Watson returned to the centre-forward position – as he had played under Alan Brown with a number 9 on his back. Lathan was dropped and Coleman was named as substitute.

'Bob Stokoe talked to me after the draw with Reading and he said that he wanted me to play at centre-forward in the replay,' Watson says. 'We lost the aerial battle against them at home and he wanted to put me up front. I was happy to go along with that. I was always happy to play at centre-forward when asked.'

The plan proved to be a masterstroke. Elm Park was an old ground set tightly within rows of terrace houses and could be a difficult and intimidating place to play, particularly on a cold winter night, but

Sunderland were 1–0 up within ninety seconds, 2–0 up after quarter of an hour and 3–0 up after half an hour. The game was all over before half-time.

The Rokerites took the lead when Tueart intercepted a square pass by Wagstaff and played it through to Kerr on the right. A return pass from Kerr to Tueart led to a shot that was cleared off the line by John Hulme, but this was picked up on the edge of the box by Watson, who brought it under control before striking it firmly into the net.

Reading had claims for a penalty on thirteen minutes when Young dispossessed Chappell in the box, but nothing was given. One minute later it was 2–0 when Watson won possession on the left, cut inside and played the ball in to Tueart, who chipped it over Death.

Watson was winning everything in the air and on thirty minutes he knocked down a Porterfield throw-in into the path of Tueart, who played in Kerr, and the Sunderland skipper slammed the ball home to essentially settle the contest. A few minutes later Watson and Tueart linked up again to play in Kerr, who smashed the ball against the crossbar with an angled drive.

Reading's goal on seventy-eight minutes was a mere consolation prize. It came from the penalty spot by Cumming after Pitt had brought down Chappell in the box. Stokoe then signalled for Watson to go into defence for the last twelve minutes to make sure his side protected their lead.

It was Sunderland's best performance yet under the new manager: Jim Montgomery was largely untroubled; the defence of Ron Guthrie, Ritchie Pitt, Dave Young and Dick Malone was strong throughout; the midfield of Ian Porterfield, Micky Horswill and Bobby Kerr controlled the match; Billy Hughes and Dennis Tueart were outstanding down the wings; and Dave Watson won everything in the air and led the attack well up front.

'We played extremely good football at Reading,' Cox says. 'I remember it well. It was my first match with the team after a couple of training sessions and – with respect to them – Reading never had a chance. Dennis Tueart immediately stuck in my mind that night.'

'Dennis Tueart was on fire in the replay,' Youlden says. 'I was supposed to be marking him and within a minute we were a goal down. He was an exceptionally good player and I found that out that night. We were totally outclassed. Those two wingers were functioning superbly and with Dave Watson up front it was very hard for us.

'The pressure had completely turned on to us for the replay, we felt that we were in with a chance after drawing up there, and with the prospect of playing against Liverpool or Manchester City there was definitely a different feeling around the place. It was a big crowd for us that night – 19,793 – and the pressure was on. But Sunderland played with a lot more freedom and played very well. It was a tremendous performance by them and it was evident they were a good side with some very good players and that sixth-bottom of the Second Division or whatever was a completely false position for them to be in.'

'I think it all started to work for us because a lot of factors were coming together,' Tueart says. 'The age of the team was right; we were a group of young players maturing together at the same time. Then Bob Stokoe came in, he relaxed us and he allowed us to play.'

'I took some champagne into the Sunderland dressing room afterwards,' Hurley says. 'I had bought it for us to celebrate, but we were well beaten on the night. I fancied our chances in the replay but Sunderland hit us so early on that it threw us completely. Those two matches were the only times that I have ever wanted to see Sunderland get beaten in my life and those supporters were great to me again. They chanted my name and many of them wanted to talk to me at the end.' Hurley signed over 200 autographs for visiting supporters after the match.

The managerial skills Hurley had learned under Brown at Sunderland helped him to control one of the most talented yet wayward players English football has ever produced. Robin Friday played for Hayes against Reading in the second round of the FA Cup that season and as a result of his performance later signed for them, helping the Royals win promotion to the Third Division a few years later. Nobody could control Friday but Hurley came the closest: 'Hayes were scared of Robin,' he says. 'But he loved me as a person and I loved him. He died very young and that was very sad. His parents told me at his funeral that I was the only one with the balls to give him a chance. I told them that he was the guy who got me promotion!'

Due to the Reading–Sunderland match being played on a Wednesday evening in early February some 300 miles from home, the away support was comparatively low that night. One Sunderland supporter who did make the trip from the north-east was Bill Peverley. He expects that fewer than a thousand Sunderland fans were at Elm Park for the replay.

'I had just gone through a difficult divorce and I didn't feel too good about things so the Cup run was very important to me,' Peverley says. 'It was really all that mattered in my life at that time. I knew I just had to be at Reading for the replay. I was a machine worker in Hartlepool and I asked if I could take the day off work. I couldn't, but I took it anyway. The foreman knew what I'd done and he made my life a misery from that day forward. He didn't sack me but my position was untenable after that. Never before or since did I ever jeopardise my living like that. But it meant so much to be there. I remember a photograph in the newspapers on the day of the match of Dave Watson holding up the number 9 shirt and the number 5 shirt. He was the "nine to five" man essentially. Dave was brilliant at that time. He is my all-time favourite player and that has a lot to do with what happened that year. I had a pure feeling of failure personally, but Dave and his wife would always make time to talk to me in the Sunderland Supporters Association shop or wherever. When you're low, as I was at that time, having what I felt was the great and godly talking to you means absolutely everything.'

Fellow Sunderland supporter Pete Sixsmith adds, 'It was my first year as a schoolteacher and that was a difficult year for me. The FA Cup run got me through it. The Reading replay was the only match I missed in the whole Cup run. It was horrible waiting to hear news of the match. In those days there was no local radio, there was no Radio Five Live; there was no Sky Sports News; there was no teletext. Radio Two was all we had and it would take second-half commentary from a chosen game. That night the chosen game was the Manchester City and Liverpool replay. I remember sitting upstairs in my bedroom that night, marking my first-ever O-level mock papers. I had Radio Two on with commentary from Maine Road and at half-time someone said, "By the way, Sunderland are 3–0 up at Reading." I couldn't believe it. Fantastic news. The kids that got their papers back the next day got really good marks!'

Manchester City beat First Division leaders Liverpool 2–0 in sweeping rain with goals from Colin Bell and Tommy Booth to set up a fifth-round tie against Sunderland. In the other replay that night, Derby came from 2–0 down to beat Tottenham 5–3 at White Hart Lane. With the prospect of Second Division opposition at home in the next round, Manchester City manager Malcolm Allison confidently proclaimed that his side were going to win the FA Cup that night. The bookmakers agreed with him and instantly made them the new favourites for the competition.

But Stokoe was also smiling: he had reached the fifth round of the FA Cup for only the second time in his managerial career, and equally pleasing was the signed contract he had in his hand as he left Elm Park that night for the north-east. It confirmed that Vic Halom – a striker who had started his career under Stokoe at Charlton Athletic – had agreed to join Sunderland from Luton in a £35,000 deal. By a strange quirk of fate Halom – who would remain Luton's top goal scorer that season – was not Cup-tied either, despite the fact that the Hatters had also made it into the last sixteen of the competition.

'Everton had made a bid for me and that is why I hadn't played in the FA Cup for Luton,' Halom explains. 'It was agreed between the clubs that I wouldn't play in the fourth round at Newcastle and so when that move didn't come off I was like a bear with a sore head. I actually met Bob Stokoe in Middlesbrough the night before the Newcastle game and I told him how unhappy I was with the situation. He didn't say much but then Luton told me that Sunderland had made a bid and they would like to talk to me. Sunderland were playing at Reading on the Wednesday night and so I met up with Bob and I saw the match from the stands. Sunderland got through to the next round, I wasn't Cup-tied, I signed for them that night and everybody was happy.'

It was the final piece of the jigsaw: Halom was the centre-forward that Stokoe had been looking for. The manager now had his team from one to eleven as the signing meant that Watson could once again return to defence and resume his partnership with Young. Furthermore all eleven players were fit and available to play in the fifth round of the FA Cup against Manchester City. As Pitt travelled to London that night, the chances of him ever again wearing a Sunderland shirt looked to be very slim.

Born in Swadlincote in Derbyshire, Halom was a tough, fun-loving player who had a background and an upbringing like none of his new team-mates: 'My father was from Budapest and my mother was born in Sevastopol in the Crimea, Ukraine, near to the Black Sea,' he says. 'My parents met in a concentration camp. My father played football and my mother was a nurse. My grandfather on my mother's side was a Cossack and was killed by the Bolsheviks. My father spoke Hungarian and my mother spoke Russian, but they both understood German so they spoke to each other in that language. Until I went to school all I heard at home was German, but then German was closer to English than what was spoken in South Derbyshire in those days! I was essentially eligible to play for both Hungary and the Soviet Union, which the Ukraine was part of in those days.

'I went down to Charlton Athletic because of a local scout called Walter Slater,' Halom adds. 'I played against people like Billy Bonds and Alan Campbell and I scored a couple of goals before half-time so they offered me a contract there and then. There had been other offers for me but my father wanted me to go down there for Charlton had a good reputation. Of course, it was my relationship with Bob Stokoe that later sealed my move to Sunderland. I liked him very much, even if we did used to fight. He used to kick bloody lumps out of you on the training pitch but I could handle myself: I came from a place where there was only one street and football went on from first thing in the morning until you were shouted in at night. Miners would play in their pit boots – they were big buggers and hard as hell too – and I was playing against these men from the age of eight. I played in midfield for my father's pit team, Granville Colliery, when I was twelve. One or two would have a whack so you had to learn how to look after yourself. It was a great grounding for me. Bob used to kick ten bells out of you as well, he really did. But he also knew which buttons to press with me. He could fire me up just by winding me up.'

Sunderland were Halom's fifth league club. He moved on from Charlton to Orient at the beginning of the 1967–68 season and later signed for Bobby Robson at Fulham (just before the manager was sacked by the Cottagers) in 1968 before joining up with Harry Haslam at Luton in September 1971. Clough had also once tried to sign him for Derby. At the age of twenty-four Halom, a strong, barrel-chested striker with an eye for goal, was well respected in the game, with over fifty league goals to his name. But like three of his new team-mates – Horswill, Malone and Watson – he had yet to play in the First Division.

Sadly two young Sunderland supporters who made the long trip south to see the Rokerites beat Reading that night would not live to see Halom play in a red-and-white shirt. Kevin Bottoms, aged nineteen, of

Boldon Drive, West Boldon, and Keith Bowen, aged sixteen, of John Street, Boldon Colliery, tragically died in a car accident south of Chester-le-Street on their way home from the Cup tie in the early hours of the following morning. Stokoe and his players attended both funerals.

7.

A SLEEPING GIANT AWAKES AT MAINE ROAD

On taking up his appointment as manager of Sunderland, Bob Stokoe had been told by his chairman Keith Collings that money would be made available to him for team-strengthening. Vic Halom's transfer from Luton Town in early February 1973 took Stokoe's total spend at Roker Park to just over £100,000, and it would just about complete his signings for the season.

It is interesting now to muse whether Stokoe would ever have signed the centre-forward had John Hughes not broken down so badly on his Sunderland debut less than two weeks before. The manager had decided early on that he wanted to make three changes to the side that he inherited and Halom now completed the hat-trick: Newcastle United pair Ron Guthrie and Dave Young had settled in at left-back and the centre of defence, meaning Keith Coleman and Ritchie Pitt, who had played in those positions under Alan Brown, were surplus to requirements and therefore allowed to go to Arsenal on trial with a view to permanent deals. Joe Bolton, who had just turned eighteen, had played left-back at the start of the FA Cup run and would have a successful future ahead of him at Roker Park, but for now Stokoe kept him in the reserves and the youth team and on the fringes of the first team. John Tones, who had partnered Dave Watson in defence in the Cup match at Notts County, would make just one more appearance before being released in the summer. John Lathan, who had started every game that season under Brown, was drifting out of the new manager's plans as well, relegated to the reserves after the draw against Reading.

The Sunderland side that took the field at Sheffield Wednesday was the nearest yet to the one that would soon become famous: Jim Montgomery in goal; Dick Malone at right-back, Ron Guthrie at left-back; Dave Watson and Dave Young in central defence; a midfield of Bobby Kerr on the right, Ian Porterfield on the left and Micky Horswill in the centre; and a forward line of Billy Hughes and Dennis Tueart alongside Vic Halom.

But there was to be one more twist in the tale. Just five minutes into the match on a waterlogged pitch at Hillsborough, the Owls' full-back Peter Rodrigues – a future FA Cup-winning captain with Southampton in 1976 – clattered into Young. He was booked and received a severe lecture from the referee, but Young suffered such a bad injury to his right ankle that he could play no more part in the match. He was carried off the field and replaced by Brian Chambers. Sunderland went on to lose the match 1–0 – the first time the side had experienced defeat since Stokoe's first match in charge – but that was somewhat incidental. The knock-on effect was that Young would face a frustrating time on the sidelines while Pitt – almost sold by Stokoe and currently at Arsenal – would now unexpectedly get his chance.

'I played for Arsenal Reserves with players such as Sammy Nelson, Brendan Batson and Peter Marinello that Saturday and fully enjoyed it. Chelsea had Ray Wilkins in their team as well,' Pitt says. 'My wife Angela was three weeks away from having our first child and so I was allowed to come back home after the match and return to Arsenal on the Monday. The next day I was having Sunday lunch when Billy Elliott rang me from Sunderland and told me that Bob Stokoe had cancelled my loan. I told Billy that I didn't want to come back to Sunderland because the manager and I didn't get on and he was trying to get rid of me. I wanted to stay at Arsenal. I was on £40 per week at Sunderland and Arsenal had doubled my wages. Bertie Mee had also told me that he would like to sign me. So you can understand how disappointed I was. But in those days when a club said, "Jump," all you could say was, "How high?" For me to argue back was quite a big thing, but I told Billy that I didn't want to come back, even though I am a Sunderland lad and Sunderland was my club from the age of six. I didn't want to come back to Sunderland because of the way Stokoe had treated me. But I was told I had to come back.

'Apparently Sunderland had cancelled the loan because one of their London scouts had watched me play at the weekend and I had played well,' Pitt adds. 'I had played for the club for two years so surely they knew enough about me? But Stokoe hadn't played me. He hadn't wanted to play me. The first morning he came to Sunderland he told me to go and train with the youth team. Don't ask me why. If Dave

Young hadn't got injured I think the chances of me ever playing for Sunderland again would have been nil.'

But Young was injured and the prognosis was that he would be out for at least one month. 'By the time I came back from injury, everything had changed,' he says. 'I never really got back into the team that season because by then I had lost my place. From then on, I was just on the fringe. With everything that was happening, it was obviously a very frustrating time.'

'I have been trying to get a settled team and I thought we had reached this point,' a frustrated Stokoe told the press. 'Pitt will play on Saturday. He is the most experienced player we have for the job and he can take over from Young at the back.'

Pitt had been at Arsenal for just three days. He made his first league start under Stokoe by coming in at number 6 in the next match. Sunderland found form by warming up for the eagerly awaited FA Cup fifth-round tie against Manchester City with a 4–0 drubbing of Middlesbrough at Roker Park. Horswill, Halom, Hughes and Tueart were the goal scorers in a match watched by 26,040. It was the highest home league crowd of the season, beating the previous best set just a fortnight before by well over 3,000.

'That was my first home game and from then on we never looked back,' Halom says. 'I think the players had worked so hard for the previous manager for all those years that the jigsaw went *click* under Bob Stokoe and suddenly they could all release the talent they had. There was an enormous amount of talent in that side as well: Billy Hughes, Dennis Tueart, Bobby Kerr, Ian Porterfield and so on. Bob just said to them, "Go on then, play," and they got this release of energy and took that message on a hundred per cent. They were fabulous players and we tore teams apart. From that moment on there was never any thought to sit back and defend. Of course we had to do it from time to time but our approach was to go forward. That suited us better. It was never in our make-up to be negative.'

'It was just a natural way for us to play,' Hughes adds. 'If Dennis Tueart did a diagonal run or whatever it was just automatic for me to go out to the right-hand side and vice versa. There was no talk about that, it just happened. That was the freedom we had and the knowledge we had in our football: if he goes there and it breaks down, I am going to go there. Nobody said to us, "We want you and Dennis to do diagonals." I started doing them because I was quite quick and they gave me an advantage, coming across and then going off. That is where I started to get most of my goals, just with running off the ball and the likes of Ian Porterfield and Bobby Kerr feeding it through. It was great.'

It was this match against Middlesbrough that essentially launched Stokoe's Sunderland. It was the first time Pitt and Watson had played together in the centre of defence. Young's unfortunate injury had handed Stokoe a natural partnership at the back. Gradually and reluctantly the manager began to accept that Pitt could yet have a part to play in his future plans. The change of heart came about because there was no other choice.

'I knew I was good at my job – I could tackle, I could mark, I could run and I could organise at the back. Dave Watson was very athletic – he could jump up and head the moon if he wanted to. We were a good combination,' Pitt says. 'We were compatible in playing alongside each other,' Watson agrees. 'I think he was mainly left-footed so he played on the left and I played on the right. He became a suitable partner for me at the back.'

With so little to cheer about for so long, the trip to Maine Road was to be the biggest match the club had played in years. John Tennick, of Sunderland Supporters Association, confidently predicted that the non-all-ticket affair at Maine Road would see the greatest exodus of Sunderland fans since the 1955 FA Cup semi-final when the Rokerites had played – and lost to – the same opposition at Villa Park.

With excitement building rapidly at home, Stokoe decided to take his players and staff off to the seaside and his former town of Blackpool to prepare them for their biggest test yet as a group of players. Four of them had never played in the First Division and only two of them – Montgomery and Kerr – had ever played in the last sixteen of the FA Cup. By contrast, over half of the Manchester City side had been in the team that defeated Leicester City in the 1969 FA Cup final.

The Sunderland side was relatively young – the average age was twenty-four – but there was plenty of experience. Montgomery had the most. The oldest player in the side at twenty-nine, he was now in his twelfth season as first-choice goalkeeper at the club and had played in all six matches against Manchester United and Leeds United in the classic FA Cup ties of 1964 and 1967. He also had six First Division campaigns under his belt and had come close to winning full national honours with England. Elsewhere Kerr, Hughes, Tueart and Pitt had all made their debuts for Sunderland in the First Division as teenagers. Porterfield had played and starred in the famous final match of the 1967–68 season when Sunderland beat Manchester United at Old Trafford in front of 62,963 people to help win the First Division title for, ironically, Manchester City. Guthrie had played at Anderlecht and Porto for Newcastle in the Inter-Cities Fairs Cup. For a team so supposedly 'unknown', the Rokerites did not lack experience.

Sunderland prepared patiently and properly for the Manchester City match away from the eyes of the media. Arthur Cox, who had been head coach for less than three weeks, had already witnessed a growing confidence among an underrated group of players that would soon take the nation by storm and, in the process, become household names. He was perfectly placed to assess that talent up close: 'You don't join a Second Division club and start thinking about winning the FA Cup,' Cox says. 'But take that team across the board and look at the potential that so many of them had. Jimmy Montgomery had fantastic reflexes. Some people said that he could be beaten from distance but that was nonsense. Monty could stand in the pouring rain and not have a kick for long periods and then he could fetch one out of the bottom corner. He didn't enjoy training too much but he loved to play and, of course, he had these tremendous reflexes, which became so famous.

'Dicky Malone enjoyed going forward from right-back but Bob Stokoe always made sure that he knew his job: "Get your automatic tacklers on," he would tell him. Dicky's relationship with Bobby Kerr on the right side was brilliant. Ron Guthrie had been in and out of the side at Newcastle before he signed for Sunderland and Bob gave him a new lease of life. Ron was strong, resolute and had a good left foot. He played behind Ian Porterfield and their relationship on the left was very good. Ron was a tremendously reliable man. You knew where he was day in and day out. He would stand his corner too and he was frightened of no one, on or off the pitch.

'Then there was David Watson. I don't think I have ever worked with anyone who made himself into a player like David did. He worked so hard. He lifted his own weights in training. He was a tremendous advert for a professional. He was outstanding in the air. We had a natural balance in defence: David went right and Ritchie Pitt went left. Ritchie was good in the air too and he had an excellent left foot. He wasn't slow and he could always go that extra yard. We had an excellent pair at the back.

'Dave Young was honest and genuine. He was versatile and covered all the defensive positions – right-back, left-back and central defence – for us. He was another good man. Micky Horswill was frightened of no one. He tackled and he kept it simple and that is what we wanted him to do. He won the ball, he got the ball and he fed the ball.

'Bobby Kerr was our captain. Bobby was tremendous and he had a bloody good right foot. Bob Stokoe called him his "little general". He ran and ran all day long. He was good at set pieces and could produce a good cross from the right. He had more than enough courage for his size too. Ian Porterfield consistently produced what you knew he would produce. He was very important to us, Ian. He wasn't a quick player, he wasn't outstanding in the air but he was a natural left-sided player and he was there week in and week out for us.

'As for Billy Hughes. Well, there was nothing he didn't have: right foot, left foot, good in the air, pace to burn. He could shoot and cross. He was as brave as a lion and as fit as a fiddle. Brilliant. Dennis Tueart was outstanding. He had two good feet and he was effervescent. Dennis wasn't the quickest but he could go either side and he could shoot with either foot. He had plenty of courage as well.

'Vic Halom was the catalyst for the whole thing. You could see him and aim for him. As a centre-forward, he had special bits and pieces. Vic had little respect for the opposition. He was as confident a player as you could find. He was the focal point and he was frightened of nobody. He could hold it, he could head it and he was a bloody good starting point in that half of the field. We had Billy and Dennis either side of Vic. We played 4–3–3 religiously. We knew what we were about.

'To be honest Alan Brown had done so much shadow play with them that they could have nearly played blindfold. That is important to mention. Alan's management was rigid discipline. Bob Stokoe was clever. He came in and he eased off a little bit and allowed the players to become their own men. Everything got better and from when I saw the first kick at Reading onwards we were unstoppable. We had an us-against-the-world camaraderie, motivation, strength and encouragement from the supporters. You alloy all these things together and it is a recipe for success. When you know about the north-east it is easy to understand. These people appreciate your endeavours if you are honest and genuine. If you go about your job properly you will not only be supported, you will be idolised. We had no fear of anyone. We didn't fear Manchester City, we didn't fear Arsenal and we didn't fear Leeds.'

'Arthur Cox had this wonderful ability to come and talk to you and just point things out,' Halom says. 'He had a way of getting his message through to you and he gave you enough confidence to gee you up. It all worked very well with him and Bob Stokoe. Everybody felt very strong and very fit – both physically and mentally – and focused in a relaxed way.'

'I got on really well with Arthur Cox,' Pitt adds. 'He was a great coach and he worked us hard, but if ever you needed to go back and do extra training he was there for you. He did what Alan Brown used to do. He talked to us as individuals. He was the link between the players and Bob Stokoe. Stokoe wouldn't go into detail with an individual, he would just say, "Let's get stuck in and win our tackles." Stokoe was a motivational manager.'

Unbeknown to the press and the public, Stokoe had achieved much more than motivating this talented team of individuals to play. He had also quelled unrest among senior players. Within the first few months of the manager's arrival at Sunderland both Malone and Watson had separately spoken to him and privately asked to be placed on the transfer list, albeit for different reasons.

'I think I was the first player to ask away from Sunderland under Bob Stokoe. And, my God, he nearly took my head off my shoulders,' Malone says. 'It was during the early part of the FA Cup run, probably just after it had started but before the game at Manchester City. The two of us were always arguing at that time: he wanted me to hit a long ball all the time and I didn't want to hit a long ball all the time. He said to me, "It's a defender's favourite." I disagreed with him and I told him that I would only hit the ball on when it was on, and that is the only time that I did. I didn't want to just punt the ball up the field. So in the eighteen-yard box I would sometimes do a dummy and pretend I was going one way and then swerve and go the other way with the ball. Well, he used to shout at me, "Just get it into the stand." Dave Watson had the same problem with him because Dave liked to play with the ball too. I went to see Bob at the training ground at Washington one day and I told him that I didn't feel part of things and that I wanted to leave. He gave me a lecture for half an hour and then he told me to forget it. There was no chance and there was no option back then. But it really upset him, I could see that.'

Malone's foraging runs down the right flank would frustrate the manager from time to time, as Kerr readily recalls: 'Dick Malone used to go on his mazy runs and sometimes he could lose the ball. One day he was on this "mazy" and Johnny Watters, who used to love to gee up Bob Stokoe on the bench, shouted out, "Go on there, Santa Maria" – the name of the old Real Madrid player – and Dick then went and lost the ball. Stokoe shouts back at him: "More like Santa Claus." Now to this day if you call Dick "Santa" he will turn around. Those things stick in football.'

Watson's predicament was more sensitive: 'There were private, personal issues at that time that were affecting me at the club – nothing on the playing side – but I am a pretty placid person and I don't fall out with people easily so I just used to have to go in there and do my training and then go home,' he says. 'I wasn't happy at Sunderland and it wasn't an easy time. I had felt unsettled for a while. Bob Stokoe came to my house at Houghton-le-Spring shortly after he got the job. I told him that I wanted to leave and I told him the reasons why. He then sold me his vision for Sunderland: he told me about the players he was going to buy and his plans for getting the club back into the First Division. He said to me, "Don't do that, I'm going to do this and I'm going to do that." I said I would give it another go. He talked me into staying at Sunderland.'

Tueart had also previously asked for a transfer from Roker Park. He too decided to think again under the new management regime: 'I had been a young kid kicking up against discipline and I had been asking for a transfer under Alan Brown,' he says. 'I was after a new contract and I remember when Colin Todd signed for Derby County for a lot of money in 1971 that I went in to see the manager and said, "You can give me more money now, can't you?" But I am not sure he ever had much money to give us. When Bob Stokoe arrived, I decided to give it another chance.'

Meanwhile Hughes, another player who had previously been unsettled at Sunderland, was now beginning to enjoy the best football of his career: 'Bob Stokoe made everything enjoyable for me,' he says. 'He would give odds on us scoring goals and things like that, silly little things really. He would give me three to one that I would score and he would give the defenders odds on clean sheets too. He would go around everybody and do the same. He would pay us out of his own pocket as well, and obviously the higher the odds the more he had to pay out. It was great because we were all arguing the odds with him and there was a buzz about the place. It was just fun to have a laugh and a joke. But at the same time we all knew that when we went out on to the park there was a job to do. I had a lot of time for Bob. He was just a nice man. The fear factor went out of the window when he arrived and you felt comfortable with him: you had a laugh, you trained hard and you played hard.'

Hughes, who had been out of the Sunderland side and unhappy during the Alan Brown era, was now a markedly different player, in both persona and performance. Supporters even began to make comparisons between him and George Best. The long dark hair certainly did him no harm and along with his natural skills the confidence he was now showing on the pitch had created something that stood out from the crowd.

Everything was falling into place, and Sunderland – in the best shape on and off the field for some considerable time – approached Maine Road with confidence. Awaiting them was one of the most stylish and celebrated sides of the sixties and seventies, led by a character as colourful as any, Malcolm Allison.

As coach alongside Joe Mercer, Allison had helped Manchester City win the First Division title in the 1967–68 season, the FA Cup in 1969 and the League Cup and European Cup Winners' Cup in 1970 with a swagger and style that entertained the nation. But Mercer left the club following a boardroom takeover and subsequent fall-out, and things quickly changed at Maine Road. In solo charge, Allison had still had a chance to win the league title again in the 1971–72 season but watched his team throw it away. But on their day City were still a side of great talent and Allison took great delight in saying that in the newspapers at every opportunity he got.

'Malcolm Allison had said what they were going to do to us and all that in the press, and if any manager says what they are going to do to you it is like you don't have to do a team talk because they have done the team talk for you,' Montgomery says. 'But of course the step up for us was vast from not doing too well in the Second Division to now playing Manchester City at Manchester City.'

Gerald Sinstadt worked for Granada Television at the time and commentated on the fifth-round tie for the ITV network: 'Manchester City had a great side – and a side of footballers too,' he says. 'That particular Manchester City side was very much a side in the Malcolm Allison image as well. It was an exciting side. Although one never actually got attached to a single team at Granada there was always a special feel about City that was different. Malcolm was an interesting guy in many, many ways. I remember doing a live interview with him for *On the Ball* around Easter and he was under pressure at the time. He made a comment about Easter being "the time that people get crucified". I had to smooth it over but that was how he talked to the public. He wasn't always that person. He was actually a very quiet, thoughtful and intelligent man. As a football thinker he was ahead of his time.

'Famously Malcolm ruined the side that should have won the title the year before because he couldn't resist bringing in Rodney Marsh. If he had waited until the following season and just let Rodney sit on the bench until then it wouldn't have been a problem, but he couldn't resist a flair player and Rodney was the flair player of them all,' Sinstadt says. 'Malcolm and Joe Mercer were like Eric Morecambe and Ernie Wise. They were a perfect partnership. Joe could deal with the tricky situations and knew when to apply the reins and when to ease off the reins. He saw the talent that Malcolm had as a coach and he allowed that to develop. But Joe remained the boss and it was when that partnership broke up that Malcolm didn't have anybody to control his wildest optimism. Often it was his enthusiasm for a player that undid him. But Manchester City were still a side capable of beating anybody in the country, as they had proved by knocking out Liverpool in the fourth round of the FA Cup that very year.'

Writing in *The Times* on the day of the Manchester City versus Sunderland tie, Sinstadt was in no doubt about the outcome: 'The romance and unpredictability of the FA Cup will have to be much in evidence if anyone wishes to make a case for Sunderland to survive the fifth round at Maine Road. All other factors, status, form, motivation, history, sheer common sense, shout loudly for Manchester City,' he wrote. However, he did add, 'One reservation must be made: the shrewdness of Sunderland's new manager Bob Stokoe. In less than three months he has admirably recharged the club's batteries. But achieving Second Division safety and beating Third and Fourth Division opponents (both after a replay) does nothing to disturb my belief that Manchester City will win well.' Sinstadt and the rest of the national press were in for a surprise.

The contrast between Sunderland, edging past Notts County and Reading, and Manchester City, who had knocked out League Cup holders Stoke City and First Division title favourites Liverpool in the previous rounds, helped make the First Division side overwhelming favourites ahead of the match. Sunderland were 250–1 outsiders – from a field that now consisted of just sixteen teams – to win the FA Cup on the morning of the fifth round. Interestingly, as things turned out, the top three favourites for the trophy were listed as Manchester City, Arsenal and Leeds! The final was just ten weeks away.

The Sunderland players remained unaffected by any negative predictions. 'This was the first big team we had faced,' Watson says. 'Bob Stokoe prepared us by instilling in us that we could win. He was a very optimistic man and he would always tell us, "It doesn't matter what happened last week, it is today that matters." He gave us a belief that we could beat Manchester City. Every single one of us knew that this was now the real thing. After two lower-division sides we were now up against the big boys, but we were confident. That sounds stupid, because we had no reason to be confident, but we were. I mean if you put our team and their team next to each other on paper there was no comparison. But we didn't see that. We were confident in ourselves and that confidence came from Stokoe. He loved it when we were winning and we were now winning a lot. The momentum grew. We all loved to play and we all loved to win. I think it would have been a more difficult draw for us if we had faced Liverpool, because at that time they were like a machine, whereas Manchester City were a more free-flowing team, and we knew that would allow us to play as well.'

'We were now growing in confidence, stature and self-belief,' Malone says. 'We never once felt that we would get beaten. It never even came into the conversation. We felt we were as good as any opposition that came up against us. All the players were very confident ahead of that match, probably because we weren't expected to win and it was therefore easy to feel like that as there was no pressure on us. But even though we weren't expected to win, I didn't fear playing against anyone at that time and I think I could safely say the rest of the players felt the same way. No matter whom we were up against, it didn't mean anything. It was just another player with two legs and two arms. You just had to make sure that he doesn't go out and do better than you on the park.'

'We have done everything we can to ensure that we give ourselves the best possible chance of getting a good result tomorrow,' Stokoe said after relaxing on Blackpool promenade with his team the day before the match. 'It is a tremendous task, I know, but you can never tell what is going to happen on the day. The players could not be in better spirits and there is nothing I need to say to motivate them for the job we want to do. It has been a good week for us and it could just be a great one.'

Optimism was more common than confidence on the terraces: 'You couldn't really see us getting a result but you always hope, don't you? I think when you get to that stage – the last sixteen – you allow yourself to dream a little,' supporter Pete Sixsmith says. 'Maine Road was a decent ground. It had a new stand behind the goal that ran from the old main stand right around to the Kippax, and our fans went right around behind the goal. I was on the corner. It was a proper football ground and Sunderland must have had twelve thousand or more there.'

The Sunderland support was further boosted that day by a late postponement at Old Trafford. Manchester United's First Division match against Crystal Palace was called off at lunchtime due to a frozen pitch. Remarkably, just a few miles away at Maine Road it was sunny. Some United fans joined up on the terraces with the visiting supporters from the north-east.

'There was segregation at Maine Road but you didn't need a ticket in those days – you just turned up and paid your money – so nobody could prove if you were a Sunderland fan, a Manchester City fan, a Manchester United fan or whatever,' Sunderland supporter Paul Dobson recalls. 'Some Manchester United fans came in with us and supported us against Manchester City. They were stood on the terraces beside us and shouted for Sunderland. They weren't singing anti-Manchester City stuff, they were singing Sunderland songs. There were several hundred of them. We all started chanting, "Sunderland-United, Sunderland-United."'

'It was a massive crowd – nearly fifty-five thousand – to watch us play a First Division team at a First Division ground and that match was really the beginning of our FA Cup run,' Watson says.

'We had a good following as always but the crowd was blue basically.

Maybe three or four to one in number, I would guess. It was a surprise for us to be in that situation because normally we would have more fans than the home team. But we were outnumbered easily on the day.'

Stokoe selected the same team that had beaten Middlesbrough so impressively the weekend before. Chambers was named substitute despite being in dispute with the club and on the transfer list and an independent tribunal recently valuing the asking price for him at £25,000. But Young and Mick McGiven were both still unavailable and the first-team pool was threadbare.

Manchester City settled into their stride from the start. Rodney Marsh brought a good save from Montgomery early on, while Mike Summerbee was quickly stretching Guthrie to the limit at left-back. It was from this source that the home side took the lead on fifteen minutes. A Summerbee cross was knocked on by Mike Doyle into the path of Tony Towers – positioned outside the box – who fired home crisply from over twenty yards.

Francis Lee shot narrowly wide from a good angle as the home side dominated the flow of the game. But Manchester City then unaccountably seemed to give Summerbee less of the ball down the wing and instead concentrated their efforts through the middle. Both Watson and Pitt were on hand to stifle any threat down this path and slowly Sunderland got back into the match. In fact, such was the strength in Sunderland's central defence that the main battle was pushed into midfield, where Horswill, Kerr and Porterfield were more than able to hold their own.

On thirty-six minutes Manchester City were awarded a free-kick in their own penalty box after a foul by Tueart on goalkeeper Joe Corrigan. An anxious Corrigan played a short free-kick to Willie Donachie and, under pressure from Horswill, the left-back stepped inside the box so that the kick had to be retaken. To Donachie's astonishment Corrigan then proceeded to play the ball to him again. Donachie hesitated and Horswill pounced by intercepting the ball, hooking it over the defender and racing on to fire home. Sunderland were suddenly level.

'I was quite young at the time,' Donachie remembers. 'I couldn't step inside the box again so I had to let the ball come out to me. Micky Horswill came out of nowhere. He got the ball and he scored a goal. It immediately changed the game. We had been well on top until then.'

Sunderland grew in confidence. Horswill snapped at the heels of the Blues' creative force, Colin Bell. Kerr and Porterfield began to find more space to set up more attacks and start to pose problems. As a result Halom, Hughes and Kerr all threatened before the break.

But Manchester City were renowned as an attacking force and, with the game opening up, Montgomery was required to make good saves from Lee and Doyle early in the second half before Towers was booked for lifting his foot dangerously against Halom.

Midway through the second half Malone won the ball inside his own penalty box and played it forward for Tueart, who then released it quickly to Hughes. Positioned just inside the Manchester City half and wide on the left, Hughes made a spectacular run towards goal. When he was eventually caught by Derek Jeffries on the edge of the box, he casually switched inside and unleashed a powerful shot which Corrigan got a hand to but could not keep out. Sunderland – the 250–1 outsiders – were beating the FA Cup favourites with twenty-two minutes to go. There were tears on the terraces.

'We broke quickly out of defence and Hughesy was off with the ball – he was such a quick lad – and I was working as much as I could to get up with him,' Halom recalls. 'I found space but instead of pulling it back and giving me a tap-in, he cuts inside. I was just about to say something – and probably swear – when he then goes and smacks the ball right into the roof of the net. What can I say about him? He was a remarkable talent.'

'I think that was one of the most important goals I ever scored,' Hughes adds. 'It gave us a belief and a confidence that we could play our game to the full against those top sides.'

The Rokerites were frustratingly denied glory by a hotly disputed goal. As Summerbee sent in an in-swinging corner, Marsh appeared to obstruct Montgomery and, unable to get a clear hand on the ball, the goalkeeper palmed it into his own net. Sunderland had held the lead for all of four minutes. 'Jimmy Montgomery was fouled blatantly for their second goal,' Cox says. 'We would have beaten them at Maine Road had it not been for that. We were the better team.'

'It was an abysmal decision by the referee,' Sixsmith adds. 'It should have been disallowed. It wasn't even a legitimate challenge. Nat Loft-house might have got away with it in his day, Dixie Dean probably would have done, but even back in 1973 it was a foul. There is no doubt about it.'

Manchester City went on an all-out attack to settle the tie in the closing minutes, but not only was this stifled by the excellent Sunderland defence, it also allowed the Sunderland forwards to break. Halom produced a good header from Tueart's cross that was touched over the bar by Corrigan, while Hughes also brought a fine diving save from the goalkeeper.

An angry exchange between Horswill and Towers late on led to the Manchester City midfielder being sent off and the Sunderland youngster being booked. The match finished in a 2–2 draw. Every Sunderland player had excelled. Their reward was a replay at Roker Park.

'Manchester City had all the stars out that day – Colin Bell, Franny Lee, Rodney Marsh, Mike Summerbee, you name them – and to actually get a result there was fantastic,' Watson says. 'At one point it looked like we were going to win it as well. City made mistakes and we capitalised with goals. We played exceptionally well and we took the game to them. They were definitely not expecting us to attack them.'

'We were unlucky,' Malone adds. 'Whenever you get into a winning position you always feel that you may have missed an opportunity, but in no time at all we were just looking ahead to the replay. We had come so close to winning at their ground that we had no fear at all about playing them at home.'

The confidence among the Sunderland players was so strong that Montgomery was even able to share a joke with his team-mates about the equalising goal. 'I told the lads I was on a crowd bonus so that is why I knocked the ball in,' he says with a smile. 'It got Manchester City back up to Sunderland. There would have been no replay otherwise.'

The national newspapermen were amazed by Sunderland's front three – particularly Hughes – and the team's attacking wing play, while Watson was voted man of the match. Pitt also received accolades for his performance.

'I sat in the dressing room at the end of the game and I cried,' Pitt recalls. 'Even now when I think about it it brings tears to my eyes, because that game proved to me that I could do it. I always knew I was a good player. That is why I turned Lincoln down, because I didn't want to go into the Fourth Division. I knew I could play at the top level and

I had confidence in my own ability. But there is nothing like going out and proving it. That game did that.'

There were no surprises in all the other seven FA Cup fifth-round ties: Leeds defeated West Bromwich Albion 2–0 at Elland Road with two first-half goals from Allan Clarke – taking his tally in the competition this season to six; Arsenal saw off the challenge of a spirited Carlisle United 2–1 at Brunton Park; Derby raced into a four-goal half-time lead against Queen's Park Rangers, whom they beat 4–2 at the Baseball Ground, Kevin Hector hitting a hat-trick; John Richards secured Wolverhampton Wanderers' third successive 1–0 home win in the competition, against Millwall; Coventry City quietly and comfortably recorded their first quarter-final appearance in ten years with a 3–0 home win over Hull City; in the clash of the minnows between Second Division Luton Town and Third Division leaders Bolton Wanderers at Burnden Park, the Hatters ran out 1–0 winners in front of a crowd of 39,536, the third-highest FA Cup attendance of the day; Chelsea's 2–1 win at Sheffield Wednesday recorded the second-highest attendance (46,910) of that day. But it was the clash at Maine Road – the only one of the eight ties not to have an outcome – that was far and away the highest in terms of spectators (54,478). It was also the match that made the headlines. As Sinstadt later admitted in *The Times*, it was 'no place for faint hearts or forecasters'.

The impact of the result – and the performance – in the north-east was incomparable. Sunderland, fortunate to avoid a tragedy nine years earlier in an FA Cup match against Manchester United at Roker Park, immediately announced that the replay would be an all-ticket match. The club put tickets on sale the following morning. On hearing this news, fans began to queue immediately, through the night and into the early hours. It would be worth it. Sunderland's fifth-round replay with Manchester City would become the most famous match ever seen at Roker Park.

'On the way home from Manchester City we stopped off at Harrogate for a meal,' Guthrie recalls. 'So when we got back to Roker Park it was twelve-thirty on Sunday morning. There was already a queue about a mile long for replay tickets. It all hit you there and then.'

When the police turned up for duty at nine on Sunday morning the crowd at Roker Park was estimated to have reached 15,000. The queues wrapped around the ground and stretched into adjoining streets. Supporters had waited for hours – huddled together under the stands to keep warm – on the coldest night of the year. Many fans had joined the queues as soon as they had returned home from Maine Road. Traders turned up in the middle of the night and started selling hot drinks. The turnstiles – due to start selling tickets at 10.30 a.m. – had to open ninety minutes early to cope with the excessive demand. By mid-afternoon the home allocation of 49,000 tickets was sold out.

'I went home to get some sleep and then got down to the ground at six-thirty on the Sunday morning to queue for my ticket,' Sixsmith says. 'There were already long queues outside the Clock Stand paddock by then and they just got bigger and bigger. I brought a mate along with me. He was a Londoner but living in Sunderland at the time and he had only ever known there to be a few hardy scattered souls around Roker Park. He couldn't believe what he saw that morning – suddenly so many people would turn up at that time in the morning to queue for tickets for a football match! But we all knew what it meant. Something was stirring up again.'

8.

CUM ON FEEL THE NOIZE

The FA Cup quarter-final draw handed a home tie against Luton Town – the only other Second Division team left in the competition – to the winners of the Manchester City–Sunderland replay.

Yet despite the Rokerites' performance at Maine Road and the exhilarating confidence felt by players and supporters alike, the bookmakers and the press focused not on the possibility of an all-Second Division quarter-final but the likelihood of Manchester City getting an easy path into the last four. City's odds to win the FA Cup were shortened once more while Sunderland – 250–1 outsiders before the first game – came down to 100–1. These odds appeared to be in deference to the fact that two wins at Roker Park would achieve the club's first semi-final appearance in the competition since 1956.

Malcolm Allison repeated his boast that his side would beat Sunderland – and Luton for that matter – in the press. He was not on his own: few in the media seemed to have recognised the quality or the spirit of Sunderland's display at Maine Road just two days before. If Allison had, then he was keeping very quiet about it.

'I remember Malcolm Allison saying we were going to win the FA Cup in 1973,' Willie Donachie says. 'He was very confident about that and had actually said it early on in the competition, even before we had knocked out Liverpool in the fourth round. After we'd beaten Liverpool, he was convinced we were going to win it. The draw at home against Sunderland did not deter him in his belief at all. He was always a confident man.'

There was no question that Luton at home was the best possible quarter-final draw that either Manchester City or Sunderland could have hoped for. Elsewhere there were plenty of big teams – and plenty of big names – left in the competition. The biggest clash would come at the Baseball Ground, where Brian Clough's Derby County would meet

Don Revie's Leeds United. Another tasty tie was a London derby between Dave Sexton's Chelsea and Bertie Mee's Arsenal at Stamford Bridge; while at Molineux Wolverhampton Wanderers, managed by Bill McGarry, would take on a Coventry City side aided by the experience of Joe Mercer, who had taken over as general manager at Highfield Road alongside Gordon Milne after parting company with Allison and Manchester City. Moreover, these different permutations meant that there would be numerous opportunities for old rivalries to be reignited later, in the semi-finals: Allison and Mercer, McGarry and Revie, and, of course, Bob Stokoe and Clough – or even Stokoe and Revie.

Revie played down the clash between himself and Clough, a man who had openly criticised him and Leeds in the media: 'Naturally any draw away from home is a tough one,' he said. 'Anyway it is no good moaning – we have to get on and get it played.'

For Stokoe, a man who had spent the majority of his managerial career in the Second Division – and part of it even way down in the Fourth Division – this moment would have been the first time that he could realistically have dreams of one day matching the big boys. But those dreams had to wait, for Sunderland still to had manoeuvre past the might of Manchester City.

'The Manchester City games came along at the right time for us,' Dave Watson says. 'We had been getting good results and our confidence was growing by the week. After our performance in the first game at Maine Road I think our supporters were as confident as us going into the replay. We embraced the occasion while I think Manchester City feared it.'

The quiet confidence of the Sunderland team and staff had now reached the supporters: those who had been at Maine Road, those who had seen the highlights on television and those who had read about the performance in the newspapers or talked to fellow fans about it on the street, in the pub or at their work.

'The team were now playing well and the crowds were coming back, and there are not many clubs that have a hold on people like this club does,' supporter Pete Sixsmith says. 'Its roots are so firmly established, not so much in Sunderland itself but in the north-east, County Durham and South Tyneside communities. It has always been a club with a soul and I honestly believe there is a greater love for this football club than any other club in the country. The passion and commitment was always there and the FA Cup run revived it. There was just this buzz around the place.

'I can remember the floodlights on the night of the replay,' he adds. 'They were like a magnet attracting people through the maze of streets around the ground. Everybody was going along their own special route – past the same terrace houses with the same faces inside – and there were so many of us you literally stumbled across Roker Park when you got there. I watched the Roker End filling up from the Clock Stand paddock that night and it was a marvellous sight. There wasn't a better ground in the country at that time and that was the best night it ever had.'

The official attendance for the all-ticket match was recorded at 51,872, but both players and fans alike believe the total to have been a lot higher. Manchester City had been given an allocation of 5,000 tickets but the threat of a national strike by train drivers and railway workers on the day of the match affected away-ticket sales. A 'Football Special' train booked to bring visiting supporters to Roker Park was cancelled. But, with segregation an issue, none of these tickets were put on general sale.

'We will never know, but I would think there could have been something like as many as seventy thousand spectators there that night,' Watson says. 'I was later told that the safety officer was talking about closing the gates early on but there were so many people outside that they let in as many fans as possible. How true that story is, I don't know. But I do know that everyone wanted to see it. It was the biggest game at Roker Park in years. It felt a lot, lot more than 51,872. The Roker End, which was a massive open terrace in those days, the Fulwell End and both sides of the ground were all jam-packed with spectators.' Revie was among them.

It was officially the biggest crowd Roker Park had witnessed since the early part of 1970. It is likely that it was the highest attendance seen there since the ground improvements made prior to the 1966 World Cup. 'That night was electric,' Dick Malone adds. 'Whatever the official attendance was it felt to me like there were a hundred thousand in the crowd. It was always a tremendous stadium to run out to, but the roar that night was something else, it really was. It was just incredible and to know just about everyone in there was supporting you and your team was awesome.'

'The belief was now there,' Jim Montgomery says. 'We knew that having achieved a draw away against a great team like Manchester City that we had every chance at home. It was only the corner kick in the first match that had denied us victory. That was what had brought them back to two each. The way we played at Maine Road, we knew for a fact that with our fanbase we now had a great chance of beating them at home. But, yes, the expectation was immense.'

Stokoe selected an unchanged line-up for the replay with Brian Chambers, an unused substitute at Maine Road, again on the bench. Manchester City had to make one enforced change due to Mike Summerbee being suspended for the match. Ian Mellor, who appeared as a substitute in the first game, took his place. Tony Towers, sent off at Maine Road, played.

The Sunderland manager would later rate this match as his outstanding memory from his time at Roker Park. But when he said that, he wasn't talking about his team's performance, he was talking about the crowd. Speaking in an interview on *Football Focus* on BBC1 shortly before Sunderland vacated Roker Park for the Stadium of Light and long after his retirement from the game, his words still have resonance today and are worth repeating in full: 'I have a lovely memory from 1973,' Stokoe said.

I mean the first game against Burnley when I became manager and we lost, there was 12,000 there. Then we were drawn at Notts County in the FA Cup. We got a draw there, we brought them home and 30,000 turned up. We played Manchester City. We had to go to Manchester and we got a very good 2–2 draw, brought them home and all of a sudden it is over 53,000. You tell me any other club in the world – never mind anything else – that can go from 12,000 to 53,000 in the space of five or six weeks?

'When the teams came out of the tunnel it was just fantastic,' Sunderland supporter Paul Dobson recalls. 'We thought we had a real chance and then we saw the Manchester City line-up: Colin Bell, Francis Lee, Rodney Marsh and all the rest. Deep down you did think, but you just wouldn't – you just couldn't – let that thought come out. In terms of atmosphere and passion you can't ever better that night. It was voted the best-ever match at Roker Park, and rightly so. Bob Stokoe helped create that and he should have been immensely proud of that.'

'The replay was one of those situations where we didn't believe we could lose,' Watson says. 'We just had total belief in ourselves and the way we approached the game was all about attack and scoring goals. We wanted to make sure we won and got through to the quarter-finals. When I look back now our confidence was astonishing really – we were still in the bottom six of the Second Division!

'We came out only a few minutes before the match and I remember it was very windy and we were facing the wind in the first half. There was always an on-going breeze coming off the sea at Roker, but this night was way beyond that and it was only once we were out on the pitch that we realised the problem. We were lumbered with the wind and we quickly had to decide how deal with it at the back. We decided to play no-thrills and just knock the ball forward at every opportunity, over the opposing full-backs for Dennis and Hughesy to chase. Manchester City weren't used to playing teams who just kicked the ball forward and for the first half that is what we did. But we had no choice – if we hadn't done that we would have been anchored in our own half with City playing football around us. Normally the ball would carry fifty or sixty yards at Roker Park but that night it could only travel twenty yards, it was that windy. Our plan worked but we couldn't afford to put a foot wrong against them. The message had been clear all week: "Don't dive in, stand up." If ever we were in trouble at the back we were always told by Bob Stokoe to clear our line, get our shape back and start again. If you're out of shape at the back, you're going to make mistakes. That was his defensive philosophy and he stressed to us that we must do that every time the ball went dead. Lots of teams wouldn't even think about doing that. But we did it, particularly on that FA Cup run under Stokoe.'

Sunderland took the lead on fourteen minutes with a spectacular goal from Vic Halom. It was a breathtaking strike from the edge of the penalty box and followed a scintillating move that split Manchester City apart. It was also the best goal seen at Roker Park in living memory: Ian Porterfield and Ron Guthrie linked up well on the left side to play in Billy Hughes, who passed the ball back to Porterfield, who in turn passed to Micky Horswill, who then played it on to Bobby Kerr, who then flicked the ball into the path of Halom, who rifled it into the far corner of the Fulwell End net.

'As I saw the ball come across, I pulled out to give myself a little bit of space and then I came back in. Just as I hit it, the ball lifted a fraction and it screamed in into the stanchion at the back of the net,' Halom recalls with a smile. 'I remember Joe Corrigan shouting to his defence, "Leave it!" and Franny Lee screaming back at him, "Leave it? Leave it? You dozy sod."'

'For all the noise there was that night I'm sure you could hear Vic Halom screaming for the ball,' Dobson, who was stood in the Fulwell End, says. 'His shot just flashed past Joe Corrigan and the noise was phenomenal when it went in.' Sixsmith saw the goal from the Clock Stand paddock: 'For us to score a goal like that against a team like that in a game like that was amazing,' he says. 'It was a great goal too. It was no fluke. It was a beautiful passing move – we worked it right along the line and Vic Halom's finish was supreme. But it was a goal that we had put together as a team. It ripped the heart out of Manchester City and we now thought, If we can score one goal like that, we might be able to get another one.'

In the build-up to the goal Colin Bell accidentally stood on the right foot of Porterfield, slicing through the Sunderland midfielder's little toe. For the next eight matches – including the FA Cup quarter-final and semi-final – and unbeknown to the press or the public, Porterfield would play with a fractured toe. A hole was cut into his right boot to prevent any pressure being applied on the toe and to allow it to hang comfortably outside.

Sunderland, playing with momentum and an unbelievable noise behind them, kept piling forward against Manchester City. Just three minutes after the opening goal, Halom almost doubled the lead with another stinging strike – this time from the other side of the box – but Joe Corrigan dived to his left and stopped it. The visitors' opening chances fell to their two England international strikers. Francis Lee collected a neat ball from Rodney Marsh in the penalty box but Ritchie Pitt, racing back, put in a measured challenge and Lee shot wide. A few minutes later Marsh produced an overhead kick that beat Montgomery but came back off the inside of the far post.

The match was end-to-end and played at such a pace in such a swirling wind and in such an atmosphere, it was nothing less than exhilarating to watch. Sunderland kept to their pre-match plan of attacking at every opportunity and threw men forward whenever they could. On twenty-six minutes Hughes collected a throw-in from Kerr on the right and knocked the ball back to his captain. When Kerr put the ball into the penalty box Donachie was on hand to block the cross and then almost immediately had to charge down Hughes's instantaneous left-foot drive. Hughes reacted quickly again to pick up the loose ball, slip it between Donachie and Bell and weave into space before firing the ball into the same corner of the net as Halom had done just over ten minutes before. Sunderland were 2–0 up against the FA Cup favourites after less than half an hour with two goals of true quality. There was delirium on the terraces.

'Billy Hughes showed an awful amount of patience for that goal because he had one shot charged down and rather than just lashing at it he moved into the right place, created some space and just put it away. It was incredible to see a Sunderland player do that,' Dobson says. 'Those two goals were the greatest goals I had ever seen in my life!' Sixsmith exclaims.

But Allison's side were all about attack too. A few minutes later a shot from Mike Doyle ricocheted into the path of an unmarked Marsh in the penalty box. Marsh shot but Montgomery stayed on his line and stuck out a foot to divert it wide. Sunderland then continued to chase and harry until referee Ray Tinkler blew for half-time. It was 2–0 at the break.

After the interval Manchester City began to play a more measured game and within ten minutes of the start of the second half Lee pulled it back to 2–1. A floated pass from the left by Doyle was headed back over the Sunderland defence by Bell, and Lee slid in to score from close range. There was still over half an hour left on the clock.

'When they got a goal back to make it 2–1, I was worried and I feared the worst,' Sixsmith says. 'I think Sunderland fans are terminally depressive like that. But the team really dug in that night and they stopped Manchester City from playing. Monty made another good save: there was a scramble in the box and he managed to clear the ball. But I was worried that it would go to extra-time. I feared they would beat us if it did.' The scramble occurred on seventy-eight minutes when Montgomery made a vital close-range save from Lee.

Moments later Porterfield played the ball into space for the advancing Malone to chase in the centre of the field. Malone played the ball out to Halom on the right flank with the outside of his right boot. Halom played in Dennis Tueart, who raced into the penalty box and fired towards goal. Corrigan palmed the ball away but both Hughes and Kerr were racing in. Hughes was on hand to knock the ball into the net and put Sunderland 3–1 up. He broke away, waving his hands and soaking up the roar from the crowd. Relief had broken out around Roker Park. It would be enough: Stokoe's men were in the quarter-finals.

'Manchester City left gaps at the back and we got the third goal and wrapped it up,' Sixsmith says. 'They weren't going to come back from that, the crowd wouldn't have let them. It was a cracking match and the best game I ever saw at Roker Park. Here were two very good sides committed to attacking football, but our defence was far better on the night.'

'They crumbled in the replay,' Arthur Cox says. 'Vic Halom scored a glorious goal, Billy Hughes was unplayable and David Watson was a pillar of strength at the back. The others filled in around them. We were still near the bottom of the Second Division table and we had prepared by beating Notts County and Reading while Manchester City had beaten Liverpool in the previous round. But it was obvious as far as our league position was concerned that the team was under-achieving. We could have beaten them in the first match.'

'For me, the Manchester City replay was the defining game of the whole FA Cup run,' Montgomery says. 'That night told us we had a chance of winning it. It was the game of games.'

'We played very well,' Watson adds. 'Vic Halom's goal was a Goal of the Season contender – it was a wonderful goal – and Billy Hughes got two. Billy was a good finisher and he was quick; the only thing he lacked was heading ability – he didn't particularly like to put his head in but he had everything else: good control, he could shoot and pass, and he saw chances as well and he would often gamble where the ball would drop. Billy developed under Bob Stokoe; he hadn't been given licence to do that before. Dennis Tueart changed too, and so did Bobby Kerr and Ian Porterfield. Their whole outlook seemed to become more expansive. They went forward more from midfield and we scored more goals.'

'It was a great night and the goals were tremendous goals. Billy Hughes was a great player and the most naturally fit player I have ever seen. If Billy was firing, he was brilliant, and he was outstanding that night,' Malone says.

The celebrations in the Sunderland dressing room were to become legendary, with two-goal hero Hughes famously proclaiming – in the bath – that the Rokerites could now go all the way to Wembley and win the Cup. 'We didn't just beat Manchester City that night, we played them off the park,' Hughes says. 'They were the favourites to win the FA Cup with all these England internationals and all that, but we were brilliant that night and we outplayed them in every department. So you start thinking to yourself, We can win this. I think a lot of the lads felt the same after that match.'

'We were now comfortable with each other and we knew that as a team we weren't easy to beat,' Malone adds. 'We weren't expected to win against Manchester City but we felt we were going to win. We never thought about winning the FA Cup until that night but suddenly we were so close to the final and so when someone shouts out, "We can win this," it just hits home: we can win this!'

'I'm one of those people who always keeps his feet on the ground and I've never been one to get carried away, but when Hughesy stood up in the bath that night with a bottle in his hand and said, "We can win this," I knew he was right,' Watson says. 'I think most of the team felt the same. We had a belief that it was our destiny. From then on, we believed we were going to win the FA Cup.'

'We played pretty well and scored some well-created goals in the first match, but the replay made us feel that we could go on and win the FA Cup,' Tueart says. 'It showed us just what a good team we were. Take the Vic Halom goal for instance, and just look at the passes that led up to it. The atmosphere was absolutely rocking that night. The supporters built up a head of steam, really from the Reading game onwards. There is no question that the supporters played a big part in the whole Cup run. We had eleven, twelve, thirteen or so players and over fifty thousand supporters. The whole town was galvanised. The quarter-final draw against Luton was a big incentive for us – it was the best draw we could have had.'

'I felt we could win the Cup as well,' Guthrie adds. 'But I think that had a lot to do with us being drawn at home to Luton in the next round. If we had been drawn away at Leeds or somewhere else, for example, we may not have felt like that at that time.'

But Kerr wasn't too sure about the sudden euphoria and the confident predictions: 'I know Hughesy and some of the lads said they knew we were going to win the FA Cup but I didn't, not then anyway. That's the way I am. There is no way. Anything could have happened –

we had almost gone out at Notts County and we had a scare against Reading as well. We were in the quarter-finals but there was still a long way to go.'

'People definitely started to sit up and take notice after we beat Manchester City,' Pitt says. 'We had gone from fourth-bottom of the Second Division to the quarter-finals of the FA Cup in a few weeks and we had now beaten a top side as well. We began to get a little respect after that.'

The Manchester City players gallantly accepted defeat, and Marsh claimed Halom's strike was about the best goal he had ever seen. Allison quit the club a few weeks later with his tail between his legs and went on to manage Crystal Palace. 'That I suppose brought the curtain down on me at Maine Road,' he later said of his team's defeat at Sunderland.

'I remember well Malcolm Allison going to the Manchester City training ground to say his farewells,' Gerald Sinstadt says. 'He walked down a line of players, shaking hands with them, and he had a little personal message for each one. It was the most public departure from a football club that I can ever remember.'

'Malcolm Allison gave us his time and he gave us his advice,' Donachie says. 'He was a very positive manager to play for and he was seldom critical. We had a good side with a lot of experienced and quality players. We should have won the league title in the 1971–72 season but we threw it away. Maybe Malcolm should have considered having a clear-out after that but he didn't do that. He still believed in his team, he always did.

'The replay against Sunderland was just a typical Cup night,' Donachie adds. 'The lesser team were unbelievably fired up, the crowd was fantastic, we played below par and all the Sunderland players were on fire. To be honest Sunderland battered us that night and they deserved to win by a mile.'

After witnessing the greatest match they had ever seen at Roker Park, many Sunderland supporters raced home to watch extended highlights on Tyne Tees Television. Sinstadt again commentated on the match for the ITV network, and it was transmitted in black and white. 'It was the first time I had ever been to Roker Park and it was an eye-opener for me,' he says. 'I was sat high up on the gantry with the wind blowing in from the sea and it was a truly horrible night. At the end of the match the sense of this being one of the great FA Cup upsets was absolutely palpable and perfectly true.'

'I think it is nice that the only film of that match is in black and white,' Dobson says. 'It would be great to see Vic Halom's goal in colour but I think it has somehow got more atmosphere in black and white. It looks more historic and that is quite fitting really.'

After watching those televised highlights, Stokoe put a lead on his black Labrador Jed and went for a walk. It gave him time to think things through and put the evening's achievement into some perspective.

Writing in the *Sunderland Echo* the next day, football correspondent 'Argus' could not contain his delight: 'A legend came alive last night when the "Roker Roar" of yesteryear was revived and reverberated around Roker, Fulwell and Monkwearmouth to inspire Sunderland to a 3–1 win over Manchester City.'

News of Sunderland's victory travelled far and wide, but one of the club's famous supporters struggled to find out the result, for Sir Tim Rice was in Reykjavik, promoting a stage production of *Jesus Christ Superstar* on the night of the match: 'I remember returning to England the next day with Andrew Lloyd Webber and, of course, back then you couldn't get an English newspaper out there for three or four days unless you were lucky,' he says. 'There weren't any newspapers on the plane home either. We came back into London and the first thing I did was to find a newspaper stall and look at the back page. When I saw the result – Sunderland three, Manchester City one – my immediate thought was, Oh yes, we have a shot now. Manchester City had a very good side at that time. I couldn't believe it.'

But the thousands who were at Roker Park that night did believe. 'From the fifth-round replay onwards everyone just seemed to have this belief that we were going to win the FA Cup,' Sunderland supporter Bill Peverley says. 'It is unexplainable really but we all just seemed to know. Some of us had felt it for a while. It had been blind belief but it was now sheer hysteria. I can't remember anything like that night. I think the noise we generated actually scared the Manchester City players.'

Coincidentally, 'Cum on Feel the Noize' by Slade went straight in at number one that week. But it was another record in the charts that was taking over the terraces in the north-east. While the fantasy of glam rock dominated the airwaves and the television screens, the far-from-commercial folk-rock 'Part of the Union' by Strawbs summed up the reality of the political landscape of the time – and nowhere more than in this one corner of the country. The popularity of the song soon led to a defiant version – the last word of the title was changed to 'Roker' – being chanted by the Sunderland faithful.

The dispute at Coles Cranes was now entering its ninth week, while the Youth Employment Office reported that unemployment in the town was at its highest level since the start of the 1960s. On the very day that Sunderland beat Manchester City, local civil servants began their own form of industrial action as well.

Conservative Prime Minister Edward Heath, struggling in the polls and under pressure nationwide, had written a personal letter to the readers of the *Sunderland Echo* stating, 'There are good reasons for believing that the improvement to industrial conditions, so important for Sunderland, is on its way.' Little did he know that the biggest help he would receive in quelling this local antipathy would come from the son of a coal miner who currently managed the town's football club and who was gradually bringing a whole community back together.

9.

THE LAST EIGHT

As Sunderland basked in the success of arguably its greatest sporting moment since 1937, the local news was still dominated by job losses, soaring prices and strikes. Economic strife had really started to bite in Britain and 400 employees at the North Sands yard of Sunderland Shipbuilders came out on strike in the first week of March 1973 to join those workers still refusing to work in the ongoing dispute at Coles Cranes. Growing tensions there had led to marches by workers to the Civic Centre to see the mayor, Councillor Leslie Watson. The contrast between the mood of the town's workforce and the spirit shown by the supporters of the town's football team could not have been greater. For many of these men and women Bob Stokoe's side was offering the only tangible hope of restoring some of the pride and passion that had been lost in the area.

'There was a Tory government at the time – which never goes down well in the north-east – and things were hard,' supporter Pete Sixsmith says. 'But despite everything that was going on there started to be a general feeling that things were going quite well for the football team and therefore people became happier in their work. There was definitely an element of that.'

And so, at a time when apathy and depression could have easily taken over in the workplace, somehow production in the mines and shipyards started to increase. Miners at Wearmouth Colliery – the site where the Stadium of Light now stands – set a new productivity record, with an output per man-shift of 42.6 hundredweight compared to a previous best of 40.5 cwt in 1968.

The *Sunderland Echo* letters page was packed with good wishes, poems and old photographs of historic footballing successes, including the 'Team of all the Talents' and the 1937 FA Cup winners. Someone even sent the newspaper a Football League winners' medal from the 1891–92 season from their private family collection.

With the all-ticket operation against Manchester City deemed a success by the club and police alike, it was decided to do the same for the next FA Cup match against Luton Town. But the decision to reward 'loyal supporters' by presenting vouchers, to be redeemed for quarter-final tickets, at the next home match against Oxford United that coming Saturday would prove to be a controversial one.

Sunderland beat Oxford 1–0 with a goal ten minutes from time by Dave Watson. It was the fourth successive win at home in the league and it took the Rokerites up to sixteenth in the Second Division table with four games in hand. With the form the side was showing – there had been just two defeats in fifteen matches – a comfortable top-half finish now looked to be achievable.

After the match Stokoe was full of praise for an unsung hero: 'Ritchie Pitt was a revelation,' he said. 'I might have sold him to Lincoln earlier this season for £15,000 and I couldn't have bought anyone for £50,000 as good as he is now.'

'I remember Oxford had a centre-forward called Nigel Cassidy,' Sixsmith says. 'He was a big roughhouse player with curly hair and a classic seventies moustache. He came over to the Clock Stand paddock shortly after kick-off to retrieve the ball and he started talking to some of the Sunderland fans, saying, "Great stuff, lads, well done and best of luck for the next round." He had absolutely no connection with the north-east whatsoever. It was just a really nice thing for him to do. All of the country seemed to be cheering us on our way. We were now playing really well, we were winning games and we were taking thousands of supporters to away matches in the league.' Fellow supporter Paul Dobson, who was still at school at the time, adds: 'I didn't want to miss a game. I remember going to see them play away and my school-mates were saying to me, "Aren't you going to go to the FA Cup game?" and I was like, "I'm going to go to both!" I would have watched them every day if I could.'

Dobson and Sixsmith were two of the lucky ones. A large number of Sunderland supporters were denied tickets to the quarter-final due to something of a fiasco at the match. Some fans failed to get into the ground, and many more failed to receive vouchers. Hundreds complained, and letters poured into the local press telling stories of people who had not missed a home game in seasons being denied a ticket to the biggest fixture for almost a decade. Sunderland chairman Keith

Collings apologised in the press: 'On reflection, the club completely underestimated the response of supporters to the voucher offer at the Oxford game,' he said. But the fact remained that many true supporters were without a ticket for the Luton match.

Stokoe meanwhile was becoming national news, with the *Sunday People* carrying a two-page feature on the Sunderland manager in the wake of the win over Manchester City. 'I'm not one for coaching certificates and I've never been to Lilleshall but I understand players and get on with them,' he told the newspaper. 'I found that the players had been dominated for four years. It was easy to strike a good relationship with them, just by trusting them. They can have a drink in town if they want, a thing they were never allowed before.'

Sunderland's next league match – just one week before the Cup match against Luton – was coincidentally at Kenilworth Road against the same opposition. The Hatters' manager Harry Haslam made four changes to his side, and Stokoe left out six members of the team that had beaten Manchester City: Dick Malone, Micky Horswill, Ritchie Pitt, Bobby Kerr, Billy Hughes and Dennis Tueart were all rested. Luton won the match 1–0 with a goal from Don Shanks. Stokoe – looking at the bigger picture – remained upbeat: 'I am not too unhappy about the way things went,' he said. 'I have given the players every opportunity to get over their knocks and bruises.'

After successfully steering Sunderland into the last eight of the FA Cup just four months into his managerial reign, Stokoe was offered an improved five-year contract by the board in the week leading up to the quarter-finals. Two days before the Cup match against Luton, he publicly turned it down: 'People are fed up with five-year plans,' he said.

It will be a two-year job to take them up and then we can think about it. The club and its supporters have too many lean years behind them. I want to add this note of urgency and ambition to the club's thinking and the players too and then put it over to the supporters. This club is bigger than I can ever be and is deserving of being back in the big league. With the backing they are getting right now they should not be anywhere else. Without mentioning any names we have a lot of players very capable of playing in the First Division.

It was clear that Stokoe fever was beginning to mount, both inside and outside the club.

Looking ahead to the clash with Luton, the Sunderland manager added, 'Naturally the players are all a bit starry-eyed with the FA Cup and the atmosphere which goes with it but when you get within three hours of Wembley everyone gets a little anxious. This is the most important game Sunderland have played for years.'

Stokoe also spoke of the importance of Sunderland trying to win the tie at the first attempt. After three replays in the first three rounds the Rokerites were already approaching a seventh game in the Cup and their manager was well aware that home advantage against a fellow Second Division side, with a rejuvenated Roker Roar behind them, was handing his men the best opportunity they could wish for to progress to the semi-finals: 'We are not underestimating Luton but there will be a big-time atmosphere and I know our players will rise to the occasion,' he said. It was a sentiment felt by his entire team. After knocking out Manchester City, the players now had to focus on the equally challenging task of defeating lesser-known opposition in front of a capacity crowd that would, come kick-off, again become wild with excitement and expectation.

Ron Guthrie recalls walking to Roker Park on the day of the quarter-final with Ian Porterfield after a regular team lunch meeting at the Seaburn Hotel on the North Sea coast, about a mile from the ground. At the time the hotel was a regular holiday destination for the famous English artist L. S. Lowry, best known for his depiction of football fans at Bolton Wanderers' Burnden Park ground in *Going to the Match*. Lowry also painted *River Wear at Sunderland*, *The Sea* and *Industrial Scene* from his time spent happily in the area in the later years of his life. 'Ian was a focused player and, of course, we both played on the left side,' Guthrie says. 'I remember we had a discussion about tactics and things as we walked down to the ground before the Luton match. Ian was always thinking ahead and planning ahead. It was about one-thirty p.m. and people were wishing us good luck as we walked past them. It was a brisk walk down to the ground from the hotel and the wind was swirling that day. But we were both confident. We knew what we had to do.' Porterfield was already working on a plan to stop their wingmen, and in particular any attacks materialising down his left-hand side.

Luton had a reputation as a good counter-attacking side away from home, with John Aston and John Ryan capable of causing damage down the wings. The north-east had been a happy hunting ground for them that season, for as well as knocking Newcastle United out of the FA

Cup they had taken both points from Sunderland and Middlesbrough in the league. Luton were placed in the top six of the Second Division and, with no goals yet conceded in the Cup, their confidence was as high as the hosts.

The Hatters had been FA Cup runners-up in 1959 and were playing First Division football at the start of the sixties before slumping all the way down to the Fourth Division by 1965. A comeback began under the reign of Alec Stock, the same man who had guided Yeovil Town to that shock victory over Sunderland in 1949. They won the Fourth Division title in 1967–68, finished runners-up in the Third Division in 1969–70 and came sixth in the Second Division in 1970–71.

Haslam took over prior to the 1972–73 season as a replacement for Stock, who left the club to take over at Fulham. Haslam had had an undistinguished career as a player but made his name as a nurturer of young talent while managing Tonbridge in the early 1960s. He recommended future England international David Sadler to Manchester United in 1962, and after a brief coaching spell under Bobby Robson at Fulham was brought to Luton as a chief scout and coach by Stock in 1969. During this period he discovered the likes of Ryan and, later, Malcolm MacDonald, who played for both Fulham and Luton before joining Newcastle.

This was Haslam's first full-time managerial appointment. The resurgence of Luton under Stock and Haslam coincided with the arrival and input of much-loved comedian and national treasure Eric Morecambe, who lived nearby in Harpenden. Morecambe had once taken his son to a match at Kenilworth Road in the late 1960s and was instantly hooked. He soon became a director, and via regular gags – particularly on his popular *Morecambe and Wise Christmas Show* specials – turned the club into a household name. He brought along more than a little sunshine.

Morecambe would often visit the away team's dressing room with a handkerchief and a pair of glasses on his head, just to say hello. On special supporters' trains for away fixtures, he would entertain fans in the aisle. In one match when Luton were losing, the crowd had chanted, 'What do you think of it so far, Eric?' Right on cue, a deadpan Morecambe shouted back, 'Rubbish!'

'Eric Morecambe was absolutely magnificent for the club,' former Luton striker Viv Busby says. 'He would come into the dressing room before a game and have a little laugh and joke with us. He would do his party piece to lighten the mood and then leave us to it. He was the heart and soul of Luton and, of course, he was great for getting coverage for the club as well. But he was a sensitive man. I remember once when we had been unbeaten at Kenilworth Road for a long time and then lost 3–0 at home to Sunderland – as it happens – that we were distraught afterwards and we all had our heads on our chests in the bath. Eric came into the dressing room and tried to crack a joke with us, probably for a laugh and to lift the mood. But the time wasn't right and Roger Hoy, the club captain, told him where to go. Eric immediately walked out of the dressing room and stayed away from the club for a while after that. In the end Roger had to apologise to him. That showed how much Eric felt for the club. He came back in due course and there was no problem but Luton meant a lot to the man. All he had been trying to do that day was pick us up off the floor.

'At the quarter-final stage of any competition you've got a chance,' Busby adds. 'We felt we had a chance of getting a result at Sunderland, but it was such a massive game for both clubs, with a massive crowd expected too, and that presented a great opportunity for both of us to progress. We were pleased with the draw – we had a good away record – but we knew that we had to get over the crowd, they could almost suck the ball into the net up there.'

Busby played in Luton's 2–0 win over Sunderland earlier in the season but like many others he missed the return league fixture a week before the Cup clash: 'Harry Haslam rested me in that one but he guaranteed me a place in the quarter-final,' he says. 'We'd done the double over Sunderland in the league but the two teams were totally different in personnel when we played up there in the Cup to the match at Kenilworth Road the week before.'

Luton were dressed in a stylish new kit – paid for by Morecambe – of orange shirts with a fetching blue and white vertical stripe down the left side. The Hatters had become something of a fashionable outfit due to the comedian's involvement with them, and the new strip was in keeping with that.

'Luton were a bit of a glamour team due to Eric Morecambe,' Sixsmith says. 'He was the biggest TV star of the time and I think the national media were a little bit torn as to who to side with for that match. Did they want Sunderland with their passionate supporters or did they want Eric Morecambe and Luton?'

As it was, Morecambe stayed away from Roker Park that day. Despite Luton having already won ten times away from home that season, the comedian had seen none of those wins. On each occasion he had travelled to an away match that season, Luton had failed to win. So he took the decision to stay at home and listen to the match on local radio. Unable to find out any news from that match at Bolton, he spent that particular afternoon walking up and down Redbourn High Street biting his nails.

Stokoe named the same Sunderland side that had done him so proud against Manchester City. All the regulars returned, while the fit-again Dave Young, who had played for the reserves at Scunthorpe United and heard of the FA Cup result on the team coach on the way home, was named substitute after coming back into the first team at Kenilworth Road the previous week. Jackie Ashurst, Ray Ellison, Brian Chambers, Jimmy Hamilton and John Lathan, all of whom had started at Luton the week before, stood down.

The match definitely caught the imagination of the public. A crowd of 53,151 was by far the biggest attendance of the day and totally submerged the gates at each of the three other FA Cup quarter-finals – all of which were all-First Division affairs – as well as seven top-flight games that day. It also registered record receipts for a match at Roker Park, totalling £26,156.95, and was Sunderland's largest recorded home attendance since the FA Cup tie with Leeds United in 1967. The BBC's *Match of the Day* cameras were there as well, covering a match at Roker Park for the first time since 1968.

Before the match, and to ecstatic acclaim, Jim Montgomery was presented with a gold watch in recognition of a record 453rd first-team appearance for the Rokerites that day. The goalkeeper surpassed the total set by Len Ashurst from 1958 to 1970. 'I still have the watch,' Montgomery says. 'I wear it on the odd occasion. It was a nice gesture by Keith Collings and the club. I remember going and having a look and picking the watch I wanted. It was nice, really nice, and I still have some photographs in my collection of that presentation.'

It was somewhat fitting that Montgomery was to break the club's all-time appearance record at Roker Park during the latter stages of that season's FA Cup run. He could not have wished for a more comfortable way to celebrate his new record either, for he did not have to handle one single shot of any quality that was on target in the entire match. Luton's best chance fell to Aston in the first half, but the goalkeeper dived quickly at his feet to smother the ball.

Montgomery was protected by another solid defensive performance by the Sunderland back four. The press had predicted before the match that Aston – on the left wing – would be Luton's main goal threat. He had scored both goals in the fourth-round win at Newcastle but he was below par on the day and was totally outmarked and outplayed by Malone before being substituted in the second half. Guthrie did a similar job on Ryan on the other flank.

Sunderland were also very strong in the centre of defence, with both Watson and Pitt playing well once again. Luton – for all the talk of attacking play away from home – were cautious and defensive. Sunderland eventually broke down this rearguard resilience with two goals from two defenders from two corners in the second half.

On fifty-two minutes, with litter blowing all around his feet in the wind, Kerr urgently placed the ball by the corner flag and gestured to his team-mates before taking the kick. Sunderland – under instructions from Stokoe – were eager to get it on, get it in and get themselves into the semi-finals.

'We were encouraged to do things quickly,' Watson says. 'Throw-ins, goal-kicks, free-kicks, corner kicks, everything. We wanted to play the game at a tempo. You have to play at a tempo that you can deal with, of course, but the other team may not be able to deal with it. You have to test the opposition, don't let them rest, get your foot in, tackle, don't dive in. Do all the things that opposing players will not like and unsettle the midfield players, the defenders, anybody – that was the philosophy.'

The Sunderland centre-half opened the scoring with a thundering header from Kerr's corner kick. It was a golden example of the aerial power he had worked on since he was a boy, playing in those fields with his four older brothers near to his home in Nottingham.

'Bobby Kerr made to play it and stopped,' Watson says. 'We were all jostling in the box. I got a run on the man who was marking me and got my head to the ball. I have always believed that if you head the ball, especially for goal, get your feet off the ground. I could hardly get my feet off the ground because I was actually stooping. But, at the last minute, I did get my feet off the ground and I took off. I was only about two inches off the ground but I had the momentum of my body surging forward so I was able to push straight through and it went into the bottom corner. I remember I ran into the back of the net and collected the ball. Goals like that in games like that mean so much to a player.'

The relief in the Sunderland players' faces was there for all to see. Porterfield now started stroking the ball around in midfield a little more, and in another attack on eighty-two minutes his through-ball led to Hughes turning quickly to shoot on goal and winning another corner after a save by Keith Barber.

Hughes casually ran over to the same corner flag on the left where Kerr had stood half an hour earlier, to take the kick himself. This time Pitt went forward and Watson stayed back. Hughes gestured with both hands and aimed for the penalty spot. Pitt headed down and Guthrie – situated on the six-yard line with his back to goal – swivelled and smashed the ball into the net. Sunderland were in the semi-finals.

'Whenever we got a corner from that side of the pitch I would always try and hang around the corner of the box,' Guthrie says. 'Billy Hughes took the corner and as the ball came in I got myself into the box, but when Ritchie Pitt headed it down I was facing the wrong way. I just hit it over my head into the corner of the goal. It was a glorious feeling, sixth round of the Cup too. I just couldn't believe it, me scoring a goal like that, plus the fact it was on *Match of the Day* that night so I could see it at night-time too. I remember my friend's daughter was eighteen years old that night and we went across to their house for a party – but I came back home to watch *Match of the Day* because they didn't have the television on!'

'It was rare for me to go over the halfway line,' Pitt adds. 'That came from the days of Alan Brown. He used to say to me, "You do not go over the halfway line." I remember the goal well: the ball came over, I headed it down and Ron Guthrie knocked it in. I made one of the goals and Dave Watson scored the other one, so you could say that the two centre-backs had a big bearing on that day. But goals came from all areas in that side. We could all score goals.'

It was Guthrie's first goal for Sunderland and only the third goal of his professional career to date. These statistics had given his manager the foundations to offer odds of 66–1 against him scoring that day. Guthrie declined the bet but he has no regrets: 'I scored two goals for Sunderland and I scored two goals for Newcastle. But that is my favourite one, due to the nature of the occasion and the nature of the goal. It was absolutely brilliant,' he says.

The atmosphere on the Luton team bus after the match was far from brilliant. A sing-song started by one of the players to lift the downcast mood was immediately stopped in its tracks by an angry Haslam. The superstitions that had kept Morecambe away from Roker Park had been to no avail either. But better times were around the corner for the Hatters, and by the end of the following season both Haslam and Morecambe would be celebrating Luton's return to the First Division after an absence of fourteen seasons.

'We played badly and we deserved to lose,' Haslam said afterwards. 'We simply had no spark. It was a pity we should have to save our worst display of the season for what should have been our greatest day.'

'Sunderland battered us on the day,' Busby says. 'We didn't really get a kick. It was a great experience to play in a match like that in front of a crowd like that and there was a hell of a crowd that day too – the atmosphere was electric. You hear stories about the "Roker Roar" but until you were out on the park and heard it for yourself you didn't fully understand quite what it was like. That was a very big game and Sunderland were far more up for it than us. They had a great team spirit and if you can get on a Cup run that belief grows and grows with every round. But they also had a great team with some great footballers – as was later proved – and, of course, a great motivator as a manager.'

The Rokerites were through to the last four in the competition for the first time in seventeen years. Furthermore, for the first time during the campaign Stokoe was able to sit and listen to the Cup draw on the radio without an if, a but or a replay.

Sunderland were assured of a place in the semi-finals alongside Cup holders Leeds, who knocked out Derby County 1–0 at the Baseball Ground with a goal from Peter Lorimer; Wolverhampton Wanderers, who defeated Coventry City 2–0 with goals from John Richards and Kenny Hibbitt to reach their first semi-final since winning the trophy back in 1960; and Arsenal or Chelsea, who had to replay after a 2–2 draw at Stamford Bridge.

Stokoe listened to the semi-final draw that Monday lunchtime at a seafront hotel in Blackpool on the way to Deepdale for a rearranged Second Division fixture against Preston North End that night. Before switching on the radio, the Sunderland manager had already gone on record as saying that he wanted the winners of the Arsenal–Chelsea replay to be his side's opponents. He felt his attacking team had their best chance against both those defences.

'Wolves have just started to click and Leeds are the number one side for sheer consistency. In contrast Arsenal just seem to do enough, they peg away and get results but are never really decisive,' Stokoe said. 'It would be the right game for the players. The way Carlisle went at Arsenal in the fifth round shows what can be done.' He didn't even mention Chelsea.

The Sunderland manager privately felt that Arsenal – despite challenging for the First Division title – were the least physical side left in the competition and the most likely team to be upset by the pace, work-rate and will-to-win attitude of his team.

He was to get his wish: Sunderland drew Arsenal or Chelsea and Leeds drew Wolves. Stokoe could hardly contain his delight: 'This is the one I fancied and it suits us fine. If we have got a chance of going to Wembley then I think we will get it from this particular game,' he said.

The following night Arsenal beat Chelsea 2–1 in a hotly disputed replay to take their place in the last four. Chelsea were leading 1–0 when referee Norman Burtenshaw awarded Arsenal a free-kick on the edge of the box. He then changed his mind – following protests from the Arsenal players – and awarded a penalty. Alan Ball scored from the spot and Ray Kennedy later claimed the winner. Stokoe didn't bother to go to the replay: 'I don't need to, they are on television nearly every week,' he joked.

'I don't believe the fact that they are challenging for the championship while we are in the lower half of the Second Division will mean anything at Hillsborough,' he said after the match. 'It is what happens on that day which will decide who goes to Wembley.'

The Gunners were immediately installed as the new 11–8 favourites to win the trophy, with Leeds priced at 6–4. Even shorter odds were offered on a repeat of the Leeds-versus-Arsenal finale from the previous year. If it happened it would be the first time that identical back-to-back FA Cup finals had taken place since Blackburn Rovers played Queen's Park in 1884 and 1885.

In addition to this possibility, Arsenal and Leeds both still harboured serious hopes of winning the league and Cup double: the Gunners were positioned second in the First Division, and Don Revie's men were placed third with two games in hand. Arsenal were aiming to do the double for the second time in three years while Leeds – through to the semi-finals of the European Cup Winners' Cup – had set their sights on an unprecedented treble for an English club: 'We shall play our strongest possible team for everything we are involved in – Championship, Cup and Cup Winners' Cup,' Revie said.

Sunderland were eighteenth in the Second Division table when the semi-final draw was made and were once again largely written off by the national press. But the players couldn't wait to play the Gunners and their confidence levels continued to rise, not diminish: 'We wanted Arsenal and we got Arsenal,' Hughes says. 'As good as Arsenal were, we thought they were weak at the back and we thought that Dennis Tueart and I could get at them. We were really pleased to get them in the draw. We thought that come the day of the match we could destroy them.'

Arsenal in the semi-final and the prospect of Leeds, Revie and revenge in the final – Stokoe couldn't have asked for more if he'd pulled the maroon-coloured balls out of that velvet bag himself.

10.

HILLSBOROUGH

The Football Association selected Hillsborough, the home of Sheffield Wednesday, as the venue for the FA Cup semi-final between Arsenal and Sunderland on 7 April 1973. It was the twenty-second time that a semi-final had been staged there.

Arsenal were bidding for a hat-trick of FA Cup final appearances. Not since 1888 – the year the Football League was created – had a team reached three successive finals. For the record, the list read: Wanderers (1876–78), Blackburn Rovers (1884–86) and West Bromwich Albion (1886–88). The Gunners now stood on the verge of creating football history.

Meanwhile Sunderland were aiming to become only the third Second Division side to reach the FA Cup final since the Second World War – and the first to knock out First Division opponents in the semi-final since Don Revie and Leicester City did it in 1949. The Rokerites had played at Hillsborough in 1956 against Birmingham City and lost. That match had been the club's last chance to reach the final. This was Sunderland's tenth appearance in the semi-finals; there had been just two wins from the previous nine attempts.

They were rated as rank outsiders by the bookmakers, both to get to the final and to win the Cup. The other three teams left in the competition – Arsenal, Leeds United and Wolverhampton Wanderers – were all placed in the top six of the First Division. Sunderland by contrast had been just two points above the relegation zone in the Second Division when the semi-final draw was made.

The Rokerites were still playing catch-up with their league programme – due to the Christmas flu virus and the Cup run – and had seven games in hand on some of their rivals. This meant that their schedule ahead of Hillsborough consisted of five league games in fifteen days, starting with the visit to Preston North End on Monday 19 March and ending with a home match against Queen's Park Rangers on Monday 2 April – just five days before the semi-final.

The managers and scouts at Arsenal, Leeds, Wolves and several other First Division clubs now had ample opportunity to consider the team's talents. By doing so well since the turn of the year and reaching the last four of the most famous knock-out competition in the world, certain members of the Sunderland side were already considered to be hot property.

Most of the speculation surrounded Dennis Tueart and Dave Watson. The first reports to surface linked Tueart with interest from West Ham United and Watson with interest from Manchester United. Bob Stokoe dismissed the Manchester United rumours but did admit that a conversation between himself and West Ham manager Ron Greenwood regarding Tueart had taken place in February after the Cup win at Reading. Stokoe told Greenwood that Tueart was not available at any price.

Stokoe played his Cup side at Preston just two days after the quarter-final win over Luton Town. He should have been happy with the performance and the result, a 3–1 victory secured by two goals from Billy Hughes and one from Vic Halom. But he was far from happy. He was disappointed with the goal scored by Preston's Alex Bruce and let off steam in no uncertain terms at Ritchie Pitt in the away dressing room at Deepdale after the match. What followed was to further rock the already uneasy relationship between the two men.

'It was absolutely chucking it down at Preston and my hair went flat; it was right out here at that time but with so much rain it looked the same as Dave Watson's that night,' Pitt says, indicating the fullness of his hairstyle. 'Obviously the vision from the touchline wasn't great because of the rain, but Dave was marking the Preston forward when he scored their goal. At the end of the match we walked off the pitch and Stokoe came straight up to me and went into this rant about it being my fault that Preston had scored. I just walked past him and went into the dressing room. When we got there, he started again. I said to him, "It wasn't me, I wasn't marking him, you're getting at the wrong person." But he went on and on and eventually I got so frustrated that I swiped the cups off the table and walked into the shower. He followed me into the shower and told me to go and see him in his office at nine the following morning. When I did that, he gave me another roasting and then told me that Dave Young was his first choice and that if he got the chance, not only was he going to drop me but he was going to have me out of the club. He told me he didn't like me, he didn't want me in his team and he didn't want me at his football club. This was just days after I had reached the semi-finals of the FA Cup. You can imagine how I felt.'

But Joe Bolton was the only change to the side for the visit to Fulham the following Saturday, coming in for Ron Guthrie. (The tough-tackling left-back was ruled out with an Achilles tendon strain.) Arthur Cox took control of the side as Stokoe planned another player-vetting mission in Scotland. Sunderland won 2–1 at Craven Cottage with a first-half penalty from Tueart and a second-half winner from Halom. Tottenham manager Bill Nicholson was sat in the stands by the River Thames that day, prompting more transfer speculation in the press afterwards. Such stories would now come and go on a regular basis.

A crowd of 40,930 turned up for the next match, against Carlisle United at Roker Park three days later. After complaints over the voucher system used for the Luton game, Sunderland decided on a ballot system for their allocation of 22,000 tickets for the semi-final: 4,000 season-ticket holders were given priority, with the remaining 18,000 tickets – seats were priced at £3 and £2 while standing was 70p – balloted using cards given out at the next two home games against Carlisle and Bristol City. The gates opened two and a half hours before kick-off that Tuesday night to deal with the demand and the attendance was proof – if proof were needed – that no solution was going to be that simple. Sunderland, again unchanged, defeated Carlisle 2–1. Hughes and another Tueart penalty settled the points.

The wins over Preston, Fulham and Carlisle lifted Sunderland up to thirteenth in the table, and with games in hand plus the class and confidence that were evident on the pitch, any fears of relegation were fading fast. The message to Stokoe when he arrived had been: 'Keep us up and bring the crowds back.' Survival had essentially been achieved, with eight wins and two draws in thirteen league games; furthermore the average home attendance of less than 13,500 under Alan Brown early in the season had now shot up to over 31,000 under Stokoe – and was still rising. There was also, of course, an FA Cup semi-final to look forward to.

Before then Sunderland still had to play Bristol City and QPR. Stokoe was keen to keep his first team playing all the way to Hillsborough if he could, and was buoyed by the return of Guthrie against Bristol City. But a badly bruised toe and calf ruled out Halom. The manager shuffled his pack and moved Watson – now the most sought-after centre-half outside the First Division – back to centre-forward once more. It would be the very last time he did so. Young was recalled to partner Pitt in defence.

This match gave Stokoe a much-needed warning sign when, leading 2–0 after fifty minutes thanks to an own-goal by Geoff Merrick and a second-half strike from Watson — the last of his career at centre-forward – Sunderland were pegged back to 2–2. Furthermore Bristol City's equaliser came in the eighty-eighth minute. Stokoe was furious with his team's performance and the lost point and said so in no uncertain terms afterwards. But the schedule was so demanding that he could do little more than prepare his side for another match forty-eight hours later at home to QPR.

The never-ending fixture list was becoming stressful for all concerned, not least the manager. Luckily snow, sleet and driving rain came to his rescue, howling across the north of England and making Roker Park unplayable. The match against QPR was postponed just hours before kick-off. It was a slice of good fortune for the Rokerites; the path was now clear to prepare for Arsenal.

On the Tuesday morning Stokoe took a fourteen-man squad – Jim Montgomery, Dick Malone, Ron Guthrie, Micky Horswill, Dave Watson, Ritchie Pitt, Bobby Kerr, Billy Hughes, Vic Halom, Ian Porterfield, Dennis Tueart, Dave Young, Brian Chambers and Joe Bolton – down to the Derbyshire spa town of Buxton, deep in the Peak District, to prepare for the match. The team stayed at the town's quiet and spacious Palace Hotel, the same retreat used by Stokoe and the Newcastle team in 1955 ahead of their FA Cup semi-final against York City at Hillsborough.

The plan was to train on Buxton's Northern Premier League pitch at Silverlands – the highest football ground in England, at over 1,000 feet above sea level – but three inches of snow had settled on the town and the pitch was unplayable. Instead the Sunderland squad trained at a sports ground at nearby Fairfield, where they did light work for most of the week; after an exhaustive run of games there was little need to do anything more.

'I don't worry about the opposition,' Stokoe said. 'I suppose 95 per cent of the country would back Arsenal to beat us but we are not frightened of them. They have a lot to lose. We have had a bit of luck in the Cup but – from what I have seen – so have Arsenal. So maybe it will depend on whose luck runs out at Sheffield.'

'The manager didn't have much to say to us in Buxton,' Malone recalls. 'We all knew the team by then and so all he had to do was to keep us ticking over and to keep us relaxed by stopping us from thinking too much about the game beforehand. Sometimes he would take us golfing rather than training, because when you're playing confidently you don't need as much training; there is less to correct so training is mainly about keeping your fitness and that is what he would do in training, in five-a-sides with conditions on them: often the losing side would have to buy the winning side a Mars bar or something like that – and in those five-a-sides you would do anything not to have to buy your opposite number a Mars bar!'

'Bob Stokoe and I just topped it up,' Cox says. 'We inherited these boys firing on all cylinders physically. It was then just a question of making sure the morale was right, the tactics were right and brushing up on set pieces. It's the players that do it. It's all down to the players and it always has been all down to the players. What happened in 1973 was no different.'

Training in Buxton generally consisted of four morning sessions of light physical exercise, sprints and tarmac tennis, with the odd game of eight-a-side thrown in. Such games would feature the entire fourteen-man squad plus Stokoe and Cox. 'The five-a-sides could get quite heated,' Montgomery says. 'I used to have a right battle with Bob Stokoe. We both loved to win and, of course, he hated losing. He once squared up to me and I squared up to him as well. Arthur Cox had to come in and send us both off.'

Sunderland comedian Bobby Knoxall – appropriately blessed with striking red hair – joined the squad during the week and recorded a song with them in Manchester for RCA Records. It is interesting to note that 'Sunderland All the Way', which became the club's official FA Cup record, contained more lyrics about the club returning to the First Division than anything else.

'Bobby Knoxall was the resident comedian with us,' Watson says. 'He was Sunderland through and through and he came along with us a lot on the Cup run. He was a bit clownish and helped relax the mood, especially for the local players in the team. But I couldn't understand him. I remember talking to him on my own one day after a match and I didn't understand a word he said. Dicky Malone had to act as my translator!'

Stokoe spoke to the press on a daily basis at Buxton, but the players were kept away from the national spotlight. The manager essentially took the pressure off them by single-handedly dealing with the mounting media requests. It was another lesson he had picked up from his time at Newcastle in the 1950s: 'I have brought them here so they are in a relaxed atmosphere and we can get them into the right mood for the biggest game they have ever played,' he said. 'We have got to live for this particular game and give it everything we have got.'

'Buxton was a good way to prepare for the game,' Kerr says. 'We had a drink, we played snooker, we played pool and we played golf. Some of the lads even went shopping. There was absolutely no pressure on us at all.'

'The weather wasn't too good but the mood among the lads was great all week,' Guthrie adds. 'Most days we just trained and relaxed. We always had a couple of pints at night too.'

Halom was the only injury doubt when the Sunderland squad arrived at Buxton, but towards the end of the week Horswill had become the big concern and physiotherapist Johnny Watters had to work overtime to get him fit. Young was on standby if a reshuffle was required, but he had a two-match suspension hanging over him after reaching twelve penalty points following a sending off – the consequence of two separate minor offences committed in a reserve team outing at Scunthorpe United. Stokoe's plan, had Horswill not been passed fit, was to lodge an appeal to the FA in an attempt to get the suspension delayed so that Young could play in the semi-final. In the end that wasn't necessary and so the defender served his ban and watched the match from the stands. Chambers took over from Young, who had been the substitute against Luton, on the bench as Sunderland fielded the same starting line-up for the fourth Cup match in a row.

In the evenings leading up to the semi-final Stokoe and Cox spent time considering a report they had received on Arsenal, sent up from Sunderland's representatives in London, Peter Doherty and

Peter Croker – the same people who had reported back to Stokoe on Pitt's performance for Arsenal Reserves against Chelsea Reserves in February.

Arsenal manager Bertie Mee was a former physiotherapist who had risen through the ranks at Highbury. Now aged fifty-four, he had taken over in a caretaker capacity following the dismissal of former England captain Billy Wright in the summer of 1966 and was appointed full-time in March 1967. Assisted by coach – and later assistant manager – Don Howe, Mee took Arsenal to two successive League Cup final defeats at the end of the 1960s before winning the Inter-Cities Fairs Cup in 1970. The league and Cup double famously followed in the 1970–71 season before Howe left the club to become manager at West Brom. Without him Mee still took the Gunners to the Cup the following season, and by the spring of 1973, he again had realistic ambitions in both major domestic competitions.

It was said that Mee's strength was a power to manage men. He produced a system at Arsenal to suit his players rather than finding players to suit a system. He was a tracksuit manager and enjoyed being on the training ground. He had watched Sunderland play once since the quarter-finals, in the 2–1 win over Carlisle.

'Bertie's big saying was "Let's get on with it." He felt that if he spent too much time talking about things it was not productive,' Howe once said of his former manager. But if ever there was a time to talk about things, it was prior to this semi-final against Sunderland.

The Arsenal manager had been desperately unlucky with injuries ahead of the match. He had major headaches in his team selection, particularly in defence. Club captain Frank McLintock, a veteran of four FA Cup finals and the man who had led the Gunners to the double two years before, was ruled out with a hamstring injury sustained in the home match against Derby County the previous weekend. His loss would prove to be monumental for them.

Jeff Blockley, a central defender signed from Coventry City for £200,000 the previous October and capped by Sir Alf Ramsey the following week in England's 1–1 friendly draw against Yugoslavia at Wembley, would have been McLintock's natural replacement at the back; but he was still recovering from a thigh injury that had kept him out of the first team for six weeks and was not yet match fit. Five days before the semi-final – in a clear race to be fit for Hillsborough – Blockley played his first full match since February in a reserve game against Oxford United and came through the test. Mee made the decision there and then to play him against Sunderland. But the defensive problems dominated Arsenal's build-up so much that serious doubts over striker John Radford – who had himself been out for five matches with a knee injury and was still fighting to regain match fitness – barely got a mention in the press.

There was still an abundance of talent in the Arsenal side – George Armstrong, Alan Ball, Charlie George, Eddie Kelly and Ray Kennedy included – but those injuries weighed heavy on the manager and, in the absence of McLintock, on his players as well.

Arsenal goalkeeper Bob Wilson – who missed the 1972 FA Cup final due to a serious injury which damaged ligaments, tendons and snapped the cartilage in his left knee – had been on the sidelines for most of the 1972–73 season, but was back in the starting line-up. He explains the selection problems his manager faced ahead of the semi-final: 'Frank McLintock was out and that was a big blow, for he was absolutely vital to us. Frank was an incredible leader and an incredible captain, and so it was a massive loss,' he says. 'Jeff Blockley wasn't match fit. Bertie Mee made an absolute error that day. He would ask us as men if we were able to play and Jeff obviously saw it as an opportunity and said that he was, but he clearly wasn't. I think Sunderland knew that. But what could Bertie do? He could possibly have put Peter Storey alongside Peter Simpson, but we were struggling because, basically, the squads were so small back then. Bertie didn't really have any other option; he needed Jeff to play – we didn't really have an alternative.

'We were struggling with a lot of injuries. I had missed the previous year's FA Cup final due to my own injury – which was a personal disappointment – and although I was back to playing in the first team my left leg and natural take-off leg was damaged due to the injury, so my take-off leg had to become my right leg, which was a massive problem for me. Nigel Harris, our surgeon at Arsenal, was fondly nicknamed "Nigel the Knife". It was the brute-force way back then, not like it is today, and maybe I came back too quickly. I was back playing and I was making my saves, but in my own mind I think I realised I was probably never ever going to play as well as I did in our double season. I was the best goalkeeper in the First

Division that season but I now knew I was never going to be that again. I suppose it was the beginning of the end of my career, now that I look back. But I was fit, I felt good and I was in a team that was sound and was challenging for the double for the second time in three years.

'Bertie Mee was very thorough in his preparation and our scouts would report back after watching the opposition two or three times,' Wilson adds. 'The crucial part of their report would have been what the opposition did at set pieces – long throw-ins, corner kicks, free-kicks and things like that. Dennis Tueart – "Dennis the Menace" we called him – was of course a very good player and everyone knew the ability he had; Billy Hughes could be an absolute thorn in your side as well; and Ian Porterfield was considered by us to be Sunderland's playmaker. We also knew all about Jim Montgomery and this incredible reputation he had for reflex saves. He was like greased lightning. But then there was this myth – if it was a myth – that had built up about Monty having an eyesight problem and that apparently his long sight wasn't clever. Jim was definitely a goal-line keeper; he stayed on his line and rarely came out to the penalty spot to collect crosses and things like that. We believed there could be a problem there and so our forwards were told to have a crack at goal from twenty-five yards, thirty yards or whatever against him.'

Now, for the first time during Sunderland's FA Cup run – but certainly not the last – Stokoe cunningly played his press card and – on the morning of the semi-final – became back-page news. Writing exclusively in the *Daily Mirror* under the headline EXIT ARSENAL, the Sunderland manager confidently predicted that his team would become the first Second Division side to reach the Cup final since Preston in 1964: 'For once Arsenal's luck will run out,' he said, referring to the late goal that had kept the Gunners in the competition in the third round against Leicester, and the somewhat fortuitous win over Carlisle in the fifth round.

For once fate will give their opponents the breaks and I am convinced of that as much as I am that Sunderland are on the verge of greatness again. Sunderland might have been called 'Slumberland' before I arrived and before our FA Cup run. Not any more.

I don't take credit for our success. I give that to the players and the thousands of Wearside fans who have come out of hibernation. It has been like rolling back the years to when all roads led to football grounds on a Saturday afternoon. No one can tell me crowds don't influence players, that players don't grow ten feet tall on a crest of fanatical support. I have seen it happen over the last few months. That is why it would be good for football for us to win today and good for football that we once again take our place among the top clubs. The players have given the club and the supporters seven great ties in reaching this stage and no one would have forecast anything like this at Christmas. They have worked hard to put Sunderland back in the big time again.

Then came the sting: 'I won't be alone in willing my lads to victory,' Stokoe said.

Every neutral soccer lover in the country will be by my side and I am sure my players won't disappoint us. Arsenal are on a hiding to nothing. That is the way I see a game which all the experts seem to regard as a trifling interruption of Arsenal's training routine. They said the same things when we came up against Manchester City in the fifth round and look what happened. That is what they will be saying when we play either Leeds or Wolves in the final and it won't worry us a bit.

Stokoe's passion for the game was now being lapped up by the national newspapers as much as by the local pressmen, and there is little doubt that the man himself realised just how powerful a tool this could be.

Interestingly, in the same article Stokoe caused some surprise in the north-east by touching briefly on his allegiances within the game, saying, 'My father was a Sunderland supporter. I feel the same as those on the terraces because I used to be there too. Although I was with Newcastle as a player, Sunderland was always my first love.' It is difficult to now assess just how much truth there was in this rare and forgotten comment. It may have been fact, it may have been due to the moment, or it may even have been another card played to fuel the passion of the Sunderland supporters ahead of the big day. But by this stage Stokoe's stock could hardly rise any higher among the fans, and his background at St James' Park had faded among most of them. It is, however, interesting to note that from this day onwards he would always be known as the 'Messiah' among the Sunderland faithful.

'He was always black and white, Bob,' Montgomery says. 'You would never take the Magpie out of him, never in this world. He was a Newcastle man and a Magpie and so for him to be seen as a messiah in

Sunderland, when everybody knew he was a Magpie through and through, was astonishing. In addition to all that he achieved with us at Sunderland, he always tried to go with the supporters in what they wanted. He tapped into the history of the club and the tradition of the club, like going back to the black shorts for example – that was Bob all over. His father was a Sunderland fan, yes, but Bob – what with winning the FA Cup with them and playing for them like he did – was always black and white.'

Stokoe was never to repeat the claim that he was a Sunderland supporter. Indeed, close to twenty-five years on from that comment and long into his retirement from the game, he insisted that his affections remained even between Sunderland and Newcastle: 'You will have to split me in two – black and white on that side as the first club and the success of the red and whites on the other,' he said. Stokoe's good friend Len Shackleton – who knew him better than most – was sitting next to him at the time and joked, 'He is only saying that because he managed Sunderland.' Maybe the man couldn't bear to disappoint or hurt supporters from either side.

Nevertheless, Stokoe was 'sickened and shattered' at comments made by Newcastle centre-forward Malcolm Macdonald in the press about how 'Sunderland will meet with glorious failure against Arsenal.' Stokoe, feeling the subtext to this may have been the fact that an FA Cup win for Arsenal (or Leeds) would mean the fifth-placed team in the First Division would qualify for the UEFA Cup (Newcastle were currently placed sixth in the table), retorted, 'If Newcastle are not good enough to finish in the top four on their own legs then they are not good enough to go into Europe. As a former Newcastle player who still glows of the memories at St James' Park, I know my former team-mate Joe Harvey, the manager of Newcastle, will not support Macdonald's comments.'

On the morning of the semi-finals, the vast majority of national football writers predicted a repeat of the 1972 FA Cup final. But some remained cautious: 'Logic says Leeds against Arsenal on May 5, yet there is little logic in football. Thus the ball skips and spins on the roulette,' Geoffrey Green wrote in *The Times*. 'The odds, I repeat, are on another Leeds v Arsenal final but I have a tickle behind the left ear, which suggests it will not be so.'

The *Yorkshire Post* did not use any such caution: LEEDS AND ARSENAL

FOR WEMBLEY REPEAT it screamed across its back page. 'My view is that the monopoly of Wembley by Leeds and Arsenal will continue,' wrote the newspaper's football correspondent Barry Foster.

The headline in the *Sunderland Echo* simply quoted Stokoe and said: WE CAN GET TO WEMBLEY. It was the Sunderland manager's last message at his final press conference ahead of the match. 'I keep reminding myself that Arsenal have no right to go to Wembley three years running and we have got to see that it doesn't happen,' he said. 'We are not world-beaters but we won't be lacking in effort. We are a team of fighters.'

But Raich Carter – the Rokerites' FA Cup-winning captain in 1937 – did not share Stokoe's optimism: 'I think I shall be the only Sunderland captain to collect the Cup for some time yet,' he wrote in the *Sun*. 'I doubt if anyone outside Sunderland regards this game as anything except a foregone conclusion.' Alan Ball, the Arsenal and England star with a World Cup winners' medal in his collection, had publicly stated that winning a Cup winners' medal was now his last remaining ambition in the game. He agreed with Carter's viewpoint: 'There is no way we can lose this match,' he confidently predicted.

Stokoe's 'fighters' boarded the team bus outside the Palace Hotel in Buxton at around noon on the day of the match and made their way down from those scenic Derbyshire hills to Hillsborough, twenty miles away. Spirits – as was by now the norm among the Sunderland players – were high. But there was the odd case of nerves as well.

'I admit I felt a bit nervous on the coach, what with it being an FA Cup semi-final and everything,' Guthrie says. 'I remember there was snow when we left Buxton and there was snow on the way to the ground as well. Then as we came into Sheffield there were lots and lots of Sunderland fans. It was all Sunderland fans. When you see all those fans, you get boosted.'

Watson was recovering from a severe kidney infection at the time and had been unable to sleep the night before the match, but he remained as focused as ever: 'I just felt this occasion was what I was born for and this was my place,' he says. 'Rudyard Kipling: triumph and disaster: you should treat those both the same; I firmly believe that and I always tried to do that. It is sometimes difficult but it helped me to have a calm approach to matches. When we were drawn to play Arsenal we weren't worried at all, which now sounds

crazy because they had about nine or ten internationals in the team –
all big stars with big reputations. But we looked at their strengths
and weaknesses and we just set out to play our game. Our philosophy
was simply to enjoy football and we looked forward to playing
matches. Winning had a domino effect on us and when you're
winning, the more, the better.

'One of the key figures for me was my wife, Penny,' Watson adds.
'She would drive me on and used to make sure I was in the right mood
for every match. She would go through a little routine to make sure
I was sharp before a game, maybe even slapping me across the face to
make me angry. She did this in the Cup run and it helped me a lot.
I relished playing against the bigger teams.'

'As far as I was concerned the semi-final was the big one, because
if we could win it, we knew we were going to play in the final at
Wembley with all the trimmings and all the pomp, in front of millions
of people worldwide,' Pitt says. 'The FA Cup final was the biggest Cup
match in the world at that time.'

'I thought we were going to do it and get to Wembley,' Hughes adds.
'It was the Arsenal thing. We didn't want Leeds. History might have
been different if we had drawn Leeds in the semi-final. But we drew
Arsenal. We wanted Arsenal and we got Arsenal.' 'It was a chance of a
lifetime for us,' Kerr says. 'We all knew what it meant and we were all
up for it.'

Sunderland supporters travelled from all corners of the country to
reach Hillsborough that day. Sir Tim Rice made the journey on a coach
from London: 'Andrew [Lloyd Webber] and I had been lucky enough
to have a bit of success, and David Land became our manager,' he
explains. 'David was a lovely guy and an Arsenal fanatic. He had a
season ticket there and used to go to every game. He was also manager
of the Dagenham Girl Pipers – a bunch of ladies who used to play the
bagpipes – and he would book them for semi-finals and things like that.
I remember going up on the coach with the Dagenham Girl Pipers all
the way up to Hillsborough that day, which was quite fun. They were
there with their bagpipes in the tunnel at the start of the match, and it
was a great occasion.'

An estimated 23,000 other Sunderland supporters travelled down
from the north-east on nine special trains, 200 coaches and an armada
of around 2,500 cars. Most of them would settle on the old Kop end, a

high, open, banked, uncovered terrace behind the goal to the right side of the Hillsborough tunnel and the dugouts.

Hopes were high among those supporters. The previous weekend Red Rum had caused a sporting surprise in the world of horse racing by hauling back Crisp from over twenty lengths to win the Grand National at Aintree in a record time. Why could a Second Division side not now achieve something similar in the world of football against a team that had won the double two years before?

'We drove down to Sheffield and everyone was in great spirits,' supporter Pete Sixsmith says. 'It was the day of the university boat race and I remember winding the window down as we came into Sheffield – after about four pints – and asking anyone who could hear me, "Who won the boat race then?" Like I cared! We were all on such a high. Some fans were stopping wedding cars and kissing the brides. It was a great atmosphere.'

'A lot of Sunderland fans travelled in hope with no tickets. I had a ticket for the Arsenal end but I swapped it with an Arsenal fan and went on the massive open terrace on the Kop,' fellow fan Paul Dobson recalls. 'We were confident we could win. We felt we had beaten Manchester City and so there was no reason why we couldn't now beat Arsenal.'

'I was sat in the seats – opposite the dugouts – and everyone around me was a Sunderland fan. Arsenal had a pen behind one goal and it seemed that we had the rest of the ground,' Sunderland supporter Steve Hodgson adds. 'I was very confident that we would get a result from the moment I heard that Frank McLintock wasn't playing. McLintock held that team and that defence together. He was Arsenal's leader and they were not the same when he wasn't playing. If I could have picked any one player in advance to be missing from their side that day, it would have been him.'

The inclusion of Blockley in the Arsenal line-up dominated the pre-match press coverage. It was clearly an issue in the Arsenal dressing room and it gave Sunderland supporters encouragement. Yet Sunderland players seemed unaffected by it all. 'I wasn't bothered about it and I never thought about it,' Halom says. 'We didn't really think about the opposition. I would have been as happy playing against Frank McLintock as Jeff Blockley. In fact I might have preferred playing against Frank McLintock. Jeff Blockley is a big lad and I'm not that big – I'm only five feet ten and a half – so in the air he had a natural advantage.'

'The situation with Jeff Blockley made no difference to us at all,' Tueart adds. 'We were flowing once we had beaten Manchester City. After Vic Halom arrived we stuck with the same eleven players all the way through. Vic was the final piece of the jigsaw. Billy Hughes and I were both, in essence, not wingers – we had been brought up as forwards, were two-footed and could play on either side. We could be flexible and support the team and once Vic arrived we had a centre-forward to play with. He was a fantastic central point to revolve around and a good target. We had a well-balanced side. There was a lot of quality in there.'

'The most important thing was that by buying a centre-forward like me it freed Dave Watson up to go back to centre-half,' Halom adds modestly. 'That was the big thing – Dave moving back from centre-forward to centre-half. He was an exceptional centre-half and he locked the defence. Anybody will tell you that is where any team starts; the rest you can build on.'

The teams – led out by captains Bobby Kerr and Bob McNab – walked out of the tunnel and were welcomed on to the pitch by those Dagenham Girl Pipers. The deafening noise of sheer emotion and heartfelt hope generated by the many thousands of Sunderland supporters was exhilarating. Locals claimed it was the loudest noise the ground had ever witnessed.

McNab won the toss and decided to defend the Kop end, against the biting wind. There was no snow in Sheffield but the temperature was very low for early April. Both sides had chosen to wear their away kits: Sunderland wore a new all-white kit, dispensing with their regular round-necked shirts for a new Umbro design featuring collars, while Arsenal played in yellow and blue, the two colours associated with their FA Cup triumph two years before. So for all the red and white in the stadium, there was to be none on the pitch.

With Sunderland attacking the Kop end in the first half, Wilson stood alone in front of nearly 20,000 raucous Rokerites as the match kicked off: 'The noise was exceptional,' he says. 'It was an absolutely incredible noise and I will never forget running out from the dressing room that day. We ran out and we hit daylight and, of course, we saw red and white. Now we were used to seeing red and white wherever we played, but on that day the difference was, this was Sunderland red and white and not Arsenal red and white. It struck me there and then that this was the opposition, and this was a Second Division side too! Our fans were great – they followed us everywhere – but this was something else. We were well aware of how good the Sunderland team were and the players they had, but now we were facing the full effect of their supporters as well.'

'Our fans were out of this world that day,' Sixsmith says. 'We had the entire Kop at Hillsborough, half the cantilever stand and half of the main stand as well. There were Sunderland fans all over the Arsenal areas too. We outnumbered them by about two to one.' 'We made some noise, I can tell you,' Bill Peverley adds. 'But it wasn't just noise; it was a passion of support for the team that just oozed belief.'

The blustery conditions wrapped this passionate air around all four corners of the ground, bringing the Roker Roar down to South Yorkshire that afternoon. On top of the main stand a flag with the Sunderland crest fluttered excitedly in the wind, while a flag with the Arsenal crest wrapped itself around a pole and remained unmoved for the duration of the match. The image was to prove poetic.

'I remember coming out on to the pitch, looking across the ground and seeing thousands upon thousands of our fans stood on the high banking section behind the goal,' Tueart says. 'That was an incredible sight. The support for us was truly amazing that day.'

'It was just an incredible noise and an incredible atmosphere,' Watson adds. 'The stadium was absolutely packed and it was a sea of red and white. The stage was set and I felt very comfortable. I felt this was my stage. I couldn't wait for the match to start.'

Sunderland approached the semi-final in the same attack-minded manner as they had the fifth-round replay against Manchester City: firm in the tackle and fast down the flanks, breaking down the strengths of the opposition by imposing themselves, setting the pace and setting the agenda straight from the kick-off.

'If we had allowed Arsenal to play we would probably have lost,' Pitt says. 'We were playing against a team that were in a division higher than us so obviously they had better players in terms of skill and ability. But we worked very hard, closed them down quickly and stopped them playing as much as we could. That was Micky Horswill's job in midfield – to stop the passes coming through. Billy Hughes and Dennis Tueart worked very hard on their full-backs as well. We stopped the opposition from playing and when we had the ball we had the ability to play and create chances for ourselves as well. We were a team and we worked as a team. We had enough confidence in ourselves to know what we could do. We were never intimidated or frightened.'

Horswill had earned rave reviews after his performances in the two games against Manchester City, when he won the midfield battle against Colin Bell – a World Cup quarter-finalist with England in 1970. Now he had to do the same against Alan Ball – a World Cup winner in 1966 and another current England international. The twenty-year-old's task at Hillsborough was to stop his fellow redhead opponent from controlling the semi-final from the middle of the park.

'Micky Horswill had quite a battle with Alan Ball in midfield,' Watson says. 'Bally was a tenacious player but so was Micky. They clashed a number of times in the semi-final, kicked each other and so on, but Micky came out on top.' It was Horswill who had the first shot on target in the match, after eighteen minutes. A cross into the penalty box was headed clear by Kelly, and McNab – under pressure from Hughes – kicked the ball out of play. Kerr's long throw-in into the penalty box was partially cleared by McNab but only as far as Horswill – positioned on the edge of the box – who swung his left foot at the ball to produce a good save from Wilson. The goalkeeper then crashed into his left-hand post after tipping the ball over the crossbar.

Two minutes later a long kick from Wilson reached the Sunderland half; Storey made an attempt to head the ball on but failed to connect with the bounce, and Horswill was on hand to hoof the ball back into the direction of the Arsenal goal with his right foot for Halom to chase. With a fierce wind carrying the ball, it went high over the heads of Halom and Arsenal's two central defenders – Blockley and Simpson – before falling into the path of the retreating Blockley.

The question mark over the match fitness of Blockley – the big talking point in the pre-match build-up in the press – was to become abundantly clear within seconds. It was seen by all other twenty-one players on the pitch and witnessed by the baying crowd of 55,000. Possibly uncertain about using the right foot that had caused him to be out of first-team action for six weeks, Blockley allowed the ball to move across his body and then attempted to play a back pass to Wilson with his left foot. The pass was too weak and too short – it bounced on the edge of the penalty box – and allowed Halom to nip in and get a foot to the ball to take it away from the oncoming goalkeeper. The striker stumbled but quickly recovered and, with Wilson stranded, managed to push the ball into the empty net. Although the connection was not a clean one – it came off Halom's ankle – the shot was on target, bobbled twice and crossed the line: Sunderland were ahead in the semi-final.

'I managed to get a little touch on the ball and knocked it around the goalkeeper. I took a nudge, and some players would probably have gone down and tried to claim a penalty but I was strong enough to go on,' Halom recalls. 'Then just as I was about to shoot the ball lifted and I mishit it, it just came off the turf, flicked up and came off my ankle. For a split second I feared the worst but it trickled across the line, with no pace on it. I was so pleased when I saw it go in. The first feeling I had was relief, sheer relief, and then there was joy, absolute joy.'

The Arsenal goalkeeper felt the opposite emotion: 'It was a ridiculous opening goal and Jeff Blockley totally underhit the pass,' Wilson says. 'Once we felt there were jitters down the middle of our defence, we were vulnerable. We felt vulnerable and we were vulnerable.'

As the ball was collected from the Arsenal net, Halom was jumped on by half of his team-mates in front of the Kop end. Once the group celebration had died down the goal scorer then fulfilled a promise he had made to a friend in the local press that morning by waving to the crowd. The story goes that, on meeting a woman the night before the match, the journalist had told her he was the Sunderland centre-forward and that should he score in the semi-final the next day he would dedicate the goal to her by waving. Halom was asked if he would do his friend a favour. When the moment came he duly obliged, smiling and waving to the crowd on his way back to the centre circle. Halom confirms that this story is true; and this underlines a remarkably relaxed feeling among the Sunderland players that day. After putting his team 1–0 up against Arsenal in an FA Cup semi-final, his first thought was to remember to do that!

Sunderland had the lead. But for five minutes the underdogs had to work hard to retain it. A free-kick on the right-hand side of the Sunderland half was taken by Pat Rice and headed goalwards by Blockley. Horswill back-tracked to clear the ball from near his own goal line with his left foot, and then Montgomery made his first save of the semi-final by blocking the rebound from Armstrong with his feet. Porterfield coolly ran the ball out of danger.

Moments later, neat work by George and Ball opened up another chance for Arsenal. Armstrong – smothered by the close attention of both Watson and Guthrie – was unable to shoot at the first attempt but still managed to hook in an effort when the ball ran free, which scraped the outside of Montgomery's left post.

Sunderland responded in the only way they knew, by attacking. Another long ball upfield from Horswill and another mistake from Blockley almost led to Halom doubling his own tally – and Sunderland's lead – just before the half-hour mark. But on this occasion Wilson saved Arsenal. Horswill had punted a high ball towards the Arsenal goal from his own half. Halom and Blockley again gave chase and this time, under pressure again from Halom, Blockley fell to the ground. The ball eventually ran free for Halom – after he out muscled Simpson in the box – and he was faced with a one-on-one against Wilson. The goalkeeper produced a magnificent save, hauling himself at the ball to charge down Halom's shot. But the Gunners were evidently completely rattled by Sunderland. Wilson's screams at his defence immediately after he made this save summed up the seriousness of the situation.

'That type of save was my *pièce de résistance* really,' Wilson says. 'I usually came out with the ball in that type of situation – I once took the ball off George Best's feet – and it was the best thing I did. I always went hands first and head first. After Sunderland took the lead, the noise was incredible. Whatever it had been like before the goal, it was now absolutely deafening. This lifted Sunderland. They played with such belief for a Second Division team.'

That moment in the game also gave further evidence – if any were needed – that Blockley was out of his depth that day. Fit or otherwise, the Arsenal defender was clearly unable to handle the pace or the power of Sunderland's centre-forward. 'While Jeff Blockley was a big bloke, Vic Halom was a big bloke too, and if someone could out muscle Jeff then it could be a problem, and on that day that is what Halom did really,' Wilson admits.

A less sympathetic view comes from the Sunderland faithful, who were gathered in their thousands behind the very goal that Sunderland attacked with such purpose in the first half: 'Jeff Blockley was smashed to bits in that game,' Sixsmith says. 'Vic Halom just took him apart. It was perfect for Vic as he was quite a quick player and Blockley was coming back from an injury and was slow. He was a traditional centre-half who followed the centre-forward everywhere. Vic pulled him across the back four and he didn't know what to do.'

Halom by contrast was enjoying his finest performance yet in a Sunderland shirt. Another chance came his way shortly before half-time, when a cross from Kerr caused problems in the Arsenal penalty box and Halom prodded the ball towards the goal. Wilson was beaten but McNab cleared the ball off the line, just before Hughes was able to pounce. The sublime Scot was also causing the Arsenal defence endless problems, and before the break Storey was booked for bringing him down to the ground after he had effortlessly skipped past McNab down the right flank.

Sunderland ended the first half on a high, and it is no exaggeration to say they could have been three or four up. Halom himself could have had a hat-trick. But the final moments of the opening half almost produced an equaliser for Arsenal. On the stroke of half-time Armstrong took a corner from the left that was headed out of the penalty box by Pitt but then hooked back towards Armstrong by Kennedy. Armstrong cut inside the box and shot towards the goal. The ball ricocheted violently off Halom's shins and almost crept inside the near post, but Montgomery's agility once again saved Sunderland. He was moving to his left then reacted superbly to dive back to his right, push the ball away from his goal and then knock it out for a corner before an alert Ball could connect with it. It was a crucial save and as important as any other Montgomery had ever made. Ball instantly showed his respect by shaking his head and ruffling the goalkeeper's hair.

'The end of the first half is always a bad time to concede a goal and if they had gone in at one each at half-time it might just have changed it a little bit to their advantage,' Montgomery says. 'But by going in at 1–0 we had something to hold on to. It was important to do that.'

So it was 1–0 to Sunderland at half-time. But Arsenal were used to being behind in FA Cup semi-finals. The Gunners had famously trailed Stoke City in 1971 and 1972 and had come through on both occasions. But this time there was a difference: there was no McLintock in the Arsenal dressing room.

'We had been there before,' Wilson says. 'We played Stoke at that very ground two seasons before in the FA Cup semi-final, and we were trailing 2–0 at half-time. Everyone was demoralised that day as our double hopes looked to have gone. But Frank McLintock was a real "Braveheart" – just like William Wallace – and his message was clear: "Let's get at them." Frank was amazing, particularly in situations like that. He never accepted defeat and his voice was always important to us, particularly on that day. We got a 2–2 draw, won the replay, won the Cup and then won the double. So we knew we were never out of a game at half-time but, of course, Frank's voice wasn't with us in the dressing room against Sunderland. He was missing. And we missed him.'

For the thousands upon thousands of Sunderland supporters unable to get tickets for the semi-final came some unexpected good news. After Frank Bough had announced the half-time score from Hillsborough on *Grandstand* at just after 3.45 p.m. on BBC1, BBC Radio 2 then decided to switch live and uninterrupted second-half commentary from the Leeds–Wolves semi-final, which at that stage was deadlocked at 0–0, to Hillsborough, where the story of the day – and the season so far – was unfolding.

The second half at Hillsborough began in the same way as the first had: Hughes and Tueart caused problems down the wings, the Sunderland midfield was in command and the defence was strong and firm, ably led by the outstanding Watson, who seemed to be winning everything, on the ground and in the air.

'I can still remember individual tackles I made in that game,' Watson says. 'I remember cutting the ball away from Alan Ball and as I slid in I knocked it out of play. I remember making a lot of headers that day too. On one occasion, I was in mid-air and hovering, waiting for the ball to come, and heading it away. I remember those moments well.'

Mee decided to substitute Blockley with Radford early in the second half. The defender later left Arsenal for Leicester after failing to establish himself at Highbury. He was never able to recover from that difficult day against Sunderland. 'Even though Jeff Blockley had been a terrific player for Coventry, had cost us £200,000 and had played for England, he never really got to terms with Arsenal and the size of the club,' Wilson says. 'Sometimes it's not just about whether a player has the talent, it's also about whether he can cope with the pressures of playing at the club that he is playing at. That sounds pompous but it's true.'

'Jeff Blockley was blamed for the first goal against us and people remember mistakes like that in your career, especially in FA Cup semi-finals,' Guthrie adds. 'I can imagine how he must have felt at that time. It must have been dreadful for him. I am glad it wasn't me.'

George was moved into the Gunners' midfield and Storey took over in defence. Within ten minutes the move backfired. A lack of height in the Arsenal box – something Blockley had in abundance – was exacerbated by headers from two of Sunderland's smallest players on the pitch, and the result was another goal for the underdogs.

Kerr's throw-in was knocked on by Tueart and then flicked on by Hughes beyond the retreating stretch of Wilson, who could only palm the ball into his own net. Sunderland led Arsenal by two goals to nil after sixty-four minutes of the semi-final.

'It was purely a reflex action,' Hughes says. 'Luckily Bob Wilson was by the near post. I didn't know too much about it because I was moving backwards.'

'It was bad defending in many ways,' Wilson concedes. 'I remember how close I was to keeping it out. It wasn't the power of the header, it was the loop, and with me pushing backwards I just couldn't get it up and over and I touched it over the line.'

Seven Sunderland players ran over to the touchline to once again celebrate in unison, to cries of 'Easy – Easy' from the stands and the terraces situated close to the benches. These relatively unknown players were now as close to Wembley as any of them had ever dared to dream.

But Watson was not among them: 'I didn't run to the bench to celebrate,' he says. 'I never did that, running forty yards to congratulate somebody. I thought it was a waste of time, I really did. I always wanted to get back into my position on the pitch. I was never one for kissing and stuff like that.

'We overwhelmed teams – whatever the reputation – and in a very exciting way,' he goes on. 'There weren't many teams playing with two wingers at the time – especially in the First Division – and it worked for us. We deserved our 2–0 lead, we were outplaying them.'

Montgomery – stood in front of the hordes of Sunderland fans at the Kop end – was transfixed by what he saw after Hughes doubled

Sunderland's lead: 'I just turned around and looked up at all our fans celebrating on that big terrace behind me. It was an unbelievable sight,' he says.

With fifteen minutes remaining on the clock, Radford tussled with Malone just outside the Sunderland penalty box. Malone eventually brought Radford down – almost pulling his shorts off in the process – and Arsenal were awarded a free-kick on the edge of the box. George fired the free-kick just wide of Montgomery's right-hand post, and Arsenal's best chance of the match so far had gone, accompanied by immediate cries of 'Nice one, Dicky, nice one, son. Nice one, Dicky, let's have another one' from the Sunderland fans – exhausted with excitement – on the open terrace behind the goal.

'John Radford was through on goal and it was a blatant foul,' Wilson says. 'If Dick Malone had got sent off – and he could have been for that challenge – eleven against ten would have made it a different game. I think it would have set up a really close finish.'

With less than ten minutes to go, George and Guthrie were involved in a scuffle in front of the two benches – an incident that resulted in both being shown yellow cards by referee David Smith. 'Charlie George was a great player but he was a feisty character as well,' Guthrie says. 'I got the ball and I knocked it past him and he had a little kick at the back of my shin. I pushed him, he had a slight swing at me and in the end I had him around the throat. We would probably have got sent off today. But it was done with in seconds. End of story.'

'Charlie was our one free spirit,' Wilson adds. 'When anyone got into Charlie we often became defensive as a result. So it was a bad sign to see that.'

As it was it was George who gave Arsenal hope, when he scored on eighty-five minutes. Simpson ran down the left flank and cut the ball back for Kennedy, who, closely marked by Guthrie, failed to connect and the ball ran on to George to stab a left-foot shot past the diving Pitt and outstretched Montgomery. The goalkeeper managed to get a hand to the ball but could not prevent it from trickling over the line. George then raced into the net, collected the ball and ran back to the centre spot. Arsenal – the comeback kings – were back in it.

'We were so close by then,' Dobson says. 'When Arsenal got that late goal, the whole of the Kop end was trying to blow it away from the net. It seemed to take a long time to cross the line. We were all stood there helpless, trying to keep it out.'

Arsenal had one last chance. It came from another long kick by Wilson, which was picked up in midfield by Ball, who fed Simpson, who in turn played in Radford, who was running down the right flank. Radford put the ball high into the Sunderland box, where a trademark header from the towering Watson again cleared the Rokerites' lines. As Radford and Armstrong stood by the corner flag and discussed who should take the resulting corner kick, the referee blew his whistle. The long wait was finally over – Sunderland were back at Wembley after an absence of thirty-six years.

'I remember the corner kick at the end,' Montgomery says. 'John Radford decided not to take it and so Geordie Armstrong came across to take it and as he did so the referee blew. I just remember little Geordie Armstrong running away up the line and Charlie George too. They were away – gone – and we had won. It was so emotional at the end. Ritchie Pitt came up to me and all I could say to him was, "We're there." The crowd played a tremendous part in getting us to Wembley. The fans were magnificent, phenomenal, they really were. They got us through it. But we put a shift in that day as well.'

Most of the Sunderland players were mobbed by delirious supporters on the pitch and almost all of them were later hugged on the touchline by a tearful Stokoe. By then some of them were in tears themselves.

'I ran straight down the tunnel,' Watson says. 'I presumed everyone else was following me but I must have been in the dressing room on my own for at least five minutes. It was strange, I never let myself enjoy that game or that win. I didn't let myself enjoy the feeling or the moment. I left the pitch too quickly and I regret that now. I have actually regretted it ever since I did it. But it was one of those things; I was so focused on the game and the game was now over and we had won. My instinct was to get down the tunnel, get my boots off and get into the bath. I was completely on my own, soaking myself and thinking, Where are all the boys? Then they all came in with champagne and it dawned on me what I'd missed.

'I found that the higher the standard of football, the more concentration I had to give,' Watson adds. 'Often I came off the pitch and I wasn't physically tired, but in big games such as this I would be mentally tired because I had needed to concentrate for ninety minutes. I particularly found that in those big games when I had to go up a level in performance. Thankfully I was able to do that. That level of mental ability can only be tested in matches like that.'

'In those days we just went straight down the tunnel at the end of the match, even if we had won 5–0; maybe we would wave at the crowd but nothing more than that,' Guthrie adds. 'The only time you did a lap of honour was if you had won something at the end of the season; otherwise you just went straight down the tunnel. But Hillsborough was something else, it really was. It took a while to get off the pitch.'

For over ten minutes after the final whistle the Sunderland supporters remained inside the ground, unmoving, shouting constantly for Stokoe to re-emerge from the dressing room and salute them. In the end the police had to go inside the ground and ask Stokoe to come outside once more. It was at this moment that the title 'Messiah' came into its own, on this occasion, for this unfathomable achievement and one man's heartfelt emotion. Stokoe came out and saluted the supporters. As he did so he wiped tears from his cheeks and blew kisses. This unashamed reaction summed up Stokoe. Those who saw it later on national television – regardless of which team they supported – could only warm to the man. Football neutrals got completely caught up in it. From this moment until the Cup final four weeks later, Stokoe was a popular hero throughout the country.

'When it was over and I finally got to him we just looked at each other and burst into tears,' Stokoe's wife Jean – now in the media spotlight herself – said after the match.

'I didn't know what to do or how to deal with it,' Stokoe later told biographer Paul Harrison in *Northern and Proud*.

People, grown men, were crying and bowing to me as though I was some kind of god that they were worshipping. It was then that I heard thousands of them calling me the 'Messiah'. I think that is when the press picked up on it. Tears rolled down my cheeks. Never in my life had I received such an ovation. I wanted to tell each and every one of them that this wasn't just my doing – it was a collective effort that included them. I walked off the pitch as I could feel myself breaking down with emotional joy.

'In some ways that day was more emotional than Wembley, with Bob Stokoe wiping tears from his eyes at the end,' Watson says. 'He took the accolades but it was very much a team effort. I think the main difference that had taken place over those five months was that Alan Brown had felt personally responsible for the team, whereas Bob allowed the players to take that responsibility. The atmosphere changed and a confidence spread throughout the team. We became confident – individually and collectively – and our confidence was sky high by the semi-final.'

'I have a photograph on my wall at home of Bob Stokoe in tears looking up at the Kop end at Hillsborough after the semi-final,' Sixsmith says. 'You can't buy a moment like that.'

'Hillsborough was the only time in my life that I ever saw my dad cry,' Peverley adds. 'He cried at the final whistle; Bob Stokoe wasn't the only grown man who was in tears at the end of the semi-final.'

'Bob Stokoe was a very emotional man and he could cry at the drop of a hat,' Montgomery says. 'That was really the moment when the Sunderland fans started calling him "Messiah". He just knew how the fans felt about it all – even if he was a Geordie in his heart deep down. He still knew what it meant to our supporters.'

'On my dying bed I will lie there and I will think about when we went back out on to the pitch after the semi-final,' Pitt says. 'I went out there in my stockinged feet and I was crying – I'm nearly crying now just thinking about it – and Stokoe was crying as well. What a fantastic moment that was. The ground was a mass of red and white. It was one of those moments that makes the hairs stand up on the back of your neck and you get this shiver down your spine. It is one of those moments in your life that you just never forget and even after all this time it still brings tears to my eyes and makes me shiver because Sunderland was my club. I had gone to Roker Park with my two uncles, Uncle Tommy and Uncle George, and they had taken me when I was six years old to stand at the back of the Fulwell End. They used to stand me on the fence and then go into the middle of the Fulwell End and shout and chant and come back and collect me at the end of the match. So for me to be a Sunderland supporter and to have gone through everything that I had gone through that season under Stokoe and then to end up playing in an FA Cup final was just – well, how can you explain that?'

'I think I became more aware of what had been achieved when I saw the highlights on the television later on and Bob Stokoe with tears in his eyes and all that,' Hughes adds. 'That was the moment for me. It was a while before it all sunk in that we were actually going to Wembley.'

'We really didn't have much time to think about what we had achieved,' Tueart says. 'Things were happening so quickly to us. We were a young team – even though the majority of us had been together for quite a long time – and it was like a whirlwind for us.'

'The great thing about the semi-final was that we beat Arsenal on merit,' Kerr adds. 'We took them on and we beat them well. We fully deserved our place in the Cup final.'

'I guess I'd look at it that seven times out of ten we would have beaten Sunderland, maybe twice there might have been a draw and on one occasion Sunderland might have won – and that was the occasion when we played them,' Wilson says. 'It is all about the day and how people react and everything else that goes with it, and on that day there was no fluke about what Sunderland did. They had a fantastic group of players who all had a huge respect for each other, knew each other's strengths and weaknesses and had togetherness and belief. But a team can only achieve something like that if they've got the support. Those fans were behind them all the way, literally willing them on and driving them on to Wembley. I will always remember those Sunderland supporters.

'It was desperate in our dressing room afterwards. It hit me hard personally, after all the effort and hard work of getting fit and after the disappointment of missing out on the 1972 FA Cup final. As it turned out for me, that was my last chance. I never played at Wembley again and I don't think there was anything worse at that time than being on the losing side in a semi-final. It was absolute dejection, despondency, letting the fans down, letting yourself down. I got no sleep that night. I just went over and over the game in my head.'

'We didn't want to lose the semi-final and I wouldn't have liked to be a loser that day,' Watson adds. 'We went into the match feeling we could win, but then it was the first semi-final we had all played in. We were all new to it and we didn't know what it was like to lose. Although it was 2–1 in the end, we were better winners than that. The scoreline didn't reflect the game. We were comfortable winners on the day.'

'We could have been 4–0 up by half-time,' Hughes says. 'Arsenal had a lot of great players, people like Charlie George, who I thought was one of the greatest players I had ever seen. But he just didn't seem to be on the ball that day. Maybe that was because we didn't allow them to play. We just played our natural game: when we got the ball we went forward; when we lost the ball, we all got back. Arsenal didn't seem to have the teamwork that we had for each other. They were more individuals rather than a team. We had great individual players but we would still die for the next guy. We worked our socks off for each other. The only one that was running about in the Arsenal side in the way all of us were running about was little Geordie Armstrong. He worked like a beaver, but one against eleven is no contest.'

'That was most certainly the game to do the business in,' Malone says. 'We believed in ourselves. We had nothing to fear because we weren't expected to win, but we knew what to expect from them and they didn't know what to expect from us, so they got a shock when we hit them with our style of play. We were playing really well by then as well.'

Arsenal were still very much involved in the First Division title race. That same afternoon Liverpool lost 2–1 at Birmingham City to leave the Gunners one point behind them with five matches still to play. But that was of little consolation to the Arsenal players sat in the dressing room at Hillsborough. 'No, none at all,' Wilson says, shaking his head.

'I remember walking into the Arsenal dressing room sometime after the match and Alan Ball was in there on his own,' Cox says. 'He still hadn't dried himself properly. I knew Alan from working with his father, Alan Ball Senior, at Preston. Alan said to me, "We were terrible, Arthur." But I said to Alan, "No, *we* played well." We did play well too.'

'They never stopped coming at us,' Ball later reflected. 'They were harassing, chasing, fighting back for the ball. We could never settle.'

'It was our worst performance of the season,' Mee said. 'We were way below par. Sunderland deserved to win. They were better than us on the day.'

'My brother and my father had gone in the Kop end and I had been sat in the seats so I hadn't seen them at all during the match,' Sunderland supporter Steve Hodgson says. 'I walked back to our car and when my brother and I saw each other we just raced towards each other and started hugging. It was a truly fantastic day. I was never worried at all during the match, which for me is unusual. Maybe I had trouble taking it in that we were beating Arsenal so comfortably!'

Arsenal's form faded badly after that defeat at Hillsborough. One win from those remaining five league matches was to be nowhere near good enough to challenge Liverpool for the title. In the football classic *Fever Pitch*, author and Arsenal fan Nick Hornby suggests Sunderland may have marked a change in the direction of the Gunners that day. The team of double winners began to break up shortly afterwards – as soon as McLintock left the club to join QPR at the end of a season that finished with a 6–1 thrashing at Elland Road against Leeds.

'That result still hurts to this day,' Wilson says. 'We knew we had finished second by then but it was 1–1 with twenty minutes to go. We were on a plane the next day for the end-of-season tour and everybody's mind was on going away the next day, which is disgraceful really. There were rows in the dressing room and on the bus after that match about wearing the shirt of Arsenal and what it meant. The senior players were very upset and it was the only time in my career that I ever let in six. I remember Bob McNab was screaming at everyone afterwards. It was a horrible experience.'

The Sunderland players boarded the team coach at Hillsborough to chants of 'We shall not be moved' from over a thousand Sunderland supporters waiting outside to wave them off from the ground with their red-and-white scarves.

The players celebrated their achievement in reaching the FA Cup final with a dinner at the Hallam Towers Hotel in Sheffield that evening. 'It was some party,' Montgomery says. 'My mate used to work away on the rigs but he was there – he made sure he came to the final too – and we had our wives and our parents with us. It was a great night. It was a massive win for us that day. To get to Wembley and everything that went with it was just phenomenal.'

Amid the celebrations news came through that Leeds had beaten Wolves 1–0 in the other semi-final at Maine Road. Billy Bremner had scored the only goal of a fiery encounter that saw Jack Charlton limp off injured, John Richards hit a post and Derek Dougan go close with a header late on. The 1973 FA Cup final was to be between Leeds United and Sunderland.

Peter Lorimer, one of the stars of that Leeds side, remembers hearing the shock news that Sunderland had beaten Arsenal to deny a repeat of the previous year's final: 'We couldn't believe it,' he says. 'We all expected Arsenal to win. So when we heard the result we just felt that it would be a formality for us in the final.'

This air of confidence soon spread from the Leeds players to their supporters. 'We were travelling back home from Hillsborough and to this day I can still see some Leeds fans standing on one of the bridges over the motorway with a big banner that said LEEDS UNITED, FA CUP WINNERS 1973. It was literally just a few hours after we had beaten Arsenal,' Dobson recalls.

Wolves manager Bill McGarry had made a point of not congratulating Don Revie after the game. 'People expected me to do the polite thing and say well done to him,' he said. 'I couldn't. They are words that would have stuck in my throat. I was staggered during our semi-final at the way Billy Bremner went the whole ninety minutes disputing every decision given against Leeds.' A thoughtful Stokoe would later read those words with interest.

And so began the build-up to what was, on paper, potentially the most one-sided FA Cup final in history. Sunderland's wins against Manchester City and Arsenal appeared to count for nothing as virtually everyone outside County Durham predicted a comfortable win for Leeds. It was nothing new and the Sunderland players – confident and relaxed all the way through with not a care in the world – continued to enjoy their celebrations in Sheffield.

'We didn't care who we played in the final,' Tueart says. 'Leeds, Wolves, it didn't matter to us. We believed in ourselves as a group of players and we really didn't care about the opposition.'

But there was one man who did care about the opposition. Everything had now come full circle for Stokoe, all those years after his first managerial encounter with Revie back in Bury in 1962. For all the Leeds manager had since achieved in the game, the Sunderland boss had now been handed an opportunity to pit his wits against him on the biggest stage of all. There could have been no bigger stage. For a man who could not forgive and could not forget, this was his chance for retribution.

'It is so unbelievable,' Stokoe said that night. 'We were the better team in every way today and after beating Manchester City and Arsenal we are now ready for Leeds United. We will be just as full of confidence at Wembley.' That final comment would prove to be an understatement.

11.

LEEDS! LEEDS! LEEDS!

Allan Clarke's diving header had won Leeds United the centenary FA Cup final of 1972 against Arsenal and put the league and Cup double within their grasp, an achievement that would surely have brought comparisons with the great sides of the past – Real Madrid included – and also some much-needed respite for the club's long-suffering manager. But it was not to be. Something got the better of Don Revie's men at Molineux against Wolverhampton Wanderers just over forty-eight hours later, and yet another opportunity for his team to be recognised as one of the greatest sides of this era had slipped through their grasp.

By the summer of 1972 Leeds had won five major trophies under Revie – the 1968–69 league championship, the 1967–68 League Cup and the 1967–68 and 1970–71 Inter-Cities Fairs Cups – but there had been a multitude of runners-up disappointments as well. Five of them had come in the First Division, with three more in various Cup finals, including two in the FA Cup. These near-misses were celebrated far and wide across the country, for this team was known as 'Dirty Leeds' – the most loathed side the nation had ever seen. Whatever Revie's men had achieved had been dissipated by a reputation for gamesmanship and a variety of other misdemeanours.

It was a far cry from the ideals Revie had adopted in his playing days, which had convinced Harry Reynolds and the Leeds board to give him the job in the first place. This had been replaced by a will to win at all costs as Leeds kicked their way out of the Second Division, into the First Division and Europe. They were resolute and rugged; victorious but often vicious. The sad part was that there were tremendously talented players in their ranks. There were moments during the 1971–72 season when public recognition of this ability finally replaced headlines about their armour. It had taken ten years, but Leeds were now playing the type of football associated with the Spanish greats Revie had idolised so much and set as a benchmark for his own ambitions.

One match stood out above the rest: the 7–0 thrashing of Southampton on 4 March 1972. At the end of this match there was an unbroken sequence of twenty-six Leeds passes that pushed the skills of this side to the fore, epitomised by an audacious back-heel flick from Johnny Giles on to the chest of Clarke. 'Oh, look at that,' BBC commentator Barry Davies remarked on *Match of the Day* that night. 'To say Leeds are playing with Southampton is the understatement of the season.' Elland Road had become a fortress. A fortnight earlier Leeds had defeated Manchester United 5–1, and by the end of March league champions and FA Cup holders Arsenal had succumbed 3–0, while Nottingham Forest would be thrashed 6–1. The reason for these performances and results was quite simple: the team Revie had created was at last being allowed to be creative.

'Leeds were really at their pomp then and that was brilliant to watch,' Davies says. 'There was an arrogance about them, it was almost cruel. But there wasn't enough of that on show in that side in my view. Don Revie was an artistic player and a real thinker but when he came into management his instincts were to make sure that you won the ball and you were somewhat conservative. I believe if they had played with more freedom then they might have got more credit. Leeds were one of the great sides at club level during my time as a commentator, but they could have been even better and their record should have been better, and sadly a large part of that was down to Don.'

Peter Lorimer agrees with Davies's assessment: 'I don't honestly know if Don Revie ever realised just how talented our team was,' he says. 'There were many games when we went one up and we could have gone on and swamped teams but Don wanted us to sit tight and not give the ball away. We had a great work ethic and that is the way Don liked it to be, but when he relaxed the reins and allowed us to show what we could do I think he was amazed by what a group of talented individuals he had in his squad. It was probably one of the finest periods of football and as good as anybody will ever see. The quality of the goals and the individual ability of the players came to the fore at that time and I think it surprised a lot of people who thought that Leeds were just a machine that grind out wins week in, week out.

I think this was the time when people saw just how useful a side we were.

'That game against Southampton, the reason it was only seven – it could have been ten or eleven – was because Don was pretty friendly with their manager, Ted Bates, and he actually told us to cool it down a bit,' Lorimer reveals. 'Don was trying to say to us that this was sort of embarrassing for Ted. Well, of course, passing the ball around at the end was featured on television more than the goals anyway, so that made it bloody worse for Ted in fact. It certainly made it worse for their players, lads like Mick Channon and Ron Davies. Southampton had some very useful players and they just couldn't get a touch of the ball. But that was the reason why that came about at the end of that particular match – it was Don saying to us, "OK, putting the ball in the net is easy for you, so just keep the ball now." But that was easy for us as well.

'I think we were all a little bit older and we had a lot more belief in ourselves as individuals,' Lorimer adds. 'In the beginning we were a manufactured team, a bit like robots who performed in a certain way that Don wanted us to. But the way he had the unit working was successful so you keep to the plan, don't you? We would always verge on the safety side rather than the adventurous side at that time, so it was great to finally show what we could do on the pitch and score lots of goals too.'

Leeds had made their name in the 1960s and early 1970s by grinding out one-goal wins at home and abroad, mainly because Revie was so anxious and uptight about the prospect of losing matches. He would do anything in his power to maintain control, and those early superstitions that had reared their head during his playing days would go into overdrive during his managerial career: rituals soon became a science to him.

The signing of Bobby Collins in March 1962 not only saved Leeds from relegation; it defined the way the team would play for a generation. The following summer more money was made available to Revie and he set about bringing the crowds back by re-signing John Charles – a hero in the days of blue and gold at Leeds – for £53,000 from a successful period with Italian giants Juventus. Charles brought the good-will factor back to Elland Road but featured just eleven times for the new all-white outfit before returning to Serie A with AS Roma.

However brief it may have been, the return of Charles crucially bought Revie time. When the Welshman went back to Italy the look of the Leeds side had changed dramatically, with three teenagers emerging as regular members of the first team: Norman Hunter, Paul Reaney and Gary Sprake. Revie was fortunate to inherit these players – plus the likes of Terry Cooper and Paul Madeley – from the junior side left behind by his predecessor Jack Taylor, but the rest was undoubtedly down to him. Hunter – who was almost released shortly before Revie's appointment – had joined the Leeds ground staff as an inside-forward; Reaney was a centre-half; while Cooper had been playing on the left wing. Revie began to mould these players into the talent they would become. When Hunter and Reaney made their league debuts at Swansea Town in September 1962, Hunter played at left-half and Reaney played at right-back; when Cooper later joined the first team, he did so at left-back. All of these players would go on to play for England in these new positions, each one handed to them by Revie.

Three weeks after the Swansea match Lorimer was given his league debut, at the age of just fifteen years and 289 days, at Southampton. The player had been plucked from under the noses of several interested British clubs by Revie, who was so keen to get his signature that he was stopped for speeding in his blue Ford Zephyr on his way up to Dundee. Another Scot, Eddie Gray, who hailed from Glasgow, turned down no fewer than thirty-five clubs the following year due to the lure of the persuasive Leeds boss and his amazing plan to turn an unfashionable Second Division side into one of the best teams in the world. Scottish scouts alerted Revie to the best local talent around, but getting the youngsters to sign on the dotted line was down to him and him alone.

'Don Revie had a vision from the start,' Lorimer explains. 'We all came through the youth system and that was something he planned. You have to be lucky sometimes with young boys that it all happens, but it all happened at Leeds, so you have got to say that he was ahead of other managers in his way of thought. There were strict rules: we were one of the first teams to have a training regime and a doctor. We had suggested diets, ate the proper foods and weren't allowed to drink twenty-four hours before a game. The training schedules were very tough. The stamina training we used to do was unbelievable actually.'

With a back-room team of assistant manager Maurice Lindley, first-team coach Syd Owen and trainer Les Cocker, Revie created one of the toughest training schedules in the country through constant running and intensive gymnasium work, making his young charges one of the fittest sides in the league. He also set about creating a family spirit at the club, well supported by his wife Elsie.

'He wanted us to meet a nice girl and get settled down rather than be young, footloose and fancy-free,' Lorimer says. 'Elsie was very much involved. They were a good team and they worked well together. She was involved in everything. But at the end of the day it was about winning football matches for him. We always went away the night before a match, even for home matches. It didn't always suit our families, but it was accepted. He always involved the families, every chance he got. He encouraged that kind of thing. This was the team spirit he wanted us to have.'

'That Leeds team was a family unit and Don Revie got more support and loyalty from his players than any team manager I have ever come across,' Davies says. 'I can't remember ever talking to a Leeds player who had a bad word to say about him.'

Due to a much tighter defence and the goals of Jim Storrie, Leeds finished the 1962–63 season fifth in the Second Division. It was a substantial improvement on the previous campaign, which had so nearly resulted in relegation to the Third Division, and Revie was rewarded with an improved contract to become the highest-paid manager outside the top flight.

An example of his man-management skills was the way in which he secured the long-term futures of Billy Bremner and Jack Charlton at this time. Both players had been first-team regulars but both had become problematic: Bremner was homesick; Charlton, who had been at the club since 1952, was by his own admission 'a one-man awkward squad'.

During his own playing days at Elland Road, Revie once told Charlton that if he had been manager of Leeds he would not play him in his side. During the early days of Revie's managerial reign at Leeds, Charlton refused to sign a new contract and on one occasion travelled over the Pennines to speak to Manchester United manager Matt Busby about a move to Old Trafford – the deal only fell through when Busby suggested putting it on hold until the new season so that he could look at the merits of another player already at the club. As Charlton recalled in his autobiography *Charlton*, he immediately changed tack and told Busby so in no uncertain terms:

I have caused ructions at Elland Road. I have refused to sign a contract. Nobody there is speaking to me. I have caused bloody havoc in the club. I have been offered a deal and turned it down – and now you are telling me I have got to wait until the beginning of the new season, until you have had a look at someone else? No, I am not going to do that, I am going back to Elland Road, and I am going to apologise for what I have done. I am going to sign a new contract with the club and I am not bloody well coming here.

That was a turning point for player, manager, club and country. Charlton never looked back, and a few months later Revie suggested to him that if he tried harder and changed his attitude he could one day play for England. By 1965 Charlton was in the England team and the following year he won a World Cup winners' medal.

Bremner and Revie were once room-mates as well as team-mates at Leeds, but shortly after Revie became manager his young protégé asked to be put on the transfer list, citing his wish to return to Scotland to be near to his girlfriend. Hibernian offered £25,000 for Bremner, who at that time was playing at inside-forward or on the wing, but Revie – still unsure of the player's best position but nevertheless reluctant to lose him – rejected the bid. He then upped the asking price to prevent any possible move materialising.

Revie also threatened to leave Leeds if the board forced him to sell Bremner. He was determined not only to keep the young Scot but to build his future team, hopes and dreams around him. In the end he drove up to Scotland to visit the player's girlfriend and told her of his plans and vision for the club, and Bremner was persuaded to come off the transfer list. The fiery Scot became the club's driving force and inspiration and went on to make 586 full league appearances for them. Charlton made a club-record 629.

Bremner was moved into midfield to play alongside Collins. This was to create one of the most forceful midfields the game had ever known when, within a week of the start of the 1963–64 season, Republic of Ireland international winger Johnny Giles signed from First Division Manchester United for £33,000. Giles had won an FA Cup winners' medal with United just three months beforehand, but had surprisingly been left out of his team's opening league fixture of the new season at Sheffield Wednesday. He asked to be put on the transfer list and Revie snapped him up within a day.

Leeds won the Second Division title and promotion to the First Division. But success came at a price: with Bremner, Collins and Giles pulling the strings, the drive to the top flight was based on a team spirit that often bordered on physical intimidation, epitomised by a sign hanging in the home dressing room at Elland Road that said KEEP FIGHTING.

'I think the "Dirty Leeds" tag started in order to get them up into the First Division in the first place,' Davies suggests. 'There is no doubt that Leeds strong-armed or strong-footed their way out of the Second Divison. They had probably the hardest player – in terms of his mental view – in Giles. There was a cruel, calculating side to a brilliant player. Most successful teams need a ball winner, but there aren't too many teams who've had ball winners who could be as creative as Giles, Bremner and Collins. These were three small, hard-nut players who could really play.'

But just how hard did Revie believe his players to be? 'I recall that I once went to do a radio interview with Billy Bremner at that time when Leeds were staying in London,' Gerald Sinstadt recalls. 'I met Don Revie beforehand and he invited me up to Billy's room to do the interview. We went into the room and he was there in his bed, fast asleep. Don turned to me and said, "Look at him, he's like a little cherub." I was taken aback. It certainly wasn't the Bremner image I was used to. That phrase has always stuck in my mind whenever I think of those two.'

A more brazen analysis comes from Giles: 'You had to establish a reputation that would make people think twice about messing with you,' he wrote in his book *Forward with Leeds*. 'You had to get respect,' he added, 'in the sense that people could not clog you without knowing you would clog them back.'

Ahead of the 1964–65 season, the Football Association produced a league table of English clubs' disciplinary records; Leeds had the worst. 'Dirty Leeds' was a nickname that was known up and down the country. The question now was: would First Division sides be better equipped to cope with Leeds' much-criticised but ultimately successful style of play than their Second Division counterparts had been?

The answer was no. Leeds won their first three matches – including a 4–2 victory over defending champions Liverpool – to surge to the top of the Football League. The First Division didn't know what had hit it.

In a match against Everton at Goodison Park in November, referee Ken Stokes had to take both teams off the pitch as matters came to a head with a chest-high tackle from Leeds' Willie Bell on Everton's Derek Temple. The teams walked off to shouts of 'Dirty Leeds – Dirty Leeds.' Leeds won the match, 1–0.

George Best once said that the only time he wore shinpads was when he played against Leeds. In his autobiography, *The Best of Times*, he also claimed that less than a month after that Everton-versus-Leeds match he was kicked by Collins as the Manchester United and Leeds players walked down the tunnel at Old Trafford before a crucial top-of-the-table clash and was then told, 'And that's just for starters, Bestie.' Leeds also won that match 1–0.

As Leeds supporters Rob Bagchi and Paul Rogerson put it in their book *The Unforgiven*:

Over the next five years as Manchester United conquered Europe and Best was at his peak, he tore countless teams to shreds, but for all his sublime ability he never once dominated a game against Leeds United. It wasn't because Best was physically frightened by Leeds, simply that Leeds were prepared to use every weapon at their disposal to stop him playing, whether physical, psychological, tactical or, like the tunnel assault, borderline criminal.

Best later referred to Bremner and Giles as an 'unusual mixture of delicate skills and hard man tendencies'.

Going into the final week of his first season as a First Division manager, Revie stood on the threshold of winning Leeds' first major honours. Against all the odds his uncompromising side stood at the top of the table – albeit having played one game more than second-placed Manchester United – and had reached the FA Cup final, where they were due to meet Bill Shankly's Liverpool. It was possible Leeds could win the double just three short years after narrowly avoiding relegation to the Third Division.

But Leeds did not win either the league or the FA Cup that season. They lost the First Division title on goal average to Manchester United after a bizarre match at bottom-of-the-table Birmingham, which they drew 3–3 after being 3–0 down after an hour. With the game and the title seemingly lost, Revie urged his players to ease up with the Cup final in mind, yet they fought back and miraculously almost clinched the title: Hunter hit the post in injury time. The following weekend a tired Leeds were beaten 2–1 after extra-time by Liverpool at Wembley.

The club's highest-ever league finish and a first Wembley appearance meant little. Collins was also voted the Football Writers' Footballer of the Year, but the headline was that Leeds had won nothing. But the First Division runners-up spot did at least mean that European football came to Leeds for the first time, in the shape of the Inter-Cities Fairs Cup, and subsequently a growing education was now to come from a hard school.

Leeds defeated Italian side Torino in the first round but at a massive cost; while defending a 2–1 home-leg advantage in Turin, Collins was stretchered off with a broken thighbone – an injury that was to effectively end his career. Leeds held out for a goalless draw to go through, but things would never quite be the same again. Bremner took over as team captain.

By the time of the next round, against SC Leipzig of East Germany, Giles had been moved into the centre of midfield and Lorimer had come in on the right wing. Six inches of snow overnight made for treacherous conditions in Leipzig and a match Lorimer remembers well:

We played in studs and Don and his coaching staff had shaved off the bottom layer of the leather so that the nails poked through, allowing us to get a foothold on the ice. They knew our studs would be checked, so on each of them they affixed a cardboard tip to hide the nails. We kicked off the cardboard as we came out for the kick-off. Within minutes blood was oozing from all of their players' legs and they were complaining furiously to the referee.

Their protests fell on deaf ears, with the official insisting that he had already checked our boots he recalled in his autobiography *Leeds and Scotland Hero*. Leeds won the match 2–1, and a goalless draw at home put them into the last sixteen. Revie's side had arrived in Europe.

The visit of Valencia to Elland Road in the third-round second leg of the competition secured the infamous name of 'Dirty Leeds' in the annals of European football, when Dutch referee Leo Horne took all twenty-two players off the pitch after a twelve-man brawl was sparked when Charlton was spat at in the face and retaliated with his fists. Charlton and two Valencia players were sent off and the police had to restore order. Leeds again went through, 2–1 on aggregate.

'One of the great things about that Leeds side was that we could play anybody however they wanted to play: if a team wanted to play football, we could play football; if a team wanted a battle, we could out-battle anybody. It used to finish up that teams got more than they bargained for when they played us and they certainly never looked forward to coming to Elland Road,' Lorimer says. 'That was one of our great assets: we were all in it together – you kicked one and you kicked us all – and we seldom lost in European matches because we were prepared for anything.'

Preparation also meant dossiers on the opposition. Revie remembered to good effect how Septimus Smith's reports had helped Leicester City reach the FA Cup final in 1949, and from the early days of his managerial career at Elland Road he would study pages and pages of information on opposition teams and players, carefully recorded by Lindley and Owen. These listed all the strengths and weaknesses of the opposition – no matter how strong or how weak. The detailed information was then passed on to the players in a pre-match meeting.

Revie's dossiers became a bureaucratic spine to his careful match preparation. His focus usually centred on the other team and not his own. A defensive policy to stop them playing grew at a pace and, it could be said, at a cost: Leeds had talent, but the purity of it was seldom allowed to shine through at this time.

'When we played in European matches the dossiers were important because you didn't see these guys week to week,' Lorimer says. 'But we did this for every game, no matter whom we played. We may have been playing some no-hope Fourth Division team in the FA Cup at home and by the time Don had had them watched three times and had finished with his dossiers, we used to be saying to each other, "How the hell are they in the Fourth Division?" Sometimes he would get a little bit carried away and I think, looking back on it, maybe he was a little bit over the top with it. But that was Don. He thought that if he didn't prepare us and tell us everything a team did – free-kicks, corner kicks, players who had to be watched – we could lose the match and then he would have blamed himself. He felt that as long as he had covered everything he had done his job and it was then down to the team.'

Leeds beat Ujpest Dozsa of Hungary 5–2 on aggregate in the quarter-finals of their first European campaign to set up a semi-final clash against Real Zaragoza of Spain. They lost the first leg away from home 1–0 and won the second leg 2–1. With no away-goals rule in place, the toss of a coin determined that Elland Road would be the venue for a deciding third match. Revie summoned the fire brigade down to the ground and asked them to flood the pitch with gallons of water, turning it into a quagmire. The opposition complained but the match went ahead. But it was all to no avail: Leeds were beaten 3–1.

If defeat in the Fairs Cup semi-finals was disappointing, so too was another runners-up spot in the First Division, this time to Liverpool. In his autobiography *Biting Talk*, Norman Hunter suggests that Revie's superstitious thoughts may now have started to impact on some of the players' minds: 'For our first two seasons in the top division our achievements were fantastic but having been runners-up in the championship twice, beaten Cup finalists and losing in a European semi-final, we began to wonder if there was some sort of jinx on us,' he wrote. If there was a jinx then Revie hoped he had found the answer to it when he invited a gypsy over to Elland Road to exorcise the ground that summer.

Leeds came a step closer to Fairs Cup success in the 1966–67 season but had to settle for a runners-up spot when Dinamo Zagreb beat them over two legs in the final. There was also a controversial exit from the FA Cup at the semi-final stage against Chelsea at Villa Park when they were on the receiving end of a debatable decision by referee Ken Burns. Chelsea led through a Tony Hateley goal when – with just one minute left on the clock – Leeds, who had already had one goal by Cooper disallowed, were awarded a free-kick outside the Chelsea penalty box. Giles rolled the ball to Lorimer, who hit a scorcher into the net, but the strike was ruled out on account of the Chelsea wall not retreating the ten yards to where Burns was standing. Leeds protested but the referee was unmoved. 'In effect, he punished us for the failings of the opposition,' Hunter commented. The free-kick was retaken and cleared and Chelsea went through to the final to face Tottenham, but the disallowed goal remained the big talking point. 'You'll have to look in the rulebook backwards to find a reason,' mulled *Match of the Day* commentator Kenneth Wolstenholme. Burns joined a growing list of officials who had upset Revie.

Charlton was crowned the Football Writers' Footballer of the Year in 1967 – the second Leeds player to win the award in three years – but after three seasons in the top flight the club had still won no silverware. With journalists now using words such as 'bridesmaids' and 'chokers' to describe the team in their match reports, Revie signed England international striker Mick Jones for a club-record fee and set his side a target: win any two trophies from the four competitions entered the following season – First Division, FA Cup, League Cup and Fairs Cup.

The club's first major silverware finally arrived in March 1968, when a volley from Cooper was enough to beat Arsenal in a highly physical League Cup final at Wembley. The physical nature of the match set the agenda between these two sides for several seasons and did nothing to help Leeds' reputation down south.

'We were hated in London,' Lorimer says. 'The press hated us because we always went down there and won, so we weren't liked. We were an aggressive team and so we were the team that people loved to hate. The London clubs were also having a hard time. I know Arsenal did eventually win something but most of the success came in the north – Leeds, Liverpool, Manchester United, Manchester City – at that time. We became the targets of the London journalists and Don used to use that all the time. He would get all the London editions of the newspapers on the Friday night and show us what they were saying about us. He loved doing that. He would then tell us, "Get out and show them, so they will write something really bad about you on Sunday morning when you have stuffed them." He used it all as a positive and it worked. Nobody likes unfair criticism and they were criticising us because we were consistent, we were good, we were strong, we were ruthless. We also had a lot of ability, but they never mentioned that.'

A second trophy followed six months later, in September 1968, when Leeds defeated Hungarian side Ferencváros in the held-over final of the Fairs Cup over two legs. But Revie's men failed to land either of the big two trophies – they totally floundered in the league by losing their last four matches to finish fourth in the table, and went out of the FA Cup in the semi-finals again, this time to Everton.

Some Leeds players started to consider that Revie's reluctance to rotate his squad, despite the enormous number of fixtures his team consistently had to play on all fronts – 127 matches in the last two seasons alone – was contributing to the now common collapse at the end of a campaign. But the manager remained unmoved and stubbornly proved his point by playing only twelve players regularly throughout the 1968–69 season as his team were eventually crowned Football League champions.

Leeds won the title with a record number of points, just two defeats and in front of a sell-out crowd of 53,750 at Anfield against their nearest challengers Liverpool. After the match the home supporters chanted, 'Champions!' as Revie and his players applauded the Kop. 'It was a fantastic moment and one of the greatest gestures I have ever experienced,' Bremner said. Shankly visited the Leeds dressing room after the match, shook Revie's hand and told him, 'You're worthy champions. If it wasn't going to be us, you're the next best.' Revie never forgot it.

Leeds now had a league championship to defend and, at long last, a European Cup campaign to enter against the likes of AC Milan, Benfica, Celtic, Feyenoord and – to Revie's delight – Real Madrid. In preparation he went out and smashed the British transfer record in the summer of 1969 by signing Allan Clarke from Leicester for £165,000. The league champions set their sights on creating history. The aim was to win an unprecedented treble of Football League, FA Cup and European Cup. It was some plan in this season of all seasons: the forthcoming World Cup in Mexico had led the FA and the Football League to end the domestic season in mid-April to allow England as much time as possible to defend their crown, and as a result the FA Cup final was scheduled for 11 April – the earliest date it had been played since 1894.

Revie's men kicked off their European Cup campaign with purpose by recording a 10–0 home win (16–0 on aggregate) against Norwegian champions SK Lyn Oslo. By late March things looked to be going to plan: Leeds were top of the First Division with just seven games to go, and had reached the semi-finals of both Cup competitions. But an insurmountable problem loomed: fixture congestion. To make matters worse Leeds then drew twice with Manchester United in the FA Cup before eventually defeating them at Burnden Park to reach Wembley and a final against Chelsea.

Faced with an almost impossible schedule, Revie decided he had to concede on one front to try and succeed on the other two. He chose to concentrate on the two trophies Leeds had not won – the FA Cup and the European Cup – and jettisoned the league by fielding inexperienced reserves. With one Cup final place already achieved, he prepared for the first leg of the European Cup semi-final clash against Celtic on 1 April by resting half of his side for the First Division match at home to Southampton on 28 March, and then fielded a reserve side at Derby County on 30 March. Leeds lost both matches (3–1 and 4–1 respectively) and then received a £5,000 fine from the Football League and the wrath of its secretary Alan Hardaker for fielding an under-strength side at the Baseball Ground. Revie and Leeds were now as unpopular with the authorities as they were on the terraces and in the media.

Leeds played nine matches in twenty-five days during this time, including five games in just over a week. Two days after the Derby defeat they were beaten 1–0 at home by Celtic in the opening leg of the European Cup semi-final. Jock Stein's side – well on their way to a fifth successive Scottish League championship – were now clear favourites to progress to the final. With Revie giving up on the league, and any hopes of European Cup success requiring a victory in Glasgow, winning the Cup final against Chelsea became imperative.

On an awful pitch – damaged by the staging of the Horse of the Year Show during the previous week – Leeds led twice through goals from Charlton and Jones and stood a few minutes away from glory. Television pictures clearly showed Revie battling past a police cordon to instruct his players to close it up. But his players couldn't hear him. Ian Hutchison equalised for Chelsea on eighty-six minutes and the match finished 2–2. Princess Margaret sympathised with Bremner after the final whistle, telling him, 'I am sorry you haven't got the Cup yet,' from the Royal Box. It was the first Cup final replay in fifty-eight years.

Before that replay came the task of overturning Celtic's advantage in the European Cup. In a fascinating BBC television documentary entitled *United We Fall*, which details the end of Leeds' exhausting 1969–70 season, there is an illuminating section, filmed behind closed doors, which shows Revie talking his players through the pre-match dossiers on Celtic. In the film Revie concentrates on the strengths of winger Jimmy Johnstone and midfielder Bertie Auld, both of whom, he says, require special attention: 'What we have to do is get close to Jimmy Johnstone so that he doesn't start them twists and turns, pulling players out of position every time he gets it.' But the Leeds players, sitting and listening, appear tired and in some cases even distant. 'Push up on Bertie Auld to stop him picking up loose balls out of the box to set Celtic going,' Revie tells them.

After the dossiers, the Leeds players often relaxed by playing bingo, dominoes, cards or carpet bowls. Revie felt that such preparation was vital ahead of big matches and no match came bigger than a European Cup semi-final second leg played in front of a record attendance for a football match between two British clubs of 136,505 at Hampden Park.

Leeds took an early lead through Bremner in Glasgow, but two goals in six minutes at the start of the second half from John Hughes and Bobby Murdoch gave Celtic a 2–1 win (3–1 on aggregate) and a place in the final against Feyenoord. At 1–1 Sprake was stretchered off after a collision with Hughes. Replacement goalkeeper David Harvey picked the ball out of his net less than thirty seconds after coming on to replace him when – just as Revie had feared – Johnstone was allowed to twist and turn and create the winner for Murdoch. Feyenoord, led by the great Austrian manager Ernst Happel, went on to beat Celtic in the final, 2–1 after extra-time. Meanwhile Everton – with a midfield of Alan Ball, Colin Harvey and Howard Kendall – lifted the league championship trophy. With three points from their last six games, Leeds drifted away to finish nine points behind in second place.

The FA Cup final replay – held at Old Trafford on 29 April – was now all or nothing for Leeds. Revie told his players to go out and prove to the watching millions on television what a great side they were. Instead the match became notorious as one of the dirtiest games ever seen in English football. The basis for this was the switching of Chelsea full-back David Webb, who had been embarrassed by Gray on the left wing at Wembley, to central defence, with Ron 'Chopper' Harris taking over at right-back. Harris man-marked Gray out of the game, often using cynical and illegal tactics – one kick to the back of the knee virtually immobilised the Scot. Leeds took a first-half lead through Jones, who scored minutes after colliding with Peter Bonetti in a goal-mouth collision that injured the Chelsea goalkeeper. This only fired up an already heated contest, which by the end had featured almost fifty fouls plus a few instances of players squaring up to each other and trading punches.

Leeds stood twelve minutes from winning the FA Cup when an unmarked Peter Osgood equalised with a diving header. In the closing stages of normal time Eddie McGreadie's studs connected with the head of Bremner in the Chelsea penalty box, but nothing was given by referee Eric Jennings. The replay went into extra-time, making it the longest FA Cup final in history. Webb headed Chelsea into the lead after a long Hutchison throw-in on 104 minutes. It was the first time Leeds had been behind in the final, and it proved to be the winning goal of the contest.

The Leeds players trudged up the tunnel as one, disconsolate. Charlton was too upset to collect his losers' medal. A season that had promised so much had once more ended with nothing. After sixty-three matches Leeds had again finished empty-handed. There was some consolation in the award of Manager of the Year for the second year running to Revie, who was also awarded the OBE, while Bremner was overwhelmingly voted Football Writers' Footballer of the Year. But as the Leeds captain said himself in the title of his book, published at around this time, *You Get Nowt for Finishing Second*.

'We would probably have won a lot more had we not tried to win too much, if you know what I mean,' Lorimer says. 'Don wanted to win everything every year and I think this became a burden come the end of most seasons, because the players were getting tired. He believed in using just twelve or thirteen players and that was it. But I certainly think that team could have matched any team at any time. We were one of the finest teams.'

Revie would do anything in his power to change the fortunes of his side for the better. His habits of wearing the same lucky blue suit and walking to the same traffic lights before every home game were now well known, and this ritual became so obsessive that once, after breaking a zip, he wore a safety pin in his trousers so that he did not have to change his lucky attire. But how could he prepare for what was to happen to Leeds in the 1970–71 season, when they came up against a Colchester United side called 'Grandad's Army' in the FA Cup and later, at Elland Road, a referee called Ray Tinkler?

In February 1971 Leeds once again stood at the top of the First Division and were through to the last sixteen of the FA Cup. The draw appeared to have been kind to them, handing them an away trip to Fourth Division Colchester in the fifth round and therefore avoiding the likes of Arsenal, Everton, Liverpool and Tottenham, who were still in the competition.

Colchester, managed by Dick Graham – the man who had once kept Bob Stokoe in the game when he was down on his luck in the 1960s – had six first-team players aged over thirty, hence the team's nickname. The star player at Layer Road was striker Ray Crawford, a First Division winner with Ipswich Town back in the 1961–62 season and the owner of two England caps.

Graham prepared his players by telling them, 'Little old Colchester are taking on probably the greatest team in Europe. It's going to be a match everyone will be talking about and looking at. Everybody's going to be here: television, radio, all the papers. It's going to be something you remember all your lives. No nerves, no tension, just relax and, you know what, I think we can win.' It was a motivational speech straight out of the Stokoe handbook.

Leeds hired a private plane and travelled down to Essex in style. This only irritated the local fans and played into Graham's hands. Bremner was out injured and the home side attacked from the start on a rock-hard pitch with the wind behind them. Leeds went 3–0 down due to two goals from Crawford, one from David Simmons and a catalogue of errors by Sprake and his defence. The dossiers were now redundant. Revie desperately pushed Giles up front and his side fought back to 3–2, but it was too little too late. Amid a cacophony of whistles and several late goalmouth clearances, Colchester held on for one of the greatest shock results of the century.

Revie rallied his troops and focused on the title race. Leeds were clear favourites to win it again and were top of the table with just four games to go, with only Arsenal anywhere close, when West Bromwich Albion – without an away win all season – visited Elland Road. West Brom led 1–0 in the match when, twenty minutes into the second half, Tony Brown intercepted a misplaced pass from Hunter in his own half and, as the ball ran over the halfway line, Colin Suggett was flagged offside by linesman Bill Troupe. The players stopped but the referee ignored the linesman's flag and waved play on. Brown, who had slowed down while the ball was at his feet, now quickened his step and advanced into the Leeds penalty box, where he passed to Jeff Astle, who also appeared to be in an offside position, to score. Tinkler controversially allowed the goal to stand.

'And Leeds will go mad, and they have every right to go mad because everybody stopped with the linesman's flag,' Davies screamed on *Match of the Day*. 'Leeds have every justification for going mad, although one must add that they played to the linesman and not to the whistle.'

That wasn't the half of it. Revie came on to the pitch to appeal, encouraging Troupe to talk to Tinkler as he did so, and was waved away. Aghast, Revie looked up to the heavens in disgust. Grown men in suits and ties ran on to the field to remonstrate with the referee and were led away. It was pandemonium inside the ground and Troupe was hit on the head by a missile thrown from the crowd.

'In many respects it was an injustice,' Davies says. 'There was a distinct moment when everybody stopped, but play was then allowed to go on. I think that was unfair. Tony Brown didn't score, he passed the ball to Jeff Astle, who was in some danger of being offside himself, I recall.'

Clarke pulled a goal back but Leeds lost the match 2–1 and, despite winning their remaining three fixtures, went on to finish the season one point behind Arsenal, who celebrated winning the double after defeating Liverpool in the FA Cup final. Revie felt that one man and one man alone had cost Leeds the title that season, and as a result he called for full-time referees to be appointed.

'After the match Don Revie came to be interviewed on *Match of the Day* and he was absolutely breathing fire,' Davies says. 'I sent him back to the dressing room. I said to him: "Don, do yourself a favour, go away and count to ten." He was prepared to take my advice and he came back later to do the interview. There is no doubt that Leeds were going to win the title that season and that match cost them the championship.'

(Revie had crossed swords with Tinkler before. In October 1965 the referee had cautioned Bremner for dangerous play during a match against Northampton Town and Revie had asked afterwards if he would not report the incident. The Leeds manager was given short shrift and later warned about his future conduct by an FA disciplinary commission.)

At the end of the 1970–71 season Leeds beat a Juventus side featuring the likes of Roberto Bettega, Fabio Capello and Franco Causio on away goals after two draws (2–2 away, 1–1 at home) to win the last ever Fairs Cup – the competition's name was changed to the UEFA Cup from the following season – and claim their first silverware since the 1968–69 league championship. But the tags of 'bridesmaids' and 'chokers' were now as popular in describing Revie's side as 'Dirty Leeds' had ever been. There was also a sense that luck was never on their side. The superstitious Revie now went into overdrive and responded by ordering the motif of an owl to be removed from the left breast of the team shirt. Revie had a problem with birds anyway and believed the badge, which was loosely based on the City of Leeds coat of arms, was bringing bad luck to the club. It was replaced with the initials LUFC, written in italics, for the forthcoming season.

'I do believe that if you are a superstitious person then you are likely to think there is possibly something in things like that always going against you,' Davies says. 'Don would certainly have thought about that long and hard. He was a worrier and he had a belief in these things.'

It could be argued that Tinkler's decision at Elland Road in April 1971 inadvertently led to Leeds not wrapping up the First Division title the following season too, as punishment for the pitch invasion and the injury to the linesman meant Leeds played their first four home games away from Elland Road at three neutral venues – Huddersfield Town, Hull City and Sheffield Wednesday. The first two of these matches ended in draws in a season when Leeds were to be undefeated at home. Those two lost points against Wolves and Tottenham would prove to be costly. Ultimately a win in either game would have sealed the title by the time Leeds walked out to play Arsenal in the FA Cup final at Wembley.

If ever Leeds looked at their most complete it was surely in the spring of 1972. Five players – Madeley, Cooper, Bremner, Giles and Gray – all made it into the *Rothmans Football Yearbook* 'Golden Boots' Team of the Year. As the Leeds players and supporters sang 'Leeds! Leeds! Leeds!', the club anthem written and composed by Les Reed and Barry Mason (the same songwriters who penned the number one hit 'The Last Waltz' for Engelbert Humperdinck) and recorded to coincide with that year's Cup final appearance, Revie's men looked invincible. Eight back-to-back wins at Elland Road were achieved with an arrogance befitting the talent on show. This was the year Leeds introduced numbered sock tags to their kit and began home matches by standing in the centre circle and saluting the crowd before kicking footballs on to the terraces. After so many false dawns Leeds now looked unstoppable in their quest for the double. But, again, it was not to be.

'The defeat at Wolves was heartbreaking,' the missing Jones said some years later. 'I have never known a quieter dressing room. It was far worse than 1970 because we really deserved the double that season. We were by far the most adventurous and entertaining team. The closure of the ground at the beginning of the season had proved costly but the decision to play the final game so close to the FA Cup final ultimately cost us the title.'

This was not the first time Leeds had finished runners-up in the First Division. Neither was it the closest they had come to failure. But it was the closest they would ever come to doing the double and therefore possibly the most painful disappointment. It left a feeling of failure that overshadowed the Wembley win of just a few days before. But there was little sympathy at the home of the Blackpool manager on the north-west coast.

Bob Stokoe always looked out for Leeds' results, checking up on what his great nemesis was up to. The 1972–73 season had gone reasonably well for Revie, with progress to the finals of both the FA Cup and the European Cup Winners' Cup. Liverpool had knocked Leeds out of the League Cup and had also set the pace in the First Division as well. A troublesome thigh injury and subsequent operation kept Eddie Gray out of Revie's plans for large parts of the campaign, but with the climax of the season approaching and two Cup finals on the horizon, including the Wembley clash against Sunderland, Revie decided that the time could be right to bring him back.

12.

WEMBERLEE

Sunderland's build-up to Wembley was gathering pace: local politicians rejoiced and told of what the team's success could mean to the region, fans waited anxiously to hear news on ticket allocation, and Bob Stokoe considered how on his earth his team of heroes could play ten Second Division fixtures in the three weeks leading up to the FA Cup final.

'A few months ago no one seemed to want to know about Sunderland but now everybody wants to know,' Sunderland mayor Leslie Watson said. 'I don't think you can measure the value of this but I do know it is helping Sunderland as a town. Bob Stokoe's young team of heroes have become ambassadors for the town and their effort has generated a high morale in Sunderland.'

Production in the local factories, mines and shipyards continued to increase. Contracts at the shipyards of Austin & Pickersgill, Dexford and Sunderland had topped £98 million for the year so far, already surpassing the 1972 total. Absenteeism was reported to be at an all-time low in the workplace, and the Coles Cranes dispute was finally over.

As a thank-you gesture for rising sales Vaux Breweries had started to supply each of the twelve Sunderland players on FA Cup duty with crates of Vaux Norseman lager after every win in the competition. 'By the time we'd reached Wembley my garage was literally full with cans of lager!' a teetotal Dick Malone recalls.

The 'Messiah' was already the best football news story of the season and Tony Pawson, writing in the *Observer*, offered a candid analysis of the man in a special feature: 'He is a player's manager who knows his own success is dependent on coaxing the best from them,' he wrote.

He took over at Sunderland from Alan Brown, who has a remarkable record of achievement in developing young footballers without matching success on the field. Brown was a strict disciplinarian and the players responded at once to Stokoe's less formal approach. He encouraged them to enjoy their football and to enjoy their social life, provided they were unstinting of effort in a match. He believes that the professional player wants to improve, wants to win, and that the worthwhile footballer will always respond to encouragement.

At around the time that the *Observer* published this article, Alan Brown broke his silence on Stokoe's rapid achievement at Roker Park, saying: 'The present success is not the overnight miracle most people imagine it to be. It was built on solid foundations.' Stokoe immediately retorted: 'When I first came I was not worried about relegation, I was frightened to death. Enthusiasm as well as supporters had disappeared!'

Sunderland were allocated 20,000 of the 100,000 tickets for the FA Cup final. These tickets were priced at £8, £5, £4, £3, and £1 for standing. The day after the semi-final win over Arsenal, the club announced that another draw of the vouchers distributed at the Carlisle United and Bristol City home games, played at the end of March, would again decide which fans – along with the 4,500 season-ticket holders – would be lucky enough to get a place inside Wembley Stadium on 5 May 1973.

The streets of Sunderland were now full of men, women and children wearing red and white. Anything red and white was snapped up, including certain items that had stood unsold in shops for years. The demand on red wool in the town for scarves was so great that some fans had to settle for orange ahead of the big day. Many workers wore red-and-white boaters and rosettes, and it seemed almost every primary-school class in the area was making models or painting pictures of Sunderland players, Wembley Stadium and the FA Cup.

'I vividly remember making a life-size replica of the FA Cup out of silver foil,' says former World Championship 1,500m gold medal winner, world record holder, Olympic silver medallist and renowned Sunderland fan Steve Cram, who was a twelve-year-old schoolboy at the time. 'I was so proud of that.

'Football was all that seemed to matter at that time,' he adds. 'Nothing else was going on in the north-east. I stood in the Fulwell End for the Manchester City game and in the Roker End for the Luton Town game. The atmosphere and the noise at that time was fantastic.'

'Sunderland's success springs from team spirit – that and the remarkable resurgence of support which has brought back the halcyon days of North East soccer and with them, the "Roker Roar",' 'Argus' wrote in the *Sunderland Echo* after the win over Arsenal. 'Sunderland's players – believing in themselves but most of all in manager Bob Stokoe – played the game of their lives to give everyone with a Sunderland interest their biggest moment in 36 years.'

Fans sent the newspaper even more letters, photographs and memories of the Rokerites' 1937 FA Cup win. There were many stories of the FA Cup final defeat at Crystal Palace in 1913 too. John Hodgson of Hasting Street, aged eighty-six, had been at both matches and already had his ticket sorted out for the 1973 FA Cup final. 'If this is the last match I ever see, I am determined to be there,' he said.

There were plenty of poems too, the pick of the bunch coming from Alex Winter of Pallion, who wrote:

The night Sunderland beat Arsenal,
I am sure you all know,
The clouds shook with wonder,
And down came the snow;
'Can it be Christmas?'
A friend of mine said
As, amazed by events,
He scratched at his head;
'Well, one thing is certain,'
Quick came my reply:
'If this lot beats Leeds,
Look for ice in July.'

An anonymous wordsmith even suggested that the powers of Stokoe could heal the political strife that was enveloping the nation:

Bob Stokoe is Prime Minister,
It happened in a dream,
And he inspired the nation
Once again to be supreme;
As the masses listened to him,
They learned to play the game,
And even union leaders
Were inclined to do the same.

Meanwhile Southwick couple George and Ethel Howey, aged seventy-eight and sixty-six respectively, made the local newspaper by opening up a 'vintage' bottle of Newcastle Brown Ale dating from 1937, which they had kept as a souvenir from that year's Wembley win and had pledged to open and drink the next time Sunderland reached the FA Cup final. 'That day is nearly here now but I dread to think what the beer is going to taste like,' Mr Howey, of Yewtree Avenue, said.

To echo the town mayor's words, away from the north-east and the world of sport, Stokoe and his side were becoming the darlings of the nation. The BBC subsequently commissioned Houghton-le-Spring-born Harold Williamson to present and narrate a programme entitled *The Pride and Passion of Sunderland*, to be broadcast on BBC1 on the Thursday evening before the FA Cup final, to try and explain just what was happening in Sunderland and what it all meant to the town.

National reporters and photographers trekked to the north-east to speak to the local people and try to fathom how – against a backdrop of strikes, job cuts, wage demands, high inflation and an impending energy crisis – the mood was so buoyant and jubilant. No one on the outside seemed to be able to understand just how much Sunderland's Cup run meant and why. It went far deeper than the pictures of ships with SUNDERLAND FOR THE CUP written on them, but those were printed anyway. Most of the articles generally focused on one man and one title: 'Messiah'.

John Motson returned to Sunderland for the first time since he had interviewed Stokoe on the day of his managerial appointment at Roker Park on 29 November 1972. Motson visited Wearmouth Colliery to talk to miners about the big day against Leeds United. The mood in the town had changed significantly in those five months since his last visit; all of those interviewed were in no doubt about the outcome of the FA Cup final: 'We'll win it,' they said. 'We're the better team.'

But there remained an air of caution at Harry Kirtley bookmakers, on High Street West, with odds of Sunderland winning the Cup priced at 5–2 while Leeds were 1–3. So many locals had already backed their heroes that it was predicted at least £10,000 would have to be paid out in the town alone if Sunderland won. The final was still three weeks away.

Meanwhile, over at Tyne Tees Television, head of features Leslie Barrett had to decide how to tell the story of Sunderland's historic weekend at Wembley to the people of the north-east. 'We felt we should do something about Sunderland getting to the FA Cup final, so I went to see Bob Stokoe and Keith Collings about it,' Barrett recalls. 'It soon became fairly clear that we weren't going to get into Wembley. The team hotel looked to be our best option, but the BBC and ITV had that covered to the hilt. It was very expensive too, so it was a problem for us. On the way back from my meeting a thought came into my head and I asked myself, Why am I thinking about Wembley? All the joys and disappointments will be magnified in Sunderland. When I got back to the office and told the production team, they were disappointed not to be going to Wembley but I said to them, "If we win, we have got a hell of a programme here." We then started to plan blanket coverage of the town from five a.m. to midnight on Cup final day.'

Barrett and his team didn't know it at the time, but they were about to produce an absorbing social document and one of the most treasured television programmes ever to come out of the north-east. It would be entitled *Meanwhile Back in Sunderland*.

In early April Stokoe and club secretary Ron Linney were again in contact with the Football League in a bid to ease the burden of Sunderland's fixture list ahead of Wembley. Once again the club got a result: it was agreed that two of the outstanding fixtures – away at Cardiff City and at home to Queen's Park Rangers – could be held over until the week after Wembley. But the match at Orient would have to be played in Cup final week.

That did not look as though it was going to be too much of a problem, after Billy Hughes put on a Man of the Match display to hit the first hat-trick of his first professional career – one with his right foot, one with his left foot and one from close range – as Sunderland defeated relegation-threatened Huddersfield Town 3–0 at Roker Park. 'I owe everything to the new manager,' Hughes said afterwards. 'He makes you want to play for him and, for me, it was part of the repayment to him for all the help he has given me.'

Jim Montgomery also saved a penalty late on from Alan Gowling. All eleven players that had beaten Arsenal at Hillsborough played against Huddersfield as a thank-you to the loyal support. (A crowd of 32,251 turned up.) But another booking for Micky Horswill meant he was unavailable for the Easter programme and Stokoe would soon have to make changes to his marauding team.

But not yet: Stokoe named an unchanged side for the home match against Portsmouth, with Dave Young – available again after suspension – taking over as substitute from Brian Chambers. Sunderland won 2–0 with a header from Bobby Kerr and a penalty from Dennis Tueart, and with eleven points from the last twelve, the Rokerites now sat in the top half of the Second Division table for the first time since the days of Alan Brown. Promotion was out of the question – Burnley and QPR were more than a dozen points clear of them – but with games in hand third place was still possible, and that became the team's new target: to keep up their winning mentality ahead of the FA Cup final.

The result of the ballot for Cup final tickets was announced after the Portsmouth match, with holders of pink X, green A, pink C and pink U vouchers successful. Essentially the luck of the draw depended entirely on which turnstile fans had used for those two Second Division matches a fortnight before. Not everybody was happy but there was never going to be an easy way to do it.

Within days of the ballot, tickets started to circulate on the black market in Sunderland for upwards of £25. Stokoe issued a warning in the local press: 'If anyone buys a ticket over the odds, I would like them to bring the ticket to us and we will identify the original holder and report the matter for action.' It was a noble act by the Sunderland manager but there remained only one topic of conversation in the pubs and the clubs, at work and on the street: 'Have you got a ticket for Wembley?'

One supporter who had not got a ticket was local shipyard worker Colin Thompson. He had torn up his season ticket in disgust a few months earlier. 'It was a pound for a match ticket and we complained about it,' supporter Pete Sixsmith recalls. 'It was another £3 for the train. I remember going into the bank and asking for £24 to pay for six train tickets to London, and the manager coming out from the back and asking me why I wanted to cash £24. I told him and he said to the cashier, "Cash it." I was earning £18 a week at the time, so £24 was a lot of money to take out of the bank.'

A sore throat and other minor injuries to Vic Halom and an Achilles tendon injury to Hughes meant that Stokoe had to rework his attack for the trip to Burnley on the Monday before Easter. Tueart took over at centre-forward, with Young playing on the left, Kerr playing on the right and Chambers moving into midfield. Burnley – needing just a point to win promotion to the First Division – won 2–0. Stokoe responded to this defeat by giving his entire squad two days' complete rest before planning how to negotiate three games in four days over the Easter weekend.

Both Halom and Hughes were fit to return for the match at Hull City on Easter Saturday, but with Horswill suspended, Dave Watson – one of the few players to avoid illness at Christmas – struck down by flu and Ritchie Pitt ruled out through gastroenteritis, Stokoe had to change the team around once more and played Jackie Ashurst alongside Young in defence, with Chambers taking over the number 4 shirt in midfield.

Those who saw the match at Boothferry Park – the attendance was only 12,637 – were in for a treat, as they were to witness what is regarded as the finest save of Montgomery's career. There is no question that the goalkeeper was enjoying a rich vein of form in the early part of 1973. Two awe-inspiring reflex saves against Notts County and Arsenal in the FA Cup were now followed by a truly brilliant reaction save from Hull striker Roy Greenwood.

A goal from Halom early in the second half had given Sunderland a 1–0 lead. On seventy-three minutes Young conceded a free-kick on the edge of the penalty area after a challenge on Stuart Pearson. Terry Neill took the kick and sent it into the middle of the box, where Greenwood – moving in from the far post – connected and sent it wide of the Sunderland goalkeeper, who momentarily looked to have committed himself. Montgomery appeared to be beaten by the change of direction but he checked, dived back along his line and somehow managed to scoop the ball away with one hand. The Hull players stood as one to applaud him. The spectators – regardless of which team they supported – did the same.

'Monty was completely wrong-footed,' Sixsmith says. 'Roy Greenwood put the ball towards the other corner from him but Monty just turned and knocked it away. It was a truly fantastic save. In my opinion, it was the man's best – and there are quite a few to choose from.'

'I think it was my best save,' Montgomery says. 'It was more or less a Gordon Banks type save, if you know what I mean? I went from one end to the other, getting a touch on the ball and putting it over the bar. But there was something like twelve thousand people there. No media coverage, no nothing. It was all very different to what happened a few weeks later at Wembley!'

Ironically Stokoe did not see this save, as he was on yet another of his vetting missions in Scotland, with the target once again believed to be Drew Busby. The Sunderland team was under the guidance of Arthur Cox that weekend. 'Monty was a special person and that was a truly great save,' he says.

Another man who saw it was Leeds chief coach Syd Owen, who was busy compiling Don Revie's dossier on Sunderland ahead of the FA Cup final. Revie had pledged to have the Rokerites watched in every match they played leading up to Wembley, and Owen was sat in the stands that day. It would be interesting to know what he wrote about Montgomery's reflexes.

A late goal from Hughes – a header from Halom's cross – gave Sunderland a 2–0 win at Hull. Hughes had now notched eight goals in eight games, while Halom had scored six times since his move from Luton Town in February. The press quickly nicknamed the pair 'the "H" Bombs'.

'We were an attacking side with players that loved to get forward,' Halom says. 'To have Dennis Tueart and Billy Hughes – who had got natural pace – was something that made my life very easy. I would set things up and go and finish them off. But while I loved to be creative and imaginative and worked hard to create problems, the one thing I didn't have was pace. I had broken my left leg twice when I was five and I was in plaster for the best part of six months. My left leg didn't grow but my right one did. So I had one leg longer than the other – my right leg is bent – and this meant I had to work at it. I lost pace that I could have had. I think the Alan Brown regime was a factor too. After talking to them, I think the players did all the graft, all the hard work and all the nasty things to learn the business under him and then suddenly they were allowed freedom – freedom of thought and freedom of movement – by Bob Stokoe. They provided the service. All I had to do was work hard and get on the end of things.'

Hughes scored another goal on Easter Monday in the 2–1 home win over Cardiff, to give Sunderland both points after another penalty from Tueart had cancelled out Leighton Phillips's first-half goal. With eighteen points from a possible twenty, Sunderland were now up to ninth in the Second Division table with five league matches still to play, while the next five teams above them each had just one game left. Stokoe's record in all competitions as manager of the club was an impressive seventeen wins and six draws from twenty-seven games in charge.

Sunderland were now playing very much as a squad and not just a team. A virus ruled out Ron Guthrie against Cardiff, meaning Joe Bolton came in at left-back again. With Horswill, Pitt and Watson still ruled out, only seven of the side that beat Manchester City, Luton and Arsenal in the FA Cup played against the Bluebirds. Mick McGiven, back from the hamstring injury that had forced him to miss three months of the season, was fit again and named substitute. If the first eleven – when fit and well – picked themselves, the race for a place on the bench at Wembley was well and truly on, with five players – Ashurst, Bolton, Chambers, McGiven and Young – all staking claims by playing in the first team.

As Sunderland's league programme progressed, those five were joined by two other hopefuls – John Lathan and John Tones – who were both recalled to the first team for the trip to Nottingham Forest the following night. In fact, when Guthrie was withdrawn at half-time, no fewer than six of the side were reserve-team players. Forest won the match 1–0, with former Sunderland striker Neil Martin scoring the only goal of the game twenty minutes from time.

A few hours before Sunderland's match had kicked off in Nottingham, supporters who had collected green K vouchers from the Carlisle and Bristol City games a month before – and still had them in their possession – were told to queue at Roker Park on a first-come-first-served basis to claim 800 or so leftover tickets for Wembley. These tickets were like gold dust. It was announced that the extra allocation of tickets was to be sold from 11 a.m. the following Thursday. The queues began to form at 5 p.m. that Tuesday. The cold snap that had affected the north of the country for most of April restrained few of the hopefuls. So much so that only those fans who were certain of making the trip to Wembley travelled down to the City Ground.

When the Sunderland team coach arrived back at Roker Park from Nottingham in the early hours of Wednesday morning, the players were met by the sight of fans – most of them children as it was the Easter holidays – wrapped in sleeping bags and blankets, drinking tea from flasks to keep warm. Stokoe could only praise them: 'This is an indication of the tremendous enthusiasm in the town,' he said. 'I am only sorry that Wembley does not hold a lot more people. It is sad we do not have a stadium that holds 250,000. There will be thousands of genuine football supporters who cannot get a ticket for the game.'

The last Sunderland supporter to collect a Cup final ticket from Roker Park was twenty-six-year-old civil servant Kenneth Lightburn, who queued for eighteen hours from five o'clock on Wednesday afternoon before finally getting his hands on the much-coveted prize at eleven on Thursday morning.

That same night Don Revie conceded that Liverpool had all but won the First Division title after the Reds beat his side 2–0 at Anfield. 'They have won it now and they thoroughly deserve it. If we don't win anything at Leeds, we like Liverpool to win it,' he said, recalling Bill Shankly's tribute to his side in the Anfield dressing room in 1969.

Sunderland's final home match before the Cup final came the following Saturday against Blackpool. The town of the Golden Mile was already trying to hook into the euphoria in County Durham by placing advertisements in the north-east wishing the Rokerites well and pertinently suggesting summer-holiday celebrations for supporters on the north-west coast.

The build-up remained relentless but Halom, Hughes and Ian Porterfield – who had been troubled with a bruised toe – all responded positively to treatment, while Pitt and Watson both recovered from illness to enable Stokoe to play his first team against the Seasiders. It was the first time that Owen – the busy Leeds coach who was totting up the miles as well as his notes – had been able to see Sunderland play in all their splendour.

A defence-splitting pass from Porterfield set up Hughes, on the edge of the box, to score the only goal of the game in a 1–0 win. But there were two injury concerns: Montgomery went over on his ankle and had to receive treatment, while Tueart was badly fouled and there were fears he could be a doubt for Wembley. 'I had a knee injury,' Tueart says. 'I thought I was struggling at one stage on the Sunday – just six days before the FA Cup final – but Johnny Watters assured me there was no ligament strain and thankfully after a day or two I was OK.'

Young came on to replace Tueart against Blackpool and now appeared to be the favourite to make the bench at Wembley, particularly after Stokoe agreed to sell Chambers to Arsenal for £25,000 that very week. Chambers had been an unused substitute for Sunderland against Arsenal at Hillsborough while Young was suspended. He went on to make just one league appearance for the Gunners, although, rather bizarrely, he did appear in the FA Cup third-place play-off for them against Wolverhampton Wanderers in the summer (Wolves won that match 3–1 and so officially finished third in the competition).

As with the build-up in Blackpool and Buxton, Stokoe intended to keep his squad out of the media spotlight as much as he could for the week leading up to the Cup final. He had chosen the private and spacious grounds of the Selsdon Park Hotel in Croydon to achieve that. The hotel was famous in political circles for the term 'Selsdon Man', a phrase used by former Prime Minister Harold Wilson to describe Edward Heath's shadow cabinet meetings, which were held there to discuss Conservative Party policy ahead of the 1970 general election.

Once in London, Sunderland had to play one more league match – at Orient – before the Cup final preparations could begin in earnest. Porterfield, who was now struggling with a hamstring strain, Tueart, who was still receiving treatment on his knee, and Montgomery were all rested. It was the first match the goalkeeper had missed all season. His replacement, Trevor Swinburne, who had helped win the club the FA Youth Cup in 1969 at the age of fifteen, made his first-team debut at Brisbane Road.

Young played on the left side of midfield in place of Porterfield and scored his first and only goal in a Sunderland shirt in the second minute. It would be enough to secure his place on the bench for the final. Derrick Downing equalised in the second half and the match ended in a draw. It also ended with no injuries, and with the three absent first-team players responding well to rest and treatment, the Rokerites were set to be at full strength for Wembley. 'The worst of our fears are over now,' a relieved Stokoe said after the match.

Halom was another relieved man. An over-exuberant reaction to some foul play by two former Orient team-mates could have proved very costly. But luckily for him – and Sunderland – it went unnoticed and therefore unpunished. 'Two apprentices during my time at Orient – Terry Brisley and Paul Went – were winding me up. At one point I was trapped by both of them and so I went over the top and flattened Terry. It was one of the worst tackles I have ever seen – and I did it! Immediately I thought to myself, You dozy bugger. I certainly didn't want to get involved in anything like that so close to the Cup final. But they were going to sandwich me and there was no way I was going to allow myself to get injured. I quickly apologised. I feared I would be suspended.'

'I played really well in that match and the goal probably cemented my place for Wembley,' Young says. 'I had experience, I was quite versatile and with just one substitute in those days that gave options, for I could play at the back, in midfield or at full-back, and the fact I scored that night meant that I could get goals as well. But I had no clue at the time if I was going to be the sub. The first eleven picked themselves by then, but there were five or six of us in the back-up squad who travelled and trained and hoped. That match did my chances the power of good.'

Stokoe gave his squad the next day off. Some players enjoyed a round of golf on the course adjoining the hotel's grounds, while others relaxed in their rooms. 'I don't want to bring them to the boil too early and run the risk of them draining emotionally,' the manager explained to the press.

Swinburne and Bolton travelled north to play for Sunderland Reserves in the second leg of the Northern Intermediate League Cup final against Middlesbrough at Roker Park. Sunderland lost the match 3–2 – losing the final 5–4 on aggregate – but some joy had come with the Sunderland youth team winning the North Midlands League title. All in all it had been a successful season for all three of the club's sides. The future looked bright.

But such success may have been achieved at something of a cost to the Sunderland manager. The devoutly private Stokoe opened up his heart in an interview with Brian Gearing in the *Radio Times*, which was published that day: 'It's sad really,' he said. 'I know I'm a poor husband and an inadequate father. I provide for my family to the very best of my ability but I know that I am remote from them. I just can't help it.

'My whole life is football. We've lived in twelve different houses and my daughter has been to five different schools,' the journeyman manager added. 'The people here had been waiting for a sign and once we started to win, they came pouring back. It made me afraid at first in case they expected too much. But when we beat Manchester City in the fifth round and followed that by knocking out Arsenal – well, I knew I'd given them something.'

Following a light training session on the Wednesday morning, the Sunderland players went to Wembley to look at the pitch and check out the facilities ahead of the big game. Some of them were unimpressed with a playing surface that still showed scars from the previous week-end's FA Trophy final between Scarborough and Wigan Athletic.

'We were excited to be playing at Wembley,' Tueart says. 'But when we went down there to train I thought it was a tip. There were bare patches on the pitch – but these were all covered in sawdust by the day of the match!'

Stokoe was very unhappy at Leeds being given the England dressing room and the tunnel end for their supporters – without so much as a draw to decide either. 'I have no quarrel with Leeds but I must protest against the favouritism they appear to be enjoying,' he said. 'We appreciate that we are a Second Division team but we are definitely not second rate, although that is the way we are being treated. We have had no say in the matter at all. We would have been quite happy to spin a coin for choice of ends and dressing rooms.'

Apparently unknown to the Sunderland manager, the dressing rooms were traditionally allocated on alphabetical order. Furthermore, while Leeds had been given the North dressing room, used by England in international matches, the greatest success the national team had ever achieved – winning the World Cup in 1966 – had come when England emerged from the South dressing room, due to the draw order of the competition. The majority of recent FA Cup winners had also used the South dressing room, and soon it would become known as Wembley's 'lucky dressing room'.

'The stadium looked huge with nobody in it and the goals looked so far apart,' Watson recalls. 'When we got back on the coach, we were all up for it. We'd got a taste for it and now we wanted it there and then. Saturday couldn't come too soon.'

That afternoon the Sunderland squad went shopping in London. Some of the players hit the King's Road in Chelsea, mostly looking for a shirt, a tie or a suit to wear on the big day. Although the club had supplied the team with official blazers – complete with the new club crest featuring a ship – not all the players chose to wear it.

That evening Hughes, Porterfield and Tueart travelled up to BBC Television Centre in Shepherd's Bush to watch a recording of *Top of the Pops*, hosted by Tony Blackburn. They saw live performances by Hot Chocolate, Sweet and 10cc. Tony Orlando and Dawn were number one with 'Tie a Yellow Ribbon Round the Old Oak Tree'. The programme was broadcast on BBC1 the following night.

'I would have loved to have gone to *Top of the Pops* but I couldn't go,' Halom says. 'In fact I would have been lucky if Bob Stokoe would have let me watch it on the telly. I was under lock and key at that time and he wouldn't let me out. I certainly couldn't leave the hotel grounds. Players had to bring meals and beers and pass them through the window to me.'

While grounded, Halom was at least able to hire a Rolls-Royce – decked out with a huge red-and-white rosette – and chauffeur to take his mother, father, sister and brother-in-law to Wembley on the big day. His mother would later tell him that she felt like the Queen of England!

Malone and a few others went to the Gallipoli restaurant off Old Threadneedle Street. 'It was a fantastic night out,' Malone remembers. 'The owner put quite a bit of money into the players' pool and the food was out of this world.'

Most of the others stayed at the hotel and played snooker, watched television and had a few drinks. 'I just had a couple of pints to relax with the rest of the lads,' Guthrie says. 'Bob Stokoe and Arthur Cox were with us. Bob didn't drink and Arthur didn't drink, but they both came along. We were all in it together.'

But Pitt had something on his mind: 'A few weeks before the FA Cup final my daughter Louise was taken into hospital in Gateshead with gastroenteritis. She lost a fair bit of weight and so that was a bit of a worry. The week before Wembley she was still in hospital. The nurses decorated her cot in red and white for the final. I knew she was OK and that she was going to be fine, but she was less than two months old and it was difficult being away from her that week. It was a worrying time for me and my wife.'

On the Thursday afternoon Stokoe and Cox sat down with the players to talk through tactics. The plan was to nullify the Leeds attack on the ground and in the air: Stokoe openly questioned Leeds' pace, and so Malone would refrain from his attacking runs and sit back more at right-back to soak up the threat of Eddie Gray on the left wing. Stokoe's 'little general' Kerr was there to assist him whenever it was necessary. Guthrie would try to keep Peter Lorimer as far away from goal as he could on the other flank. If this worked, the result would be that a lot of Leeds' attacks would come in to Allan Clarke and Mick Jones from deep. Pitt and Watson – two great headers of the ball – would then have the task of dealing with that. Horswill and Porterfield would concentrate on Billy Bremner and Johnny Giles in midfield, and the front three would have to get back to help out their defence at every opportunity. Whenever they could, Sunderland would of course attack in numbers and with pace – just as they had throughout the FA Cup run – and try to take the game to Leeds, as was their wont. Hughes and Tueart would be key down the wings.

'Leeds wouldn't have expected what we gave them that day,' Malone says. 'But we knew exactly what they were going to give us. So it was easy for us to work out our pre-match plans, but it wouldn't have been that easy for them. We knew we had to keep on top of Leeds in every position on the pitch. All they could do was react once the game started. We caught them on the hop.'

Midway through the team talk there was an interruption when a workman began drilling outside the hotel. A disbelieving Cox was sent down to see him: 'There we were discussing our tactics when this pneumatic drill goes off in the driveway below us, just underneath the window where we were having our meeting,' the coach recalls. 'I went downstairs and shouted to the chap, "Give us a break, please – we're trying to plan how to win the FA Cup final up there." Eventually Bob was able to explain all his thoughts to the players and he had an impact on them.'

That evening Stokoe took his entire squad off to the Football Writers' Association Footballer of the Year awards dinner. The title was won by Pat Jennings of Tottenham Hotspur. This broke with protocol – it was the first time that any FA Cup final team had arrived *en masse* at the dinner, traditionally held just two days before the showpiece event. No Leeds players were present at the function.

'All sorts of people were coming over to us all night, saying hello and wishing us luck,' Guthrie says. 'Michael Crawford – who played Frank Spencer in *Some Mothers Do 'Ave 'Em* at the time – was there. He came over to our table, patted us all on the back and said, "Come on, lads, I want you to win the Cup final on Saturday." Everyone wanted us to win. There were no Leeds players there. I don't think Don Revie would have let them go.'

'Of course they can have a few beers,' a relaxed Stokoe told a surprised press. 'I never talk about this point. I know them well enough to appreciate they can look after themselves.' 'We were trying very hard to get the players' minds off the FA Cup final,' Cox explains. 'But we made sure we left at ten-thirty p.m. We were always back to our beds on time. We always did things properly.'

While the Sunderland players enjoyed the awards dinner, *The Pride and Passion of Sunderland* was transmitted to the nation on BBC1 between 8.30 and 9 p.m. It featured Stokoe, the team, four members of the club's 1937 FA Cup-winning side, local dignitaries, townspeople and lots of local schoolchildren.

Harold Williamson had become famous due to his 'Children Talking' feature on *Braden's Week* on the BBC. He had a natural talent for eliciting animated and humorous tales from youngsters. In the documentary he asks one boy to explain why the Leeds players in his painting look unhappy while the Sunderland players are laughing. 'Leeds are losing,' the boy replies. 'Or they should be!'

Williamson also spoke to Stokoe on the golf course in an interview filmed a week or so before. He asked the Sunderland manager how he felt about being called the 'Messiah' by supporters. 'It is something that, because of a lack of success in the town, they have got something to cheer about again and obviously I am delighted they hold me responsible for it,' Stokoe replied. 'I still feel the players have done it, although I have made them tick in certain places and that. But, hey, football is football and if you are going well the manager is a great guy and next season they might want to kick me in the backside or knock me off the end of the pier or something like that. But I will accept it whichever way it comes.'

At Tyne Tees Television, Leslie Barrett and his team were all set to film their own documentary. Across the country football fans of all persuasions were keen to support the underdogs – Sunderland were the most popular FA Cup final side in television history – with millions of neutrals cheering them on, many watching the match in colour for the first time. If the Queen's coronation in 1953 had been the boom year for television sets, 1973 was the year that colour television exploded. Television rentals reached an all-time high in the north-east that week and many of those not fortunate enough to have a colour set of their own arranged to go to the homes of family or friends who had one, to watch the match.

'I had a ticket for Wembley but I remember we still got a colour television the day before the game,' Sunderland supporter Paul Dobson says. 'I got back from school on the Friday afternoon and there it was.'

Another viewing option in Sunderland was at the cinema. Austin &
Pickersgill and Sunderland Shipbuilders took over the town's Top
Rank and Odeon cinemas respectively and installed massive screens
for local fans to watch the match. By now the majority of businesses
and shops in Sunderland had announced they would be closed for
business throughout Saturday afternoon. Most if not all the shops
were bedecked in red and white, with team photographs in the
windows. Local hospitals did the same. Schoolgirls wore red and
white ribbons in their hair and family pets wore red and white
collars. It looked like Christmas had come early. The entire town had
sold out of red and white carnations and crêpe paper long before
closing time on Friday afternoon.

Fashion writers Terri Moore and Sue Mullen wrote in that evening's
Sunderland Echo: 'If you don't suit red and white you are out of fashion.
To be without an outfit in the triumphant Sunderland team's colours is
to have missed the fashion boat.'

Down in London, after one final light training session at Selsdon Park
watched by cameramen hidden in the woods, Stokoe spoke to the press
for the final time. It is fair to say that his gun was loaded. 'I want
Ken Burns to referee the Cup final against Leeds tomorrow, not Billy
Bremner,' he said.

He [Bremner] is wearing a little armband but there is still no law that says a
captain can appeal against decisions. I sincerely hope Mr Burns will not allow
him to do that. The referee is going to be vital. I don't want any favours from
him, just a fair crack of the whip. We know that Leeds are going to be thoroughly
professional but they can have only twelve players on call, the same as ourselves. They do not worry us. We have no nerves and no fear because we have
nothing to lose. I am not trying to knock Leeds in any way but we are playing
a professional side and – let's face it – the word professional can embrace a
multitude of sins as well as virtues.

It is good for the game that we have got through to Wembley and it
will be good for the game if we can topple Leeds. We seem to have everybody
rooting for us. All over the world – outside of Leeds – people would love to
see us win. Nobody gave us a chance against Manchester City and Arsenal
and the difference against Leeds is that everybody wants us to win. Managers
from all over the country have told me so. The crowd, I am sure, will be
on our side.

When I came back to the north-east I did not expect anything quite like this. You get fairytales and this must be one. The way people have welcomed the success of the club is incredible. I can't get out of the house or take the dog for a walk without someone coming up and patting me on the back. The way the town has reacted to our Cup run is frightening to me. I am so dependent on the players. I get a lot of credit which I don't think I deserve because I don't go out on the field and do it.

Unlike Sunderland, Leeds only arrived in London forty-eight hours before the match, but quickly settled into their headquarters at the Hendon Hotel, the hotel they had used the previous year before defeating Arsenal at Wembley and the hotel England had used the night before the 1966 World Cup final. 'The less fuss before the final, the better we like it,' Revie told the waiting press.

The Leeds manager may not have wanted fuss, but in his final press conference ahead of the Cup final the next day he seemed to be trying to engender anxiety in his opponents: 'We know all about Cup final morning, when anxious minutes seem like hours; we know all about driving up Wembley Way; we know what it is like to stand in the tunnel twenty minutes before kick-off when the wait in the tunnel makes your legs feel like jelly and your throat a little dry the first time; we know what it is like to step out into that wall of thundering sound, which really shakes you; we also know that strange feeling just after kick-off when men become a little slow in their thinking and their legs begin to feel heavier than ever before. For Sunderland this is an experience still to come.'

Responding to the criticism of his captain, Revie said, 'If we are as bad as people say we are, we should be in jail instead of Wembley. We have been successful for ten years and it appears that is too long for some people. It hasn't annoyed us because we've become used to it over the years. We'll probably get the blame if something goes wrong with the ball tomorrow.'

Revie also gave his take on growing press talk that Eddie Gray would prove to be an unstoppable match winner: 'This is his occasion and when he turns it on, he can be magic. He really enjoys the big match atmosphere and tomorrow's pitch, after the recent rain, should suit him. If he is flying tomorrow, it will be something to watch,' he said.

Gray had terrorised the Chelsea full-back David Webb in the 1970 FA Cup final, and the media believed the Scottish international would now do the same against Malone. They were seemingly undeterred by the fact that he had missed a large part of the season through a series of thigh injuries, and they also totally underestimated the intelligence and the resilience of Sunderland. It was to be a popular prediction but it was way off the mark.

Revie concluded his press conference by saying:

I don't expect an easy final against Sunderland. They will be quite a handful. Sunderland did a fantastic job in getting to Wembley, beating two great sides, and we will treat them with the respect they deserve. I saw them beat Manchester City and they were magnificent. They have tremendous ability and we don't agree with those who say they have got where they are by running and chasing. I have a feeling they will hit us with all they have got in the first half-hour or so and this is going to be the critical time. If they nick a goal it is going to lift them even higher. If we hold them, however, then the advantage will turn our way. I think we will win because we have a lot of skill in our side and we have the experience of the big occasions that we have earned the hard way over the years.

Allan Clarke was in no doubt about the support of the neutral ahead of the FA Cup final: 'Leeds United aren't simply playing Sunderland at Wembley,' he told the *Daily Mirror*. 'We are taking on the whole country – Leeds supporters excluded.'

Clarke sat out Leeds' final training session, but the England striker was not injured. The reason he did so was because he had missed the final training session before the previous Cup final against Arsenal and it had appeared to be a lucky omen. 'It was just superstition,' Revie admitted. 'He did not play in the last practice match last year and we won the Cup.' The Leeds manager's superstitions knew no bounds. Clarke would also be the last Leeds man down the tunnel the following day, given the retirement of Jack Charlton – another Revie habit designed to bring much-needed luck.

Syd Owen, the man who had watched Sunderland on numerous occasions home and away for Revie during the past few weeks, presented his dossier on the Rokerites that night. The one major concern was the aerial threat of Watson at corners. Revie spoke to his team about this at length and gave his instructions on how they should deal with it: the tall centre-half would get special attention at set pieces and was to be man-marked at all times when necessary.

Back at the Selsdon Park Hotel, with all the hard work done and preparations completed, the Sunderland players settled down for the night in their twin rooms – Jim Montgomery and Bobby Kerr; Dick Malone and Dave Watson; Ron Guthrie and Dave Young; Micky Horswill and Joe Bolton; Ritchie Pitt and Mick McGiven; Billy Hughes and Vic Halom; Ian Porterfield and Dennis Tueart.

The team was known: Stokoe unsurprisingly stuck with the eleven players that had taken Sunderland from 250–1 outsiders at Maine Road just ten weeks before, past the challenges of Manchester City, Luton and Arsenal in the last three rounds. Young was named substitute. 'I was resigned to that fact that Ritchie Pitt was going to play and that the first team was settled,' Young says. 'You couldn't dispute that. So I was absolutely thrilled to bits that I was going to be on the bench with a chance to get on at Wembley and be a part of it all.'

Stokoe later met up with journalists and friends Jackie Milburn and Len Shackleton, plus BBC commentator Barry Davies, who had been with the Sunderland camp at Selsdon Park for three days preparing his report for *Cup Final Grandstand*. The four men went up to Stokoe's suite to watch the late-night ITV programme *Who'll Win the Cup?*, presented by Brian Moore and Jimmy Hill and featuring the opinions of Malcolm Allison, Jack Charlton and Paddy Crerand.

'Why necessarily I should have been there, I don't know,' Davies says. 'I was just one of that particular group that night. The four of us went up to Bob Stokoe's suite and watched the programme together. Bob could get very irritated when people criticised his players. His irritation – and indeed his temper – when the ITV panel went through the various categories of the teams and gave points to the two sides had to be seen to be believed. On every part Leeds came out on top. Bob got further forward on his seat and you could see him bristling away. I recall he got very upset when they did a thing about creativity. They also made a big fuss about Eddie Gray winning the match down the left flank against Dick Malone. Bob had to then be pushed back in his seat by Messrs Milburn and Shackleton, helped by me. It was a very interesting evening to be part of that quartet.'

As a seething Stokoe switched out the lights and bade the men from the media good-night, Shackleton's parting shot to the Sunderland manager is one that Davies remembers to this day: 'Len said to Bob, "Hey, Bob, they've just done your team talk for you, man." They had as well.'

13.

THE FIFTH OF THE FIFTH

Rain started to fall all over London early on the morning of 5 May 1973. By the time the Sunderland players awoke and caught a glimpse of the wet grounds surrounding the Selsdon Park Hotel, the scene was well and truly set. It was the same story with the weather at Wembley. It would be the same story for the rest of the day.

The night had passed smoothly for the Sunderland players, and by the morning of the FA Cup final there was no evidence of any pre-match nerves in the camp. Instead there was the same growing confidence that had surrounded the team for the last ten weeks, since their visit to Maine Road and the 2–2 draw with Manchester City that really kick-started this whole run. Individuals with different talents, different needs and different personalities were all preparing in their own way for the biggest day of their lives.

'I had my six Weetabix for breakfast as usual, with masses of sugar too,' Dave Watson recalls. 'Dicky Malone, my room-mate, was astounded by that but that is what I had. It gave me energy, roughage and carbohydrates – everything I needed for a football match. I felt good and supremely confident we were going to win. Nothing had changed. We were all confident in our own ability and what we had to do come the final.'

'I had a good night's kip,' Billy Hughes remembers. 'Vic Halom and I had a few cans of Vaux Norseman lager tucked under the bed – I don't think Bob Stokoe or Arthur Cox knew about it – and we used to have four cans the night before a match, otherwise we would have been tossing and turning all night. It just seemed to get us off to sleep, without wondering what was going to happen the next day. I'm not saying all the lads did it – some of them, the likes of Dave Watson and Dick Malone, were virtually teetotal – but it did the trick for Vic and me that night.'

'I remember waking up on the morning of the Cup final and just saying to myself, OK, this is it,' Ron Guthrie says. 'I had a bowl of cornflakes, some toast and a cup of tea. I was so focused on the match that if somebody had telephoned the hotel and told me that my house had burned down, I would have just said, "OK, so what?" From the Thursday night onwards I hardly spoke to anybody. I completely focused on the match from the Friday morning after training.'

All the Sunderland players woke with confidence, focus and unity in abundance. None of them cared that most of the morning's newspapers had gone with the same line that had dominated the ITV preview programme the night before – that Eddie Gray would be Leeds United's 'match winner' and that Dick Malone was the 'weak link' in the underdogs' line-up.

'Sunderland seem destined to be second up the Royal Box steps for all the reasons that have been advanced and argued endlessly for weeks – all of them associated with the undeniable truth that Leeds are a side of far greater quality,' Frank McGhee wrote in the *Daily Mirror*. 'For me the Leeds player who, more than any other, illustrates the man-against-man difference in class between the two sides is Eddie Gray. I am convinced that Leeds manager Don Revie has for weeks now seen Gray as his Cup final match winner, and for this reason was prepared to sacrifice what was left of his team's slender championship chances by leaving out his most skilful ball player, reserving him for Wembley.' McGhee's comments were echoed all around Fleet Street and beyond.

'I could understand why they all said that,' Malone says. 'I liked to attack, so therefore they all thought Eddie Gray could be the match winner. If you're working on theory then that is really what should have happened. But there were two things about that day: firstly Eddie wasn't really match fit – not mentally – and he had been out for a while, and secondly Leeds didn't know what we were capable of. They didn't know that I might decide not to attack and not give him the space, and they didn't know that if I did attack, Bobby Kerr was there to drop back, and vice versa: if I sat back then Bobby had the freedom to go forward.'

'Jack Charlton said that Eddie Gray was going to rip Dick Malone apart,' Kerr recalls. 'Dick and I spoke about what we were going to do but everybody in the team had to be involved in the plan because obviously if we were going to be doing something like that then every-body needed to know – I wasn't going to be available for other things if that was going to be my role. Eddie was some player. I played in one game against Leeds and all you could hear on the pitch was, "Give the ball to Eddie." It was getting switched to him all the time.'

The last Second Division team to win the FA Cup had been West Bromwich Albion, in 1931, and the last team to win it without a single full international in the line-up was Barnsley in 1912, two years before the outbreak of the First World War. Few in the media therefore gave Sunderland a chance of upsetting the odds.

Writing in the *Sun*, Arsenal goalkeeper and BBC pundit Bob Wilson rated each of the twenty-two players on show out of ten. Leeds came out on top by six points, with only Watson winning his respective numerical battle, against Paul Madeley. Perhaps critically, the biggest man-to-man gap was in midfield at number 4, with two whole points separating Billy Bremner and Micky Horswill. 'Everybody predicted Leeds to win and I predicted Leeds to win,' Wilson recalls. 'But one thing I was certain about was that the Leeds fans would be out-sung and out-shouted by that remarkable noise that I had witnessed at Hillsborough by those Sunderland supporters.'

The FA Cup final dominated the television schedules in the 1970s. It was shown by two of the three terrestrial channels and was sport's biggest TV event of the year, often attracting the biggest audience of the year too. With the battle for viewing figures rife, the build-up began well before noon, with ITV's *World of Sport* being transmitted from 10.30 a.m. and *Cup Final Grandstand* coming on BBC1 at 11.15.

'It was an arms race,' Gerald Sinstadt, a reporter for ITV that day, remembers. 'The previous year we had been on slightly later, but then the BBC would decide to come on a little earlier and so then so would we. If it had gone on like that for much longer we would have been on air at six o'clock in the morning!'

The television battleground was an intriguing one in 1973: ITV had made a request to put cameras on the Leeds and Sunderland team coaches on the way to Wembley. Don Revie had refused the request but Bob Stokoe had accepted it, making Sunderland the first team ever to do this. ITV had also flown the European Footballer of the Year and Ajax star Johan Cruyff to Wembley as their special guest. The BBC went for a wider appeal by inviting the Soviet Union's international star of gymnastics Olga Korbut – who had enthralled the world the previous year at the 1972 Munich Olympics – into the studio. It also mounted a special Cup final version of the highly popular BBC1 entertainment show *It's a Knockout*, presented by Stuart Hall and Eddie Waring. It featured teams from both supporters' clubs, plus present and past players such as Billy Bremner, Johnny Giles and Raich Carter. Comedian Nat Jackley also took part. It was filmed at Leeds' Greyhound Stadium and all the games had a football theme: one particular challenge had a goalkeeper defending his net on wheels, pushed along by his team-mates. Sunderland – wearing an old kit with white shorts – won the contest.

Raich Carter, the only Sunderland captain ever to lift the FA Cup, could now, at long last, sense a shock in the air himself: 'If I was Don Revie I would be a bit apprehensive,' he said. 'The teams are wearing the same colours as we did then, 1937 twisted round is 1973, and once again it's Sunderland's ninth game. All little superstitions but . . .' Revie, of course, knew all about little superstitions. The viewers' appetite for a giant-killing had been whetted early on by the words of a Sunderland legend.

Before the respective powers of David Coleman, Brian Clough and Bobby Charlton on BBC1 went head-to-head with Brian Moore, Jimmy Hill and Jack Charlton on ITV just before kick-off, there would be a combined total of almost eight hours of coverage on the two channels. The BBC struck gold first by going live to Barry Davies at the Selsdon Park Hotel at 11.30 a.m., where he was set to interview the Sunderland team live. What happened next not only provided a moment that has since gone down in FA Cup final folklore; it also set the agenda for the rest of the day.

There was a relaxed humour among the Sunderland players that morning, which seemed as surprising to viewers as it was remarkable, given the occasion and the task that lay ahead. But now many who had thought the final was a foregone conclusion suddenly began to consider Sunderland's chances of creating the biggest shock in Wembley history.

'The plan was to come to us first and then show the interviews from the Leeds hotel, which was to be very significant as it turned out,' Davies recalls. 'I had been with the Sunderland team for three or four days by then and so I knew them pretty well. All the players came into this room for the interview just before they sat down for lunch. It was all very relaxed. I told the cameraman where I was going to start and so forth and off we went. We were just getting into full flow – there was a buzz about the interviews and the players were joining in – when suddenly this laughter starts coming from this little machine. It made a hell of a row for a small machine. I realised I was being set up in some way and I started to think, I'm live on air here, what on earth are they going to do? It became a bit of a worry.'

Hughes had unleashed a laughing box – bought for a pocketful of pesetas in Tenerife – on a shocked and bewildered Davies. It certainly wasn't the protocol to do this type of thing live on television on Cup final day, and those that saw it immediately sat up and took notice.

'I remember Barry Davies asked Dave Watson if he was as good a centre-forward as he was a centre-half, which, to be fair, he wasn't. I mean Dave was an excellent and an exceptional centre-half,' Hughes says. 'That seemed as good a time as any for me to just let it go; it could have been a question for somebody else but that was what came out and off it went. Dave didn't know I had it, hardly any of the lads knew I had it. None of the camera crew knew I had it, that's for sure.'

The laughing box had been given to Hughes's room-mate Halom by a friend, Steve Smith, to lighten the mood during the week. Neither of them had expected it to be used to embarrass Davies live on BBC1. 'I bought the laughing box on holiday in Playa de las Américas in Tenerife just a few weeks before the Cup final,' Smith explains. 'I saw this street seller pressing this box and laughing along with it and I thought to myself, I have to get one of those, so I bought it off him. I gave it to Vic Halom to lighten the mood and give the lads a bit of a laugh during the week. Billy Hughes got hold of it and the next time I saw my laughing box, it was going off live on television!'

'Everyone laughed along with it,' Watson says. 'We were relaxed anyway but that relaxed us even more. It might have been a case of "lambs to the slaughter" in a sense but we didn't feel overawed at all. We had a relaxed confidence, we felt good and we were enjoying ourselves.'

'It was very funny because in those days whenever anyone appeared on television they behaved. Those interviews were more or less officious at that time but we altered all that,' Malone says. 'We all doubled up,' Jim Montgomery adds. 'Barry Davies was trying to ask us all these questions and when the noise went off, well, it just ended everything.'

'That was Billy Hughes all over,' Halom says. 'I used to like to read, but every time I got to the end of my book I would find that he had ripped the pages out of the back. He would chuck the pages away and just be sat there watching me, patiently waiting for me to get to the end of the book. He did all sorts of things when we roomed together. But that is an example of the team spirit we had. The team spirit in that side was so strong.'

'I don't know how much the viewers would have heard what was being said at that time,' Davies says. 'I mean it went on for well over a minute – maybe even ninety seconds – until somebody turned it off. I don't know how the hell we got off air in our allotted time either. Obviously I had somebody talking to me in my ear but I can't remember what the reaction was. I expect they started laughing too. It was good, live television. These were a bunch of young guys enjoying the day and we just about held it together to make some sort of sense of it all. We got off air and then we fell about laughing again. It was hysterical.

'*Grandstand* continued and the picture then cut to the Leeds team hotel,' Davies adds. 'As it did so one of the Sunderland players shouted out, "Look at that lot!" Leeds were dressed in these pin-striped double-breasted suits and seemed to be terribly tense as they were being interviewed. The Sunderland players didn't know it but I knew those Leeds interviews had been recorded the day before the match because Don Revie would not allow his team to be interviewed by the BBC in the hotel on the day of the match. This was another one of Don's superstitions and an attempt by him to protect his players. The contrast between the two hotels was enormous and you could sense the difference immediately: Leeds looked to be so uptight.'

'It is true to say that Leeds were very sombre and sober in their pin-striped suits,' John Motson, the BBC reporter at Hendon Hall, remembers. 'There was not much give in the interviews at all, even though I had interviewed the same players at the same hotel the year before, ahead of the FA Cup final between Leeds and Arsenal, which they had won. I thought they were very stiff and very tense.'

'If we had cut just briefly from those Leeds interviews back to the Sunderland players watching the television screen at Selsdon Park it would have been quite telling,' Davies adds. 'Of course we didn't do that, for there would probably have been hell to pay if we had and Don

Revie would have got very upset. But the growing feeling in the country that a shock could be on the cards would have been even greater if the viewers had seen what I saw.'

'The contrast was unbelievable: our laughing box versus the tailor's dummies,' Watson says. 'It was a picture for us. We laughed at Leeds because we couldn't believe what we were seeing. We made fun of them and it gave us a lift. Leeds looked like robots. I can still remember seeing Paul Madeley's face to this day. All of them looked full of dread and fear at what might happen. I thought to myself, What's wrong with them?'

'That was the moment I felt we were going to win the FA Cup,' Sir Tim Rice says. 'I was sitting watching the warm-up to the match at my house before setting off for Wembley and the Sunderland team came on and looked so casual, fooling around, while Leeds looked deadly serious. We seemed to have a great team spirit – summed up by that laughing box – and if the players were nervous, they didn't look it. I felt confident we would do it from then on.'

'Leeds were in their suits and ties and were quite regimental, if you want,' Hughes says. 'We were just having a laugh. That was the way we were. It may have come across as though we had nothing to lose, but that was far from the truth. We had everything to lose. We were in an FA Cup final at Wembley! Bob Stokoe just gave us this feeling we could do nothing wrong now. His message to us before the match was "Go out and enjoy the day. Do what you have been doing and whatever happens happens." So, again, there was no fear attached. We had no fear at all.'

'Maybe the difference between us was that we had never played at Wembley before and we had never lost at Wembley before,' Watson adds. 'We didn't know how that felt and so we had no fear. But Leeds had been there and got beaten in the past so they knew how that felt.'

'The week we had down at Selsdon Park was the total opposite to what any other club had ever done,' Malone says. 'It took all the pressure off us. We turned up for that television interview so relaxed. It is not unfair to say some of us looked like tramps in comparison to Leeds at their hotel. We were dressed as casual as anything and they looked immaculate.'

'We were correct, don't worry about that,' Cox says. 'The players were focused and, underneath all the laughter, we knew what we were about. Bob Stokoe's make-up could be serious – as mine could be – and it was important that the players felt they were not going to Wembley just to take part. If you can overcome Manchester City and Arsenal – two of the best teams in Europe – you have a self-belief that you can overcome Leeds as well, another team of household names and probably, at that time, I would say the best team in Europe. We needed to concentrate on our strengths and how to eliminate their strengths.'

Stokoe later told of how he and his coaching staff had done their homework on Revie's side: 'What I didn't know about Leeds in the build-up to that final wasn't worth knowing,' he said. 'I had them watched and went to see some of their games myself, although I wouldn't have accepted Leeds' hospitality – had there been any on offer! They were a tough lot, physical and ruthless. They played with a win-at-all-costs attitude. If they couldn't match the opposition on a football front, they were cunning enough to play it rough.'

'Bob's policy was that he wanted us to take the game to Leeds,' Porterfield said. 'He didn't want us to sit back and try and pace ourselves in the game, he wanted us to have a go.'

After lunch the Sunderland team set off on the twelve-mile journey through the rain and the red-and-white banners, flags and scarves that carried them all the way to Wembley.

'I remember Bob Stokoe got on the bus and just said, "Hi, lads," to the camera crew and off we went to Wembley,' Montgomery says. 'There was no pressure on us at all, which, looking back, is unbelievable really. The relaxed mood was definitely down to Bob, but we had two good men in Arthur Cox and Billy Elliott as well. Arthur was a placid man, never aggressive, and while Billy would kick his granny on the pitch, off the pitch he was mild and meek. So there were no aggressive people around us. They were all a calming influence on us and that was important.'

The mood on the Sunderland coach could not have been any better. ITV's cameras beamed back live pictures to the nation and gradually – on one channel or the other – the infectious camaraderie and feel-good factor among the squad was getting through to the viewers. The jokes that had kept coming all morning and into the afternoon could be shared by those at home, whichever channel they were watching, despite the fact that the satellite link from the team bus broke up now and again – something else that was just lapped up by the confident and carefree Sunderland players.

'Certainly the confidence of the Sunderland team seemed to soar after those interviews with me in the morning,' Davies says. 'They bubbled through lunch and they were still bubbling on the way to Wembley. It was like they were going off to a party. They were a decent bunch and such good fun that I found myself getting well beyond what you should do in a situation such as that and I so wanted them to win. I got so involved with wanting them to do well. If you were a reporter with a particular team you hoped that team would go on to win, and during the course of the day my belief grew that Sunderland were going to win. There was no logic involved in that except the attitude that the players were taking.'

On the coach Dennis Tueart told Stokoe that he had felt more nervous watching previous Cup finals on television than he now did travelling to Wembley to play in one. 'We didn't know what nerves were,' he recalls. 'There were no nerves at all. We didn't know what it was all about. We didn't know what pressure was.'

'When the coach turned into Wembley Way all you could see was red and white,' Davies says. 'That was purely by chance – because the Leeds supporters were at the other end of the stadium – but it was another factor. It looked as though there were only Sunderland sup- porters there.'

'All the way to Wembley it was red and white,' Malone says. 'Everyone in London seemed to want Sunderland to win that day. Maybe that had a lot to do with Leeds, of course, but it was a tremendous feeling to see that support. I don't think I saw a Leeds supporter.'

'My father had a friend in the Merchant Navy and he told him that his boat was full of Scousers, Scotsmen, all sorts, and no one was shouting for Leeds,' Guthrie adds. 'Everyone wanted Sunderland to win. The support we had from all pockets of the country was incredible.'

'That day couldn't come soon enough for us,' Sunderland supporter Pete Sixsmith recalls. 'We left Sunderland at midnight and there was a stream of special trains that got us into London at six o'clock in the morning. One of my mates suggested we went over to a cartoon theatre at Victoria Station to warm up. So we trailed over there and it was closed – he wasn't Mr Popular after that, I can tell you! There were nine hours to kill before kick-off so by the time the teams were on the way to the stadium we were more than up for it.'

Miss Sunderland, Jackie Short, travelled in comfort on one of the special supporters' trains to London with a red 'Miss Sunderland' sash across her chest and a red-and-white boater on her head. She confidently predicted a final score of Sunderland 3 Leeds United 1 on account of the three red ribbons and one white ribbon that sat on top of her hat. This would not be the correct scoreline, but these numbers would be uncannily relevant to how the match turned out.

Hundreds of Sunderland supporters went down to London in the hope of buying tickets on Wembley Way on the day of the match. The asking price for a £1 standing ticket was upwards of £15, with reports that as much as £50 passed hands between desperate fans and touts.

'I was stood on Wembley Way when our coach went past,' Sunderland fan Bill Peverley says. 'I saw Dave Watson sat looking into emptiness, he was that focused. I put my thumb up to him and he mouthed back at me, "We're going to win." I can't tell you what that felt like. The hairs stood up on the back of my neck. The belief was there, from all of us.'

'Supporters were banging on the bus all the way down Wembley Way, cheering us on and waving at us,' Montgomery says. 'If that wasn't going to frighten us then nothing would; and it didn't frighten us. When we drove through the big arch at Wembley and those doors closed behind us, it went from all that noise and support outside to suddenly just total quiet. It was just us then – for the time being anyway.'

Wembley's dressing rooms were austere and quite unwelcoming. Each was set out over two levels, with a large bath, and showers and individual baths some steps above the changing-room area. The ceilings were high and the white tiling was clinical, almost cold in character.

Montgomery had been in these dressing rooms once before, as an understudy to Gordon Banks when England beat France 5–0 in a friendly in 1969, but he had never played at Wembley before – only one of his Sunderland team-mates had. The goalkeeper had sat in the North dressing room that night with the national team, across the passage from the South dressing room that he was using today.

Ritchie Pitt had done likewise when representing England Schoolboys against Scotland Schoolboys. He was the only member of the entire

Sunderland squad to have previously played on the famous turf.

Watson had been to Wembley on FA Cup final day seven years before, as a spectator, when he watched Sheffield Wednesday – managed by Alan Brown – lose to Everton. The fact that today was almost like a day out for the Sunderland squad was summed up by the following comment from their centre-half: 'I had just joined Notts County when I went to Wembley in 1966 and I thought it was fantastic. But I never thought one day in the future I would play there in a Cup final of my own.'

The future was now. The Sunderland players walked up the tunnel and stepped out on to the rain-soaked pitch, greeting the early arrivals in the crowd as they did so. There were less than ninety minutes to go until kick-off.

'It all hit home to me when we walked out on to the pitch,' Malone says. 'All I wanted to do then was to get out and play. I just wanted to have the first touch, because the first touch tells you how you're going to play on the day. It had poured down as well and the pitch was wet.'

'There was hardly anybody in the stadium at that time and it was just fabulous to soak it all up,' Montgomery adds. 'I made the decision there and then that I was going to have to punch if anything came my way. The gloves we had in those days were like gardening gloves and I was never comfortable with them when it was greasy. It would have been perfect if it had been dry conditions and I didn't have to wear gloves, but it wasn't dry, it was very wet. So rather than try and get the ball under pressure I decided I was going to get it away. If you punch it out then you can get back and get settled if anybody comes in and shoots again. I decided very early that I was going to do that.'

'We were all looking at the weather conditions – the pitch wasn't good and it had rained an awful lot – and trying to decide which studs to wear and all that, for it was important to get the studs selection right,' Halom adds. 'I got it wrong, I admit it. I put inch-long studs in the front of my boots to get a good grip on what was a very wet pitch and it turned out to be the wrong decision.'

Pitt and Watson were standing together in the centre circle quietly discussing tactics when Cox walked over to them. It is a conversation that Pitt remembers well: 'Arthur took me to one side and said, "Allan Clarke is a top-class striker but I'm not sure how brave he is, so the first chance you get – well away from goal, thirty yards out – let him know you're there."'

At this time the Leeds squad – resplendent once more in those charcoal-grey pin-striped suits with matching waistcoats – arrived at Wembley. The Sunderland players had been issued with official club blazers but were given freedom of choice over whether to wear them. Most of them decided against wearing the blazer and therefore, in contrast to their opponents, gave the impression of rather random group attire on the day – not that it mattered to them. 'There was a club suit so I am not sure why some of the players wore their own suits,' Malone, one of only three players to wear the blazer – Guthrie and Halom were the others – says. 'Maybe we all just wanted to wear our twenty-one-inch trousers and flared suits and all that,' Young suggests.

Motson was assigned the task of pre-match player interviews on BBC1 and quickly grabbed a word with a group of Sunderland players behind the goal at the tunnel end. 'We feel that the onus is on Leeds,' Montgomery told him. 'We are the underdogs, we can relax. It's up to Leeds – they have got to watch us.' When asked what Stokoe had said to his players regarding the opposition, Hughes replied, 'Nothing much. We don't need to talk about them. We know all we need to know.' Asked about the playing conditions and the suggestion by some that the wet pitch would favour Leeds, Watson answered confidently, 'I wouldn't think so. We'll do well on it.' Kerr agreed with him: 'We can play in anything,' he said. Guthrie and Tueart were asked about the relaxed mood that enveloped the squad and was amazing all onlookers: 'It's a good carry on,' Guthrie said. 'What's wrong with it?' Tueart joked. 'Is it wrong, like?' No question could faze them. The underdogs remained carefree and confident.

Derby County manager Brian Clough – a man with more interest in the situation than most – was sat high up in the BBC television studio looking down on the interviews as they went out to the nation. He remained unconvinced about the growing notion that Sunderland had a chance of causing an upset: 'I'm not trying to be rude to them but they looked like a little kindergarten side coming out, as though it is a fairytale and they can't quite believe it,' he said. 'They are so blasé about it, it is nothing short of a miracle. I hope Leeds don't catch them in this mood because if they do it will be over in the first ten minutes.'

'That's the miracle man. The question is, can he produce another miracle for Sunderland this afternoon?" ITV commentator Brian Moore said over live pictures of Stokoe on the Wembley turf. In a live pre-match interview on ITV, reporter Keith Macklin asked him, 'Bob, you looked tremendously confident as you walked down there and waved to the crowd. You know, everybody thought you would be bowled over by the atmosphere.' A calm and composed Sunderland manager replied, 'We are all very thrilled and excited but not overawed because we expected it. Greatest supporters in the land up at the other end there, and we are going to do everything we possibly can to make them proud of us.' Macklin also asked, 'Don Revie says that his side will have the psychological advantage because they have been here before, do you accept that?' A smiling Stokoe replied, 'No. No I don't, not in the least.'

As the Sunderland squad walked back down the tunnel, the Leeds players emerged from it, waving to their families and friends, smiling and chatting to each other. Motson asked David Harvey about the wet playing conditions: 'It doesn't help very much but these things you have got to overcome,' the goalkeeper replied. Mick Jones, responding to Motson's observation that the mood in the Leeds team appeared apprehensive compared to the fun and frolics of Sunderland, warned, 'Once we get out there, there will be no laughing or joking.' Peter Lorimer added: 'If we could score an early goal I think we will put a performance on like you have never seen before. I think it all hinges on the early goal.'

'My memory from those pre-match interviews is that the only Leeds player who seemed to show any sign of confidence was Peter Lorimer,' Motson recalls. 'My impression was that Sunderland had nothing to lose and they were going to enjoy the day come what may. It was an amazing turnaround from where they were in late November when Bob Stokoe had taken over up there and we did that interview at Roker Park. But I sensed that Leeds were on edge.'

'I personally felt we were very confident that day but maybe, looking back, we were too confident,' Lorimer reflects. 'I think we thought, We can go out here and we can take them apart, do it with a bit of style and put on a show for the millions of people watching at home.'

All those years of playing to the defensive Revie method were about to explode. As tense as many of them looked, Lorimer confirms that this may have been too good an opportunity for Leeds to miss: a live television audience, Second Division opposition and a chance to try and redeem themselves and their reputation in front of a previously unforgiving nation.

As the Leeds players retreated down the tunnel to the North dressing room, Sunderland's players and coaching staff were already getting into their pre-match routine. Stokoe and Cox were walking around the South dressing room having individual chats, geeing players up if necessary. Billy Elliott and Johnny Watters were doing the same.

'That last hour was my hour and I would never leave the dressing room at that time,' Stokoe explained. 'I would have a little chat here and there. Some would need a little fist under their nose, some an arm around them. You learn about your players and you try to get the best out of them.'

But one man was left to his own routine. 'Everyone knew just to leave me alone, and the Cup final was no different,' Montgomery says. 'Five to two was always the time for my last cigarette; home or away that was my ritual. I used to have it in the toilets – you could see the smoke coming up from the cubicle and so everyone knew where I was. I would finish my cigarette and then I would start to get changed and go through my routine, bouncing the ball off the bathroom wall to get a feel of it and that kind of thing. My jersey would be the last thing I put on. Nobody ever spoke to me during the last fifteen minutes or so before we went out because they knew I had to get focused and that was it.'

'It became a standing joke that Bob Stokoe would come into the dressing room to give us his team talk before the match and always ask where Jimmy Monty was, and every time he was always in the toilet,' Pitt adds.

'The changing rooms at Wembley were so ancient, with big old baths and everything,' Young recalls. 'I remember looking at the souvenir FA Cup final programme before we walked out and Brian Chambers was in it, named as the substitute. I remember thinking at the time, Well thanks very much, Bob, that's just fantastic. The FA Cup final programme and I haven't even got my name in it!'

High up in the Wembley television studios the respected pundits gave their final pre-match verdicts. The BBC panel of Brian Clough, Bob Wilson, the injured Leeds and England full-back Terry Cooper and Bobby Charlton, who the day before had been appointed Preston North End manager, voted 3–1 in favour of a Leeds win. Charlton was the solitary voice that gave Sunderland a chance. 'The more I have seen since I came into the stadium – and around the stadium – convinces me that what I thought this morning is right, that I think Sunderland have a great chance of winning,' Charlton said. 'I think they have every chance of creating a mild sensation today.'

'I don't think there is any way that Sunderland can win the FA Cup this afternoon. In the semi-final against Arsenal they never stopped chasing and running. From my own experience playing out there, you just can't chase about for ninety minutes on that pitch,' Cooper said. 'It's got to be Leeds.'

'You have got to have reservations because it is still a Cup tie. Despite the fact it is a Cup final, it is still ninety minutes and anything can happen,' Clough added. 'But, clinically, there is not a single solitary thing apart from the physical side – running power – where Sunderland can possibly win. We all used to believe in fairies at the bottom of the garden. We like these things to come true and if that happens today then obviously everybody's dream would come true and Sunderland would win. But it is impossible to be – I don't know – anything but certain that Leeds will beat Sunderland in today's Cup final.' Clough also knew that a Leeds win would mean that Derby would qualify for the 1973–74 UEFA Cup. 'It's like Ted Heath, in actual fact, voting Labour, but that's how it's got to go,' the former Sunderland legend said.

One guest in the BBC studio that afternoon who was shouting for Sunderland was Korbut, the Olympic gold medallist. She was dressed for it too, wearing a white blouse and red skirt. She had told anchorman Frank Bough via a translator earlier in the day that she was supporting 'the smaller ones'. But Korbut's compatriot and fellow member of the Soviet Union gymnastics team Ludmilla Turitsheva decisively and determinedly opted for Leeds.

Attention then turned to the pre-match entertainment of international athletics, with the British record holder at 5,000 metres and 10,000 metres, David Bedford – wearing red socks, to the delight of the Sunderland fans – running in a field including Britain's Olympic 5,000m bronze medallist Ian Stewart and the Olympic 5,000m silver medallist and 3,000m world record holder Emiel Puttemans of Belgium in a six-man 3,000m event around the Wembley pitch. Puttemans won the race comfortably, with Bedford second and Stewart third.

The Ayr Majorettes then entertained the swelling crowd before singer Frankie Vaughan, accompanied by the Band of the Coldstream Guards, took to the pitch. Vaughan had connections with Sunderland – his wife was born in the town and during the 1972–73 season he had performed at La Strada nightclub, on Fawcett Street, on more than one occasion. He wore a white tie beneath a light-grey suit and warmed the crowd up with a rendition of 'You'll Never Walk Alone' before performing 'Abide With Me', the traditional hymn that had been performed at every FA Cup final since 1927. It was sung from the heart by the 100,000 fans packed inside the stadium, and the emotion was particularly visible among the Sunderland supporters, reading the words from their programmes and reclaiming their place on the big stage after so many barren years.

Television viewers could now see for themselves the vast quantities of red-and-white support inside Wembley, dominating the West End of the stadium but also visible in many other parts, even in the East End – the tunnel end – that Stokoe had commented on earlier in the week. There were plenty of Leeds scarves and flags as well, of course. In fact the one banner that caught the eye more than any other was written in blue and yellow on a white background and simply read NORMAN BITES YER LEGS. The scene was well and truly set.

'It was the first match I had ever seen in colour on television and I couldn't believe how green the pitch was,' Steve Cram says. 'The grass was lime green.' Other first-time colour-television viewers later commented on how rich Sunderland's red and white stripes looked. 'We didn't have colour television at our house at that time and so I watched it two doors down,' Cram adds. 'I would have loved to be at Wembley and I was disappointed not to be there because my dad was offered two tickets for the final by a neighbour. The story goes that he did Vic Halom's garden and got offered them through him! Sadly my dad had to work and he wouldn't let me go down to Wembley on my own. So I had an early lunch and sat down to watch the whole afternoon – in colour – on the BBC.' The focus – and the tension – now switched to the Wembley tunnel, where referee Ken Burns, a forty-three-year-old legal executive from Stourbridge, Worcestershire, made a late decision that was to make this FA Cup final unique. Due to the overcast weather conditions Burns elected to use an orange match ball in preference to a white one. An orange ball – synonymous with

England's World Cup win of 1966 – had never been used in an FA Cup final before and this would be the only time it has ever been used at the showpiece event.

The night before, the BBC programme *Nationwide* had gone to great lengths to film an item showing the Cup final ball being stitched and prepared for the big occasion. But that ball was white. Like the coloured ribbons of the losing side, it was never used on the big day. Burns was in his thirteenth year on the Football League list. He had refereed Sunderland's opening game of the 1972–73 season against Middlesbrough. Much more importantly – in Revie's mind – he had also refereed the 1967 FA Cup semi-final between Leeds and Chelsea and was the man who had cancelled out Lorimer's late goal which would have taken the contest into extra-time. The referee had been subjected to a lot of coverage in the press during the week due to Stokoe's public pleas concerning Bremner. He now knocked on the North and South dressing-rooms' doors.

The South door was the first to open as the Sunderland team took their place to the right side of the tunnel. First out was Stokoe, unveiling his unusual Cup final attire. Instead of dressing in a traditional suit and tie – which incidentally he had been wearing pre-match – the Sunderland manager appeared in a bright red tracksuit with his name emblazoned on the back in big white capital letters for all to see. Stokoe later made light of this by joking: 'I hadn't got a lucky suit like Don Revie, so I just came dressed as one of the lads.' But Young remembers another reason for the Sunderland manager being so keen to break with FA Cup final protocol: 'Bob Stokoe had a friend who became our agent and acted as his agent as well,' he says. 'I think he got about two grand in sponsorship for wearing that tracksuit, which was a huge amount of money.

'The players were all guaranteed some money if we wore new boots as well,' Young adds. 'But it takes a few weeks to break boots in. We tried them on and feared we would get crippled. Some of the lads just wouldn't wear them. So Billy Elliott – the boot man on the day of the final – had to black out several pairs of old boots and paint them with the logo of the new ones. Of course it was a wet day and in no time at all all the bloody paint had run off them.'

Behind Bob Stokoe stood his 'little general' and captain Bobby Kerr, goalkeeper Jim Montgomery, Ritchie Pitt, Micky Horswill, Dick Malone,

Dave Watson, Ron Guthrie, Ian Porterfield, Billy Hughes, Dennis Tueart, Dave Young and Vic Halom. Although he was the substitute Young was not the last man in the line-up. 'I was planning to go last,' he says. 'But Vic Halom always had the same superstition, hence he magically appeared behind me in the tunnel.' Some moments later, when Leeds emerged from the North dressing room, Allan Clarke, as predicted, similarly took his place in their line-up behind substitute Terry Yorath.

Stokoe tried his best not to make eye contact with Revie or any of the Leeds players, one of whom he later claimed mouthed obscenities at him. His professional ambition was now matched by his own personal vendetta: 'This was the one game I was desperate to win, the ultimate challenge of wits and strategy against a man and a manager who, in my opinion, was fortunate to be in charge of any football club,' he later said. Stokoe's players generally followed their manager's lead, and ignored their opponents as the teams gathered in the tunnel.

'Bobby Kerr and I were the only ones still there from the FA Cup games with Leeds in 1967 and we were stood at the front,' Montgomery says. 'I know Bob Stokoe didn't admire Leeds that much. He wasn't a great lover of them and he certainly wasn't a great lover of Don Revie. But then not many people were really, in the methods he used and whatever. There was still a big rivalry with them, but I think it was mainly between the managers and among the supporters.'

'I didn't speak to any of the Leeds players in the tunnel,' Watson adds. 'I didn't know any of them personally as I had never come across any of them before. I do remember they looked different to us. We were more with the era and had longer hair and so on. Don Revie wouldn't have liked long hair. He would have wanted his team to look the same, in orderly fashion. Then again, Bob Stokoe didn't like long hair too much either. He would say to me, "Get your hair cut!" but I never did. We all had long hair. I had hair down to my shoulders. So he must have been saying it to all of us!'

The players stood in the tunnel waiting for the cue to walk out on to the famous turf. It was an anxious wait and for some it seemed to last for an eternity.

'I will always remember standing in the tunnel at Wembley,' Kerr says. 'I was bouncing the ball and chewing gum like an idiot. My gob was going like the clappers and the ball was bouncing up and down because we were just stood there waiting. It was just sheer tension.'

At 2.50 p.m., the teams were led out. Stokoe gave a wry smile and a shake of the head as he tried to put his anguish and anxiety to one side and visibly shared a word with Revie in front of the watching television cameras; Kerr stopped bouncing his ball but continued chewing his gum; Montgomery made the sign of the cross across his chest. Then the noise hit them.

'I had sat at home and watched FA Cup finals at Wembley on the television but I never ever thought that I would ever be walking out there. I mean: the FA Cup final at Wembley! The noise when we got to the top of the tunnel was deafening and the first thing I saw was that anybody in the stadium who wasn't supporting Leeds seemed to have some red on them,' Kerr says. 'We never knew what to expect walking up that tunnel and maybe that was a blessing in disguise,' Montgomery adds. 'We were stood there and we could see nothing apart from the sky, then – as we started to walk – we could see all the Sunderland fans facing us. The crescendo was unbelievable and to see that mass of red and white and hear the roar was absolutely awesome.'

For all Stokoe's careful and cunning pre-match planning and preparations, the one fact that appeared to have escaped his attention was that when both teams emerged from the tunnel at Wembley the first sight the players would see would be the Sunderland supporters at the far end of the ground. Stokoe had spoken publicly about his unhappiness concerning the allocation of ends, fearing it gave Leeds an unfair advantage for their fans to be situated at the tunnel end. In fact, it proved to be the opposite. The sight that met the Sunderland players as they walked out on to the pitch that day could not have been bought at any price. It provided a moment and an emotion that would live with them all for the rest of their lives.

'We walked out on to the pitch and it looked to me to be nine-tenths Sunderland supporters,' Malone says. 'I couldn't believe the red and white. It was the same inside the stadium as it was outside on the roads and virtually all around the ground was red and white.'

'When you walked up the tunnel at Wembley all you could see was the sky because the tunnel slopes,' Watson explains. 'When you got over the crest you could see the crowd but only when you left the mouth of the tunnel could all of the crowd see you, and then the noise hit you. It was like a sound wave knocking you over that day. It was so loud you couldn't talk to each other because you couldn't hear each other.'

'I can't remember too much pre-match because I think I was so focused on the game,' Hughes adds. 'But I can remember walking out, hearing the roar and seeing there was red and white everywhere. I can remember that – and the realisation that millions of people were watching us at that very moment.'

'I don't remember a lot,' Halom says. 'I think you begin to focus on things at that time. It is a team game but it is also very singular. It is about you. I don't remember anything about the dressing room. That wasn't important. I do remember walking out with the tracksuit top on and the reception we got. The red and white that was in the stadium was awesome and the noise was incredible too. It was like no place where I'd played could ever match Roker Park in terms of atmosphere with a full house of over fifty thousand people – but when we walked out at Wembley and saw the red and white all around the stadium it was an enormous lift. It was like sucking in fresh air. Your power and your strength and your determination all come out.'

Once out on the pitch, Pitt, with his full head of hair, began to engage himself in some head tennis to ease the pre-match tension. 'That was sheer nerves, sheer nerves. It was just a case of doing something,' he says. 'By then I just wanted to get out there and get the match started. I was a little nervous so I just did a few keepy-ups to pass the time. I remember looking up to the stands to see my wife. She waved and gave me the thumbs-up so I knew everything was OK back home.'

Other Sunderland players looked up to see if they could spot their wives and girlfriends too. 'I remember glancing up to where our wives were sat near to the Royal Box – just for a split second to see if I could see my wife – but I couldn't see anyone I knew. All I could see was red and white. I just kept walking and remained focused on the game,' Guthrie says.

'My wife was there and she was pregnant with our first child,' Young adds. 'The roar when we came out was incredible and my heart was in my mouth, it really was. It was like the gladiators going out to fight. It was such a thrill to hear that roar, absolutely fantastic.'

'There was a big luncheon before the match which I had to attend, which is regrettable in many ways,' Sunderland chairman Keith Collings recalls. 'I was virtually at the centre of the top table but I wanted to be outside to see what was going on. I remember there was a panic trying to get to my seat in time. It was annoying but you are waiting for the official guests to go up before you can go up and, of course, we were sat in the front row of the Royal Box and so we had to wait. The volume of noise hit me as soon as I got up to my seat and the magnificence of the occasion. I don't think you can put into words what it is like seeing your home-town team in an FA Cup final. It was just a pity we couldn't have had twice as many tickets or more.'

A brief and rare ray of sunshine greeted the players as they emerged from the tunnel, but as both teams gathered either side of the halfway line below the Royal Box the rain came down again. The teams stood for the national anthem and the Duke of Kent was introduced to both teams and both managers by the club captains, the two shortest skippers in FA Cup final history, Billy Bremner and Bobby Kerr. At five feet five inches tall, the Leeds skipper was the taller of the two by just half an inch.

'The royalty came along and I introduced them to the team,' Kerr recalls. 'The officials had told me not to converse with the royalty unless they conversed with me but when I did talk to them I found myself talking the way they talked. I introduced Ritchie Pitt as "Richard Pitt". I can remember doing that.'

'I was the only one in the team that the Duke of Kent stopped to talk to as he came down the line,' Pitt says. 'He had heard that my daughter was in hospital and he asked me how she was. I said she was fine and that I was looking forward to seeing her.'

At the end of the line of Sunderland players stood Stokoe. After having a word with the Duke of Kent, he gently turned to his team, clapped his hands in encouragement, shook Kerr's hand and then sent them on their way. He then took his place on the bench and put on his raincoat and trilby. As his players ran over to applaud the Sunderland supporters at the West End of the stadium, a deafening jeer rang out around them as Bremner led the Leeds players into the centre circle and they turned to salute all sides of the stadium. It was a pre-match gesture Leeds did at Elland Road every week, but it didn't go down too well with the Sunderland fans.

Kerr walked to the centre circle to shake hands with Bremner. Kerr won the coin toss and elected to attack the Sunderland supporters' end in the first half. Leeds would kick off.

As the teams changed ends, Burns placed the ball on the spot and there it stood until Hughes ran along, flicked it up and started to knock it about to get a feel of it. When the time was right he casually lofted the ball into the arms of the waiting Jones so the Cup final could start.

The match got under way: Jones tapped the ball to Giles, who played it back to Hunter, who attempted to swing the ball out to Reaney but his pass was cut out by the on-rushing Tueart. Within five seconds of the match starting, Sunderland were on the attack and Leeds were back-tracking. Halom and Hughes advanced towards the Leeds penalty box as Tueart ran on and fired towards the goal. His shot was blocked by Hunter. Horswill and Kerr – both running forward in support of Tueart – slipped on the wet surface at the same time, immediately indicating what the playing conditions were like.

Giles collected the ball for Leeds and coolly played it out to Jones on the left flank. With both Watson and Malone in attendance, the Leeds striker played the ball back to Giles, who took a touch and allowed Clarke to run inside with the ball, about thirty yards from the Sunderland goal. Clarke made space for himself and neatly pushed the ball forward. The watching Pitt timed his run to perfection and then clattered into him. The defender's left leg connected with the striker's right knee. Clarke was down, Leeds trainer Les Cocker was on, and Pitt was fortunate to avoid a caution.

'This was a tackle, for me, that in any normal match I think might have resulted in a name-take,' ITV co-commentator Jimmy Hill said. 'It was really late, no question about it.'

'It wasn't intentional to hurt him but it was intentional to let Leeds know they were going to be in a game,' Pitt says. 'I had to make sure it didn't happen near the penalty area because Lorimer would have just lashed one and we didn't want to give them a chance like that early on. There is no way I would ever hurt another professional, but part of our game plan was to show Leeds that we weren't going to be intimidated by them and we were going to give them a game and, of course, we had to do that early on. I think that tackle set the tone for the game.' Burns awarded a free-kick but took no action on Pitt; the pre-match plan had worked to perfection and gone unpunished.

'It was a terrible tackle and if it had happened in the second half or maybe even later in the first half he could have gone for it,' Watson says. 'There was no plan on getting the ball. He just whacked him. It could have broken Allan Clarke's leg and ended his career. But it didn't, he got up and he played on. If it set any agenda I think it set the agenda for Allan Clarke and Ritchie Pitt. I think it was a personal thing between those two players but to my mind it didn't make any difference to me or the rest of us.'

Pitt's foul on Clarke was actually typical of Revie's Leeds. In his autobiography Hunter admits, 'The gaffer used to say to me: "Norman, when your man gets the ball for the first time, let him know you're there. Hit him hard and let him know you're on his case."' There were no complaints from the Leeds players as Clarke returned to his feet.

Sunderland formed a four-man wall – Horswill, Hughes, Tueart and Porterfield – but Giles moved the ball along to his right, to the waiting Lorimer, who lashed it well wide of the goal. Montgomery's goal-kick was quickly picked up in the centre circle by Bremner, who played in Madeley, who sent the ball back into the Sunderland half towards Clarke, who was again challenged by Pitt, who was again penalised by the referee – this time for a push in the back – but there was still no booking, despite there being only ninety seconds on the clock. Lorimer took the free-kick and lofted the ball deep into the penalty box. It sailed over the heads of both Jones and Malone.

The wet conditions were continuing to prove hazardous. Both Bremner and Giles misplaced passes. When Kerr took advantage of a mistake by the Leeds captain, he promptly played in Hughes, who was then upended by Cherry. Watson went forward for the free-kick and was immediately man-marked by Hunter. The information in the Leeds dossier concerning the tall centre-half meant that special attention would be given to him whenever necessary, and that was carried out to the letter. On this occasion Kerr's free-kick went high over Watson's head.

From the resultant goal-kick Harvey rolled the ball out to Gray on the left flank. It was the Scottish winger's first touch of the ball. After linking up with Hunter, Gray sent the ball forward for Jones to chase, but Pitt was on hand to slide in and play the ball back to Montgomery. In an end-to-end opening sequence Montgomery then played the ball out to Guthrie, who played a long ball forward for Halom to chase. This time Madeley mopped up any danger before inexplicably playing a casual pass into the path of Tueart, who looked up, saw Hughes in the box and quickly crossed. Cherry was on hand to clear for Leeds.

Moments later the ball broke to Gray on the left. Running towards Malone and pursued by the back-tracking Kerr, Gray suddenly found himself losing possession. Another agenda had been set early on. The television cameras briefly picked up a shot of Revie sat pensively on the Leeds bench with a towel wrapped around his head to keep out the rain and Harvey's tracksuit top on his knees to keep out the cold.

The Leeds manager would have been encouraged by what he saw next – an eight-pass move that took the ball from deep inside their penalty box to just outside the Sunderland penalty box. The authority and assurance of the move was textbook Leeds. But the way Guthrie dispossessed Lorimer and Porterfield, then calmly collected the ball and showed great close control to set Sunderland off on another attack, should have been a reminder to the Cup holders that they could not rest on their laurels.

Halom then took advantage of a mistake by Giles to play in Tueart, who made a short pass to Horswill close to the edge of the Leeds penalty box. Horswill turned to shoot but his effort was blocked by Bremner. It was the first one-to-one collision between the two red-haired number 4s. Bremner was left checking his shins.

More assured play from Porterfield in midfield led to Hughes running down the left flank and playing a neat ball between the bodies of Bremner and Reaney into the penalty box that was just too fast for Tueart. Leeds responded: Lorimer played the ball forward for Jones to chase, but Watson intercepted quickly to break up the attack. Leeds kept up the pressure: Giles swept the ball out to Reaney on the right. Reaney headed the ball into the path of Lorimer, who took a touch and then lofted a deep cross into the penalty box aimed at Jones's head. It was the first time that Montgomery had been called into action. The goalkeeper gave a shout and came off his line to fist the ball away. Horswill was on hand to clear Sunderland's lines.

A foul by Bremner on Porterfield brought boos from the Sunderland fans. It also left a gaping hole in the Sunderland midfielder's left sock and a gash on his left leg. When Porterfield got up from the floor and smiled sarcastically at Bremner, the Leeds captain told him, 'You're as mad as your bloody manager.' 'His reference to the boss made me grin,' Porterfield later said. 'Bob Stokoe had got stuck into Billy Bremner before the match, accusing him of trying to referee games by his constant bleating and the point had apparently found its mark.'

'Ian was such a calming influence in our midfield that day,' Watson says. 'You always knew that if you gave him the ball, he wouldn't give it away. He was a good passer, had good control and was always very cool under pressure. He was a positive influence on the team.'

Sunderland's resultant free-kick, taken by Malone, was aimed for Halom in the penalty box but the centre-forward couldn't connect. A long kick from Harvey was then challenged by both Clarke and Pitt and the defender was subsequently penalised for a third time in the opening ten minutes, on this occasion for another push on the Leeds and England striker. The free-kick – again taken by Lorimer – came to nothing and once more flew over the head of Jones, closely watched by Watson.

Sunderland created a good opening for Hughes on twelve minutes. Kerr dispossessed Gray and linked up well with Halom, who was already having to spend a lot of his time in midfield. Halom moved the ball out left to Porterfield and continued his run towards the Leeds penalty box. Porterfield crossed the ball to the edge of the box and, although Halom slipped, Hughes was on hand to take it on the run and send in a left-foot shot that flashed past the goal. 'A sign of the growing confidence in this Sunderland side,' BBC commentator David Coleman remarked. 'They have started well and really most of the flowing moves and the better midfield play have come from Sunderland.'

But Leeds started to press. Harvey's long goal-kick was headed into the path of Giles by Clarke. Giles played it neatly down the left flank for Jones. But Jones was tackled well by Watson. The ball fell to Clarke, who touched it on to Giles, who smashed in a drive. Pitt blocked the shot but the ball broke to Reaney on the edge of the box. Reaney sent in a low cross that deflected off Guthrie and spun across the penalty area. Bremner and Horswill fought to get to the ball first. The Sunderland youngster won the race, but could only hook it back into the path of Clarke, who steadied himself and then delivered an effort that was charged down by Watson. Sunderland were holding strong at the back. It was 0–0 after quarter of an hour.

Sunderland's best chance of an early goal came moments later. From Porterfield's throw-in on the left, Guthrie whipped a cross into the Leeds penalty box that was headed out by Reaney towards Horswill, who took a touch before unleashing a measured drive that skidded a fraction wide of the outstretched Harvey's far post.

Leeds' best chance of an early goal quickly followed. It resulted from a free-kick by Bremner – awarded when Guthrie was adjudged to have tugged the shirt of Reaney – just outside the penalty box on the right-hand side. Sunderland placed Guthrie and Porterfield in a two-man wall. Bremner floated the ball into the box, but it was cleared by a diving header from Kerr. The ball dropped to Giles, who swung it back to Reaney, who tapped it into the path of Bremner, who this time sent in a much deeper cross. Montgomery punched the ball clear as far as Cherry, who knocked it straight back into the box to an unmarked and waiting Clarke, who was stood by the penalty spot. Clarke took one touch with his left boot, one touch with his right boot and lined up to shoot. Watson then made up yards in a nanosecond and slid in to make a brilliant saving tackle, blocking Clarke's shot with his outstretched left boot. Clarke's face was pure disbelief.

'Watson saved what surely was a certain goal there as Clarke was lining it up,' Moore remarked on ITV. 'When Clarke lines it up from that range that usually means just one thing.'

'It was relentless pressure at that time,' Watson recalls. 'It could be Mick Jones one minute and Allan Clarke the next. Peter Lorimer had chances too. But we held on and held it together.'

'I can think of two or three instances in the first half – in the first ten or fifteen minutes in fact – when we had some outstanding chances to get the ball in the back of the net, but we were trying to beat somebody or go around them or take an extra touch and pass it to somebody else and then put it into the net,' Lorimer says. 'That was probably a lack of professionalism on our part on the day, and of course professionalism was something that we were famed for. We had chances that we would normally have put away but we were trying to walk them into net and make it look what a good side we were rather than getting two goals up and then doing that.'

A few minutes later Clarke's name was the first to go into the referee's notebook, which was somewhat ironic given the nature of the foul that went unpunished against him in the first minute of the match. He was booked for pulling down Hughes, although it has to be said that the challenge by Hunter on Tueart shortly afterwards looked far worse. This ensured that for a while the Leeds defender – a Newcastle supporter in his youth – suffered as many boos from the West End terrace as those being directed towards his club captain. Those boos were still ringing out when, moments later, Hunter showed tremendous confidence, composure and skill to take the ball past three Sunderland players along the edge of his own penalty box.

The first corner of the match went to Leeds. A searching ball aimed deep into the Sunderland penalty box by Giles was headed behind by Malone, although the full-back did appear to be impeded by a challenge from Clarke at the time. Lorimer's corner kick was met by the head of Madeley and swiped away from the feet of Cherry in the six-yard box by another quick-thinking interception from Watson.

A second corner – also taken by Lorimer – was half cleared by Kerr's head. When the ball was knocked back in dangerously by Lorimer, both Watson and Montgomery left nothing to chance. Watson went in with his head and Montgomery with his fists. Between them, the ball was cleared. 'I was in front of Monty and I headed it away but everyone thought Monty punched it. His fist was right next to my head, I could feel it,' Watson says.

Hughes then showed a flash of inspiration when linking up beautifully with Porterfield and Guthrie on the left side. The fast, flowing move was stopped in its tracks by a foul on Guthrie by Bremner. Porterfield nudged the free-kick to Hughes, who managed to get a shot in but sent it wide. At the other end Malone cleared Sunderland's lines once again by heading clear when under pressure from both Clarke and Jones, after some neat work and a nice cross from Lorimer.

After half an hour Sunderland were more than matching their illustrious opponents. The commanding aerial power of Watson and Pitt was there for all to see; Kerr and Malone were silencing Gray on the left flank; Horswill was winning his personal battle with Bremner; Porterfield was beginning to find space and spray the ball around well in midfield; the wide men – Hughes and Tueart – were causing headaches for the Leeds defence; Guthrie was solid and breaking forward whenever he could; Halom was doing his bit too – either up front or in midfield where he was having to spend a fair amount of his time; and Montgomery's decision to punch rather than catch had been absolutely the right one so far. Yet still Leeds showed class. Sunderland had to be on top of their game.

Montgomery kicked the ball high in the air from the left-hand side of his six-yard box. Halom rose on the halfway line to head it on for Hughes, who sent it out to Porterfield on the left. Porterfield looked up and sprayed the ball over to Kerr, in space, on the right. Kerr looked up towards the Leeds goal but as he connected with the ball he slipped on the wet grass. Harvey, under pressure from the oncoming Hughes, jumped to tip the ball behind his crossbar for a corner.

'I have always said that I was the first man to try and chip a goalkeeper from that range,' Kerr says. 'In other words, yes, I slipped. The foot I was standing on – which was my left foot – slipped. I only used that for standing on, I used the right one for everything else.'

'A bad ball into a good one, you see,' Hughes adds. 'Bobby Kerr had tried to cross it in so I just tried and put as much pressure on the goalkeeper as I could. If I hadn't run in to put him under pressure I think he would have just plucked it out the air and we wouldn't have got the corner. If I hadn't done the run, he just jumps up and catches it. He would have caught it.'

Sunderland had won their first corner of the match on thirty-one minutes. Hughes ran over to the left-hand side to take it. Watson came up from the back and made his way into the Leeds penalty area alongside Halom and Porterfield. Tueart positioned himself on the edge of the six-yard box, close to where Hughes was. Guthrie waited on the edge of the penalty box for any half-chances. Horswill and Kerr stood waiting just outside the area as well. Sunderland had four men in the box while Leeds had nine, with only Gray and Lorimer stood outside.

'It was our first corner so we made sure we didn't do anything silly and leave the back door open for them to punish us,' Watson says. 'Breakaways can easily happen from a corner. Bob Stokoe would have told us not to leave ourselves open to that and may even have indicated so from the bench when we got the corner. I normally took up a position at corners where I could run a few yards to get some momentum or to take somebody with me.'

'My plan was to aim for the penalty spot,' Hughes says. 'I wanted to keep it away from David Harvey and then leave the rest to Dave Watson.'

Hughes's plan worked. Although Watson didn't connect with the ball, the centre-half's presence in the box took both Jones and Madeley with him. The ball sailed over all three of them and was met by Halom, closely marked by Hunter, whose momentum knocked the ball forward – off his thigh – to Porterfield, now unmarked and standing just outside the edge of the six-yard box. Porterfield had time to cushion the ball on his left thigh and volley it into the net with his right foot. For such a naturally left-sided player, it was a rarity. For it to come in an FA Cup final, it was a goal and a half.

'Hughes with the kick,' Coleman said on BBC1, before announcing with trademark effect: 'Porterfield.' Peter Jones told Radio 2 listeners: 'Porterfield has scored and the Second Division side Sunderland go into the lead against Leeds United.' Moore, on ITV, called it as follows: 'Watson is right in there, so too is Halom and Porterfield; oh, Porterfield has scored and Sunderland, the underdogs, are in the lead.'

'When Billy's corner came in I knew fairly quickly that I wasn't going to get the ball, but I knew there were a couple of players around me and we created that hole which was exposed so well by Ian,' Watson says. 'I jumped up and got half a yard on both of them by making the first move. If the ball had come to me I would have got there first. As it happened they were trailing me across the box and none of us got it. I knew I wasn't going to get the ball – I realised it was too high – but my instinct was to jump anyway and take the Leeds players with me. The ball came over the top of all three of us, hit Vic on the thigh and Ian was left in space to finish. The ball just popped up for him. He hit it with his right foot and found the net. He seemed to have so much time and space to pick his spot that it appeared to have been scored in slow motion. I think that every time I see it. It's beautiful, isn't it?'

'As the ball came over the top, I lifted up to have a look at it – or get a better look at it – but the momentum of those players in front of me stopped me being able to attack the ball or to get a header on the ball,' Halom says. 'It came at me at an angle that wasn't quite right for me, so I had to adjust. I let the ball hit my legs and came back to push it on and take a shot at goal. I was ready to hit it with my left foot and Ian came in and smacked it with his right foot and scored. If he hadn't hit it, I would. Ian stuck it in on the volley. It was a good strike.'

'I brought the ball down on my left thigh and as it dropped I hit it right-footed with all my strength from twelve yards,' Porterfield said. 'Football is all about instinct and reaction and things like that. I mean you can plan tactics and you can do lots of things but incidents happen and, you know, it is a reaction and your ability to manoeuvre and adjust. It just all fell perfect for me in lots of ways.

'When I scored it is the first time I have ever felt emotion in my life,' Porterfield added. 'I am not an emotional fellow but I could feel the tears come into my eyes. Billy Hughes said: "Porter, you've scored, you've scored." When he said that I think I began to realise I had scored. What a magical moment. Our fans, penned behind David Harvey's goal, must have seen it all the way. They went mad.' So did the Sunderland players. Porterfield was quickly engulfed in a sea of red-and-white shirts.

'I was the first one to congratulate Ian,' Guthrie says. 'I was hovering around the edge of the box just looking for anything that might happen and come my way. Nobody ever told me to do that, I just did it myself. I always used to hang around that area, like I did in the sixth round against Luton Town when I scored. Of course Ian was in the right place at the right time in the final. It was a great goal. He used his wrong foot as well. I went up to him and said, "Good on you, Porter, you beauty."'

'I took up a position, hoping for any knock-downs or any bits of scrap,' Tueart says. 'The main target was always Dave Watson or Vic Halom. Both Dave and Vic were good headers of the ball. Dave took two defenders with him, Vic got a touch and it fell for Ian. I don't know what Ian was doing in there. He was normally on the edge of the box. He hit it so well. It got a little deflection off Allan Clarke's shoulder and went in.'

'The only thing I can remember seeing is the ball hitting the back of the net,' Hughes says. 'I didn't even realise it was Porter's right foot at the time. I think that was the only time he ever scored with his right foot, God rest his soul.' 'For Porter to score a goal with his right peg, I would never have believed it,' Kerr adds. 'But I have to believe it because it's now history. Amazing. It was a hell of a goal.'

'I had a great view of the goal and I can see it now: Porter scoring in front of a sea of red and white,' Montgomery says with a smile. 'My first thought when we scored was, If we can keep a clean sheet, we've won the Cup. But that is easy to say. There was still a long way to go.'

'I was back in the right-back position when Ian scored,' Malone says. 'That is an example of me not really getting forward during the game. Ian took his chance so well.'

'I was on the halfway line when we scored,' Pitt adds. 'But it didn't take us long to get to Ian and celebrate with him.'

'I didn't celebrate the goal like the others did,' Watson says. 'I stretched out my arms like an aeroplane and ran straight back to my position, thinking, Let's get on with it and let's finish it. The goal seemed to give our fans extra belief, and that came through to the players. I felt it.'

'We were very grateful Ian Porterfield scored with his right foot. He could paint, he could shave, he could do anything with his left one but the right one was just for standing on, so that was a very special occasion,' Stokoe said. 'Inside I was bursting with emotion but the last thing I wanted to do was to physically release that feeling. I wanted to keep it under control, harnessed to use to motivate my players through the remainder of the game.'

'I felt we had won it there and then,' Sunderland supporter Steve Hodgson says. 'I was stood behind the goal with my brother and it was fantastic when we scored. One minute we were mauling each other and the next minute we were twenty yards apart. When everything calmed down – a bit – I said to him, "We've won it. They'll never get one past Monty now." I was confident they wouldn't score. I just felt sure they wouldn't, in my heart – you know?'

But Leeds *had* to score if they were to prevent the greatest FA Cup final shock of all time. Revie's side had just under an hour to do that. The television cameras showed Cocker on the bench with his head in his hands. Revie – having now discarded the towel from his head – looked on motionless. Somewhere in the stadium Miss Sunderland threw her boater – with three red ribbons and one white ribbon – up in the air. There were thirty-one minutes on the clock: Miss Sunderland's 3 and 1.

'The goal we conceded against Sunderland was a mistake that we very seldom made,' Lorimer says. 'It was very, very surprising that one of our players would drop three yards off a guy like Ian Porterfield in the penalty area to allow him that amount of space, but that is what happened on the day and once it has happened there is nothing you can do about it. The disappointing thing that Don Revie would have felt would have been that he had designated a man to mark Ian, because he was a big lad. Ian was in there and so we would have had somebody designated to pick him up. So what would really have upset Don was that what we had been told at these meetings beforehand we hadn't carried out on the day.'

Leeds' frustration began to show itself immediately. Within a minute of the goal, Bremner lost his cool twice, first by retaliating after being tackled by Porterfield and then by producing a strong challenge on Horswill. The referee had words with the Leeds captain.

Wembley Stadium was now showcasing the 'Roker Roar', packed with red-and-white scarves and featuring a selection of the day's football chants, from 'We Shall Not Be Moved' to 'When the Reds Go Marching in' to 'You'll Never Walk Alone' and then breaking into the resolute mantra of 'Haway the lads – Haway the lads'. The Sunderland fans were singing themselves hoarse.

'Look at them,' Moore remarked. 'After all the thin years with so little success that Sunderland have had, how can you deny them an afternoon like this? The unbelievable is happening that Sunderland – 250–1 outsiders when the FA Cup started in January – are leading in the final against one of the finest teams in Europe, Leeds United.'

A ball from Bremner was cut out neatly by Watson and Porterfield sprayed it out to Hughes on the right, who – after a neat one-two with Tueart – found space to attack and whipped in a deep cross that was just too high for the head of Halom in the penalty box. A challenge by Giles on Horswill moments later led to a stoppage in play. It was noticeable in the minutes that followed the goal that Bremner was now concentrating a lot more on the presence of Porterfield, while Giles had switched his attention to Horswill.

'It is an interesting battle in the middle of the field between Ian Porterfield and Micky Horswill, who are really looking stronger on this heavy ground maybe than Billy Bremner and Johnny Giles,' Jimmy Hill, the ITV co-commentator, said. 'It is the canny, elder players against the younger, strong ones. At the moment it is the younger, strong ones, I feel, that are on top. Bremner has become irritated a little bit because he can't get the space he needs to dictate.'

When play resumed Tueart chested down Guthrie's throw-in and – with a neat touch of the heel – took the ball past Reaney into the path of the advancing left-back. Guthrie, who was finding himself increasingly in forward positions, fired in a cross that went over Harvey's bar. Once again the Leeds goalkeeper powered the ball back into Sunderland's half from the goal-kick but, once again, the height and head of Watson immediately put Leeds back on the defensive. Another throw-in, this time by Kerr, led to a delightful and incisive pass through a group of Leeds players by Tueart into the path of Hughes down the right flank. Hughes – under pressure from both Cherry and Hunter – then casually back-heeled to Kerr, who lofted the ball into the heart of the Leeds penalty box. Hunter managed to cut out the cross.

Leeds looked out of sorts and unsettled as another long kick from Harvey was again won by the head of Watson to send Sunderland back on the attack, stopped this time when Reaney pushed Tueart firmly in the back. No action was taken. Sunderland looked comfortable and confident as they won a series of throw-ins down Leeds' left side and managed successfully to slow the pace of the game down.

But then suddenly there was danger at the Sunderland end as Madeley found himself in space in midfield and advanced rapidly before playing the ball into the penalty box for Clarke. On this occasion Clarke didn't waste any time and quickly turned to shoot towards goal. Watson – seemingly out of nowhere – again slid in to divert the ball away for a corner.

'I should have been closer to him when he shot, really,' Watson says modestly. 'It shouldn't have happened like that but at least I got there in the end. He was shooting and I just managed to get there with my studs. It was a saving tackle.'

Lorimer's corner was punched away by Montgomery – under pressure on his own goal line from Bremner – but the ball eventually found its way back inside the penalty box to Lorimer, who was able to power in a shot from close range. Montgomery positioned himself well and beat the ball away with his fists.

Sunderland then broke forward with Porterfield, who quickly opened up a chance for Hughes, whose shot was blocked in the penalty box by the diving Cherry. In a frantic end to the first half Giles also produced an effort on goal that flashed high and wide. The half came to a close when Hughes was fouled by Reaney to produce the nineteenth free-kick of the opening forty-five minutes; Sunderland had been awarded eleven of them. As Burns blew his whistle and the players left the pitch, Stokoe went straight over to talk to Porterfield and Malone, while Cox did the same with Watson.

'Wherever you look in this Sunderland side you will find a player who has played well, and by comparison Leeds United, the FA Cup holders, carrying the responsibility of being favourites, expected to win, really haven't found their rhythm at all,' David Coleman said at the interval. 'The scoreline really is a deserving reflection of the play.'

'Bob Stokoe told us we had done a good job in the first half but he stressed that we were only halfway through the match and we had another forty-five minutes to get through,' Watson says. 'Arthur Cox was an agitator. He was enthusiastic and he would gee people up. He used to get hold of your hair by the back of the head and squeeze it tightly. Arthur went around everybody, rallying the troops. The goal had given our fans extra belief and the longer the game went on the realisation of the crowd that we could do it grew and grew. That realisation came through to us as well. We felt good at half-time but we knew it would be a battle for us in the second half.'

The Sunderland players could have done no more for their manager. The pre-match plans had worked: Gray had been marked out of the game, the shots from Lorimer had been limited, Bremner and Giles had been silenced, and Clarke and Jones had been handled. Furthermore the Rokerites had a precious goal to their credit and had a lead to defend.

Across the passage, Revie was far from happy. He wanted more direct pressure put on the Sunderland goal. If required, Cherry, Hunter, Madeley and Reaney were to get forward more. A fully loaded assault of white shirts was set to be unleashed in the second half. Leeds had forty-five minutes to prevent the greatest FA Cup final shock of all time.

The half-time entertainment was provided by the Bands of the Coldstream, Scots, Irish and Welsh Guards. As they departed the arena, a group of Leeds players walked out on to the pitch looking somewhat dejected. Hunter was staring at the ground, Lorimer was scratching his head and Madeley was walking with his hands on his hips. Montgomery and Kerr – the first Sunderland players to emerge after half-time – ran past them. Watson put his hand up to the crowd as he chatted with Tueart.

Sunderland kicked off. Halom played the ball to Hughes, who cut it back to Pitt, who launched another attack into the Leeds half. It came to nothing. Leeds had changed their tactics and it was apparent early on that their defenders had been encouraged to get forward.

In Leeds' first attack of the second half Reaney took the ball past Pitt and played in Clarke, who was dispossessed by Watson, to raucous cheers from the West End terrace behind the goal. Moments later a move involving Clarke, Madeley and Bremner broke down when Horswill took the ball off Giles's feet. But Leeds already looked to be much more attack-minded than they had been in the first forty-five minutes.

The biggest change to Sunderland's armoury involved Kerr on the right side of midfield. The Rokerites' captain was finding more space for himself early on and skipped past Hunter at pace after good work from Porterfield and Tueart.

Moments later a good cross from Lorimer on the right was directed towards Jones in the Sunderland penalty box. Montgomery came out to punch again but this time was only able to connect with his fingertips as he turned it away from goal. Gray collected the ball and played it back to Cherry, who passed it along to Bremner. A neat turn by the Leeds captain with his right boot on the edge of the box took him past Pitt and opened up space for a left-foot shot. Bremner hit it first time and then watched as the ball bounced off Montgomery's chest in the six-yard box. Malone had to react quickly to turn the ball away for a corner. Lorimer took the corner kick and Jones headed wide.

Montgomery's goal-kick was picked up by Gray just inside the Sunderland half and the Scottish winger began a flowing six-pass attack which was eventually cut out by Guthrie in the Sunderland penalty box. In response a neat move involving Halom, Tueart and Hughes again found Kerr in space down the right. Kerr produced a low drive into the Leeds penalty box that was cut out by Bremner.

On fifty minutes Leeds had the ball in the Sunderland net, but it was rightly disallowed for a foul on Montgomery. The goalkeeper had comfortably collected a Bremner free-kick in his hands but was then floored by an illegal challenge from Clarke. Cherry had then put the ball over the line to a chorus of boos from behind the goal.

It was now an open, end-to-end contest. Hunter was joining in Leeds' attacks and, with Sunderland defending deeper, the red-hot favourites were finding more space in midfield. Lorimer managed another shot on target, which was easily collected by Montgomery. Gray found Clarke on the left, but the Leeds striker ran into Watson, who immediately put Sunderland on the attack. Halom and Malone linked up to begin a passing move between Tueart and Hughes which ended with Horswill sending in a left-foot drive from thirty yards just wide of Harvey's post.

Then came a telling moment. The Leeds goal-kick was headed on by Jones, but cut out by the head of Pitt, who found Porterfield in space. Porterfield was then fouled by Bremner but kept moving forward, only to be called back when Burns awarded Sunderland a free-kick. Showing no sign of frustration, Porterfield casually ruffled Bremner's hair and while doing so winked cheekily at Guthrie. Psychologically he was playing a blinder against the Leeds captain.

Watson took the resultant free-kick and fired it all the way into the Leeds penalty box. There followed a goalmouth scramble and three shots on goal by three different Sunderland players. Hughes, with his back to goal, played the ball back to Tueart, whose shot was charged down by Madeley. Porterfield immediately connected with the rebound and saw his shot cannon off Hunter into the path of Guthrie, who whipped in a shot at pace that hit the side-netting. 'My natural game was to go forward, so whenever we went forward in the final I tried to join the attack and then I would get back into defence,' Guthrie says. 'I was never frightened to have a pot at goal. I had a couple of shots here and there at Wembley and I nearly scored when I hit the side-netting.'

Back came Leeds, with Bremner driving them on from midfield. He found Lorimer and continued a run towards the left-hand side of the Sunderland penalty box. When Lorimer cut the ball back, Bremner had time and was in space. When Watson went across to challenge, Bremner played the ball past him with the outside of his right boot and then rather theatrically fell to the floor. Leeds appealed for a penalty but Burns waved play on and immediately gestured that it was a dive. 'No penalty given!' Moore screamed. 'The referee won't even listen or look. He decided that Billy Bremner made far too much of it.'

'My recollection is that I went to play the ball and Billy Bremner dived over my leg,' Watson recalls. 'He threw himself up in the air and bent his legs as though he'd been kicked but he hadn't. I didn't touch him. If he hadn't picked his feet up I would have kicked him, because I wouldn't have been able to get my foot out of the way. So if he hadn't dived it would have been a foul. But he dived and there was no contact at all. It wasn't a penalty.'

The Leeds captain's forlorn expression suggested that he felt everything was going against him. Stokoe – who had played an ace card concerning Bremner and Burns in the pre-match build-up in the press – sat back, smiling and relieved, as the referee ignored all pleas for a penalty.

'Luckily the referee was in the right place,' Kerr says. 'If he hadn't been where he was, he could have easily given a penalty.'

Moments later Bremner was roundly booed when he played the ball out to Giles, who whipped in a cross that once more was punched away by Montgomery. 'It is a sensible thing to do under the circumstances because those Leeds strikers go in hard,' Hill observed. 'It only needs one drop and it can be a tap-in for a goal.'

A long ball forward from Pitt – intended for Hughes to chase – was cut out by the head of Madeley but only as far as Guthrie, who immediately fired in another shot across the face of the Leeds goal and past the far post. Moments later, from a Porterfield throw-in on the left, Madeley again headed the ball into the path of Guthrie, who this time tried his luck with his right foot. His attempt flashed wide of the near post. But Leeds kept coming forward from the back, and another good forward run from Madeley led to Lorimer whipping a shot into Sunderland's side-netting from just inside the penalty box.

Then came the moment of the final: Hunter and Giles linked up well in the Sunderland half. The ball was played to Jones on the edge of the penalty box, who had his back to goal. Jones played it back to Reaney, who sent a searching cross deep inside the box towards an unmarked Cherry at the far post. Cherry headed goalwards but his effort was pushed away by a diving Montgomery into the path of the oncoming Lorimer, the man with the hardest shot in football. Lorimer – positioned inside the six-yard box – steadied himself and placed his shot back towards the goal.

Montgomery somehow flung himself in the direction of the ball – which was travelling at pace from no distance at all – and made contact with his flailing left forearm. The ball ricocheted off him on to the underside of the crossbar and bounced back into play. Cherry – lying motionless on his stomach – lifted his right heel in hope of a rebound, but the ball spun to Malone, who without thinking hooked it clear for a throw-in with his left foot.

'Leeds are really pushing forward, Cherry, brilliant save, and Lorimer makes it one each – no!' Coleman screamed. 'It must be a goal, it's a goal, it's not a goal, it's off the upright. I have never seen anything like it,' Radio 2 summariser Bryon Butler reported. 'Reaney, the high one in, and Cherry going in, and a great save, and a goal – no. My goodness, I thought Lorimer had got that one,' Moore said.

'Well, we better look at it now because this is very vital. I must say it looked as if the ball had hit the stanchion at the back,' Hill said over the ITV slow-motion replay. 'Let's look closely: underneath the bar and out! That's the verdict – no goal!' Moments later Hill was given another replay to talk over from a better angle: 'We can look at it now from behind the goal. As it turns out to be an incredible miss. There it is: Lorimer coming in, oh, in fact it wasn't, it was a save. In fact it was a fantastic save from Montgomery.'

'Well, really that was astonishing,' Coleman reflected. 'Lorimer tried to side-foot it in, it came off the goalkeeper and the underside of the bar and that is as close as Leeds have been – and will ever be – without scoring. Lorimer thought he had scored, most of the crowd did, but it wasn't in.'

'As Trevor Cherry's headed it across me, I've gone and parried it,' Montgomery says. 'Some say I should have held the header, but I maintain I would always have pushed it away; maybe I would have tried to catch it if it had been dry and everything but it wasn't dry, it was wet. As I've knocked the ball away, I've gone down and I look up and I can see a white shirt – I don't know who it is, but I'm up because if I stay down, he scores. I knew I had to get off the ground as quickly as I could and the only place he can hit it is back across the goal because I believe Dave Watson is blocking the left-hand side, so I've gone there. I've seen him hit it and I stick my hands up to make a save and fortunately the ball hits my arm. As I turn around off the floor I see the ball come down off the crossbar and Dick Malone volleying it clear.

'I trained to make saves like that,' Montgomery adds. 'It was all about trying to get up without using your hands. Your momentum takes you down and so you have to quickly push yourself up. That's the way I worked in training. The other thing to say is that if you make a save and you stay down you'll never get a rebound. So the first thing for me if I was down was that I had to get up. That was always in my make-up. I never dived and stayed down.'

'Ninety-nine times out of a hundred that shot would have flown in, but that day Jim Montgomery threw himself off the floor, the ball hit him on the arm, hit the underside of the crossbar, came down and went out,' Lorimer says. 'I had so much time coming in that I thought to myself, Don't blast it, just get a really solid contact back into that corner and we're out of trouble. I did exactly that. I hit it exactly as I wanted to. I did everything I wanted to. If I had mishit it, it would have gone in. If I had topped it, it would have gone in. But I hit it really well with my instep, nice and solid. It was flying and it was going in. I turned away with my hands up but Jim somehow made the save. It was amazing how he got to it. One moment he wasn't there and the next moment he was.'

'The ball flashed past me,' Watson says. 'Monty dived towards Peter Lorimer, and as Lorimer shoots the ball goes between Monty's arms, hits his left arm and then rebounds up on to the underside of the crossbar. It all came down to a matter of inches. I think the ball had to probably hit his trailing arm at that speed and that angle to rebound off the bar in the way that it did. It was fate. I mean how could that all happen? It couldn't happen.'

'For a split second I thought, He's scored, and then I thought, No, he hasn't. I thought it had hit the stanchion at the back of the goal at first, I thought he couldn't miss,' Guthrie adds. 'I couldn't believe it when the ball bounced out and the game continued. I yelled out to Dick Malone to just get it clear and get it away.'

'It would have been an injustice if it had gone in and a goal was given because I was tripped in the penalty box as the cross came over from Paul Reaney,' Malone says. 'Allan Clarke put his foot around my leg just as I was going to make a run to head the ball away. I stumbled and so the ball goes to Trevor Cherry, who's free. Cherry gets the header in, Monty makes the save, Peter Lorimer shoots, Monty saves again, it comes back off the bar and I clear it. It was just instinct to clear it. I was thinking to myself, Thank God, it hasn't gone in. I expected it to go in so when it bounced down I took no chances and just whacked it away. But I was panicking in case they got a goal because it would have been totally unfair and I probably would have got sent off because I would have said quite a bit to the referee because it was totally ridiculous for him not to have seen it. He must have seen it. It was impossible not to have seen it. So I would have said something to him, it wouldn't have been complimentary and I would probably have been sent off as a result.'

'Monty makes the save, it hits the bar and Dicky Malone clears it. Well, after that you have to think there's no way they're going to score now,' Pitt adds. 'Mind you, our legs were getting tired due to the Wembley pitch being very sapping and the fact we had all done a lot of running. Our game was based on running so we were bound to tire in the last ten or fifteen minutes. But being a goal ahead in the FA Cup final keeps you going and it makes you fight that little bit harder. I think you get to depths that you don't know you've got in a situation like that. Monty's save kept us going, it certainly did.'

'It was a truly great save that Monty made from Peter Lorimer,' Tueart says. 'Norman Hunter was stood near by and he just turned to me and said, "It's your day now, Dennis!"'

'I was stood fairly low down behind the goal where Monty made the save,' Sunderland supporter Paul Dobson recalls. 'Peter Lorimer shot straight towards us. I tell you, the collective heart at that end of the ground stopped. Lorimer had one of the hardest shots in football and he was lining up to blast the ball into the open goal right in front of us all. Time just seemed to stand still and you could literally feel it in your chest. Then Monty's hand came up and he turned the ball on to the underside of the bar. When Dick Malone cleared it, all of us behind that goal seemed to breathe again as one. It was like watching it in slow motion.'

'I thought it was in,' Pete Sixsmith adds. 'Monty made a great save from Trevor Cherry's header and then the ball dropped for Peter Lorimer. Well, how could he miss? I was resigned for the inevitable. I can see Mick Jones now with his hands in the air, celebrating a goal. But somehow Monty saved it. I was bouncing on those terraces like I was bouncing on a bed.'

Young had been sent to warm up before Montgomery made the save, but now the word on the Sunderland bench was to keep things as they were. 'Bob Stokoe turned to me and said, "I can't change it, I can't make it any better." I totally agreed with him,' Cox says. 'I couldn't see how we could make it better. The players had an incessant work rate and they played so well, every one of them.'

Leeds piled on the pressure: Reaney sent in a searching cross for Clarke, which Malone once again headed away. 'He really hasn't made a mistake so far, Dick Malone,' Moore said from the commentary box. 'Everybody thought that the left-hand side of the Leeds attack with Eddie Gray in particular might make him look a bit silly but he's done Sunderland proud this afternoon.' A little later Moore offered his opinion on the second part of that equation: 'He really has been almost anonymous, Eddie Gray, and everybody thought that he could well be the man to set this Cup final going for Leeds.' But Moore still posed the question: 'I am just wondering whether Sunderland's hearts are big enough to withstand this pressure from Leeds United for another quarter of an hour or so?'

Sunderland were defending deeper and deeper. Both Halom and Hughes were often found back in their own penalty box helping out. Clarke still found space to slip the Sunderland defence, latch on to a through ball from Giles and fire in a shot across the goal. Leeds' urgency was summed up by the fact that Madeley played for over three minutes with one boot. Halom – socks rolled down around his ankles – was the first Sunderland player to suffer evident cramp.

'I can't recall ever having cramp before or after that – it just never happened to me – but that was down to me being on my toes all the time,' Halom says. 'I could probably have got away with an ordinary set of studs, but you live and learn. I actually thought Bob Stokoe might have subbed me late on and put an extra defender on but to his credit he didn't. It did go through my mind in the last few minutes that he might do that.'

With fifteen minutes remaining Revie made his substitution and brought on Welsh midfielder Yorath for – of all people – Gray. Malone and Kerr had done their jobs perfectly. Their plan to stifle the skills and the threat of the talented Scottish winger had worked.

'Nobody was more below his best than me,' Gray wrote in his autobiography *Marching on Together: My Life With Leeds United*.

This was by far my worst performance at Wembley, and what made it doubly frustrating was the player marking me, Dick Malone, was a right back against whom I had previously done well. Throughout my career the full backs who tended to have the best games against me were those in the strongest teams, because these were the teams in which players could always be relied upon to work for each other; the teams in which the men responsible for marking me were less liable to be isolated.

This FA Cup final was one occasion when Malone, supported by Bobby Kerr, also had the right backing.

Kerr was now left with something of a dilemma. 'When Eddie Gray went off, our job was done,' he says. 'Terry Yorath came on and he started to cause a few problems down on the right side. He started to knock cracking balls in so I went there to mark him. I just took it upon myself to go over there and do that.'

Yorath soon produced a save from Montgomery. Another good ball from Madeley found the substitute in space on the right. Yorath ran into the box and drove a low shot towards the near post that was blocked by the goalkeeper.

It was now generally a white wave of Leeds attacks. But Sunderland still had chances on the break, and the Rokerites also showed composure in possession. Halom took the ball off the feet of Cherry and played it along to Horswill, who played it to Hughes, who played it back to Horswill, who played it to Tueart, who delightfully took it past Madeley. Tueart advanced on goal and was just about to size up his shot when Madeley intervened brilliantly and poked the ball back to Harvey. Moments later an intricate passing triangle between Hughes, Malone and Porterfield was killing more vital seconds until Cherry broke it up and Hughes had to pull him back, conceding a free-kick and earning himself a booking. A goalmouth scramble followed Giles's free-kick before Pitt cleared well.

'Our job was to keep a clean sheet and to stop Leeds scoring, and although they probably had seventy-five per cent of the possession we did manage to limit the number of opportunities they had to score to a minimum,' Pitt says. 'But it was relentless at the end and I would think it was probably easier for the players – because we are able to concentrate on the game – than it was for the fans. It must have been really nerve-racking for the fans, especially because Sunderland hadn't won anything for so long and here we were 1–0 up against one of the best teams in the country – if not *the* best team in the country – and under such pressure.'

'The pressure is still enormous on Sunderland,' Moore said. 'Not only the physical pressure but the mental pressure: each of them knowing now that one mistake by any of them could mean the end of a dream. So you can imagine how these fellows must be feeling – full of hope and yet with their own worries as well.'

Hunter was then fouled by Porterfield two yards outside the Sunderland penalty box. Giles and Lorimer sized up the free-kick. Porterfield, Malone, Kerr, Hughes and Pitt made up a desperate five-man defensive wall. Clarke hovered in front of it and Jones stood at one end, beside Pitt. Giles touched the ball to Lorimer, who lashed it straight at Clarke's feet. Malone booted it clear.

As the clock ticked on Elliott put his hand up from the Sunderland bench to show the players there were five minutes left to play. The

Sunderland supporters, who had sung throughout, now burst into a rendition of 'You'll Never Walk Alone', breaking off only to whistle deafeningly whenever a Leeds player touched the ball. The homeward stretch was near and, as if to symbolise the fact, the sun came out.

'I will always remember that in the last few minutes of the final we were just trying to keep possession,' Hughes says. 'I got the ball and Norman Hunter was backing off me. He's looking at me in the eyes and saying, "Don't take the piss, Billy, or I'll kick your arse!" So I thought about it for a second and then I just put the ball inside to Micky Horswill'

Revie, now covered in a dark sheepskin coat, sat pensively on the Leeds bench, looking across the pitch towards the centre circle, holding his hands down between his legs and flexing his fingers, almost counting the ticking seconds in his head. There was still time for his men to force an equaliser.

Giles linked up with Reaney and another dangerous cross was floated into the Sunderland penalty box. Watson rose majestically to head clear once again. Halom picked the ball up in space and slipped it past Madeley towards Tueart, who tried to find Kerr, but his pass was cut out by the Leeds defender. Kerr then raced to win the ball back for Sunderland and played it back to Tueart, who just managed to steer it along to Halom, who immediately drove in a shot that rebounded off Madeley. Halom then composed himself and fired in another effort that brought an acrobatic diving save from Harvey. Late on, Sunderland had come close to scoring a second.

'I had two chances. One that I hit particularly well ricocheted off Paul Madeley's shins and then David Harvey made a good save,' Halom says. 'But I was absolutely shattered by then because all I had done during the match was chase and chase. But that was the job I had to do.'

Burns kept looking at his watch. Stokoe, Cox and Elliott were doing the same, gesturing to the Sunderland players to get back down the field as they jumped up and down on the bench. The long grey blanket that covered their knees was on and off and off and on.

'We've got one of the biggest upheavals of all time at Wembley,' Moore said. 'It seemed, the experts said, there was no way that Sunderland could win, except that it looks as though they are going to.'

Deep into injury time Kerr floated the ball towards Harvey's goal and Halom body-charged the Leeds goalkeeper into the net. Leeds were awarded a free-kick. Harvey quickly played it out to Reaney, who passed to Giles. Against a cacophony of screeching whistles, the referee blew his whistle for full-time: Sunderland had won the FA Cup.

Stokoe instantly leapt from the bench and, evading the attention of a policeman, sprinted – trilby, tracksuit, mackintosh and all – towards Montgomery. The moment was pure Stokoe. The emotion epitomised the man and summed up Sunderland's triumph from start to finish.

ITV match director Bob Gardam covered the run in full. His pictures – along with Moore's commentary – made it the most momentous and memorable full-time celebration ever seen at Wembley. 'Where's he going, Bob Stokoe?' Moore asked. 'To Jimmy Montgomery, the goalkeeper, whose punching and saving saved the day for Sunderland.'

'Brian Moore was fantastic to work with,' Gardam says. 'He knew what I was going to cut before I cut and I knew what he was going to say before he said it. Bob Stokoe looked so agitated at the end of the match, he was up and he was down. I saw him get off his seat and I said to Brian, "Keep an eye on him, he's going to go potty." I decided I was going to hang on to Bob at the final whistle, I just had this feeling he was going to go over to Jim Montgomery because of that fabulous double save. Brian thought he might do that too. The cameraman who got the shot was Mike Patterson on camera three. Mike did very well and he kept Bob in his shot all the way. It is lucky that it wasn't blocked at all. I stayed with it and it was amazing to see. Bob had his mac flapping about and everything. I had spent a few hours getting to know him quite well and I was not surprised when he did it. He was that kind of guy. It means quite a lot to me to be associated with it but I think it was an obvious shot at the end of the game.'

'That was Bob Stokoe all over,' Jimmy Armfield says. 'He was that type of man. He was that excitable that if Sunderland had lost he would probably have ran all the way down the tunnel.'

'I had turned around and was facing the crowd behind the goal when suddenly Bob Stokoe was ten yards away from me,' Montgomery recalls. 'Still to this day I have never known what Bob said to me when he got hold of me. Ron Guthrie came up, Bobby Kerr came up and there was a fan in there with us as well. It wasn't until I spoke to Bob later on that he said he did that because of all my saves during the Cup run, the ones from Les Bradd and Geordie Armstrong – and yes, the one in the final too.

'It must have been fantastic for our supporters behind the goal,' Montgomery adds. 'It was at that end where Ian Porterfield scored, they were behind me for the save and they were there for the celebrations at the end. They were fantastic. It was phenomenal to have them stood behind us.'

'I knew there wasn't long to go for Arthur Cox was up and down on the bench,' Guthrie says. 'I kept saying to myself, It must be time up, it must be time up, and Please blow your whistle. When the whistle went, my mind just erupted inside. I couldn't believe it. Ritchie Pitt was the first one I saw. He said to me, "We've won the Cup." I then ran towards Monty and Bob Stokoe went flying past me. Bob was only in his early forties back then and he kept himself fit. He was basically a non-drinker and he played five-a-sides with us. I didn't realise Bob was coming, it was just that Monty had made that save and that was the end where all the Sunderland fans were. Bobby Kerr came on the scene and pinched Bob's hat. Bob was quite bald by that time and so he liked to keep his trilby on if he could. There was a fan there too. I don't know who he is to this day.'

'Seeing Bob Stokoe run on the pitch at the end like that showed us all just what he thought of Monty,' Kerr says. 'I then ran over and put Bob's hat on my head and he picked me up. There is only one photograph where I have no teeth in for as soon as he puts me down I go straight to the bench to collect my teeth. One of the lads had my teeth and Billy Hughes's teeth in his jacket pocket. There is talk about it being Joe Bolton and there's talk about it being Micky McGiven. One of them had our teeth, I don't know who, but I do know I didn't get them in until after that photograph.'

'At the final whistle Norman Hunter was the first one that greeted me,' Hughes adds. 'I collapsed and I was lying on my back and as I got up he came over and he put his arm around me and said, "You deserved it, son." I then went looking for my own players. But Norman was the first player that I saw after the final whistle. He had just lost an FA Cup final as well. I don't think I would have been that gracious had we lost. Even to this day I never think what we would have done if we had got beat.'

'When the referee blew, Micky Horswill came up to me on the

touchline and the tears were flowing,' Halom says. 'It was just a release and a relief that it was all over and we had come out the victors. One of the greatest feelings in the world must be lying victorious on a pitch after you've given everything you could possibly give. That is what it felt like. It happened in seconds. It was an emotional rush. But it was over. It was tight. How tight it was! We could have easily lost it. At times during the game I was praying when they attacked, Please don't let them score, and things like that. Then all of a sudden it was over. It was like a pressure valve being released at the end and that is why the tears came so easily. My mum had felt that as well; she had clasped her hands so tightly towards the end of the match that her rings left marks on her hands!'

'I just didn't know what to do at the end,' Pitt says. 'I just went down on the turf. Eventually I ran to Mick McGiven. We had a hug and then everything just went off after that. Mick was so excited he left my brand-new coat on the bench. I had bought it in Carnaby Street and it cost me a fortune. I loaned it to him and he left it behind at Wembley. That was the last time I ever saw it!'

'When the final whistle went I couldn't believe it was all over,' Porterfield said. 'I hugged Dave Watson, and Johnny Watters, our physio, joined us in our wild excitement. The Cup was ours.'

'I felt drained, completely drained,' Watson says. 'I just stood there and thanked God. We all thanked God. We had a bit of help on that day. Leeds looked shell-shocked at the end. It was odds-on they were going to win so it was nice to prove people wrong. But I remember the relief just drained out of my body when it was all over. It felt fantastic.'

'We deserved it,' Tueart adds. 'The balance of that team was perfect. We had height, mobility, a strong centre-forward, a creative midfield, wide men, a strong defence, an outstanding goalkeeper and a tremendous team spirit. People should never underestimate that team. The level of quality in that side stood the test of time.'

'When the crowd started whistling, I knew the end of the match was near and I wanted it to be over and finished. When it was, it was a tremendous feeling. That day gave me a moment in my life to be proud of and a moment that will always stay with me,' Malone says.

'Of course you're thinking to yourself, I want to get on, and the clock is counting down and the final whistle is getting ever closer,' substitute Young admits. 'But when the whistle blows all that just disintegrates. The bigger picture is we won. Yes, I could have got on but I could have made a cock-up, I could have slipped. They could have got an equaliser and it could have been extra-time and we could have lost and whatever, whatever, whatever. So the result was the right result for the club and for the team and I just had to take my medicine. It was a near-miss but I just had to live with it and I have lived with that. If you could rewind the clock I would do it all just the same again and again and again. It was a very special time.'

'I ran straight over to David Watson on the final whistle,' Cox says. 'We didn't have anyone who played below par on the day but David was brilliant. Leeds were a great side and Don Revie and Les Cocker were giving instructions to put it in there from forty yards or fifty yards towards the end of the game. Most of the aerial stuff was aimed towards Michael Jones and that is where David did so well for us. He headed the ball so much that he had blisters on his forehead at the end.'

Well-respected author and Sunderland fan James Herriot – alias veterinary surgeon Alf Wight – who was fifty-six at the time, summed up the feelings of thousands: 'When the referee blew the final whistle at Wembley and I found myself dancing with my arms around a distinguished-looking gentleman in a camel coat who was a total stranger, I felt that from that moment on I could die happy.'

Stokoe made sure that he embraced each of his players before they walked up the thirty-nine steps to collect the FA Cup from the Duchess of Kent. As Stokoe moved from one to the other all he kept saying was just one word: 'Marvellous.'

Kerr led his team up the famous steps, followed by Montgomery, Pitt, Horswill, Watson, Hughes, Halom, Guthrie, Malone, Tueart, Porterfield and Young. Kerr wiped his hands on his shirt and then received the trophy. He kissed it once before lifting it high above his head in the direction of the West End of the stadium, packed full with Sunderland supporters.

'When I get the FA Cup, I forget to pick up my medal so I have to turn around and tell Monty, but by that time Monty has picked up his medal so he has to tell Ritchie Pitt, and Ritchie is the one who picks up my medal,' Kerr says. 'There were these three little quarter-steps at the top before you went back down and I missed them. I was so busy turning around asking about my medal that I slipped and I dropped the

Cup. You could hear me drop it on the television. If you turn the volume up on the tape today you can still hear it.'

'It meant everything to me – being a local lad – to get to Wembley and receive an FA Cup winners' medal,' Montgomery says. 'We won the Cup due to the camaraderie between the lads, from number one to number twelve. It was never about him or him or him, it was always about us.'

'It was just a fantastic moment, to stand up there with the FA Cup for the team and the club that you love,' Pitt adds.

The last two Sunderland players to walk up the steps and receive their medals were Porterfield and Young. 'Ian was fantastic to me,' Young explains. 'As the team were walking up the steps, I wasn't sure whether I could go up or whether I even got a medal. I asked Ian, "Do I go up there, Porter?" and he said, "Of course you do." So we went up together. Ian had so much enthusiasm and energy and drive and motivation and he was passionate, really passionate. It is just so sad that he has gone so early.'

The Sunderland chairman was there to greet all the players from the Royal Box. His wife, Toni, gave them all a congratulatory kiss as well. 'The greatest moment of all for me as chairman was standing in the front row of the Royal Box and seeing my own team come up the steps and then shaking Bobby Kerr's hand as he came up to collect the FA Cup,' Collings says. 'To be at Wembley was marvellous, to be in a decent seat was marvellous, to actually be in the front row of the Royal Box and see your own team coming up those steps was something else. There's not really anything that could better that.'

'A tremendous result this for Sunderland and – with true deference to Leeds United – a tremendous result for football as well,' Moore commented as Leeds – led by Bremner – walked up the steps to collect FA Cup runners-up medals for the second time in four seasons and the third time in nine seasons. 'Bremner, smiling in defeat, and his side today for once, well, they have looked human,' Coleman remarked.

Stokoe, having now removed his raincoat and trilby, lined up with his players in front of the Royal Box. As they did so, the request from the Sunderland fans was clear and deafening: 'We want Stokoe,' they roared. When the Leeds players came back down to pitch level, the national anthem was played again. Kerr – holding the Cup below his waist – simply bowed his head. Stokoe held his head high. His team stood in a line while Leeds looked bedraggled and forlorn; the favourites couldn't wait to exit the arena.

Revie cut a lonely figure as he walked off towards the tunnel by himself. 'I don't think that you could ever put into words the feeling of seeing him trudge off Wembley,' Stokoe later said. 'It is difficult to describe how it felt. I wanted to go up to Revie and look him in the eye and say: "Revenge is sweet, Revie, cheats never prosper" but I refrained from doing that.'

The Sunderland players chaired Kerr in front of the Royal Box and posed for photographs before sprinting off on a lap of honour. When they reached the West End of the stadium they stood as one and applauded their supporters. Above those delirious fans stood the famous Wembley scoreboard with the words LEEDS UNITED 0 SUNDERLAND 1.

'It was like we were on the park with the players,' Peverley says. 'We felt we had won the FA Cup – the team and the fans. It wasn't just the players that had won it, it was us. Nobody can ever take that away from us. What happened and what it meant. The collective feeling – of the team and the supporters – made it even more powerful. Nothing could ever match 1973.'

'I feel so privileged to have been there,' Dobson adds. 'If I could leave something in my will for my two sons I would leave them my experience of seeing Sunderland win the FA Cup final in 1973. If I could give them anything, I would give them that.'

'Up to that time, whenever anyone asked me which team I supported and I told them, they would think it weird,' Sir Tim Rice, who was sat behind the Royal Box with singer David Essex that day, says. 'So it was quite satisfying to be there and to see Sunderland win the Cup. It was terrific, actually. That team had such a great team spirit. There was only one goal but it was *our* goal.'

As the celebrations continued, Guthrie momentarily glanced up to the television studios. 'I saw Johan Cruyff stood on his feet and clapping us,' he says. 'That remains a nice memory.'

The players took it in turns to parade the trophy around the pitch, and as they did so the Sunderland supporters continued to chant Stokoe's name. So Cox took it upon himself to put the Rokerites' manager – now donning a red-and-white bowler hat made of plastic – on to his shoulders. Surrounded by the men who had just won the FA

Cup for him, Stokoe beamed as he took the applause from the Sunderland fans and players.

'It was just a spontaneous thing to do,' Cox says. 'I can't really explain it. But it was tremendous for him to enjoy that moment in that way.'

'They came down in their thousands from the north-east,' Moore commented. 'They came down with hope and they go back with the Cup.'

'What an achievement for this man, who has known the hard times at lowly clubs – at Bury, Charlton, Rochdale, Carlisle, Blackpool – but now tastes the big time in the most major way possible. A moment to taste and really savour,' Coleman said. 'This really is a piece of fiction – if you don't mind the contradiction – that has come true, a true fairy story, even in FA Cup terms: a manager who took over this side in mid-season when they were nineteenth in the Second Division.'

'After the game finished the Sunderland players took their manager, Bob Stokoe, on a lap of honour,' Jack Charlton later wrote in his autobiography. 'As he passed the gantry, he looked up at me – and he stuck two fingers in the air.' The pre-match analysis on ITV the previous night had hurt Stokoe deeply and he wasn't a man to forget grudges, especially at a moment like this.

The Sunderland players left the celebrations on the pitch moments later and departed down the tunnel. As they did so, the emptying East End terrace above them showed plenty of red-and-white scarves. Sunderland fans had evidently been everywhere inside the stadium.

'The first thing I wanted to do after the match was to get down and see the team – which I did at all the normal matches – but that was not that easy to do at Wembley,' Collings says. 'FA secretary Denis Follows gave me his personal pass for the ground and there were some special steps where the royalty go down to do the greetings on the pitch. I went down those and walked across the pitch. I remember a policeman came up to me and told me I couldn't go through and I said to him, "I am the chairman of Sunderland and you are not going to stop me." My father followed me down; he was still on the Sunderland board and also a member of the International Committee so his seat was in the Royal Box as well, and so he could use the same access as I did. We both got into the dressing room. Everybody was hugging each other and shaking hands. Thankfully they didn't throw me in the bath or anything like that.'

Some of the players were called into the television studios to do post-match interviews. Barry Davies was the BBC reporter who was assigned that duty, and Gerald Sinstadt the ITV reporter. This part of proceedings was as competitive as any other for the small-screen rivals.

'We always had the insurmountable problem of the commercial breaks,' Sinstadt explains. 'On FA Cup final day we would have had the second half plus all the shenanigans on the pitch, with the players going up for the Cup and so on, so we would have been without a commercial break probably for over an hour and then eventually we've got to come away from the pitch and go to a commercial break. I'm in the interview room and players are being wheeled in, they have the Cup with them and all the rest of it and I have to keep saying, "Hang on, lads, we won't be long." Meanwhile I can hear Barry Davies next door doing his third interview and his fourth interview. By the time they had come over to us, the atmosphere was gone. We had to get the commercial break in – it pays the rent – but it was a killer doing those interviews. I would say ITV obviously scored by getting the famous shot of Bob Stokoe running on at the end – everyone was delighted about that – but the BBC probably led the way with the post-match interviews. We couldn't really compete.'

'The Sunderland players were not that keen to leave our studio,' Davies recalls. 'I interviewed Ian Porterfield, Jim Montgomery, Bobby Kerr and Billy Hughes and they were all living the moment and had lots to say. I was very conscious that this was good stuff but I also knew that the moment I spoke to a Leeds player the whole mood of the interviews would change. Then Don Revie came up and I took the decision to physically put my arm out and stop him coming into the interview with the Sunderland players. I genuinely felt it was their moment and I didn't want anything to spoil that moment. Bob Stokoe arrived and joined his players and I talked to him. After a little while I brought Don into the interview. Don was extremely magnanimous. He congratulated Bob and it was really a nice moment to end the whole interview. I was absolutely ecstatic about it. You could never plan anything like that because you didn't know who was going to come into the interview room at any given time. It was the best possible way to end it all.

'Personally it was a very special time for me to be so close to a team and such a fabulous story,' Davies adds. 'I so wanted Sunderland to win. I have always backed the underdog and they did it with a style and enjoyment that was shared, I think, by the rest of the nation. Bob Stokoe running towards Jim Montgomery at the end is one of the great moments of Wembley history.'

In terms of viewing figures the BBC won the battle of the television channels, attracting 21 million viewers while ITV was watched by 8 million. The total British audience was 29 million. A further twenty-four nations worldwide – a new record – also received live pictures of the final.

Montgomery's double save was the moment of the match, and would go down in history as the finest save ever made in an FA Cup final and one of the greatest saves of all time, rivalled only by Gordon Banks's brilliant save from Pelé when England played Brazil in the 1970 World Cup finals in Guadalajara, Mexico.

'Jim's save that day was an exceptional save, a really exceptional save, and it won Sunderland the Cup really,' Banks says. 'There are two saves that are always talked about, that one and the one from Pelé. The agility that Jim had was incredible. He was slim and athletic and he made fabulous saves throughout his career. But that one, of course, is the famous one.'

'Everything in that final hinged on the time of Jim's save and the manner of it,' Bob Wilson adds. 'It was truly amazing and one of the quickest movements I have seen. As a goalkeeper you walk a tightrope of excitement and fear and Jim's save that day was the epitome of that. Had Peter Lorimer scored, the press boys – without question – would have said that Jim should have done better with the initial save from Trevor Cherry, for the fact is he could have done better with it as there was still a chance of a goal. But Jim's reaction off the floor to then get his body in front of Lorimer is what made that save. It is adrenaline-driven – pure adrenaline – due to the occasion. You see many great reflex saves but not from off the floor. Given the importance of the game as well, it was a truly miraculous moment. In my little list of great saves, Banksy's has to be top due to the occasion and, of course, Pelé – but, of its type, Monty's save remains unequalled.'

'It was only when I was in the interview room after the match and everybody started talking about the save and asking me about it that it twigged with me just how significant it was,' Montgomery says. 'I didn't even know what they were talking about until they showed it back. Jimmy Hill didn't realise I'd got a hand to it until he saw the replay.'

'We had no fear of Leeds,' Stokoe said. 'We discussed our own tactics, analysed Leeds and decided they didn't have the acceleration to get past our back four. We have never doubted that we could win this Cup. We have improved with each round. We took on and defeated Manchester City and Arsenal and the result was we had every confidence against Leeds. We had many heroes – eleven in fact – but I must single out Jimmy Montgomery. This lad is one of the best goalkeepers in the game. He made the save of all saves.'

'It is one for the archives for me. Jimmy has done it several times in the FA Cup this season but that particular one, I thought, won the Cup for us,' Stokoe said. 'If Leeds had got an equaliser then it could have been over for us.'

'Monty won it but we had it won before the match,' he added. 'We have proved that propaganda is codswallop. You press lads, even though your hearts were with us, said we could not win.'

'It was the greatest save I have ever seen and it decided the match,' Revie, who had been the BBC co-commentator when Banks made his save from Pelé in Mexico, said afterwards. 'We didn't play well and when Montgomery made that double save, the doubts started to come. Wembley does funny things to people.'

'Bob Stokoe's preparation was spot-on,' Watson says. 'Our team was a mixture of immense talent and players who just did their job. In Billy Hughes we had a player who could have become a world beater, he had everything; Dennis Tueart was very outgoing and confident as well. But the most important thing was that eventually everybody in the team was supremely confident. It wasn't just two or three players, it was every single one of us. We were all confident in our own ability and what we had to do come the final. We defended for our lives and we contested every ball. We were all dying for the cause: tackle, tackle, tackle. All of us did that, not just the defenders but the forwards and the midfielders as well. We wanted to win so badly. We created a need for it and we wanted it so much that we made it happen.'

'The biggest thing on Cup final day was that we realised who we were playing and Leeds didn't,' Kerr says. 'Somebody at Leeds never did their homework properly, because we had some very good players in our side. I don't think they set their stall out to stop the likes of Billy Hughes, Dennis Tueart or Ian Porterfield. I think we took them completely by surprise.'

'Leeds were a very good side with some great players who had taken teams apart, like Southampton who they beat 7–0 and then played something like thirty passes at the end. They were that good. But Leeds couldn't do it against our defence or our team on that day,' Halom adds. 'We were essentially an attacking side, but sometimes you have to defend just to save your skin and that is what we did that day. I spent the best part of ninety minutes chasing shadows, trying to get hold of Paul Reaney, Paul Madeley, Norman Hunter, Trevor Cherry. I spent virtually all the time chasing those players and trying to get a bite at them. But everybody in our side worked their tail off. Our strength was that we were a complete side in many respects. We had lovely ability going forward and we could attack and take teams apart if they let us, but we could also defend when necessary and under those circumstances the strength of our defence and our midfield was awesome. Billy Hughes and Dennis Tueart worked their socks off defensively. It was an awesome defensive performance by us for seventy minutes or more, and that takes some doing, it really does.'

'All the pressure was on Leeds, not just to beat us but to produce a performance,' Hughes says. 'We didn't allow them to do that. You take a young kid like Micky Horswill getting stuck into Billy Bremner. He was maybe not the most talented guy under the sun, but when it came to digging in he was one of the guys you wanted in your team.'

'I remember leaving the television interview room and seeing Don Revie stood there,' Guthrie says. 'I just said to him, "Hard luck, Mr Revie," and he replied, "You deserved to win, son," and we shook hands. All the Leeds lads were quite sporting at the end. They all shook hands. But, you know, the top four teams in the country at the time were Leeds, Arsenal, Manchester City and Liverpool. We beat Leeds, Arsenal and Manchester City, and Manchester City knocked out Liverpool before we knocked them out, so it was no fluke. We were a good team.'

'We have always got pots to go at. We always will have pots to go at. We are used to disappointments. We accept praise, we have got to accept defeat too,' Bremner said afterwards. 'I think we could have probably played until twelve o'clock at night and we still wouldn't have scored a goal. Sunderland did well. But in the first half we were a disgrace. We tried to give Wembley the Pelé or Beckenbauer bit instead of playing our normal simple game. We ignored the Leeds law.'

'The thing about that Sunderland side was they had some good young players coming through – future England and Scotland international players – and at the time we played them they were all young laddies and we were maybe caught out by that,' Lorimer says. 'They had some wonderful players and I feel that in the match we didn't treat them with the respect we should have done. That was nothing to do with Don Revie, it was maybe our own casualness, if you like, and over-confidence. We got caught flat and it was obviously a major embarrassment to us, a real embarrassment to us. Don prepared us properly and told us what to do but I think we probably thought we could go out there and turn it on. We finished up with egg on our faces but on the day there wasn't one person in the country who gave Sunderland a chance, and probably our big mistake was to fall for that. We made two mistakes – over-confidence and not being aware of how talented these young laddies at Sunderland were. They were an underestimated side. I don't think anybody was actually aware of the talent they had in that team. They would go on to prove that as the years went on.'

'The players won the FA Cup deservedly,' Cox says. 'I don't know if any of them really know what it meant to me and what they mean to me. My fondest moment was probably seeing my father's face and my three daughters – then aged twelve, ten and seven – in the tunnel after the final. That was a very proud moment.'

After all the supporters had departed the stadium, three of the Sunderland players walked out into the arena to soak up the occasion for one last time: 'After we had got changed and all the euphoria had died down, Dick Malone, Dave Watson and myself, we walked out on to the pitch again and just sat down and reflected by ourselves,' Montgomery recalls. 'I remember looking up to the big scoreboard and it still had the score up there: Leeds United 0 Sunderland 1. The crowd had gone and there was nothing in there, just us.'

As the Sunderland team travelled from Wembley to meet up with their wives and girlfriends at the Grosvenor Hotel in the centre of London before leaving for a celebratory banquet at the Park Lane Hotel, back in the north-east young boys were playing outside and re-enacting the famous moments from the match. 'There were probably about fifteen of us in all and it was good fun,' Cram says. 'We did the goal time and time again and we all changed roles at different times so that we could all play the part of Ian Porterfield.'

Emily Dawson was a nurse at Sunderland Royal Infirmary and also remembers the day well: 'The rest room on ward E7 was littered with red and white ribbons and other paraphernalia brought in by nurses and visitors,' she says. 'It also had a small television set which had been donated. The room was bursting at the corners and patients had priority. When Sunderland scored, the roar from the wards literally shook the hospital. I do believe Sunderland winning the Cup was better treatment for the patients than we were giving them. They certainly responded to something, as the discharging figures went up.'

'I was confined to my bed at home with a slipped disc,' Tom Howell adds. 'My doctor gave me permission to lie on the settee downstairs and watch the game on condition I took things nice and steady. When Sunderland scored the pain in my back stopped me from jumping up and down but I could still shout and applaud. My next-door neighbour knocked on the window and the astonishment on his face was something to see. I think the best sound I have ever heard was the referee blowing the final whistle that day. What a game. What a result.'

'It was the best football match I have ever seen,' the late Peter Jeffrey, aged ninety-four when interviewed for this book, said. 'I still get a marvellous feeling when I read, see or talk about the 1973 Cup final – even now I'm getting a tingling sensation.'

Pubs and clubs in Sunderland would take more money that evening than on New Year's Eve. But before Stokoe and his coaching staff could even sit back, relax and enjoy the moment in their London hotel rooms, the reality of what the future would bring instantly hit them.

'I was in my room, the telephone rang and it was Bob Stokoe,' Cox recalls. 'He asked to see me straight away and I couldn't imagine what it could be about. When I saw him, Bob told me that as soon he'd got back to the hotel, Bill Nicholson, the Tottenham Hotspur manager, was waiting for him in the foyer. After offering his sincere congratulations for our success he promptly offered Bob £200,000 for David Watson there and then. Bill was a true professional and he was professional about it, he said to Bob, "I don't want to spoil your celebrations but we're here with a £200,000 offer if ever you decide to sell." That was the sort of professional Bill was. But, looking back, I think that from that day on there was always the risk that our best players would leave us. It started straight away, enquiries about David, enquiries about Billy Hughes, enquiries about Dennis Tueart.'

There were no such concerns in the players' rooms. 'We felt stone-cold sober and just high on life,' Montgomery says. 'Bobby Kerr and I had the FA Cup in our room but the lid had gone missing; I think one of the lads had the lid in his room. My mate who was offshore on the rigs and his young daughter came up to the room and had a photograph taken with it. That same night he was off overseas again. I later gave him my boots from Wembley. He lives in Australia now and he still has them.'

At the banquet, entertainment was provided by musician Alan Price, a Sunderland supporter himself, and, among others, glam-rock star Suzi Quatro, who was just a few weeks shy of reaching number one with her first British release 'Can the Can'. After the party the players and their partners were taken to a private room to watch and take part in that evening's *Match of the Day*. Highlights of the match were shown, with comments from the BBC panel. Bobby Charlton, the only guest to correctly predict the winners, said, 'I think Sunderland deserved it a hundred per cent.' The injured Leeds player Terry Cooper graciously accepted defeat: 'Full marks to Sunderland,' he said. 'I would have put my life on this result today that Leeds would have won and, as it turns out, I would have lost it. After this I believe in fairy stories now.'

Brian Clough gave his verdict straight down the camera lens: 'Sunderland have done football a great service today because they have taken the FA Cup against all odds,' he said. 'They have given the game such a tremendous boost. It is an incredible sight to have seen it this afternoon. All credit to Sunderland, they were superb in defence, they were superb in attacking, they played without any inhibitions whatsoever. The professionalism, which hides a lot of cheating in the game, never came into their play and they won it as pure as I have ever seen a Cup final won.'

As Stokoe stood watching and listening, Clough continued, 'Everything stems from the manager at the football club, at least a good manager, whether it be good or bad, and he obviously takes full credit for today, full credit from the second he took over,' he said.

'For everybody that has played for Sunderland, they are the side that they want to play for and they are the side that they want to manage in actual fact,' Clough said. 'When the job was vacant a few months ago, before Bob took it over, I personally was dropping hints out left, right and centre but apparently the credentials weren't good enough and Robert got it before me.' Both Clough and the watching Collings knew there was more to it than that.

Clough then gave his verdict on why Leeds came so close so often and yet consistently missed out on the prize: 'I don't think Leeds allow themselves to blossom as much as they should,' he said. 'I think they have far more ability than is expressed and I believe that if they'd played it open, if they'd played it off the cuff, if they played it straight at all times, I believe they would have won everything in the last ten years.'

After watching the highlights, analysis and comment Stokoe and each of the Sunderland team were interviewed live on air by David Coleman. Tottenham's interest in Watson had by now made the evening editions of the London newspapers. The speculation was so strong that Coleman asked Stokoe for a comment. 'I think probably I will get one or two problems from this sort of thing but I have told the players that I will jump off the pier if any of them leave,' Stokoe said. 'We are going into next season to scrap it out together. These are my feelings about it. We have got a wonderful team spirit at the club and we have got to do it together.'

'I knew that Bill Nicholson and Spurs had been interested in me when I'd signed for Sunderland,' Watson says. 'But I knew nothing at all about any offer that might have happened on the night of the FA Cup final.'

The best quote of the night from the post-banquet interviews came from Malone who, when asked by Coleman, 'Everybody was saying – there were quite a few professional comments as well – that Eddie Gray would "murder" you in this match?', replied with a smile: 'Oh, he murdered me. He did murder me. I must admit he murdered me. He got took off.' There was a roar of laughter from the entire Sunderland team, Stokoe clapped in response and Hughes shouted out ecstatically, 'I like it, Dick, I like it!' The Sunderland party rolled on into the early hours. After more drinks some of the team even ended up at a Wimpy Bar for an impromptu breakfast of burgers and chips in the early hours of Sunday morning. When a jubilant Halom returned to his hotel room, he ordered himself a celebratory prawn cocktail from the kitchen for breakfast.

Montgomery had summed up Sunderland's achievement in winning the FA Cup perfectly on *Match of the Day* when he said, 'It is a hell of a day.' It had been monumental and would be life-changing for everyone involved in it. The rest of their lives would begin the moment they woke up.

14.

A SORT OF HOMECOMING

The morning after the day of their lives, Bob Stokoe and Ian Porterfield were collected from the Grosvenor Hotel and taken to the studios of London Weekend Television for the ITV FA Cup final review programme *How the Cup Was Won*. Porterfield would give a one-on-one interview with Brian Moore, while Stokoe would sit alongside Jimmy Hill and the panel that had upset him so much just over thirty-six hours beforehand, in particular Malcolm Allison and Jack Charlton.

'We know Malcolm's thinking has been so wrong since we hammered Manchester City. To say that Leeds were going to beat us 3–0 after we had scored five goals against Manchester City, oh, his thinking has really gone,' Stokoe retorted on air. 'We have got to excuse Jack because he knows a lot about Leeds and not really a lot about Sunderland. Obviously he knows all the strengths of Leeds and he doesn't really know our strengths and the fact that he hasn't seen us in a Cup tie, he hasn't really seen us because this is when we have been at our best.

'We have got all the experts in the Second Division next season,' Stokoe went on, referring to the fact that Crystal Palace were managed by Allison and Middlesbrough were set to announce Charlton as their new manager the next day. Along with Sunderland, these clubs were already being discussed as two of the favourites for promotion in the 1973–74 campaign.

Before thoughts could turn to the following season, however, Sunderland still had to complete their fixture list for 1972–73, with matches against Cardiff City and Queen's Park Rangers. Stokoe also wanted to spend some time enjoying reading the Sunday newspapers with a true sense of honour and vindication.

'This most romantic of results was the reward of the most prosaic of common sense,' Tony Pawson wrote in the *Observer*. 'Bob Stokoe has instilled into his players his own level-headed approach to the game. When he talks there is a simplicity, a realism and a confidence in all he says, and that was the style of his team.'

'Bob Stokoe's beaming, tearful face told it all at Wembley,' Ken Jones recalled in the *Sunday Mirror*. 'The triumph was complete. Sunderland, from the Second Division, and the very depths of improbability, had won the FA Cup.'

'Eleven weary, mud-stained heroes in red and white defied all the odds, all the predictions, all the traditions,' glowed Maurice Smith in the *People*. Raich Carter, now one of *two* men to have lifted the Cup for Sunderland, added pertinently in the same newspaper, 'It is not the chances you make, it is the chances you take that decide a game.'

Frank Butler put it succinctly in the *News of the World*: 'Wembley will remember Sunderland as long as men talk football.'

The plaudits in the press continued the following day and throughout the whole week: 'Sunderland's victory will do as much for football as the 1966 World Cup did,' Frank Clough wrote in the *Sun*. 'It will renew the faith of the Darlingtons, the Newports, the Crewes and the like to carry on.' 'Have you ever seen such a delightful toothy grin in all your life?' asked Peter Batt in the same newspaper. 'Stokoe's secret is a lesson to us all – he bloody well knows how to enjoy himself. There can be only one reason why Lady Luck flashed her smile upon him and that was because she loved the way he smiled right back at her.'

'Sunderland smashed the most consistent team of the last decade, such a shattering blow to pride, composure and self-respect that the cracks will not be easily repaired. It may well be that Leeds can never completely recover this time; can never climb back to where they were, what they were,' Frank McGhee proposed in the *Daily Mirror*. 'Sunderland played with their hearts – and in this game, hearts trumped all the Leeds aces. For me, the real stars of the day were red and white – and despite how well they fought, how magnificently they gave everything, I don't mean the Sunderland players. The hordes who follow them, lift them and love them are the reason I will remember this game.'

With the trip to Cardiff having been rearranged for the Monday night, the FA Cup winners had to go to south Wales before the north-east. The homecoming in Sunderland could not take place until twenty-four hours later, which would be three days after the triumph.

A late-Sunday-morning finish to the celebrations in London was followed by the wives and girlfriends returning to Sunderland with the trophy as the players travelled to the Welsh capital. 'My wife Joy told me it was the nearest to fame she has ever been,' Jim Montgomery says. 'Whenever anybody went past them on the motorway they were looking up to see the Cup. They stopped off at the Wetherby Grill on the way back for something to eat and they took the Cup in with them. Apparently the supporters who were in there couldn't believe it.'

'When we got to our hotel in Cardiff there was a crate of champagne in each of our rooms,' Ritchie Pitt says. 'I don't know where that came from!'

A crowd of 26,000 gave Sunderland a standing ovation as they entered the stadium and cheered Stokoe to his seat. The Rokerites turned on exhibition stuff at times in the match, with an artistic and stylish performance against a dogged, determined but nervy Cardiff, who, managed by Stokoe's former Newcastle team-mate and the 1955 FA Cup-winning captain Jimmy Scoular, needed a point to stay in the Second Division. However, Gary Bell missed an early penalty for the home side after Pitt brought down Tony Villars, and Bobby Woodruff gave them the lead just before half-time. Vic Halom equalised for Sunderland after goalkeeper Bill Irwin had touched a cross from stand-in left-back Joe Bolton on to the post. Halom had another chance late on, but Cardiff held on to secure the point they needed to stay up. Huddersfield Town were relegated, along with Brighton & Hove Albion.

'The Cardiff directors invited us all up to the boardroom afterwards and the champagne flowed once again,' Billy Hughes says. Sunderland's celebratory party was back in full flow.

The teetotal Stokoe retired early to his hotel room that night. Back in the north-east, Tyne Tees TV broadcast Leslie Barrett's production *Meanwhile Back in Sunderland*, and certain ITV regions took it, including Wales, which enabled the Sunderland manager to watch it. The programme was to become a local treasure in the north-east.

It began with coverage of FA Cup final day in Sunderland at

5.30 a.m., with a long shot facing southwards towards the Wearmouth Bridge and a pull-down from the newly created tower blocks above the train station to find fans walking, shaking their rattles and screaming at the tops of their voices as they began their long journey south.

Inside the train station, Montgomery's mother-in-law predicted a 1–0 win for Sunderland. All other fans – resplendent in the new red, white and black scarves that had become so popular during the Cup run – were equally confident. The trains headed to London's Kings Cross station via Newcastle while at the same time a fleet of buses headed south towards the A19.

At 8 a.m. the town centre was deserted. Then, gradually, the early shoppers began to emerge, with babies in prams clad in as much red and white as the shops they passed. By midday the cameras had found a side street opposite Roker Park where a group of young boys were playing football with a small dog wearing a red-and-white rosette around its neck.

The attention briefly switched to Sunderland Register Office at lunchtime and the one and only marriage planned for the day in the town featuring – it has to be said – a quite unhappy-looking groom with his mind clearly on other things. The best man explained that the men were soon heading off to watch the Cup final on television while the women were going back to the bride's house.

At a house party on Beatrice Street, near to Roker Park, women and children bedecked in red and white huddled together in a living room to watch the match on colour television. Some less fortunate ladies gathered around Vision Hire on Fawcett Street to watch and cheer through the shop window. One excited woman summed up the mood of the wives outside Vision Hire: 'I have come out of the house to get away from it because the tension built up too much,' she said. 'But I just can't stay away from the television!'

Elsewhere the town was completely empty. One policeman walked the streets.

Those men and boys not lucky enough to be at Wembley gathered in pubs, clubs and local cinemas to watch the match together. The goal, the save and the final whistle were celebrated in accordance with the occasion and what it all meant. After the drama of the match was over one gentleman summed up the feeling of confidence that had swept the region in the weeks leading up to the final: 'Before the game it was a foregone conclusion that Sunderland would beat Leeds, because the people of this town willed it,' he grinned.

Immediately after the match was over, men and women raced into the streets to celebrate together. Passers-by sat on car bonnets while drivers happily hooted their horns in response. Everyone was singing and shouting. Interestingly there were as many chants of 'Stokoe!' as there were of 'Sunderland!'.

The late Bill Simmons – a Sunderland historian – summed up his feelings of the day in the first edition of *The History of Sunderland AFC*: 'My only personal regret through all this was that I could not be in two places at once,' he wrote. 'Having been part of the Wembley atmosphere was tremendous but I would have liked to have been in Sunderland when the final whistle went.'

When the Tyne Tees cameras moved inside the many clubs and pubs hosting parties – still frequented by more women than men – the party mood completely took over. One young lady showed off her 'Sunderland' knickers for the cameras as everyone took part in a rendition of 'You'll Never Walk Alone'. The half-mix to Stokoe's run at the end of the match under the emotional voices of these Sunderland locals was a fitting and poignant ending to the documentary.

'We had four single-camera units out and about and we shot everything that moved,' Barrett says. 'At kick-off the whole town just switched off. We edited all day Sunday and Monday and we knew instantly that we had a very good film. We had never done anything like this before – it was blanket coverage of one event – and it was pure gold, a dream come true in fact.

'Sunderland wasn't the most well-off town in 1973, and the programme became a great social document of its time,' Barrett adds. 'There was no reporter and no voice. The programme was about the people of Sunderland; without them there was nothing. Geoffrey Cox, who was managing director at Tyne Tees, tried to get the network to take it but sadly he failed. But Yorkshire took it and so did Wales. Bob Stokoe saw it and wept, apparently. I must say it did make the hair stand up on the back of your neck. We had some tremendous footage. That sort of thing only happens once in a lifetime. Thank God we were there to cover it.'

'I worked on *Meanwhile Back in Sunderland* as an assistant camera-man,' Dave Dixon recalls. 'The mood in the town was great. There was an air of excitement and the whole place just shut down. It was like Christmas Day: nobody was around. There can't have been one person in Sunderland who wasn't interested in the Cup final and wasn't watching the match. The team had got to the final on achievement and there was a sense of great pride.

'I have to admit I was not the world's greatest football fan but I got caught up with the euphoria and I could have cried with all those supporters on the full-time whistle,' Dixon adds. 'It was amazing to experience it all – from the pent-up excitement before the match to the celebrations afterwards. The people were so proud of the team. The pub that we filmed in at night – the one with the famous shot of the girl with the knickers – was on John Street. It was mayhem: we finished filming there at eleven p.m., but I think the party went on well into the small hours. It was fabulous to work on that programme. Films like that just don't get made today.'

'*Meanwhile Back in Sunderland* was a brilliant piece of television,' Sunderland supporter Pete Sixsmith says. 'It still gets repeated from time to time and it is still fascinating to watch. Everything about it, from the families crowded around television sets, watching in colour for the first time, to the scenes in the streets on the full-time whistle.'

The emotions featured in the documentary were an indication of the welcome that the team would receive on its return to Sunderland. Yet nothing could prepare the players for what they were about to experience the following night.

The homecoming was set to be even more spectacular than the one that had greeted the 1937 FA Cup winners. Then the team had arrived by train at Monkwearmouth Station, but this had since been closed as a result of the 'Beeching Axe' in the 1960s. This time the team would return north by coach and be paraded through the streets of County Durham on an open-top bus all the way to Roker Park.

'Well before we got to Wetherby on the way home we could see red-and-white scarves and people waving to us on the flyovers,' Montgomery recalls. 'We couldn't believe it at first and wondered what they were doing. We were still in Yorkshire at this stage but people were already turning out to cheer us on our way home. It was truly unbelievable and the further we got up the country, the more people there were.'

The Sunderland team coach pulled off the A1 at Carrville round-about in County Durham. There the players moved on to a double-decker bus, which had become an open-top vehicle following a recent accident. The plan was to travel the twelve miles to Sunderland on the A690 Durham Road and then go via Fawcett Street, North Bridge Street, Roker Avenue, Gladstone Street and Roker Baths Road before arriving at Roker Park just over an hour later. In effect, it took well over double that time.

It was estimated that as many as 750,000 people may have turned up to welcome the Sunderland team home that night. To put that figure in context, the 1971 census had a registered population of 217,079 in the town and 1,409,637 in County Durham.

The players moved along to the front of the top deck as the coach went near to their homes: Dave Watson held the Cup aloft as the parade passed Houghton-le-Spring, and Porterfield did the same at East Herrington. Fans climbed trees, stood on rooftops and hung out of windows, while wheelchair-bound patients were taken outside the hospital to see their heroes in the flesh.

'It was frightening,' Dick Malone says. 'Supporters were stood on the roofs of three-storey buildings, hanging off the ends, waving scarves and cheering. The streets were twelve-deep with people.'

'The crowds really started when we got to Durham,' Ron Guthrie adds. 'From the Carrville roundabout it was packed all the way to Roker Park. It was incredible and wonderful to experience that. I remember seeing a small pony in a field and it had a red-and-white strip on! The reaction was absolutely amazing.'

By the time the coach reached Sunderland town centre it was almost at a standstill. The multi-storey flats that now dominated the skyline were full of faces, bodies, scarves and flags. One banner proclaimed HAIL THE RETURN OF THE MESSIAH. 'It must have taken us something like three hours to get to Roker Park,' Hughes says. 'We are talking about thousands and thousands and thousands of people here. When we did eventually get there, there were another fifty-five thousand people waiting for us inside. I think that is when we realised what we'd done.'

'I was stood near to the ground and saw the team come up from the seafront towards Roker Park,' Steve Cram says. 'I took my replica FA Cup with me for the homecoming and I kept it for years and years afterwards. The Cup win was my happiest childhood memory. I suppose it was such an iconic time and I felt something exciting was going on in my life.'

'The stadium was chock-a-block,' Montgomery says. 'It was another great night, running around with the Cup and doing interviews. It was absolutely fantastic seeing all the people back home. It then really hit us what it all meant for the people and for the town.'

Bobby Kerr led the team out from the tunnel with the FA Cup in tow. 'We are very pleased that we have been able to give you this Cup,' he announced to the crowd.

'I cannot express how much we appreciate this reception tonight,' Stokoe added. 'You have given us a night we will never, never forget. We believe we did something for you on Saturday but what you have done for us tonight is something I will always remember. Royalty could not have received a reception like we have had tonight. It makes you feel you have got to run away now because nothing can ever touch this.'

Stokoe certainly had a skill in finding the right words on the right occasion – whether it was to make referees and opponents think, or to milk the rapturous response he always got from the Sunderland supporters, by simply being one of them. But it was his passion – epitomised in that glorious run to Montgomery at Wembley – that resonated with the hearts of the people.

'We didn't realise what we had done, to be honest,' Kerr admits. 'The only thing I wish now is that we had come home on the Sunday just to taste it. The Cup win meant such a lot to such a lot of people, and it still does.'

'I walked down the tunnel and somebody wrapped a scarf around my neck,' Pitt says. 'I was also given this red-and-white teddy, which I gave to my daughter Louise when I went to get her out of hospital. She lives in New York now and she's still got that teddy with her!'

After another exhausting night of celebrations Sunderland had to finally complete their league campaign, against QPR. The visitors had been promoted to the First Division while the Rokerites required just a draw to finish the campaign fourth in the table. Before the match there were three presentations: Kerr presented QPR skipper Terry Venables with a miners' lamp in recognition of his team's promotion, Kerr was presented with the *Sunday Mirror* 'Giantkillers

Cup', and Stokoe collected the Second Division Manager of the Month award.

It was still a party atmosphere at Roker Park, but one man came to spoil the party: QPR midfielder Stan Bowles. 'Seeing as it was the last game of the season, the Sunderland management decided to display the Cup on a trestle table by the pitch,' Bowles recalled in his autobiography, *Stan the Man*. 'I couldn't believe this at all: it was asking for a bit of mischief.' Bowles then proceeded to have a £10 bet with friends that he could knock the trophy off its stand.

'So the whistle goes, the game gets under way. Pretty soon the ball comes out to me, only problem is I am on the other side of the pitch to the FA Cup,' Bowles continues. 'However, seeing as there is a tenner involved, I am not about to let this geographical inconvenience interfere. With the ball at my feet, I tear straight off across the park. Everyone on the pitch is just staring at me. Then, bang, the FA Cup goes shooting up in the air. The whole ground knew that I had done it on purpose. Everything goes deadly silent for a couple of seconds, then the Sunderland fans go ape-shit. They want my balls in their sandwiches!'

Bowles went on to score two goals that night in a 3–0 win for QPR, but that wasn't the story. Before he scored, referee Peter Greaves had sent Micky Horswill off after he had retaliated to a foul by the QPR star. Two minutes later, when Pitt also retaliated at the same player, the teams had to be taken off the pitch.

'Stan Bowles was a right niggly little devil,' Pitt says. 'He was up to all sorts and I ran forty yards to kick him that night. He broke two toes in my right foot because he kept backing into me with his studs and just stamping down on my foot and then running off. He also kept elbowing me in the stomach and running off. I went after him, the referee saw me chasing and kicking him, but of course he didn't know what had gone on before. Micky Horswill had already been sent off and the game was getting out of control. The referee took us all off the pitch, put us all in the same dressing room and gave us a real tongue-lashing.'

There followed a pitch invasion, and at the request of Chief Super-intendent Ronald Kell, the head of Sunderland police division, Stokoe came out on to the pitch ten minutes later with a megaphone and made the following plea to the fans: 'Let's not spoil one of the best seasons the club has had for many years. We have learned to win but if we have to lose tonight, let's do it in the Roker tradition. Let's get the game finished, whatever the result, then we can come back again next season and start again.' Stokoe's words were heard and the game was completed.

The following week, Stokoe and Sunderland were honoured at a reception held at the town's Civic Centre. Town mayor Leslie Watson said in his speech, 'Last December we were candidates for the Third Division, now we are FA Cup winners, we are in European football and the country is in the European Community. This will do great things for the town. Sunderland is on everybody's mind.'

Each member of the FA Cup-winning team was allowed to take the trophy home for a day. For Pitt and his three-month-old daughter this was an accident waiting to happen: 'We sat her in the Cup to take a photograph and because it was metal and because it was cold, she had a little mishap in it,' he says. 'Of course we washed it out, but every year when we saw the players celebrating at Wembley and drinking champagne from the Cup, we always had a laugh about it.'

Throughout the summer months Sunderland paraded the Cup around the area. On one occasion, the two players present were a little worse for wear at the end of the evening and the trophy was taken into police custody for the night. Cram, whose father was a policeman, remembers it well, 'At six o'clock the following morning my dad woke us up. My brother and I got dressed in our Sunday best blazer and jumper. We didn't know where we were going but in the car my dad told us we were going to the police station. We went through the back door into the offices and standing there was the FA Cup. We couldn't believe it. The next thing, the crime photographer took us outside to a field at the back and we had our pictures taken with the Cup. It was fantastic.'

The Sunderland players were now household names. Wherever they went that summer they were instantly recognisable. Apart from, it seems, in Majorca, where on a post-season celebratory tour of the island there was a moment that brought the winning goal scorer at Wembley back down to earth. 'It was very funny,' Halom recalls. 'We were trying to get into this nightclub and the men on the door weren't having it at all. So Ian goes up to them and tells them in broken English, "Me Ian Porterfield, we are Sunderlando." It didn't work and we didn't get in. But it was a very funny moment and it is now a lovely memory.'

15.

WHAT NEVER HAPPENED TO THE LIKELY LADS

The Sunderland bookmakers who had paid out handsomely on the Rokerites lifting the FA Cup offered such low odds on Bob Stokoe's side winning promotion back to the First Division in the 1973–74 season that few supporters even placed a bet. With a new three-up, three-down promotion and relegation system introduced by the Football League, Sunderland, at 5–4, were the hottest favourites in years to win promotion from the Second Division.

Stokoe enjoyed the first few weeks after the Cup win. He picked up a special 'Outstanding Achievement' honour at the Bells Manager of the Year awards ceremony at the Café Royal in London, was pleased to promote coach Arthur Cox to the new position of assistant manager, and watched Sunderland beat Cannes 3–2 in an end-of-season friendly in the south of France after the trip to Majorca. But before the month of May was out, he suddenly issued a 'Give us a break' plea in the local press.

'I am very delighted that we won the Cup but will life ever be quite the same again?' Stokoe asked in the *Sunderland Echo*. 'I have no experience of this sort of situation and, quite frankly, I just don't know how to deal with it. There is no privacy, no breathing space. I dare not begin to accept the offers which are pouring in for a continual round of social engagements and even the quiet walk along the sea front which was possible before the final is now an invitation for autograph hunters.'

These were not the kind of words that had been associated with the 'Messiah' in his time at Sunderland so far, where everything had been possible and nothing had been impossible. Some supporters feared that cracks were beginning to show in his character. Such fears grew when the manager suddenly fired Billy Elliott from his coaching staff a week later, before taking a month-long break. Elliott had never really been in his plans, and with the season and the FA Cup win out of the way, he was given his cards. Stokoe subsequently spent most of his leisure time in the early part of that summer walking his dog and playing golf.

By the time he returned to his desk at Roker Park – after watching golfer Tom Weiskopf win the Open championship at Royal Troon – the first-round draw of the European Cup Winners' Cup had taken place: Sunderland were to play against Hungarian Cup winners Vasas Budapest.

Having avoided the likes of defending holders AC Milan, 1972–73 UEFA Cup runners-up Borussia Mönchengladbach and fancied teams such as Anderlecht, Banik Ostrava and Sporting Lisbon, this was seen as a good draw in the thirty-two-team competition. Incidentally, the Rokerites also avoided Cardiff City and Glasgow Rangers plus Atlético Bilbao, the Basque team that was reportedly formed by Sunderland miners and shipyard workers at the turn of the century and given a strip of red-and-white shirts and black shorts as a result. In readiness for the club's first-ever European campaign, the floodlights at Roker Park had to undergo £20,000 worth of improvements, and fourteen new private boxes were installed in the upper enclosure of the main stand.

The prospect of European football excited local politicians, who clearly saw it as a marketing opportunity for the town. It was also a new experience for the club, the manager, the players and the supporters. But Stokoe insisted that promotion was the priority: 'It is essential Sunderland gets back into the First Division as quickly as possible,' he said.

The Rokerites travelled to Scotland to play pre-season friendlies against Aberdeen and Celtic at the beginning of August, and Stokoe – reported to be frustrated with the lack of transfer business he had been able to do with English clubs that summer – took the opportunity to go on another of his vetting missions north of the border.

Aberdeen beat Sunderland 3–0, but there was better news a few days later at Parkhead when the FA Cup-winning side beat Jock Stein's eight-times Scottish League champions 2–1 with goals from Dennis Tueart and Billy Hughes. 'Naturally the lads are pleased with them-selves,' Stokoe said after the match. He then talked up possible transfer activity: 'We are thinking in terms of really big money but the men we have in mind are just not available at the moment.' Alas, he left Scotland empty-handed.

Two more pre-season matches followed in Ireland, at Shelbourne and Cork. Sunderland won both 2–1. League Cup winners Tottenham Hotspur then won 1–0 at Roker Park in front of a crowd of 21,000 in the club's final pre-season warm-up match.

This game was seen by some as an unofficial – even consolatory – Charity Shield contest after league champions Liverpool had pulled out of the traditional pre-season curtain raiser to play in Germany and Japan that summer. Sunderland consequently opted to play in a prestigious international tournament in Portugal, but that fell through and the tours of Scotland and Ireland were then hastily arranged.

As it was, Second Division winners Burnley played Manchester City in the Charity Shield that year. The Football Association subsequently moved the match to Wembley from the following season – it had previously been held at one of the two competing sides' grounds – and insisted that the league champions and FA Cup winners should always contest the trophy. The showpiece event that it is today began in earnest from the following year.

Stokoe played Mick McGiven and Dave Young against Tottenham, in readiness for the forthcoming suspensions acquired by Micky Horswill and Ritchie Pitt in the ill-tempered final match of the 1972–73 season against Queen's Park Rangers that would affect the beginning of the forthcoming campaign.

Both McGiven and Young started in the opening league match against Orient at Roker Park; otherwise the team was the one that won at Wembley. Everyone anticipated a comfortable home win. But it didn't happen. In fact the Rokerites were lucky to escape with a point from a 1–1 draw after Derrick Downing had given Orient a sixty-ninth-minute lead. Hughes equalised late on.

Stokoe responded to this result by making what appeared to be his first new signing of the season, when he agreed a £70,000 fee for the talented Burnley midfielder Alan West, who travelled up to Sunderland and even trained with his new team-mates. But the deal fell through on medical advice. 'There is no panic and I will not panic,' Stokoe told the press.

A 4–1 win at Notts County – secured by two goals from Vic Halom plus one apiece from Tueart and Hughes – was encouraging. But another

1–1 home draw against Cardiff frustrated an expectant crowd of 29,495. Sunderland again trailed in this match, with Ron Guthrie firing in an equaliser midway through the second half. Another Halom goal and another 1–1 draw followed midweek at Portsmouth. One win and three draws was not the start Sunderland supporters had expected. Still, it could have been worse: Malcolm Allison's Crystal Palace were rooted at the bottom of the table. By contrast Jack Charlton's Middlesbrough were sat at the top.

What Stokoe did not need at this time was a drawn-out court case, but that is what he got when an industrial tribunal in Newcastle heard Elliott's claim of unfair dismissal following his sacking in the summer. Stokoe told the tribunal that he regarded it as important to have his own right-hand man working with him, and that he had told Elliott this the day he arrived at Sunderland. Stokoe also believed Elliott could not carry out first-team coaching in the way he wanted it done. Cox had joined the club in February and therefore, Stokoe said, two coaches were looking after the first team. Elliott went on to win the case and Sunderland were ordered to pay him £1,448 in compensation. The whole saga was an unwelcome distraction at the beginning of the season, but it makes sense of John Motson's recollection of his visit to Roker Park in November 1972.

In mid-September Stokoe was finally able to select his FA Cup-winning side for the first time that season, for the visit to Oxford United. Horswill had served his four-match suspension and replaced McGiven in midfield, while Pitt was also back. With Young on the bench again this was man-for-man the same line-up that had walked out at Wembley four months before. Sunderland won 1–0 with a stunning volley from Tueart. But Halom lost his front two teeth in the match, something that could not have come at a worse time for him.

'I had been so excited because we were due to fly out to Hungary – where my father was born – to play Vasas Budapest in the European Cup Winners' Cup and I was going to take the opportunity to meet up with some members of my family who I had never met before,' Halom says. 'The weekend before at Oxford I whacked one or two of their players before half-time. As the second half kicked off somebody tapped me on the shoulder and smacked me right in the mouth and knocked my front teeth out. I had no time to go to the dentist and so I went to Budapest with no front teeth in.

'We were in the Nep Stadium doing a few exercises when this lady appears and turns out to be my Aunty Ila,' Halom adds. 'I had never met her before and I smiled at her with no teeth. Can you imagine? The lads were beside themselves. It was ridiculous. She couldn't speak English and I couldn't speak Hungarian so we had to speak through an interpreter. She was made guest of honour at the match. I have to say Bob Stokoe was really good to me during that whole trip. He let me off training so that I could go and spend time with my family and this allowed me to have a couple of days with them.'

The trip to the Nep Stadium – the site of Hungary's 7–1 mauling of England in 1954 – gave Sunderland supporters an opportunity to travel behind the Iron Curtain for the first time. 'I always said I would go to see Sunderland if ever we played in Europe and so I took a day off work and flew from Teesside Airport to Budapest on a Dan Air Comet,' Sunderland supporter Pete Sixsmith says. 'It bucketed it down but the city was fascinating. There were still bullet holes in the stadium walls from the 1956 rebellion. There was no cover at all, just this great big Communist bowl. But this was the place where the great Hungarian side of the 1950s had played and the team that I remembered from the 1966 World Cup when Hungary had played at Roker Park. It was a fantastic experience to be there.'

It was a trip that Dave Watson would remember for the rest of his life: 'Dicky Malone and I were walking around the city when one of the football journalists from back home came up to me,' he recalls. 'He asked me if I'd heard the news. I said, "What news?" He then informed me that I had made the England squad to play Austria later that month. It didn't sink in. He asked me how I felt and I had to say to him, "Hang on, give me ten minutes to think about it please." I couldn't believe it. I felt like I was walking on air.' The Sunderland defender was the only non-First Division player in the twenty-one-man squad. He would feature consistently in the England set-up for the next nine years.

Sunderland's match against Vasas Budapest, managed by Lajos Baróti, who was in charge of Hungary when they played the Soviet Union in the 1966 World Cup quarter-final at Roker Park, was preceded in the Nep Stadium by Ferencváros against Polish side Gwardia in the UEFA Cup; a crowd of 35,000 had gathered by the time the Rokerites were due to kick off. Stokoe again selected his Cup-winning side.

Sunderland played well and won 2–0, courtesy of a header from Hughes and a mazy run and goal from Tueart at the end. 'That was the first time Vasas Budapest had ever been beaten in that stadium in European competition,' Watson says. 'We totally outplayed them as well. It was our typical tempo. Billy Hughes was brilliant that night. To win 2–0 over there was a great result for us.'

Things were looking up for Sunderland. Still unbeaten and with a strong platform to progress into the last sixteen of the European Cup Winners' Cup, the Rokerites now hosted Luton Town in the Second Division with high hopes. But this match would bring an abrupt end to the FA Cup-winning side, for this would be the last time they ever played together. Pitt – still only twenty-one – was stretchered off the pitch after damaging medial ligaments in his right knee. He would never play again for the first team, and ultimately his career was over.

'I was shielding the ball out of play and John Ryan came in behind me and gently pushed me,' Pitt says. 'It wasn't his fault but my studs got caught in the turf and as I was going one way he pushed me ninety degrees and I twisted. I felt a really bad pain up the back of my knee and up into my hamstring. I knew I was injured but I didn't know how serious it was. They carried me off on a stretcher, I went to hospital and I was there for a long time. I knew I had a cartilage problem and I knew it was my anterior cruciate ligament. I'm not saying they didn't know what to do with it but as medicine has improved I may have been back playing within six months nowadays. In those days that didn't happen, and if you had an injury like that they tried to mend it and if it didn't respond then you were finished. Basically that was it for me. I later played twenty-six reserve games but I never got picked for the first team again. After the FA Cup final I got a new two-year contract that took me up to 1975, but when that contract was up Bob Stokoe told me I was finished. I had been expecting to sign a new contract as well. It was a crushing blow.

'I couldn't go to another football club because I didn't have that option,' Pitt adds. 'Sunderland claimed the insurance money on me. I can only presume the club claimed the money on the strength that I hadn't recovered enough to get back into the first team, which I can only presume is why I hadn't been picked for the first team. Anyway they claimed the money and so if I had wanted to go to another club then that club would have had to pay back that insurance money to the Football League in order for me to have insurance to play again. No club was going to do that. So, in effect, when Sunderland claimed the insurance they finished my career. The alternative was to give me a free transfer and let me find a club for nothing. But they claimed the insurance and, in effect, that finished me. In those days footballers didn't have personal insurance. I knew I had to get a job to support my family, so I went to college and studied physical education and mathematics for three years on a grant. I came out of college completely broke.'

Luton beat Sunderland 1–0 to inflict the Rokerites' first defeat of the 1973–74 season, but the result was overshadowed by Pitt's injury. With no wins from three home games so far, Stokoe held private talks with his squad the following week. Watson – away on England duty – missed the meeting but later met up with his team-mates in Birmingham ahead of the trip to West Bromwich Albion, where Sunderland again drew 1–1, their fourth 1–1 draw in seven league outings. Halom scored his fourth goal of the season at The Hawthorns, while Hughes and Tueart also had three goals each so far. But it was the number of points and the club's position in the table that was becoming the concern.

Sunderland began October in the bottom half of the Second Division, in thirteenth place. Better news came when a Tueart penalty defeated Vasas Budapest 1–0 and secured the club's place in the second round of the European Cup Winners' Cup. The Rokerites were paired with Sporting Lisbon – who had knocked out Cardiff 2–1 on aggregate – in the second round.

Goals from Halom, Hughes and Ian Porterfield gave Sunderland a 3–1 win over Sheffield Wednesday the following weekend, to take them into the top half of the table ahead of a Monday night visit to the Baseball Ground to play Brian Clough's Derby County in the League Cup. Sunderland's reputation as a quality Cup side was done no harm when two second-half goals by the recalled John Lathan – making his first start of the season – earned them a deserved 2–2 draw and a replay against one of the top First Division teams.

'I know that the extra game adds to our problems but I would not have it any other way,' Stokoe said. 'If we were to decide that it would be better for us to do well in one competition than another, that would be cheating.' But the one competition Sunderland were not doing too well in was the Second Division. Without Watson – sent home from England duty with a heavy cold – the Rokerites were beaten again, 1–0 at Preston North End.

Watson now had a potential England career to distract him from the frustrations that were enveloping Sunderland's bid to win promotion. He was still to make his international debut but was sat at Wembley when England played Poland in their final qualifying match for the World Cup 1974 finals in West Germany. England needed a win to qualify and should they get it Watson had a good chance of making the squad the following summer. But England drew 1–1 and failed to qualify. Poland went through in their place and within six months Sir Alf Ramsey's eleven-year reign over the national side was at an end.

'I remember getting in my car after the match and driving all the way back to Sunderland,' Watson says. 'How different things could have felt if we had qualified. I think I would have gone to the World Cup in West Germany in 1974. I was an up-and-coming player and I made every squad after that game. I was so disappointed that night. It was such a big contrast to how I had felt at Wembley with Sunderland just a few months before in the FA Cup final.'

The day after England crashed out of the World Cup, former Leeds United striker Rod Belfitt arrived at Roker Park in a £65,000 deal from Everton. It was the highest fee Stokoe had ever paid for a player, and the manager's previous biggest signing was far from happy about the new arrival.

'I wasn't very happy at all because Rod Belfitt was a centre-forward and I was playing OK at that time,' Halom says. 'We had a training session where we played forwards against defence and Rod and Dave Watson played at the back and I battered them both. Arthur Cox walked off with Rod and said, "Don't worry, you won't face anything like that tomorrow." But Bob Stokoe had upset me that much by signing another centre-forward. I thought he was brought in to replace me and when I was wound up like that I was a dangerous animal.'

In fact, Belfitt spent most of his time at Sunderland partnering Watson in the centre of defence. He scored just four goals for the club and provided little competition for Halom up front before leaving to join Huddersfield Town. He was to be the first of a number of Stokoe signings that didn't quite work out after the FA Cup run.

At this time *Match of the Day* covered around a dozen or so league matches from outside the First Division. Sunderland featured regularly on the BBC programme at the start of the 1973–74 season, including a visit to Fulham in October when a 2–0 win was secured by a Horswill strike and an Alan Mullery own-goal. The result put the Rokerites up to tenth in the Second Division, but they were still six points behind Middlesbrough. As exciting as all the Cup matches were, Stokoe's side were already well behind the promotion pack. Furthermore, the club's fixture schedule was becoming arduous: Sporting Lisbon's visit to Roker Park the following Wednesday night would be followed by the visit of Crystal Palace three days later and the visit of Derby two days after that in a League Cup replay – three home matches in three different competitions in just six days!

Watched by a crowd of 31,568, Bobby Kerr opened the scoring against Sporting Lisbon on thirty-two minutes, and crossed for Horswill to double the lead with a header on sixty-four minutes. Tueart also had the ball in the net but was flagged offside. With just minutes remaining Sporting broke and Argentine striker Hector Yazalde – the man who would set a new European record of forty-six club goals that season, a record that still stands today – headed past Jim Montgomery. This goal, scored against the run of play, would prove to be costly for Sunderland.

The following weekend Sunderland were disappointingly held to a goalless draw by a Palace side that had picked up just three points all season. The attendance of 31,935 was the third highest in the country on the day, but those fans had now seen just one win from five home matches in the league.

Just over forty-eight hours later Derby were in town but, alas, Clough was not. The mercurial manager had walked out on the Rams after a long-standing feud with chairman Sam Longson. The final straw apparently came when Longson told Clough to discontinue his media work. Clough had taken over, somewhat surprisingly, at Third Division Brighton & Hove Albion and Dave Mackay was in charge at the Baseball Ground.

'It is always important to get priorities right but only clubs like Leeds United, perhaps, can choose what they want to be successful in,' a mischievous Stokoe said before the League Cup clash. 'We can't, so we look for a good result in every game and we certainly want to win tonight.'

In a thrilling end-to-end Cup tie watched by a crowd of 38,875, Sunderland and Derby drew 1–1 after extra-time. Tueart scored for the Rokerites, who then won home advantage for the second replay two days later on the toss of a coin.

This replay was to give Roker Park its best night of the 1973–74 season. Watched by another big crowd of 38,460, an impressive Sunderland won 3–0 with a Halom hat-trick while Watson's performance at centre-half overshadowed the display given by Derby and England number 5 Roy McFarland. It took Sunderland 300 minutes to get past the Rams and, in the end, they outplayed them in every department. Their reward was a home match against Liverpool. The Rokerites had got through the latest stage of what was becoming a punishing fixture list, and once again they had found their best on a Cup night.

'They don't ask racehorses to run four times in a week but we have played four tremendous games in seven days and the system says we have to play again on Saturday,' Stokoe said after the win against Derby.

It would not happen in any other country in the world.

We have met top opposition in the European Cup Winners' Cup, the League Cup and we have promotion to think about as well. But we have got through and got through it. The tremendous sense of these Cup matches is good for the players. No one can question that the excitement of Cup football is what is wanted in this area. The enthusiasm and fervour of last night's crowd provided the answer. They are the people that matter. They tell us what they want.

Stokoe and his players were once more clearly buoyed by the crowds – and the passion – on Cup nights at Roker Park. But was this beginning to take precedence in the manager's mind over what he had so publicly claimed was his number one aim at the start of the season: promotion? Could this relatively small first-team squad really cope with challenging on four fronts?

Something had to give. Sunderland's next two fixtures were away at Hull City in the Second Division and at Sporting Lisbon in the

European Cup Winners' Cup. And now Stokoe made a decision that backfired. The Sunderland manager decided to rest his entire forward line at Boothferry Park. Not one of Kerr, Hughes, Halom, Porterfield or Tueart played. Guthrie was moved into midfield alongside untried youngster Bobby Mitchell, who was given his debut. Lathan made his first league start of the season, McGiven was recalled after two months out and Belfitt made his first start for the club at centre-forward. Sunderland lost the match 2–0 and were now positioned fourteenth in the table and ten points behind the leaders, Middlesbrough. From this moment on, things would never be quite the same.

'I was furious,' Watson says. 'Bob Stokoe left half the team out and we lost the match. I went up to him in the dressing room afterwards and I told him how I felt. I said to him, "You've let me down." He dismissed me and said that the European Cup Winners' Cup match was very important. I told him that promotion was equally as important. We argued about that but our main priority that season had to be getting out of the Second Division.

'I stood there after Hull's second goal and looked around me and saw all these reserve players in our side,' Watson adds. 'There was no Dennis, no Billy, no Bobby, no Ian, no Vic. I felt very angry. I was the senior outfield player and I felt that Stokoe had abandoned me. I didn't like it and I had a go at him about it. I felt he had let the team down and I told him so. Stokoe shouted at me but deep down he must have known he had made a mistake. He was a shouter but he was also a realist. We didn't have a chance in that game and it was patently obvious after about ten minutes that we weren't going to get anything out of it. I lost a lot of respect for him that day.'

'I was at Hull and nobody could believe it when all these names were announced,' Sunderland supporter Steve Hodgson says. 'Bob Stokoe decided to play a weakened team and nobody knew who half of them were. He was wrong to do that. The priority was to get into the First Division and he sacrificed that. It was so disappointing to feel that he seemed perfectly willing to let two points go – two points that could have gone towards us winning promotion.'

Afterwards Stokoe told the press: 'I do not want to say too much about the game. We have been forced into this position and we are doing the best we can to keep going for everything in which we are involved.'

Four days later Sunderland were sent crashing out of Europe. Sporting Lisbon beat them 2–0 at the Estádio José Alvalade in front of 60,000 partisan spectators. Yazalde opened the scoring on twenty-eight minutes and Samuel Ferreira Fraguito settled the contest after a Mário Da Silva Mateus free-kick on sixty-nine minutes. The last twenty minutes or so were played out with home fans standing on the touchline and intimidating the Sunderland players. There were also various time-wasting tactics employed by players and supporters alike as the clock ticked down.

'There was a lot of bullying inside the ground, fans beating their chests and that sort of thing,' Watson says. 'Towards the end of the match the ball boys would collect the ball and then kick it into the crowd. It took ages to get the ball back and all the time the clock was winding down. It was so infuriating. But we should have won that tie. We were much better than them at Roker Park and we should have scored more goals in that game. We suffered for that because we didn't manage to score over there. We would have been in the quarter-finals had we won. We blew our chance really. We had a good chance in that competition.'

Sporting Lisbon were fined by UEFA for failing to control the situation inside their own stadium but still progressed to the semi-finals before losing 3–2 on aggregate to FC Magdeburg. The East German side went on to win the competition with a 2–0 win over AC Milan in the final in Rotterdam. Jürgen Sparwasser – the man who would become famous for scoring the winning goal for East Germany over West Germany in the 1974 World Cup group match in Hamburg – was their star player.

A fortnight after Sunderland's European exit, they were out of the League Cup as well. This defeat could not have been played out in a more unusual setting. In mid-November the miners went on strike over pay claims, while electrical power workers were also in dispute with the government. After a crisis meeting of the Cabinet, a proclamation was signed by the Queen which gave the government the power to safeguard the country from the effect of power cuts and a shortage of coal supplies. The impact on football was that no floodlighting could be used and therefore all kick-offs – both on Saturday and midweek – were moved to 2 p.m. A crowd of 36,208 still turned up at Roker Park on a Wednesday afternoon to see Liverpool beat Sunderland 2–0 in a one-sided contest. Kevin Keegan and John Toshack scored for the Reds. The attendance was even more remarkable given that Liverpool returned hundreds of tickets due to the early kick-off.

This was Sunderland's eighth Cup match of the season but now there was just one knockout competition left – the FA Cup. Stokoe had unquestionably got caught up with Cup fever once again. The Second Division table was suddenly a sobering sight after the European campaign and the League Cup run had both been abruptly ended.

Between crashing out of both those competitions that autumn Sunderland had been dealt another blow, and in some ways a mightier one: Tueart had asked to be put on the transfer list. After scoring a hat-trick in a 4–1 win over Swindon Town and netting again in a 3–0 win over Bolton Wanderers – the first back-to-back wins in the league for the club that season – the player had seemed subdued in the 2–0 defeat at Ashton Gate against Bristol City and made his decision later that evening. He handed in a written transfer request shortly afterwards.

This was a few days before Sunderland played Liverpool. A shocked Stokoe announced that Tueart could leave the club the day before the match. 'He wants First Division football and he is not prepared to scrap it out with us,' he said. 'I am very disappointed with him.' Tueart responded by saying, 'I am not playing in top-class football and I am ambitious. If there was the guarantee that First Division football would come at the end of the season that would be fair enough but I am fed up with ifs, buts and whens.'

In an impromptu press call Stokoe was asked if granting Tueart's transfer request could lead to other players doing the same. The clearly hurt and shocked Sunderland manager hit back angrily: 'Do I know what is going to happen tomorrow, on Saturday or next week? If anyone else wants a move we just have to wait and take it as it comes.

'Circulars will go out but he [Tueart] will not be allowed to leave this club until I have a satisfactory deal in which a player or players will be concerned,' Stokoe added. Rather prophetically, as it turned out, Ron Saunders was appointed manager of Manchester City on the same day. He was immediately linked with Tueart.

'It does not seem long since, in a moment of euphoria after Sunderland had won the FA Cup, Bob Stokoe, their manager, said that if any of his team left Roker Park he would walk off the end of the pier,'

David Lacey wrote in the *Guardian*. 'Presumably he has had second thoughts – or is a strong swimmer – for after a two-hour board meeting yesterday, Sunderland agreed to release Dennis Tueart, 24, on Tuesday, who is a forward of considerable potential. The disconcerting effect that this sort of split is apt to have on a team may present even greater problems.'

The first manager to make an official enquiry about Tueart was new Southampton manager Lawrie McMenemy. Stokoe told him he was looking for a player-exchange deal. Other First Division clubs were also interested. Everton manager Billy Bingham made a straight cash offer a few days later but was turned down for the same reason that was given to McMenemy. Derby manager Dave Mackay also made enquiries but this move went cold after Stokoe's request for John O'Hare to return to Roker Park fell on deaf ears.

Tueart remained at Sunderland but he was left out of the squad that travelled to Nottingham Forest a few days later; Lathan played in his place. Sunderland drew 0–0. Stokoe left Tueart out in the cold for two weeks before bringing him back as substitute in the 1–0 defeat at Bolton in early December. Tueart was returned to the starting line-up in the next match and scored in a 2–0 win over Aston Villa that moved Sunderland back up the table. But the manager now had another problem: Hughes had handed in a written transfer request as well.

The looks on the faces of the Sunderland squad as they stood on stage at BBC Television Theatre in Shepherd's Bush, London, to receive the Team Performance of the Year award at the annual *Sports Review of the Year* programme the following Wednesday night contrasted sharply with those that had greeted Barry Davies at the Selsdon Park Hotel just seven short months before. Hughes brought out the laughing box again, but the natural camaraderie was not there. Stokoe received the trophy from FIFA president Sir Stanley Rous and did his best to show the smile that had so lifted the nation earlier in the year. When asked by Jimmy Hill, who had now moved over to the BBC, if the FA Cup win had brought its problems, Stokoe admitted it had. 'You still don't trade that sort of occasion,' he said. 'May the fifth was our day and we thoroughly enjoyed it. Whatever comes in the future we will accept it. We'll survive it.' Hill concluded the interview by saying, 'I am sure everybody in England feels that Sunderland should be in the First Division, may it happen soon.' Hughes and Tueart looked on as he said this.

'Bob Stokoe had well and truly lost me by then,' Tueart says. 'I remember I wore an open-necked shirt that night, which didn't impress him, and he asked me where my tie was. I had asked to be put on the transfer list the previous month and he had granted it. Billy Hughes then put in a similar request but pulled a hamstring and so Stokoe asked me to come off the list to cover for him and told me that he would let me go before the transfer deadline at the end of March.'

'I personally feel the club didn't do enough to hold the team together,' Hughes adds. 'I didn't really want to go but we had a good side and instead of going forward, instead of investing in what we had and strengthening it, the club was allowing good players to go, which was very disappointing.'

As if to mirror Sunderland's plight, the country was shutting down. The following day Prime Minister Edward Heath declared a state of emergency in a televised address to the nation. Street-lighting had been cut to conserve energy, while on the roads speed limits were reduced and petrol coupons came into effect. To cope with rising inflation the government had also introduced a government pay freeze, which essentially meant that pay rises were severely restricted. This proved catastrophic to team spirit at Roker Park as the Sunderland board were stifled in any attempts to improve the wage structure or bonus system at the club.

The ruling could not have come at a worse time. The FA Cup win had made the Sunderland players household names. The problem was, they were still playing in the Second Division and they were still on Second Division contracts. Therefore they were not being paid the sort of money usually associated with household names. Many of the players had attracted – and continued to attract – strong interest from First Division clubs, who could not only offer top-flight football but also much more money. Sunderland could not improve their wage structure to anything like these levels due to the pay freeze and, as a result, the Rokerites were probably affected by this ruling like no other club in the country. The consensus among the players is that how matters were handled at Roker Park had a detrimental effect on morale. As a result, a golden opportunity for Stokoe and Sunderland to build on what had been achieved in the early part of 1973 was to be lost.

'The pay freeze came in and Bob Stokoe either used that as an excuse or he just couldn't do anything about it,' Kerr says. 'We were all after more money because we felt we deserved to be paid more money. But apparently the only way to get a rise was if you left! People don't realise how little we got from winning the FA Cup, I can you tell you: I got £1,000 before deductions for appearing at Wembley. There was nothing in our contracts about winning the Cup and so there was no win bonus at all. The minute we walked on to that pitch we could have walked back off again and we would still have got our £1,000. I was on £65 per week plus appearance money at the time. A lot of the other players were on a lot less than that. The pay freeze caused problems. People say the club could have done this and that, but we had a director at the time whose father had been there in the 1950s and he had been punished for the illegal payments and so on, so nothing was ever going to happen.'

'We had a meeting with the chairman and he told us that the club would love to give out ten per cent pay rises to us all but due to the political situation they couldn't,' Watson recalls. 'He said it was not allowed by the government. We weren't too happy about it as a team. I questioned it. I just couldn't see how the government could stop commercial activity. But there were so few details given to us by the club that suddenly there was a bit of distrust there.'

'We had a very good team,' Malone says. 'We didn't really appreciate how good we were at the time and I don't think the club did either. They probably didn't show their appreciation in the way they should have and that caused big problems. If the club had given us what we were due – we had brought a lot of money into the club – then I think the players would probably have stayed together a lot longer. I know there was a wage freeze going on but surely they could have done something for us? Other organisations found a way to do that so it was there if they wanted to do it. But they didn't want to do it. In any business, if you have good staff you shouldn't ever be in a position where they're looking for another job. But unfortunately football clubs in those days treated the players less than good and I think that is what happened to us.'

'The only criticism I can give to Bob Stokoe – because I loved him dearly – is that he needed to stand up for the players at that particular time,' Hughes adds. 'He wouldn't go and see the chairman on our behalf and it was left for us to go and see the chairman. I believe that if Bob had asked for the gates of heaven to open, they would have opened. But he chose to let us fight the battle rather than fight it for us and I found that very disappointing. But hey, he is allowed one mistake!'

'There was a recession at the time but, thinking about it now, why couldn't the club have said to us, "Right, that is your new contract and once the recession is over, that is what you will be earning"? It is very sad because it was a superb side – it really was – and if they could have just kept us together who knows what we could have achieved? But it showed – to me at that particular time anyway – what the club's ambitions were,' Montgomery says.

'We had wanted to reward the players for their sterling performance above just an FA Cup bonus, but to increase their wages was not possible,' Sunderland chairman Keith Collings says. 'We weren't able to do that because the government wouldn't allow us to. It was straight-forward and, no, sadly we couldn't pay them any more. I think that maybe we should have challenged it. Afterwards we did try and draw up contracts that paid differently in the top three divisions so if we went up or down it was automatically altered in the contracts. But of course nobody knew the government was going to do a pay freeze and unfor-tunately we weren't able to write up a whole lot of new contracts overnight.'

Sunderland ended 1973 in desperate fashion, with three defeats in four games, leaving them eleventh in the Second Division table with twenty-three points from twenty-three games. The New Year began with another defeat, at home to Notts County. The Rokerites' defence of the FA Cup – due to begin the following weekend at Carlisle United – was essentially the only thing the club had left to play for in what was becoming a disappointing and frustrating season. The Cumbrians, placed above them in the table, were favourites to progress.

'It must be a very long time since the holders of the Cup were the underdogs in a third-round tie but on league form we cannot be any-thing else,' Stokoe conceded. 'This is not new to us, though, for in many games last season we were in the same position.'

The government pay freeze was killing the team spirit that had swept aside Manchester City, Arsenal and Leeds the previous year, and the club was on a downward spiral. They hung on to their FA Cup crown by their fingertips, drawing 0–0 at Brunton Park to earn a replay; Montgomery made three fine saves to keep them in the competition. 'I was delighted for the lads,' Stokoe said afterwards. 'They responded better than they have for some weeks now and it could be the start of the big comeback we are looking for.'

The manager's optimism was short-lived. With the country now in the midst of a three-day week, the replay kicked off at Roker Park at 1.30 the following Wednesday afternoon. Sunderland – with no fewer than four changes to the starting line-up that had won the FA Cup – were beaten 1–0 before 25,712 hearty souls. Dennis Martin scored the only goal in a game where Sunderland had three penalty appeals – two by Tueart and one by Halom – turned down.

'I played in that game,' Young says. 'It wasn't a good match. There was no motivation and we struggled. The team spirit had gone a little bit by then and so we were no longer the team we had once been. I personally think there were three or four prima donnas in the team and I think that is where it started to fragment. Stokoe was also under pressure from the press, who were always asking if and when we were going to get up and whatever.'

'Bob Stokoe was absolutely gutted to lose that game,' former Carlisle player Stan Ternent recalls. 'But then he was gutted to lose any game. He was a great competitor and a bad loser.' The following day the Sunderland manager tried to put a brave face on things: 'This is how it goes in football,' he said. 'We take a back seat now because this has obviously knocked a good deal of interest out of the season. We have got to do what we can in the league.'

The attendance for the next league match, against Oxford, was 16,509 – the lowest home crowd since the 1972–73 FA Cup campaign had begun a year before. Sunderland drew 0–0 and then slumped 2–1 away at Orient, a result that left them seventeen points behind Middlesbrough in the table.

Results improved during the last three months of the season, and eleven wins from the next sixteen games gave the Rokerites a final position of sixth in the table. But promotion remained out of reach. Middlesbrough won the Second Division title with a record points total; Luton and Carlisle also went up, while Malcolm Allison's Crystal Palace were relegated to the Third Division.

Don Revie was appointed England manager after taking Leeds

United to the First Division title again. It had been an interesting year for Revie and Leeds. A week after the FA Cup final defeat by Sunderland they lost to AC Milan in the European Cup Winners' Cup final in Salonika, but that defeat had been overshadowed by Revie meeting officials from Everton just days beforehand to discuss him moving over to Goodison Park. The speculation in Greece the night before the match was that Revie would go. But once again he stayed.

Leeds began the 1973–74 season with a point to prove, and after an unbeaten start of twenty-nine league matches that was as good as done. Revie moved to his new position at Lancaster Gate at the end of the season. Clough was famously given the job of replacing him and lasted just forty-four days before being sacked. Jimmy Armfield took over and led the club to the final of the European Cup and, alas, another defeat, this time at the hands of Bayern Munich.

'The Leeds players turned to Don Revie when Brian Clough was there,' BBC commentator Barry Davies says. 'I believe Don played his part in making sure that period wasn't successful as well. I remember when I asked Manny Cussins, the Leeds chairman, "How is it that Brian Clough is the wrong man for Leeds now when he was the right man forty-four days ago?", his only answer to me was "I think we were spoiled by Don Revie." But I also think Don was spoiled by the players he had there. It was such a closely knit team. That was the secret of their success but it also had its limitations.'

'Don Revie used the FA Cup final defeat by Sunderland as motivation for the next season,' Peter Lorimer admits. 'He set us the task of not losing a game all season, and when we did lose against Stoke it was our own fault: we switched off. We were cruising 2–0 and we let in three goals in the last ten minutes. Don went mad. You would have thought we'd gone twenty-nine games without a win, not a defeat. We couldn't believe his reaction but that was how determined he was and how hurt he had been by that particular defeat at Wembley in 1973. He wanted us to prove a point.

'I think there were a few reasons why Don left us. Yes, he was offered the England job, but maybe the team was also ready for breaking up. I personally think he didn't think he was getting through to us any more. I think we now wanted to do it a little bit differently to how he wanted to do it. It was nothing against him, it was just great to show what we could do on the pitch and score lots of goals. We started to go forward more and that would never have happened in the early days. I think we just wanted to do our thing and enjoy playing with a bit of class rather than winning matches in a regimented way.

'Then there was the story about Everton,' Lorimer adds. 'I don't know what was in his head at that time. He had met them, no question. He had spoken to Sunderland years before as well. I think he felt a little bit embarrassed looking us in the face because this was the great group that would never break up and yet he was the man who was going to be the first to go! I think when the England job came along it was his way out in many ways. Jimmy Armfield later came in and maybe he had to do the dirty work that Don didn't want to do and tell some of the older guys that the time was up. Maybe Don thought the time was up too – even though we had just won the league – and so when the England job came along it was a great way for him to go out on a high.'

On taking up his new appointment the superstitious Revie immediately moved England's dressing room at Wembley from the North – which Leeds had used in the 1965 and 1973 FA Cup final defeats – to the South, which had been used by Sunderland in 1973 (and Leeds in 1970 and 1972 for that matter, when they had drawn against Chelsea and beaten Arsenal). From this moment until the old stadium was demolished in 2000, England used the South dressing room – the 'lucky' one – from Revie all the way to Keegan, the last man to manage the national side underneath the twin towers.

After failing to achieve the promotion they were expected to walk, Sunderland now had to regroup for the 1974–75 season, and they had to do this without Tueart and Horswill, both of whom had signed for Manchester City before the transfer deadline in March 1974. Stokoe had kept his promise to Tueart. He also got his player-exchange, with midfielder Tony Towers moving in the opposite direction. Manchester City paid out a further £225,000 in cash in the deal.

'It was clear we weren't going to get promoted that season and there was no guarantee we would be promoted the following season,' Tueart says. 'I could have been twenty-six years old before I played in the First Division again. Bob Stokoe couldn't add to the team and before the transfer deadline Manchester City came in for me. It wasn't about money, it was about vision, and Sunderland didn't share mine. There was no vision and no ambition to build on what we had achieved in 1973.

'It is disappointing that we didn't go forward as a team after the Cup win because we had five or six international-class players in that side,' Tueart adds. 'There is no mystery to it: England won the World Cup in 1966 because they had five or six world-class players and we won the FA Cup in 1973 because we had five or six international-class players. The level of quality in that side stood the test of time.'

'Dennis Tueart was pretty practical,' Watson says. 'He saw that a move to Manchester City was good for his career and that is how it should be. He made his mind up during the 1973–74 season that he wanted to leave, and he was gone. Micky Horswill went with him and I did start to think, Hang on a minute, we're selling the whole bloody team here. I was also beginning to worry that we were selling players that had won the FA Cup and replacing them with players that weren't as good.'

'The last thing we wanted to do as a club was to lose players like Dennis Tueart,' Collings says. 'But – as always in those days – the manager made the decision on players. The board never did that. They listened to a manager's recommendation and agreed with it.'

Dennis Longhorn was signed from Mansfield Town for £10,000 – with Lathan moving in part-exchange – and took over the number 4 shirt from Horswill. During the close season Bryan 'Pop' Robson, an Inter-Cities Fairs Cup winner with Newcastle United and the top goal scorer in the First Division two seasons before, arrived from West Ham United in a £145,000 deal, while Scottish international defender Bobby Moncur, who had captained Newcastle in their 3–0 FA Cup final defeat by Liverpool the previous month, signed for £30,000. Moncur would replace Kerr as club captain and Young at number 6.

'Bobby Moncur was working on the 1974 World Cup for television that summer and for some reason Sunderland didn't want to announce that he was coming until it was over,' Kerr says. 'But rumours were flying around and everyone wanted to know who was going to be captain. I was happy to pass the captaincy on. My game had been struggling a little bit and when your game is struggling you cannot be looking after other people. We went up to Berwick for pre-season and I spoke to Bob Stokoe and Keith Collings about it. It wasn't because Bobby was coming in as captain, it was because of the time it took them to announce it and the embarrassment it caused me. I knew what was happening but I wasn't allowed to say anything. They were thinking about him and they never gave a thought about me.'

'When I came back for pre-season training that summer my coat peg – which was in the middle of the changing room – had been moved to next to the exit door,' Young recalls. 'It was obvious to me that I was on my way. I was sold to Charlton shortly afterwards.' Young was made captain at The Valley and won promotion to the Second Division in his first season there.

Sunderland were again strongly fancied to go up in the 1974–75 season but they now faced a fresh challenge, from Tommy Docherty's Manchester United, who had been relegated from the First Division. The two clubs were neck and neck for most of the season and played out a thrilling match at Old Trafford in front of a crowd of 60,585 and the *Match of the Day* cameras. Hughes, who had invited his friend Rod Stewart to sit on the Sunderland bench that day, scored two goals – the second a delightful one-two with Robson – and Docherty described him as 'the most exciting player in Britain' afterwards. But United won the match 3–2 and went on to win the Second Division title while the Rokerites trailed in fourth at the end of the season and yet again missed out on promotion.

There was an explanation for this: midway through the campaign Porterfield – in form and on the verge of a Scotland call-up at the time – was involved in a serious car accident on the outskirts of Sunderland. The midfielder suffered a fractured skull in the crash. He recovered and eventually returned to the team, but his chance at international level was gone.

It was now two long years since the FA Cup triumph and still Sunderland were in the Second Division. Furthermore, the club would be there for at least another twelve months. Watson, who had now won fourteen England caps – a club record – at centre-half, decided it was time to go: 'I was coming up to twenty-nine years of age, I was the England centre-half but I wasn't playing in the First Division and I wanted to play in the First Division,' he says. 'Bob Stokoe was adamant that the only way I would do that would be with Sunderland.

'Stokoe said I would be sweeping the streets of Sunderland before I played for another club. I made a decision and I thought, The only way I'm going to get away from here is to annoy him – and he got annoyed pretty easily. I did that by putting this letter together and telling him exactly how I felt. He got me into his office at the training ground the next morning and he was angry: "What is this? If any of this goes to the press, I will go for you myself," he told me. Someone knocked on the door and it broke up the tension. I explained to him that it was nothing personal or anything to do with the club, I just wanted to further my career. I could have ended up losing my place as England centre-half and you just can't afford to do that.

'Within a few weeks Stokoe told me there was some interest in me,' Watson adds. 'Then when I was on England duty in Manchester, just before we flew out to play Northern Ireland in the home internationals, a journalist told me of Manchester City's interest. I was sat at an England press conference answering questions about Manchester City! I rang Stokoe and he told me that Sunderland had agreed a fee with Manchester City for £275,000 and that I was given permission to talk to them. I came back from international duty, went to Maine Road and it was done. I never shook hands with Stokoe or anything, I just left.'

In the following season Watson and Tueart won the League Cup with Manchester City. The season after that, the pair helped the club finish runners-up to Liverpool in the First Division. Watson went on to win sixty-five England caps and became the most-capped England international never to play in a World Cup finals, due to the country not qualifying in 1974 and 1978 and to his being surprisingly left out of the squad for Spain in 1982 despite playing in six of the qualifying matches. Tueart also went on to win six caps for England.

Sunderland fans would have read the England line-up to face Northern Ireland in that match in Belfast in May 1975 and wept: Watson, Tueart and Colin Todd were all in Revie's team that day.

Ron Guthrie was also on his way from Roker Park that summer: 'I don't know what happened but I wasn't very happy about it because I played thirty-four league games in the 1974–75 season and hadn't been dropped,' he says. 'I went to see Bob Stokoe and told him that my contract was due to be up. He asked me to go and see him in a couple of days' time and when I went back he told me he was giving me a free transfer. One week I was playing for Sunderland at Aston Villa in front of over fifty-seven thousand people and a few months later I was signing on the dole.

'Reporters would ask me why I had left Sunderland and I couldn't tell them. I can't tell you,' Guthrie adds. 'I think Stokoe, on the spur of the moment, thought he could save a contract and so that's what he did. I wasn't happy about it at all. I had just moved house and my daughter had just started junior school. If I had been told two or three months beforehand I could have made plans but it was a complete shock. I had a bit of interest here and there – Sheffield Wednesday for instance – but I said to the wife, "I'm finished with football now." I made a decision there and then that I wasn't going to play full-time any more and I didn't play full-time any more. The shock of what happened and the nature of what happened turned me off football. I was flabbergasted by what he did and I still can't understand it.'

Guthrie later played part-time for Ashington in the Northern League, Gateshead United in the Northern Premier League and in South Africa before returning to the north-east to play in the famous Blyth Spartans team that reached the FA Cup fifth round in the 1977–78 season and came within a whisker of making it to the quarter-finals and a home tie against Arsenal. Blyth led 1–0 at Wrexham in the closing minutes of their fifth-round clash and were only denied victory by a last-minute equaliser from a retaken corner kick. But Spartans did become the first and so far only non-league club in the modern era to go into the FA Cup quarter-final draw. In the fifth-round replay – played at Newcastle's St James' Park in front of a crowd of 42,157 – the Northern League giant-killers were beaten 2–1. Had the run continued, the plan was for Blyth to play their quarter-final tie against the Gunners at Roker Park.

'It was a great run and great to be part of it,' Guthrie says. 'That Blyth side was similar to the Sunderland 1973 team in a way, but at a different level. It would have been incredible to have gone back to Roker Park after everything to play in another FA Cup quarter-final. That would have been unbelievable. Vic Halom came down to Stoke to support us in the fourth round, when we won 3–2. I said to him afterwards, "I thought all this sort of thing was over with!" We couldn't believe it.'

By the beginning of the 1975–76 season Sunderland were almost unrecognisable from the team that had so charmed the nation just over two years before. The campaign began with just three players from the FA Cup-winning side – Kerr, Halom and Porterfield – in the starting line-up against Chelsea. By the end of the season two of those would have left as well.

Halom signed for Oldham Athletic, where he went on to score more goals than at Sunderland, while Porterfield joined Sheffield Wednesday after a loan spell at Reading. Both men later went into football management. Halom managed non-league Barrow to the Northern Premier League title in the 1983–84 season and was in charge at Fourth Division Rochdale between 1984 and 1986. He also had a brief spell at Burton Albion. In later years he moved into politics and stood for the Liberal Democrats in Sunderland North in the 1992 general election. He polled 5,389 votes, just over 10 per cent of the share. He still wears his FA Cup winners' medal around his neck to this day.

'At that time in 1973 – in that time capsule – we were as good as anybody, in fact nobody could touch us,' Halom says. 'What is disappointing is that the team was not allowed to progress for various reasons. I will always feel very sad about that because I think that side could have gone on and done fabulous things. The make-up of the side, the quality that was in the side and the team spirit was very special. That team spirit has survived: whenever the players have had hard times everybody has got together. That remarkable bond was there before we won the Cup and that remarkable bond was why we won the Cup.'

Porterfield managed five clubs in England and Scotland – Rotherham United, Sheffield United, Aberdeen, Reading and Chelsea. He took the Millers to one promotion and the Blades to two. He later managed no fewer than five international sides – Zambia, Zimbabwe, Oman, Trinidad and Tobago, and Armenia – as well as teams in Ghana, Korea and Saudi Arabia. Porterfield remained in charge of Armenia until his death from cancer at the age of sixty-one in September 2007. Only one month earlier he had received a standing ovation in Yerevan before his side earned a 1–1 draw against Portugal in a European Championship qualifier.

'The entire stadium stood up and applauded him. We had only had a short time in Armenia but when Ian walked out they all stood up and shouted his name. It was very moving,' Porterfield's widow, Glenda, says. 'I met Ian while he was manager of Trinidad and Tobago and I went with him to Ghana, Korea and Armenia. Ian's brain never stopped thinking about football. At night he would write down tactics and in the morning there would be sheets of A4 paper on Ian's side of the bed where he would have been drawing up tactics – he literally played matches on paper – until he fell asleep,' she adds. 'When Ian knew he was dying he asked me to make arrangements for a memorial service to be held in Sunderland after his death. He felt nostalgic about 1973 whenever he did an interview and I know at the time it meant the world to him.'

Both Halom and Porterfield picked up Second Division championship medals with Sunderland before they left the club in the summer of 1976. A tremendous home record of nineteen wins and two draws secured the title and – at long last – promotion back to the First Division.

For a while another trip to Wembley looked possible as well, as the Rokerites reached the last eight of the FA Cup before frustratingly crashing out at home to Third Division Crystal Palace, which was revenge of sorts for Allison – cigar, fedora and all – in front of a crowd of 50,850 three years on from Manchester City's fifth-round-replay exit there.

'We thought we were going to get to Wembley again,' Malone says. 'We should have got there again, but sadly it didn't happen. Palace scored with a break-away goal and we did everything but score. I believe we could have won it again that year had it not been for that.'

'Yes, we had a chance of getting to the FA Cup final again in 1976 but it was never ever going to be the same as 1973,' Montgomery adds. 'Nothing will ever be the same as 1973 – for anyone. I think the biggest factor is who we beat to win the Cup – Manchester City, Arsenal and Leeds United: three great sides. That will never happen again. Not like that.'

Montgomery, Hughes, Kerr and Malone were the only remaining players from Sunderland's 1973 FA Cup side that went on and played for the club in the top flight in the much-anticipated 1976–77 season. But by the end of that season only one of them would be left, and the 'Messiah' himself would also be gone.

A few things happened during the summer of 1976 that, in hindsight, may offer some clues to the background to Stokoe's decision to quit Sunderland. First of all there was a ridiculous fall-out between the manager and Roy Greenwood, who had joined the club from Hull City during the promotion season. Stokoe instructed Greenwood to shave off his beard for the official team photograph because he felt it looked untidy. When Greenwood refused, Stokoe banned him from appearing in the picture. Arthur Cox was then replaced by Ian MacFarlane as assistant manager. After a short stint with Galatasaray in Turkey, Cox was appointed Chesterfield boss and began to build a highly successful managerial career that took him to Newcastle and Derby. He regularly joined up with Kevin Keegan in later years in various roles, at both club and international level. He remains hugely respected within the game.

'My personal view is that Bob Stokoe made a mistake when he got rid of Arthur Cox, a nice, decent man who had been a loyal servant to him, and replaced him with Ian MacFarlane, who I personally didn't like at all,' Keith Collings says. 'Bob felt that Arthur and he were both rather dour people and that he needed somebody to lift the dressing room. I think it took only a short while for him to realise what a mistake he had made in getting rid of Arthur.'

The 1976–77 season did not begin well for Sunderland, and by the beginning of October the club was without a win in the First Division and rooted to the bottom of the table. Stokoe brought out the cheque-book and suddenly signed four players in a few days. Goalkeeper Barry Siddall joined from Bolton for £80,000, striker Bob Lee signed from Leicester City for a club-record £200,000, central defender Jim Holton came on loan from Manchester United with a view to a permanent £40,000 transfer, and Alan Foggon, who had already had stints at both Newcastle and Middlesbrough, also arrived. Bryan Robson was sold back to West Ham.

Amid all this transfer activity, Kerr asked to be released from the club: 'The fans had always been magnificent with me,' he says. 'But they went the other way and I got it. All right-wingers and right-backs got it off the Clock Stand. I will never ever forget the Clock Stand. One of the sayings I heard – and I will never ever forget it – was "Bobby Kerr, get yourself off and take Micky Henderson with you"! I think that was their way of letting you know. It made me think, Maybe I have had my life with this club. I knew I was having a bad time and so I went to see Bob Stokoe.'

'Bobby Kerr told me that he would appreciate it if we would release him if the chance came along because he feels that this would be the right time for a change of clubs,' Stokoe told the press. 'We will not stand in his way.'

Sunderland's next match – at home to Aston Villa – brought another defeat, making it five losses in the last six league games. After the match Stokoe went to see Collings. The following day, after a hastily arranged board meeting with him, Sunderland reluctantly accepted his resignation. It was the end of an era.

'Bob Stokoe came up to me after the Aston Villa game and said, "Could you ask the directors to stay when the visiting directors have left?" He then came in from his office, which adjoined the directors' lounge, and he said he wished to submit his resignation,' Collings recalls. 'His actual words were: "I don't think I can go any further with the club. I think I have gone as far as I can, and it is only fair to you that I submit my resignation." I said to him, "Bob, oh no, please think about it overnight." I arranged a meeting for the following morning and I said we would discuss it then. We wanted him to stay. The next morning, I asked him, "Do you wish to change your mind?" He said no. So that was that.

'I think it is a credit to his honesty that he resigned,' Collings adds. 'A lot of people might have just hung on in there and tried to do something they didn't think they could do. Bob always suffered from migraines. They got him down a lot. He could get very down and so on. He did get depressed and I think he knew in his heart his time with Sunderland was over.'

MacFarlane took over team selection on a caretaker basis. In his first match in charge – a 2–0 defeat at QPR – Sunderland took to the field for the first time with not one member of the 1973 FA Cup-winning side in their line-up. MacFarlane lasted in this role for seven matches before Jimmy Adamson – who had played under Alan Brown at Burnley in the 1950s – was appointed manager, at the end of November 1976. Adamson's first two months in the job were disastrous as Sunderland went on a club-record run of ten league matches without scoring a goal. By mid-February the Rokerites looked abandoned at the bottom of the First Division, with just eleven points from twenty-five games.

Montgomery played his last match for Sunderland just before Stokoe left. The arrival of Siddall put pressure on the goalkeeper's first-team place, and the change of manager led to the man with a club-record 623 appearances behind him leaving Roker Park.

'I don't think my record will ever be beaten,' Montgomery says.

'Nobody is going to stop at the club for the length of time needed to achieve it. It means a great deal to me, especially with me being a local lad. I am proud to be the holder of that record. I never wanted to leave Sunderland, but a new manager came in and he wanted to move me on.'

Adamson gave youth its chance in the shape of three local young-sters – Kevin Arnott, Shaun Elliott and Gary Rowell – and the trans-formation was simply outstanding. Four matches were won in a row, but what made that sequence so emphatic were the results: Bristol City 1–0; Middlesbrough 4–0; West Brom 6–1; West Ham 6–0. Nine wins and five draws from sixteen matches meant Sunderland were close to completing the greatest escape. A left-footed equaliser by Kerr – a late substitute – in the penultimate game of the season away at Norwich City was wildly celebrated by players and fans alike. The impossible had almost been achieved; the Rokerites were almost safe.

Sunderland went to Everton in their final match of the season, requiring a draw to stay up. Even if they lost they would still avoid relegation if there was a winner in the other match to be played that night, at Highfield Road between Coventry City and Bristol City – two teams who were both placed below them in the table. Furthermore – and this is an important point to mention – the Sky Blues needed a win to be certain of survival.

Sunderland were beaten 2–0 at Goodison Park but would still be safe should either Coventry or Bristol City win. The only result that could send them down was a draw. But the only result that could keep both Coventry and Bristol City up was also a draw.

Controversially the kick-off in that match was delayed, and with the game deadlocked at 2–2 Coventry chairman Jimmy Hill gave instruc-tions that the Sunderland result should be announced over the ground's radio box.

Two men who played for Leeds against Sunderland in the FA Cup final were on opposite sides in that match. Norman Hunter was now a Bristol City player and Terry Yorath was now a Coventry player. In his autobiography Yorath recalls that on hearing the radio announcement he shouted out to Hunter, 'There you are, you can tell your lads to back off now.'

'It was harsh on us because there were three different ways it could have gone and it happened to go the wrong way because they cheated,'

Collings says. Over thirty years after this match, Hill, by then aged eighty, was roundly booed by hundreds of visiting supporters during a Premier League match at Craven Cottage between Fulham and Sunderland.

After a loan period at Southampton, Montgomery joined Birmingham City during the 1976–77 season and helped keep them in the First Division while his home-town club went down. He went on to make sixty-six league appearances for the Blues before signing for Clough – his former Sunderland team-mate – at Nottingham Forest, where he won a European Cup winners' medal as an unused substitute in the 1980 final against SV Hamburg in Madrid.

'It was exactly the same Brian Clough that I knew when I was young,' Montgomery says. 'He had the same arrogance, was still self-opinionated but lovable and a fabulous fellow. I had loads of time for Brian. I had three great years at Birmingham under Willie Bell, Sir Alf Ramsey and Jim Smith, and I was thinking of going to Newport County actually when Cloughie came in for me. I took my wife with me to meet him in Nottingham and after I signed he asked us where we would like to go for lunch. There was cricket on over the road at Trent Bridge between England and New Zealand, or he said we could go to an Italian restaurant around the corner. I told him we would love to go and watch the cricket. So he called his secretary and asked her to book a table for two at the Italian restaurant! Just the opposite from what I had said. That was the way Cloughie was. So we had to go to the Italian restaurant instead! After Forest, I came back to Sunderland for one season as cover for Barry Siddall but didn't play in the first team, just a few reserve games.

'In my time as a player at Sunderland I'm sad to say we missed three great opportunities,' Montgomery adds. 'The first was the 1964 squad that won promotion. We never built on it. The next was the 1973 FA Cup-winning squad. We never built on it. Then there was the 1976 squad – Gary Rowell and everyone – and we never built on it. These were three magnificent opportunities and they were all lost.'

Hughes moved on during the 1976–77 season as well. He went on to play First Division football with both Derby and Leicester. In total he scored eighty-two goals for Sunderland. In addition to his club honours with the Rokerites, Hughes was also recognised at international level when he appeared as a substitute for Scotland against Sweden in Gothenburg in 1975. It would be his only appearance for his country.

Malone also played his last game for Sunderland that season. He moved to Hartlepool in the summer of 1977 and later played for Blackpool and Queen of the South.

The one man from the Wembley win who remained at the club was Kerr. He was to stay at Sunderland until the 1978–79 season, when he too moved to Blackpool. He later played for Hartlepool as well. When Kerr finally left Roker Park he did so in the knowledge that he was the only captain to have lifted major silverware for Sunderland in over forty years. That figure has since grown to over fifty years, over sixty years, over seventy years and counting ...

'It all changed the day Jimmy Adamson walked in,' Kerr says. 'He didn't want any of the 1973 team around. So many people have wanted to get rid of this stigma around the 1973 team and I just can't understand that. You will never get rid of it. Accept it and it will go. It is just there. It will always be there. The only way people will start talking about something else is when Sunderland win something else, and by that I mean winning the Premier League or the FA Cup. But 1973 is always going to be there.

'Football is life in the north-east, and football was all they had. The people have had a really hard time up here and have had to live through pit closures and shipyards folding up. They still have this fondness for what we achieved. I get too sentimental about it all but that is how life is up here. I still get stopped in the street today. I don't know who these people are but they just want to talk to me about 1973. That's how much it still means to them.

'It personally means a lot to me as well,' Kerr adds. 'It is something that happened in my life that I never ever thought would have happened. I also never ever thought that we would still be talking about it over thirty-five years later, by the way! But that just proves that what we did was something very special. People always want to talk about 1973. They tell me, "You don't realise what you did for this town!" But we do. It was something that you cannot put into words. I don't know how you are going to do it. If you can do it, it could be a bestseller.'

At Bloomfield Road Kerr and Malone were briefly reunited with Stokoe. After taking a year out of football following his resignation from

Sunderland, the much-travelled manager spent a further nine seasons in charge of four of his former sides – Bury, Blackpool, Rochdale and Carlisle – before retiring at the end of the 1985–86 season.

He never lost his principles. During his second stint at Rochdale, Stokoe once threatened to fine his team – and himself – half a week's wages after a particularly poor performance at Tranmere Rovers. But one of his players contacted the Professional Footballers' Association and there soon became the real possibility of a strike by players at the club. Stokoe reluctantly withdrew his threat. The episode left him disillusioned: 'I can't fine them and I can't drop them because we have no one else to put in. I can't buy because of the financial situation. I feel absolutely helpless,' he said. Rochdale finished bottom of the Football League that season and were fortunate to be re-elected. Stokoe left the club soon afterwards.

Happily for him, there was light at the end of the tunnel. He began scouting for Carlisle before taking over as manager once more. He remained in charge there for five seasons, won promotion to the Second Division and achieved legendary status at the club.

After his departure from Roker Park, Stokoe's name first came to prominence again in September 1977, when he contributed his account of events surrounding the Bury-versus-Leeds match in 1962 to the 'Revie File', a series of allegations published in the *Daily Mirror* which claimed that Revie had attempted to fix matches while he was in charge at Leeds.

Revie had quit as England manager two months before these allegations were published, to take up a lucrative deal to coach the United Arab Emirates. He never managed in England again and died, aged sixty-one, in 1989.

Clough, the man who replaced Revie at Elland Road, took Nottingham Forest to a Football League championship and two European Cup wins between 1978 and 1980. His name was consistently linked with the England job but he was never offered it. 'They had a sneaking suspicion that I might have tried to run the FA and change a few things. They were right,' he famously said. The closest Clough ever came to getting the position was in 1977, when it was offered to Ron Greenwood. He remained at Nottingham Forest until his retirement in 1993. He was never to manage Sunderland and he never managed to win the FA Cup. The fact that Stokoe did both – to such great effect – against Revie of all people, and Leeds of all teams, in 1973 would probably have irked him. He died, aged sixty-nine, in 2004.

Alan Brown – the man who had both Clough and Revie as players at Sunderland – never managed again after his resignation from Sunderland in the autumn of 1972. He died, aged eighty-one, in 1996. Only he knew what thoughts were going through his head on 5 May 1973.

Billy Elliott returned to Roker Park a few years after Stokoe's resignation and enjoyed another stint as caretaker manager during the 1978–79 season. He oversaw a famous and much-loved 4–1 victory at Newcastle, when Rowell scored a hat-trick, and almost won promotion into the First Division as Sunderland finished fourth. Elliott wanted to do the job full-time but he was passed over again, this time for Ken Knighton. He later managed Darlington. He died in January 2008 at the age of eighty-two.

After his retirement from football management in 1986, Stokoe was suddenly and romantically lured back to Roker Park in April 1987 after the ill-fated Lawrie McMenemy reign, when Sunderland chairman Bob Murray asked him to return for the last seven matches of the season and try to save the Rokerites from a first-ever relegation to the Third Division. Ironically it was the same task Stokoe had been given by Collings back in November 1972. He could not achieve a second miracle, and Sunderland went down after a two-legged promotion–relegation play-off semi-final against Gillingham. Sunderland lost the away leg 3–2 and won the home leg 4–3, and therefore lost the tie on the away-goals rule. To this day it remains the only time in the history of the Football League that a club has ever been relegated on the away-goals rule.

The manager of Gillingham that day was Keith Peacock, coincidentally the man whom Stokoe had made the country's first-ever substitute back in 1965. 'That match was the highlight of my managerial career at Gillingham,' Peacock says. 'To win at Sunderland on away goals in front of a crowd like that was special. But when Bob Stokoe was sat opposite you on that bench he was your enemy. I remember Gary Bennett was moved up front and he put Sunderland 3–2 up right at the end of the match with a looping header. That made it 5–5 on aggregate and took it into extra-time. The crowd was going wild and at that moment Bob came across to me on the touchline and as good as told me that that was that.

'I remember saying to him, "It's not over yet, Bob." It was an unbelievable game: we scored again and Sunderland scored again, but they needed to score once more and they couldn't. It ended 6–6 and we won on away goals. At the end of the match Bob just shook my hand and headed inside. I admit it was a moment of total euphoria for me – there was so much at stake – but I made a point of staying out of the Sunderland boardroom. They were now a Third Division club and people were in tears in there.'

Stokoe never managed again. During his retirement he scouted for Porterfield and Chelsea for a while, continued to play golf with his old friend Len Shackleton and did some media work from time to time. He was a studio guest on BBC1 when Sunderland, once again in the Second Division, reached the 1992 FA Cup final against Liverpool and loyally predicted a win for them, but it did not happen this time. He regularly repeated his claims about Revie until his death, at the age of seventy-three, in February 2004 at the University Hospital of Hartlepool. Stokoe had suffered from a severe form of dementia for several years and his health had declined steadily since the death of his wife. He spent the last few years of his life at Elwick Grange nursing home in the town.

A huge outpouring of emotion and nostalgia followed news of Stokoe's death in Sunderland, and there was an immediate call to create a lasting memorial to him. Some £73,000 was raised to fund a bronze statue commemorating his emotional run to Montgomery across the Wembley turf on that famous day in 1973. The statue was designed by sculptor Sean Hedges-Quinn, who worked from video footage and photographs to incorporate such minute details as the correct time of ten to five on the watch on Stokoe's right wrist.

'I wasn't aware there was a statue in Sunderland,' says former ITV match director Bob Gardam, the man who was responsible for putting pictures of Stokoe's famous run out to the nation that day. 'I feel quite honoured to hear that. I suppose had we not shown the run at the end then it may not have been quite so famous. But he was the kind of guy that was always going to do something at the end, so we had to follow him. It was a glorious moment.'

The statue – which now stands outside the Stadium of Light – is a fitting tribute to Stokoe and what he and those Sunderland players achieved at that very moment. Written on the back of the plinth are the words said by the 'Messiah' on the eve of the greatest FA Cup final shock of all time: I DIDN'T BRING THE MAGIC, IT'S ALWAYS BEEN HERE. I JUST CAME BACK TO FIND IT. And so the pure emotion of the man, of that day and what that FA Cup win meant – and still means – to so many people is encapsulated for ever more.

As Bobby Kerr rightly says, it is always going to be there.

STATISTICS

Fixtures and Results

Date	Round	Opponents	Attendance	Result	Goal scorers
13 Jan 1973	3	Notts County (away)	15,142	1–1	Watson
16 Jan 1973	R	Notts County (home)	30,033	2–0	Watson, Tueart
3 Feb 1973	4	Reading (home)	33,913	1–1	Tueart
7 Feb 1973	R	Reading (away)	19,793	3–1	Watson, Tueart, Kerr
24 Feb 1973	5	Manchester City (away)	54,478	2–2	Horswill, Hughes
27 Feb 1973	R	Manchester City (home)	51,872	3–1	Halom, Hughes (2)
17 Mar 1973	QF	Luton Town (home)	53,151	2–0	Watson, Guthrie
7 Apr 1973	SF	Arsenal (Hillsborough)	55,000	2–1	Halom, Hughes
5 May 1973	F	Leeds United (Wembley)	100,000	1–0	Porterfield

Line-ups

Notts County (away): Montgomery, Malone, Bolton, Horswill, Watson, Tones, Kerr, Ashurst, Hughes, Porterfield, Tueart; McGiven (for Ashurst)

Notts County (home): Montgomery, Malone, Bolton, Horswill, Watson, Tones, Kerr, McGiven, Hughes, Porterfield, Tueart; Lathan (for Horswill)

Reading (home): Montgomery, Malone, Guthrie, Horswill, Watson, Young, Kerr, Hughes, Lathan, Porterfield, Tueart; Ashurst (for Kerr)

Reading (away): Montgomery, Malone, Guthrie, Horswill, Pitt, Young, Kerr, Hughes, Watson, Porterfield, Tueart; Coleman (unused)

Manchester City (away): Montgomery, Malone, Guthrie, Horswill, Watson, Pitt, Kerr, Hughes, Halom, Porterfield, Tueart; Chambers (unused)

Manchester City (home): Montgomery, Malone, Guthrie, Horswill, Watson, Pitt, Kerr, Hughes, Halom, Porterfield, Tueart; Chambers (unused)

Luton Town (home): Montgomery, Malone, Guthrie, Horswill, Watson, Pitt, Kerr, Hughes, Halom, Porterfield, Tueart; Young (unused)

Arsenal (Hillsborough): Montgomery, Malone, Guthrie, Horswill, Watson, Pitt, Kerr, Hughes, Halom, Porterfield, Tueart; Chambers (unused)

Leeds United (Wembley): Montgomery, Malone, Guthrie, Horswill, Watson, Pitt, Kerr, Hughes, Halom, Porterfield, Tueart; Young (unused)

Appearances

Jim Montgomery	9
Dick Malone	9
Micky Horswill	9
Dave Watson	9
Bobby Kerr	9
Billy Hughes	9
Ian Porterfield	9
Dennis Tueart	9
Ron Guthrie	7
Ritchie Pitt	6
Vic Halom	5
Dave Young	2 (+2 unused subs)
Joe Bolton	2
John Tones	2
Jackie Ashurst	1 (+1 sub)
John Lathan	1 (+1 sub)
Mick McGiven	1 (+1 sub)
Brian Chambers	(3 unused subs)
Keith Coleman	(1 unused sub)

Goals

Billy Hughes	4
Dave Watson	4
Dennis Tueart	3
Vic Halom	2
Bobby Kerr	1
Micky Horswill	1
Ron Guthrie	1
Ian Porterfield	1

BIBLIOGRAPHY

Books

Appleton, Arthur, *Hotbed of Soccer: The Story of Football in the North East* (Rupert Hart-Davis, 1960)

——*Sunderland and the Cup: From 1973 to 1884* (Frank Graham, 1974)

Ashurst, Len, *Left Back in Time* (Know the Score Books, 2009)

Bagchi, Rob, and Rogerson, Paul, *The Unforgiven: The Story of Don Revie's Leeds United* (Aurum Press, 2002)

Bale, Bernard, *Bremner!: The Legend of Billy Bremner* (André Deutsch, 1998)

Ball, Peter, and Shaw, Phil, *The Book of Football Quotations* (Stanley Paul, 1984)

Barstow, Stan, *A Kind of Loving* (Joseph, 1960)

Bass, Howard, *Glorious Wembley: The Official History of Britain's Foremost Entertainment Centre* (Guinness Superlatives Ltd, 1982)

Best, George, *Hard Tackles and Dirty Baths: The Inside Story of Football's Golden Era* (Ebury Press, 2005)

Bickerton, Bob, *Club Colours: An Illustrated History of Football Clubs and Their Kits* (Hamlyn, 1998)

Bowles, Stanley, with Ralph Allen and John Iona, *Stan the Man: The Autobiography* (Paper Plane, 1996)

Bremner, Billy, *You Get Nowt for Being Second* (Souvenir Press, 1969)

Butler, Bryon, *100 Seasons of League Football: An Illustrated History* (Queen Anne Press, 1998)

——*The Official Illustrated History of the FA Cup* (Headline, 1988)

Calley, Roy, *Blackpool: A Complete Record 1887–1992* (Breedon Books, 1992)

Charlton, Sir Bobby, with James Lawton, *The Autobiography: My Manchester United Years* (Headline, 2007)

Charlton, Jack, with Peter Byrne, *The Autobiography* (Partridge Press, 1996)

Clough, Brian, with John Sadler, *Clough: The Autobiography* (Partridge Press, 1994)

——*Cloughie: Walking on Water* (Headline, 2002)

Collett, Mike, *The Complete Record of the FA Cup* (SportsBooks, 2003)

Cresswell, Peterjon, and Evans, Simon, *European Football: A Fans' Handbook* (Rough Guides, 1997)

Cullen, Peter, *Bury FC 1885–1985* (Bury FC brochure)

Daniels, Robin, *Blackpool Football: The Official Club History* (Robert Hale, 1972)

Davies, Barry, *Interesting, Very Interesting: The Autobiography* (Headline, 2007)

Dawson, Jeff, *Back Home: England and the 1970 World Cup* (Orion, 2001)

Days, Paul, *Sunderland's Finest Matches 1940–1973* (ALS Publications, 2008)

Dykes, Gareth, and Lamming, Doug, *All the Lads: A Complete Who's Who of Sunderland AFC* (Sunderland AFC, 2000)

Evans, Jeff, *The Penguin TV Companion* (Penguin Books, 2006)

Farnsworth, Keith, *Wednesday!: The History of Sheffield's Oldest Professional Football Club* (Sheffield City Libraries, 1982)

Francis, Tony, *Clough: A Biography* (Hutchinson, 1987)

Giles, Johnny, *Forward with Leeds* (Stanley Paul, 1970)

Glanville, Brian, *The Story of the World Cup* (Faber & Faber, 1993)

Goldblatt, David, *The Ball is Round: A Global History of Football* (Penguin Books, 2007)

Goldstein, Dan, *The Rough Guide to English Football: A Fan's Handbook 1999–2000* (Rough Guides, 2000)

Gray, Eddie, with Jason Thomas, *Marching on Together: My Life with Leeds United* (Hodder & Stoughton, 2001)

Hamilton, Duncan, ed., *Old Big 'Ead: The Wit and Wisdom of Brian Clough* (Aurum, 2009)

——*Provided You Don't Kiss Me: 20 Years with Brian Clough* (Fourth Estate, 2007)

Hardwick, George, *Gentleman George: The Autobiography of George Hardwick, Captain of Middlesbrough, Oldham Athletic, England and Great Britain* (Juniper Publishing, 1998)

Hardy, Lance, *One Lost Lead Too Many* (Roker fanzine, 1987)

Harrison, Paul, *FA Cup Giant Killers* (Stadia, 2007)

Harrison, Paul, *Northern and Proud: The Biography of Bob Stokoe* (Know the Score Books, 2009)

——*The Lads in Blue: The Complete History of Carlisle United* (Yore Publications, 1995)

Hayes, Dean, *England! England! The Complete Who's Who of Players since 1946* (Sutton, 2004)

——*Football Stars of the '70s: And Where Are They Now?* (Sutton, 2003)

Hill, Jimmy, *The Jimmy Hill Story: My Autobiography* (Coronet Books, 1998)

Hopcraft, Arthur, *The Football Man: People and Passions in Soccer* (Aurum Press, 1968)

Hornby, Nick, *Fever Pitch* (Victor Gollancz, 1992)

Howey, Martin, and Bond, David, *'Meet Me in the Roker End': A Revealing Look at Sunderland's Footballing History* (Vertical, 2004)

Hudson, John, and Callaghan, Paul, eds., *Sunderland AFC: The Official History 1979–2000* (Sunderland AFC, 1999)

Hugman, Barry, ed., *The PFA Premier and Football League Players' Records 1946–2005* (Queen Anne Press, 2005)

Hunter, Norman, with Don Warters, *Biting Talk: My Autobiography* (Hodder & Stoughton, 2004)

Hutchinson, Roger, *Into the Light: A Complete History of Sunderland Football Club* (Mainstream, 1999)

Inglis, Simon, *Engineering Archie: Archibald Leitch – Football Ground Designer* (English Heritage, 2005)

——*Football Grounds of Britain* (Collins Willow, 1983)

James, Gary, *Manchester: The Greatest City* (Polar Print Group, 1997)

Jarred, Martin, and Macdonald, Malcolm, *Leeds United: A Complete Record 1919–89* (Breedon Books, 1989)

Joannou, Paul, *Newcastle United: A Complete Record 1882–1986* (Breedon Books, 1986)

Kirtley, Mel, *50 Post War Seasons of Sunderland AFC* (Wearside Books, 1996)

Lansley, Peter, *Running with Wolves* (Thomas Publications, 2004)

Leatherdale, Clive: *England's Quest for the World Cup 1950–2002: A Complete Record* (Desert Island Books, 2002)

Lloyd, Guy, and Holt, Nick, *The FA Cup: The Complete Story* (Aurum Press, 2005)

Lorimer, Peter, and Rostron, Phil, *Peter Lorimer: Leeds and Scotland Hero* (Mainstream, 2002)

Lyons, Andy, and Ronay, Barney, eds., *When Saturday Comes: The Half Decent Football Book* (Penguin, 2005)

Marr, Andrew, *A History of Modern Britain* (Macmillan, 2007)

Mason, Rob, *Sunderland: Cult Heroes* (Breedon Books, 2008)

——ed., *Match of My Life: Sunderland: Twelve Stars Relive Their Favourite Games* (Know the Score Books, 2006)

Matthews, Tony, *Who's Who of Arsenal* (Mainstream, 2007)

McKinstry, Leo, Jack and Bobby: A Story of Brothers in Conflict (HarperCollinsWillow, 2002)

Metcalf, Mark, *Charlie Hurley: 'The Greatest Centre Half the World Has Ever Seen'* (SportsBooks, 2008)

Mitchell, Mick, *Life with Carlisle United* (Ink Truck, 1996)

Moore, Brian, *The Final Score* (Coronet Books, 1999)

Motson, John, *Match of the Day: The Complete Record Since 1964* (BBC Books, 1992)

——*Motson's FA Cup Odyssey: The World's Greatest Knock-Out Competition* (Robson Books, 2005)

——and Rowlinson, John: *European Cup, 1955–1980: A History of Europe's Premier Football Club Competition* (Queen Anne Press, 1980)

Mourant, Andrew, *Leeds United 1919–1996* (Reed International, 1996)

——*Don Revie: Portrait of a Footballing Enigma* (Mainstream, 1990)

——and Rollin, Jack, *The Essential History of England* (Headline, 2004)

Murphy, Alex, ed., … *Grass in the Sky: The Book of Clough* (Toilet Books, 2007)

Murphy, Patrick, *His Way: The Brian Clough Story* (Robson Books, 1993)

Novick, Jeremy, *In a League of Their Own: Football's Maverick Managers* (Mainstream, 1995)

Pearson, Harry, *The Far Corner: A Mazy Dribble Through North-East Football* (Abacus, 1994)

Phillips, Steven, *Rochdale AFC: The Official History 1907–2001* (Yore Publications, 2001)

Porterfield, Ian, with John Gibson, *The Impossible Dream* (AK Publications, 1973)

Radnedge, Keir, *50 Years of the European Cup and Champions League* (Carlton Books, 2005)

Redden, Richard, *The Story of Charlton Athletic 1905–1990* (Breedon Books, 1990)

Rees, Dafydd, and Crampton, Luke, *Guinness Book of Rock Stars* (Guinness Books, 1989)

Revie, Don, *Soccer's Happy Wanderer* (Museum Press, 1955)

Rice, Tim, Rice, Jo, Gambaccini, Paul, and Read, Mike, *Guinness British Hit Singles* (Guinness Books, various editions)

Ronay, Barney, *Studs! The Greatest Retro Football Annual the World Has Ever Seen* (Ebury Press, 2006)

Saffer, David, *Sniffer: The Life and Times of Allan Clarke* (Tempus, 2001)

——*The Life and Times of Mick Jones* (History Press, 2002)

Sandbrook, Dominic, *Never Had It So Good: A History of Britain from Suez to the Beatles* (Little, Brown, 2005)

——*White Heat: A History of Britain in the Swinging Sixties* (Little, Brown, 2006)

Scott, Les, *End to End Stuff: The Essential Football Book* (Bantam Press, 2008)

Shaw, Don, *Clough's War* (Ebury Press, 2009)

Shaw, Phil, *The Book of Football Quotations* (Ebury Press, 2008)

Shackleton, Len, *Clown Prince of Soccer?* (Nicholas Kaye, 1955)

Simmons, Bill, and Graham, Bob, *The History of Sunderland AFC 1979–1986* (Mayfair, 1986)

Storey, David, *This Sporting Life* (Longmans, 1960)

Storey, Geoff, *Roker Roars Back: Sunderland's Return to Glory* (Mainstream, 1996)

Swan, Peter, with Nick Johnson, *Peter Swan: Setting the Record Straight* (Stadia, 2007)

Talbot, Bryan, *Alice in Sunderland: An Entertainment* (Jonathan Cape, 2007)

Taylor, Peter, *With Clough by Taylor* (Sidgwick & Jackson, 1980)

Taylor, Rogan, and Ward, Andrew, *Kicking & Screaming: An Oral History of Football in England* (Robson Books, 1995)

Tibballs, Geoff, *FA Cup Giant Killers* (HarperCollinsWillow, 1994)

Tossell, David, *Bertie Mee: Arsenal's Officer and Gentleman* (Mainstream, 2005)

——*Big Mal: The High Life and Hard Times of Malcolm Allison, Football Legend* (Mainstream, 2008)

Turner, Dennis, and White, Alex, *Football Managers* (Breedon Books, 1993)

Valentine, Ian, *Football Managers: The Lives and Half-Times* (Prion, 2008)

Wight, Jim, *The Real James Herriot: The Authorized Biography* (Penguin, 1999)

Wilson, Bob, *Behind the Network: My Autobiography* (Hodder & Stoughton, 2003)

——*Life in the Beautiful Game* (Corinthian Books, 2009)

Winner, David, *Brilliant Orange: The Neurotic Genius of Dutch Football* (Bloomsbury, 2000)

Yorath, Terry, with Grahame Lloyd, *Hard Man, Hard Knocks* (Celluloid, 2004)

Newspapers:

Daily Express
Daily Mail
Daily Mirror
Daily Telegraph
Evening Chronicle (Newcastle)
Evening Standard (London)
Guardian
Herald and Post (Luton)
Independent
Independent on Sunday
Mail on Sunday
Manchester Evening News
News of the World
Northern Echo
Nottingham Evening Post
Observer
Reading Chronicle
Sun
Sunday Express
Sunday Mirror
Sunday People
Sunday Telegraph
Sunday Times
Sunderland Echo

The Times
Yorkshire Post

Fanzines and Magazines
A Love Supreme
Four Four Two
Legion of Light
Roker Review
When Saturday Comes
Wise Men Say
World Soccer

Television
BBC archive
ITV (including Tyne Tees TV) archive

Yearbooks and Almanacks
News of the World Football Annual (various editions)
Rothmans Football Yearbook (various editions)
Sky Sports Football Yearbook (various editions)

Websites
www.fifa.com
www.rssf.com
www.safc.com
www.soccerbase.com
www.uefa.com